HANDBOOK of
TEACHER EVALUATION

HANDBOOK of TEACHER EVALUATION

Edited by **JASON MILLMAN**

Published in cooperation with the
NATIONAL COUNCIL ON
MEASUREMENT IN EDUCATION

Ⓢ **SAGE** PUBLICATIONS   Beverly Hills   London

For information address:

SAGE Publications, Inc.
275 South Beverly Drive
Beverly Hills, California 90212

SAGE Publications Ltd
28 Banner Street
London EC1Y 8QE, England

Printed in the United States of America

Library of Congress Cataloging in Publication Data
Main entry under title:

Handbook of teacher evaluation.

"Published in cooperation with the National Council on Measurement in Education."
Bibliography: p.
Includes index.
1. Teachers, Rating of—United States—Handbooks, manuals, etc. I. Millman, Jason. II. National Council on Measurement in Education.
LB2838.H3   371.1'44   80-28522
ISBN 0-8039-1597-7

THIRD PRINTING, 1983

CONTENTS

LIST OF ADVISORS

The following individuals provided commentary to the authors about earlier drafts of their manuscripts. These advisors are not responsible, of course, for the content of the chapters appearing in this volume.

Chapter 1

Gerald M. Gilmore, University of Washington
Edward F. Iwanicki, University of Connecticut

Chapter 2

D. Bob Gowin, Cornell University

Chapter 3

Jerrilyn V. Andrews, Dallas Independent School District
Gayle W. Gordon, Connecticut Education Association
M. Frances Klein, Pepperdine University

Chapter 4

Stephen D. Lapan, Northeastern Illinois University

Chapter 6

Marilyn A. Martin, Research for Better Schools
Richard L. Sweeney, Iowa State Education Association

Chapter 7

John I. Goodlad, University of California, Los Angeles
Randall C. Hickman, University of Texas
Donald M. Medley, University of Virginia

Chapter 8

Larry A. Braskamp, University of Illinois
Wilbert J. McKeachie, University of Michigan

Chapter 9

Gerald M. Gilmore, University of Washington

Chapter 10

Naftaly S. Glasman, University of California, Santa Barbara

Chapter 11

D. Bob Gowin, Cornell University
James B. Maas, Cornell University
J. C. Powell, University of Windsor

Chapter 12

Donald Musella, Ontario Institute for Studies in Education
George B. Redfern, Educational Management Consultant

Chapter 13

Fred Andelman, Massachusetts Teachers Association
Thomas P. Hogan, University of Wisconsin—Green Bay

Chapter 14

Robert L. Ebel, Michigan State University
Robert E. Greene, Burbank Unified School District
Jack Milton, University of California, Davis

Chapter 15

Ronald D. Burge, Oregon State Department of Education
Robert A. Harrell, Jackson State Community College
Daniel P. Moriarty, Minnesota Education Association

Chapter 16

Cordell Affeldt, Indiana State Teachers Association
William R. O'Connell, Association of American Colleges
Douglas A. Rindone, Connecticut State Department of Education

Chapter 17

Virginia Dalton, Virginia Education Association
John E. Dunlop, National Education Association
Barbara Lerner, Educational Testing Service

PREFACE

In the spring of 1975, a task force of the National Council on Measurement in Education, an organization devoted to improving the practice of educational measurement, recommended that a group of writers prepare a teacher evaluation guidebook for practitioners. The proposed attributes of the work were as follows:

> The guidebook should focus on the currently available approaches for evaluating teachers, detailing the strengths and shortcomings of each. Readers should, as a consequence of completing the guidebook, be in a position to know the special advantages and distinctive liabilities of all commonly employed teacher evaluation strategies.
>
> The guidebook should be written in practitioner's language. The writers should be instructed to prepare a volume which should be easily comprehended by busy educators. The writers should not endeavor to impress their scholarly colleagues in the guidebook. Rather it should serve as a guide to the practice of teacher evaluation, kindergarten through college.

This volume attempts to meet the mandate of the recommendation for comprehensibility. All articles are original and were commissioned specifically for inclusion here. The authors are recognized authorities in the areas about which they write.

Many individuals contributed significantly to the successful achievement of this book. Among the most prominent were W. James Popham, Annie Ward, and William Theimer, who were instrumental in initiating the idea of a handbook on teacher evaluation and in contributing to its early development. The advisors, listed earlier, helped to fine tune drafts of the authors' chapters. Jane Tiemann edited the text, and Shirley Preston ably performed typing functions. The biggest debt of gratitude, however, goes to the authors who, to a person, graciously provided multiple revisions of their individual chapters in an effort to maximize the value of their work.

Jason Millman
Ithaca, N.Y.

9

PART I

Orientation

The theme of Part I is that the appropriateness of teacher evaluation practices depends upon many factors, such as the purpose of the evaluation, one's concept of good teaching, and the context in which instruction takes place. Since these factors differ among institutions, no single set of procedures for evaluating teachers is always best.

In Chapter 1, the readers are reminded of the seriousness and inevitability of teacher evaluation. Several purposes of teacher evaluation are mentioned, and the distinction between the formative role (improving teaching) and the summative role (making personnel decisions) of teacher evaluation is highlighted.

A historical review of the criteria of good teaching is the subject of Chapter 2. The criteria chosen have depended considerably on what is viewed as the responsibility of the teacher and what is viewed as the responsibility of the student. When students are considered to be responsible for their own learning, the effective teacher is seen as one who manages the classroom and arranges conditions from which students can profit, if they so choose. When the teacher is seen as the sole agent accountable for student learning, the main criterion of good teaching is the achievement of the students. Other criteria of good teaching relate to teacher characteristics believed to correlate with student achievement.

The point of view taken in Chapter 3 is that if the evaluation of teachers is to serve useful and meaningful purposes, it must take into account the many contextual factors that influence teacher effectiveness. The factors discussed in the chapter are student characteristics; goals, objectives, and curriculum mandates; inservice opportunities and human support services; time and number of students; materials, media, and facilities; organizational structures and processes; leadership and supervisory skills; decision-making power; climate of professional worth and contribution; working conditions, human services, and security benefits; and community characteristics, priorities for schooling, and financial resources.

CHAPTER 1

INTRODUCTION

JASON MILLMAN
Cornell University

To evaluate, or not to evaluate,
That is NOT *the question.*

We make judgments all the time, judgments about ourselves and what we do and about others and what they do. And we, in turn, are being judged by others. We cannot escape evaluation. Every choice, every decision—to speak or not, to use this example or that—involves an evaluation, automatic or deliberate. In the context of teaching, the question is not whether to evaluate, but Who should evaluate? For what purpose? Using what means?

WHO SHOULD EVALUATE

Being evaluated can be frightening. We have the queasy feeling that we will be judged and found wanting. Even close scrutiny of oneself can be unpleasant. To minimize discomfort, shouldn't the teachers themselves be the *sole* judges of their own performance? Further, isn't what is taught and how it is taught the responsibility of the teacher? Isn't assessment by others of what goes on in the teacher's classroom an invasion of privacy?

We think not. Teaching is not a solitary activity affecting no one. On the contrary, the lives of many students are altered in far-reaching and significant ways by the instructors with whom they interact. Teaching is too important to too many to be conducted without a critical inquiry into its worth. Besides, court cases have made it clear that students have rights, and schools and colleges have a responsibility to ensure the quality of their curriculum and instruction. The protection of rights and the fulfillment of responsibility require that teacher self-assessment be supplemented by evaluation by others.

Evaluated by whom? Other teachers? Administrators? Students? Parents and the public? Professional evaluators? All of these actors can have an important role in the evaluation of teachers. But all are not equally suited to evaluate all aspects of teaching. The strengths and weaknesses of such evaluator groups are described in the chapters that follow.

FOR WHAT PURPOSE

Over a dozen reasonably distinct purposes for teacher evaluation have been suggested, such as improving teacher performance, aiding administrative decisions, guiding students in course selections, meeting state and institutional mandates, promoting research on teaching, and the like. In this volume we have distinguished between two major roles of teacher evaluation, the *formative* role and the *summative* role. Formative teacher evaluation helps teachers improve their performance by providing data, judgments, and suggestions that have implications for what to teach and how. On the other hand, summative teacher evaluation serves administrative decision making with respect to hiring and firing, promotion and tenure, assignments, and salary. Some chapters (e.g., 13, 14, and 17) are devoted almost exclusively to either the formative or summative role; other chapters (e.g., 4 and 9) have clearly divided sections on ways to use the techniques for formative and summative evaluation.

USING WHAT MEANS

The evaluator has many tools available, as the contents of this volume amply demonstrate. Although most authorities recommend multiple sources of evidence about teaching proficiency, more is not necessarily better. Techniques should be fair, accurate, legal, efficient, credible, and humane, but no technique fulfills these requirements completely. Further, the quality of a technique depends not only on its inherent characteristics but also on the context and manner in which it is implemented.

A colleague once remarked that the evaluation of teachers is a serious business, for it goes on in the midst of life and concerns the well-being of people. A process like that is not trivial. It is worth our attention and worth doing well.

CHAPTER 2

CRITERIA OF GOOD TEACHING

ROBERT M. W. TRAVERS
Western Michigan University

Across the ages, the task of the teacher has been conceptualized in many different ways. Even in modern America there is little agreement on what the role of the teacher should be in facilitating pupil learning. Teaching can involve many different tasks, and, as the tasks prescribed for the teacher vary, so too do the criteria that can be used for evaluating the effectiveness of the teacher.

Public issues related to teaching effectiveness did not arise in history until pupils were required to go to school. A Socrates talking in the marketplace, or an Aristotle walking in the Lyceum gardens, gathered around him whoever wished to engage in disputation. To be an effective teacher was to be a person who attracted students. The criterion of teacher effectiveness was objective and definite, even though the reasons why a teacher attracted students were subtle and obscure. The University of Paris, founded in the 10th century, had built into its method of operation a similar criterion of teacher effectiveness. A professor, to survive, had to be able to attract students from whom fees were extracted directly. A professor who could not attract students had no source of income. The system had a built-in criterion of effectiveness, the ability to attract students.

In antiquity organized education began at the adult level. Not until the idea developed that younger members of the community should be educated was compulsion introduced as a means of bringing students and teachers together. The grammar school that emerged at the end of the Middle Ages involved male scholars whose parents desired that their children have an education beyond that provided in the home or in the so-called *petty schools*. Pressure from parents must have been an important factor in keeping children in such schools, for they were run along monastic lines and involved a stern and disciplined routine. Such schools were private institutions and probably did not have to make any effort to attract students. The demand for education far exceeded the supply. In such a situation, there was no public pressure to evaluate teachers, although some of the masters of these schools attempted to develop criteria by which masters and ushers, or assistant teachers, could judge themselves.

Early writings referring to teacher effectiveness were largely to help teachers evaluate themselves. They were typically written around the topic of how best to organize a school and the instruction taking place in it. In other words, these writings focused on the teacher's managerial role, and they represent a good point of departure for discussing criteria of teacher effectiveness.

EVALUATING THE TEACHER AS A MANAGER IN THE CLASSROOM

Charles Hoole, a master of an English grammar school, published in 1659 a series of pamphlets on how to run a school (reproduced 1868). The main criterion of teacher effectiveness implicit in the pamphlets was a management criterion. They provided a detailed description of the management problems of the 17th-century school, describing how authority for various activities was distributed among the ushers and monitors. The discussion implied that if the school was correctly managed, then the pupils would have full opportunities to learn; any deficiencies of learning would be a result of pupil irresponsibility. The assumption made is that the teacher was not accountable for pupil progress, except insofar as management problems in the school were neglected.

The management of the school also involved what today would be called public relations. A master could function effectively only if he were held in high public esteem, and Hoole described how a master might preserve his good reputation:

In some places a master is apt to be molested with the reproachful clamors of the meaner sort of people, who can not (for the most part) endure to have their children corrected, be the fault never so heinous, but presently they must come to the school to brave it out with him; which if they do, the master should there in a calm manner admonish them before all his scholars to cease their clamor, and to consider how rash they are to interrupt his business, and to blame him for doing that duty with which he is intrusted by themselves, and others their betters. But if they go about to raise scandalous reports upon him, he may do well to get two or three judicious neighbors to examine the matter, and to rebuke the parties for making so much ado upon little or no occasion. Thus we shall see scholars abundantly more to respect the master when they know how grossly he is apt to be wronged by inconsiderate persons, and that wise men are ready to vindicate his cause. Whereas if they once see their master liable to every body's censure, and no man take his part whatever is said of him, they themselves will not care what tales they make to his utter disgrace or ruin; especially if he have been any whit harsh towards them, and they be desirous to outslip the reins of his teaching and government [1868: 301].

Until the 20th century, teachers and administrators generally maintained that the responsibility for learning was the pupil's and that the teacher's functions were to a great extent managerial. The ushers did little more than hear the pupils recite what they had learned and give new assignments. When Horace Mann visited common schools in Massachusetts just before the middle of the 19th century, he noted that the conditions of teaching were such that teachers had to spend most of their time organizing the work. Mann wrote of visiting schools with 50 or more pupils, varying in age from toddlers to young adults, who were presided over by a single teacher. Such a teacher could not spend more than five minutes a day with any pupil. Here again, pupils were regarded as being responsible for their own learning. Those who were slow in learning were called *laggards,* a term that had a strong moral implication. The common schools of Massachusetts in Horace Mann's time, like the Puritan common schools from which they were derived, were run on the assumption that all children were equally capable of learning if they would only apply themselves. Differences in achievement represented differences in motivation or, as they said in those days, differences in application to the prescribed tasks.

At the grammar school level, and even in some of the large city common schools, there was some opportunity for the teacher to engage in activities other than managerial ones. In some of the larger grammar schools, there was some segregation of pupils in terms of achievement, and the teacher might spend time with small groups instead of with individuals. At such times, the teacher would expand upon the material in the textbooks. That is why the books were called textbooks: They provided the texts that teachers used as a basis for more expansive presentations, just as a preacher derived a text from the Scriptures and then preached a sermon. Horace Mann said many times that these nonmanagerial aspects of the teacher's role needed to be developed, though he did not use the word *managerial*.

The evaluation of teachers in terms of management skills has persisted to modern times in some educational programs. Programs that make extensive use of modular materials call upon the teacher to be a manager. There is, however, one important difference between the teacher in such a modern managerial role and the teacher's managerial role in the days of Horace Mann. In the modern classroom structured with modular materials, the materials have commonly been developed in terms of the view that, since behavior is controlled by the environment, the pupils cannot be held responsible for whether they do or do not learn. If the classroom manager provides favorable conditions for learning, then the pupil will learn. If the pupil does not learn, then the conditions provided by the teacher must be blamed. This viewpoint places the teacher in a difficult position, because the teacher rarely has much choice in the modules that are available. Indeed, in a program such as Individually Prescribed Instruction, the modules come as a package; the teacher has little choice and can hardly be accountable for pupil achievement, except insofar as the program is well or badly managed in the classroom. At least, that is what the theory seems to imply. A point to note about newer programs that assume that learning, or failure to learn, has nothing to do with pupil responsibility is that every pupil has an alibi for not learning. The pupil cannot be held accountable for failure to learn, because the assumption underlying the program is that any failure is a result of the inadequacy of learning conditions.

TEACHER RESPONSIBILITY AND NEW CRITERIA OF TEACHER EFFECTIVENESS

Once the assumption was made that the teacher and learning conditions, and not the pupil, were responsible for pupil achievement, the criterion of teacher effectiveness changed. This was a change in assumption and not a change in what was known about teaching. This change took place in England in the late Victorian era, when the British government introduced a payment-by-results system in what were called the *board schools*. In this system, teachers were paid in terms of their effectiveness, and the effectiveness of teachers was determined through school inspectors administering tests to pupils near the end of the school year. Tests were administered in what today would be called *basics*, and the pay of each teacher was determined by the number of pupils who exceeded some rough estimate of the national average. The system corrupted the entire educational program, for schools became places where pupils crammed for examinations. By the turn of the century, the board schools in England came to represent the worst educational program of any civilized country. Parents became outraged by the inadequacy of the education provided their children and, mainly as a result of public outcry, Parliament brought to an end the system of payment by results in 1902. The idea of payment by results was to come to America, but not for nearly another century, and by that time the disaster it had brought to British education had been all but forgotten.

Teachers of ungraded classrooms in the last century in the United States could be regarded as managers or organizers of the school activity, but that role was soon to change. The change was brought about by the introduction, from Prussia, of the system of dividing children by age groups into grades. The division of children into uniform age groups changed the function of the teacher, who was no longer faced with 30, 50, or more children, each working at a different level. When classes in American common schools became graded, instruction took the form of giving children uniform assignments. The teacher could then discuss with the class the problems related to the completion of each assignment. The teacher was no longer just a manager, but a person who could influence learning in the classroom and perhaps even influence the overall development of each child. This new role of the teacher has been romanticized in literature through such works as *Goodbye Mr. Chips* and *The Prime of Miss Jean Brodie*.

If the main function of the teacher is to enhance learning in the student, then a whole range of criteria of teacher effectiveness may be considered. Before considering such criteria, a word of caution must be introduced. The extent to which a pupil learns in the school is a function of many different conditions, of which the teacher's mode of operation is only one. Achievement is also a function of such conditions as the extent to which the home encourages learning, the extent to which the parents participate in the learning and development of the child, perhaps genetic endowment, and the kinds of materials available for study. The teacher factor may well account for only a small amount of the differences in achievement, as Bernard McKenna notes in the next chapter of this handbook. The effectiveness of a teacher in promoting learning through intellectual interaction can be assessed in various ways, none of which has yet gone far beyond the drawing-board stage. One suggestion has been to test teacher effectiveness by requiring the teacher to teach a particular unit to a class and then having an evaluator measure the amount of learning (see McNeil, Ch. 15). The procedure is filled with unsolved problems, not the least of which is that every teacher has good and poor days. A single day of teaching may not provide a very useful sample. The situation is a highly artificial one. The Victorian system of payment by results had gross defects, but it did not have the defect of too limited a sample. It has been copied in various forms. In the early part of the present century, when a strong movement existed to apply concepts of business efficiency to education, there were scattered attempts to use tests to appraise the long-term impact of particular teachers on the achievement of whole classes of pupils. The movement never gathered much momentum, despite the fact that it was supported by the Federal Bureau of Education. A half-century later, as testing techniques became more sophisticated, some school districts attempted to use the results of statewide testing programs for the appraisal of teacher effectiveness. However, not only had testers become more sophisticated during the intervening half-century, but teachers had too. When statewide testing programs were used to assess the work of school systems, schools, classes, and sometimes teachers, the teachers soon learned ways of manipulating test scores up and down. This would not be a place to divulge the trade secrets of teachers in this respect.

CRITERIA INVOLVING CORRELATES OF PUPIL ACHIEVEMENT

The difficulties of assessing teacher effectiveness in terms of test scores of pupils seem to be almost insuperable at this time. Although such an idea has been backed with enthusiasm by some administrators, school boards, writers in the popular press, and even by some groups of parents in the present age, these groups have often been motivated by a resurgence of the idea of applying concepts of business efficiency to education. Whether this is a practical idea is a real question. There are also questions whether, in schools that have good materials, the responsibility for learning should rest with the pupil or with the teacher.

If one takes the partisan position that responsibility for pupil achievement rests with the teacher rather than with the pupil, there are criteria of teacher effectiveness that can be applied outside of the test-score criterion. The effectiveness of the teacher may perhaps be assessed, some claim, through the assessment of those aspects of teacher behavior related to the growth of pupils in achievement. This idea has fascinated research workers throughout most of this century. In the early part of the century, traits of behavior supposedly related to teacher effectiveness were selected on the basis of what was described as expert judgment, though there were no real experts for there was no real knowledge. Some real knowledge has now accumulated and has been summarized in such articles as that by Rosenshine and Furst (1973).

In order to achieve knowledge in this area, research workers had to discover what characteristics of the teacher were actually related to pupil achievement. Over the last half-century there has been a slow accumulation of studies that have attempted to discover relationships between pupils' measured gains in achievement under a particular teacher and the personal characteristics of that teacher. Such studies generally show the kind of relationship between teacher behavior and pupil learning that one would expect on the basis of common sense, though not always so. Teachers most effective in producing learning are clear in the expression of their ideas, variable and flexible in their approaches to teaching, enthusiastic, task-oriented, and so forth. Relationships are not strong, and one would not expect them to be. The relationship between what a teacher does and the products of teaching is much less strong than the relationship between the level of skill of a craftsman and the excellence of the product. Craftsmen have full control over their tools and materials, but teachers do not.

Research workers in the last decade have tended to move away from studying the teacher and toward studying the pupil. Administrators have long held the view that one only has to observe the pupils in a classroom to know the amount of learning in progress. In the early part of the century, many principals judged the effectiveness of teachers by strolling down the main corridor and taking a peek at the pupils in each classroom. Research on what pupils do and how that is related to learning is not new, but the recent emphasis on it is. Statistically significant relationships have been found between pupil behavior and academic development (see Hoge and Luce, 1979). Such research does not really validate the activities of the traditional peeking principal, for pupil behavior may well be as much a result of the influence of the home as a result of the influence of the teacher. A main conclusion from such research is the obvious fact that the amount learned by the pupil is related to the time spent in learning. This finding is hardly new, and there are many exceptions. Educational research in the last century showed that children who spent several hours a day mastering spelling did little better than those who spent 15 minutes a day. A principal who judged teachers in terms of the extent to which the noses of the pupils were kept to the grindstone might have made some very unfair judgments.

EVALUATING THE TEACHER FOR PROFICIENCY IN A CRAFT

Some educators have attempted to expand the concept of the teacher as an individual who applies the techniques of a craft. Such a concept of teaching implies that effective teaching calls for the use of a set of specific competencies. Just as plumbers pursue their trade by applying each of the skills they have learned to appropriate situations and in proper sequence, so is it claimed that teachers achieve each objective in the pupils by applying the component skills of the teaching craft. Various attempts have been made to break down teaching into a set of such component competencies. Some schools of education have attempted to identify such a set of competencies and to train teachers competency by competency, much as plumbers are trained in a set of component skills. If this can actually be done, then the evaluation of teacher effectiveness can be reduced to the simple process of determining whether the teacher does or does not manifest the component skills in the classroom. This line of thought, popularized through the millions of dollars poured into it by the U.S. Office of Education, remains controversial. No one has as yet identified a set of competencies that can be demonstrated to be related to how much pupils learn. The critics say that the competencies remain mythical entities. Others claim that clearly identifiable forms of teacher behavior in the classroom represent such competencies. The concept of teaching as an assembly of competencies lacks substance at present. It has not led to the development of any defensible and usable set of criteria of teacher effectiveness. The approach has appeal, particularly to those who know little about what has, and has not, been established about the nature of teaching. For the latter reason, it has had political attractiveness and has found some acceptance among some members of state legislatures, who have then brought pressure to bear on state departments of education to apply the concept to teacher certification, teacher evaluation, and teacher education.

THE TEACHER AS THE PROVIDER OF THE GOOD LIFE

Still one more criterion of teacher effectiveness has to be introduced in some programs. This criterion relates to the extent to which the teacher provides conditions related to a happy and rewarding life for the pupils. Such a criterion would have been implicit in Aristotle's conception of education, but it completely disappeared in the European monastic schools of the Middle Ages, from which our present schools are derived. Charles Hoole's treatises on education in the 17th century made plain the idea that schools existed for personal salvation and moral betterment and were not places where life should be enjoyed. Hoole described in detail not only how children should be whipped but also how a suitable rod should be made so that it did not harm the bones. Rebellion against this harsh concept of education was slow, for many moderns seemed to imply in their writings that a good education is necessarily irksome. For example, operant psychologists have suggested that children be reinforced for engaging in dull school tasks by being allowed to play from time to time. This is a revival of the puritanical distinction between work and play. Work was arduous and often painful, but virtuous, and play was fun, even though slightly sinful. The British philosopher John Locke, in his famous essay on education, urged that education should not be punitive. Jean Jacques Rousseau, who based his *Emile* on Locke's essay, went further and took the position that education should be enjoyable. John Dewey expanded further on the justification that education should be pleasant by taking the position that education was not just preparation for life, but it was life itself and life should be pleasant. Some disagree with the latter viewpoint, saying that merely providing pleasant conditions for living in the classroom is not teaching, and yet it may be an essential condition for developing a well-balanced philosophy of life. Regardless of any influence that the pleasantness of life in the classroom may have on learning, it is surely necessary if children are to want to continue education after they pass beyond the age of compulsory education.

A BROAD VIEW OF TEACHING

The word *teaching* refers to a very broad class of activities. The particular activities that constitute teaching in any particular situation depend upon how the school is organized, the nature of the program, the structure of the curriculum, the teaching materials to be used, the expectations of parents, and the social context of education. A method suitable for evaluating teacher effectiveness in one situation may be quite unsuitable in another. If a school encourages innovation, the teachers in different rooms may be functioning very differently and should probably be evaluated in terms of different criteria. If a school can justify evaluating all teachers through identical procedures, then the school is probably devoid of innovations. Research shows quite clearly that pupils adapt well to many different approaches to teaching, calling for very different ways of functioning on the part of the teacher. Pupils in open classrooms learn at very much the same rate as pupils in classrooms run in highly structured styles, and yet the way in which teachers function in these two different settings may be very different and should be evaluated in different ways. There is no single simple method of evaluating teacher effectiveness, because there is no single concept of what the teacher should be undertaking in the classroom.

REFERENCES

Hoge, R. D. and S. Luce (1979) "Predicting achievement from classroom behavior." *Review of Educational Research*, 49: 479–496.

Hoole, C. (1868) "Scholastic discipline." *American Journal of Education*, 17: (Originally published 1659) 293–324.

Rosenshine, B. and N. Furst (1973) "The use of direct observation to study teaching," in R. M. W. Travers (ed.) *Second Handbook of Research on Teaching*. Skokie, IL: Rand McNally.

CHAPTER 3

CONTEXT/ENVIRONMENT EFFECTS IN TEACHER EVALUATION

BERNARD H. McKENNA
National Education Association

Success in teaching, however defined and assessed, is highly contextual. Therefore, if evaluation of teaching and teachers is to serve meaningful and useful purposes, it must not only identify and define all the mitigating contexts but must also take into account their influences, both constructive and negative, in determining success. This chapter describes some ways of conceptualizing context and discusses the individual contextual factors that need to be considered in planning for the evaluation of teaching and teachers: student characteristics; goals, objectives, and curriculum mandates; inservice opportunities and human support services; time and numbers of students; materials, media, and facilities; organizational structures and processes; leadership and supervisory skills; decision-making power; climate of professional worth and contribution; working conditions, human services, and security benefits; and community characteristics, priorities for schooling, and financial ability, effort, and resources.

To discuss context as it applies to teacher evaluation in any definitive manner, the writer's concept of the purpose of evaluation needs to be clear and his definition of learning articulated. For this discussion, the major purpose of teacher evaluation is assumed to be the improvement of instruction. As an extrapolation of that assumption, the improvement of instruction should be expected to improve learning. Learning is defined as the broadest possible range of knowledges, skills, attitudes, and behaviors contained in all those goals of schooling that have been identified, articulated, and agreed to any place in the society: skills in language arts (as broadly as that term is sometimes defined to include reading, writing, speaking, listening, and forms of nonverbal communication); mathematics; knowledge in the cultural heritage (the social studies broadly conceived); a broad liberal education in the arts, sciences, and humanities; vocational competencies; interpersonal and citizenship behaviors; self-concept; and whatever other goals are selected for schooling, whether education about consumer affairs, sex, the ecology, health, safety, drug use, and a myriad of others.

Learning as defined here also takes into account the person in the process. Thus, evaluation must embrace what teaching and teachers do to make the years spent in schooling—nursery school through graduate school—as full-living, wholesome, democratic, and fulfilling as can be conceived, *to a substantial degree independent of cognitive learning outcomes.*

WAYS OF CONCEPTUALIZING CONTEXT

The ways of conceptualizing context by models or frameworks are many. Three are described here as representing different possibilities.

A Program-Performance-Outcome Paradigm

Originating with the industrial "input-ouput" model, the program-performance-outcome paradigm places teaching acts in the "middle" surrounded by program (input) factors and learning outcome (output) criteria. Figure 1 shows an adaptation of the industrial model as applied to education which, in the United States, goes back to the work of Bobbitt and Spaulding as documented by Callahan (1962). This model has been most recently propagated in approaches to evaluation adapted for the Department of Health, Education and Welfare and emanating from the Ford Motor Company, by way of the Defense Department and its then-Secretary, Robert MacNamara (former Ford president), the Brookings Institution, and such economists-turned-evaluators as Alice Rivlin (Note 1).

The paradigm provides a way of considering major elements of inputs (program components) in relation to processes (performance components) and outputs (student learning-outcome components); but it implies that if program components are present in all their forms at optimum levels, then processes will be optimal and outputs maximal. Some of the context measures, individually and in clusters, have been related statistically to criteria of quality, holding other measures constant. Although the paradigm does provide a way of considering some of the contextual elements significant for evaluation and makes possible an examination of major aspects of the educational enterprise in their linear interrelationship, it assumes analogs between the industrial arena and the educational arena that are weak at best and frequently nearly nonexistent. One important reason for this may be that industrialists view the world and their enterprises as physical scientists do. Bussis (Note 2) has observed that scientists do not study phenomena that mirror their own thought processes: "Neither atoms nor stars construct symbolic representations of the world and then 'behave' in accordance with their individual constructions of reality" (pp. 2–3). Human acts are only

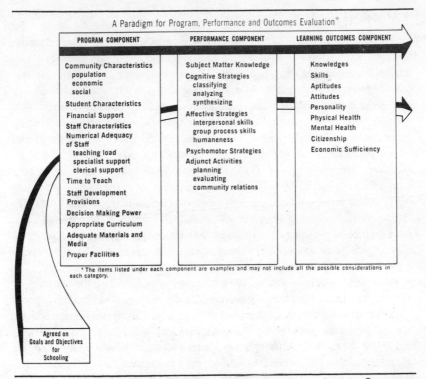

A Paradigm for Program, Performance and Outcomes Evaluation*

PROGRAM COMPONENT	PERFORMANCE COMPONENT	LEARNING OUTCOMES COMPONENT

Community Characteristics
  population
  economic
  social
Student Characteristics
Financial Support
Staff Characteristics
Numerical Adequacy
of Staff
  teaching load
  specialist support
  clerical support
Time to Teach
Staff Development
Provisions
Decision Making Power
Appropriate Curriculum
Adequate Materials and
Media
Proper Facilities
	Subject Matter Knowledge
	Cognitive Strategies
	  classifying
	  analyzing
	  synthesizing
	Affective Strategies
	  interpersonal skills
	  group process skills
	  humaneness
	Psychomotor Strategies
	Adjunct Activities
	  planning
	  evaluating
	  community relations
		Knowledges
		Skills
		Aptitudes
		Attitudes
		Personality
		Physical Health
		Mental Health
		Citizenship
		Economic Sufficiency

*The items listed under each component are examples and may not include all the possible considerations in each category.

Agreed on
Goals and Objectives
for
Schooling

Figure 1: A paradigm for program, performance, and outcomes evaluation. © National Association of Elementary School Principals. Reprinted by permission.

incidentally physical. First and foremost, human acts are characterized by the meanings and intentions of the persons who perform them. The social scientist has a first task, the "clarification of act meaning" (p. 3), then the formulation of theoretical meaning. She argues that educational research has not dealt well with the first task, and she attributes this lack primarily to methodological constraints, particularly those that equate the meaning and intention of human learning with test scores, rating scales, and preconceived observation categories.

The paradigm has been instructive in the past, but the conclusions drawn from recent experience with the model and from such postulations as those of Bussis are that its adherence to industrial systems, its assumptions about linearity in the complex arena of assessing human enterprises, and its heavy reliance on quantitative indices make it less than satisfactory for considering the effects of context on teaching and teachers.

A Models-of-Teaching Paradigm

The models-of teaching paradigm (Joyce and Weil, 1972) is based on the assumption that there is a "diverse range of alternative patterns upon which teachers may model their behavior . . . and that there is no future in our persistent effort to describe 'best teaching practice' " (p. xi). This theory conceives of teaching not "as static tenets but as dynamically interactive with social and cognitive purpose, with the learning theory underlying procedures, with available support technology, and with the personal and intellectual characteristics of learning groups" (p. xi). The 16 models of teaching identified by Joyce and Weil are grouped into four "families" on the basis of the "sources" of reality that the theorists consulted as they considered the learner and his/her environment: (1) social-interaction sources, (2) information-processing sources, (3) personal sources, and (4) behavior modification as a source. The families are not considered to be so discrete as to be mutually exclusive. They share some of the same characteristics with respect to both goals and means.

Although a teaching-models approach may appear to beg the question of context, this is not the case. For each model the authors describe the support system necessary for its implementation, that is, "additional requirements beyond the usual human skills and capacities and technical facilities" (Joyce and Weil, 1972: 16). Although the approach is much less linear than the input-output theory, it does take into account contextual factors in teaching. However, in articulating the models paradigm, its major supporters make context appear almost incidental. For example, in portraying the Developmental Model, Joyce and Weil dismiss the topic of support systems (context) with one sentence: "The optimal support system is a rich object and resource environment and a teacher well-grounded in developmental theory who can create and tolerate a free social environment that permits the student to work out the cognitive problems developed in the confrontations" (p. 197). It would appear, therefore, that, like the input-output paradigm, the models-of-teaching approach is not fully up to the task of taking into account all the complex issues of context in teaching.

An Ecological Paradigm

The ecological model is an effort currently under way at the Far West Laboratory for Educational Research in San Francisco (Dawson et al., Note 3) to develop a comprehensive approach to the study of teaching. The term *model* may be too precise for both the present state of the activity and the intended fluidity of the process by which the ecological-theory project is proceeding.

From the term *ecological* itself, one might suspect that this is a highly ambitious undertaking: to identify and define *all* the elements that constitute the classroom as an ecological system and then to recognize the interactions among the elements and take into account their relation to and effects on each other. In setting forth postulates for the theory, the investigators acknowledge that questions about what constitutes all the elements (including those contextual ones beyond the classroom), their appropriate aggregations, and defining information about each will be answered "somewhat later in the theory-development process . . . not only inductively but also deductively as our definitions are tested in exploring interrelationships among elements" (p. 6).

In the early stages of the project, 10 elements were tentatively identified for further definition, description, and confirmation (revision or rejection) in naturalistic classroom settings: students, teacher, other human elements, role, time, physical locus and arrangement, educational materials, task standards and sanctions, and communication. It is clear from the descriptors themselves that several elements are clearly contextual factors—time, physical locus and arrangement, and educational materials. In addition, if context is to be considered in the broadest possible sense, then other human elements, task standards and sanctions, and communication also need to be considered as contextual.

As is the case with the other paradigms described, ecological theory has not pursued all the contextual factors in depth, but it appears to be in the process of identifying and clarifying a broad range of them, with the intent of taking into account their complex interrelationships as teaching is studied. Its attention to interrelationships in a naturalistic setting, along with their consequences, may also have important implications for teacher evaluation.

The models described above illustrate the range of possible frameworks for considering context. They also show that complex interrelationships exist among contextual factors, which also must be taken into account in the evaluation of teaching and teachers. The remainder of this chapter describes those factors as they affect the ability of teachers to demonstrate proficiency no matter what the framework or model employed and no matter how the interrelationships among the factors are considered.

CONTEXTUAL FACTORS

Student Characteristics

The most significant contextual factor affecting teachers' success is the characteristics of the student body with which teachers must deal each day. It would appear unnecessary to state that students bring to school widely differing levels of achievement, interests, motivations, and attitudes. It would be unnecessary were it not that this important condition is so frequently overlooked. When students of differing backgrounds, in differing mixes, are placed together in an instructional setting, the potential for varying degrees of success of different teachers with differing student groups is almost infinite.

Glass (1973) has noted that "Nothing short of random assignment of pupils to teachers as an ironclad administrative necessity would ensure that the teachers were in a fair race to produce pupil gain" (p. 54). Since both the technical and practical potential for assigning to teachers groups of students whose collective characteristics are identical (or nearly identical) is very low, then any teacher evaluation system, to reflect accuracy and fairness, must take into account the characteristics of the students who arrive at a teacher's door each day for instruction, characteristics over which those who teach have little or no control.

Goals, Objectives, and Curriculum Mandates

Evaluation of the success of an enterprise is, or ought to be, based on how nearly the expressed goals and objectives of that enterprise are achieved. At the same time that contemporary rhetoric (and in some places legislative and other policy mandates) would narrow the school's goals and objectives to those that promote only learning in the basic skills and a few limited cognitive knowledges and understandings, other goals and mandates emerge that broaden the objectives schools and teachers are expected to accomplish, sometimes to an overwhelming array. For example, New Jersey mandated in 1980 that by 1983 all schools will be required to teach sex education to all students. In recent and not-so-recent times, one after another of such objectives has been assigned to schools and teachers. Driver education was mandated in many places decades ago, followed by first-aid and civil defense. In more recent years, goals and objectives have come to embrace consumer education, drug use, parenting, the ecology, energy conservation, mainstreaming the handicapped, and on and on.

Evaluation of the performance of teachers must, of necessity, take into account the full range of professional responsibilities mandated and the opportunities provided for discharging those responsibilities. Teacher evaluation must respond to the question, Just how omnicapable should an individual teacher be expected to become in managing this ever-increasing array of goals and objectives? Answers to this question are particularly crucial for those teachers who preside over classrooms where being equally enthusiastic and proficient in teaching the traditional branches of the curriculum— language arts, mathematics, science, social studies (taking into account the knowledge explosion in these subjects)—is a lot to expect, let alone achieving all the other objectives that have been added over the years and that continue to accumulate.

Teacher evaluation must also take into account the clarity with which goals and objectives are articulated, the degree of agreement to them, and the number of objectives mandated in terms of their manageability. Sometimes goals and objectives are not clearly defined and thus not fully understood by those who have the responsibility for accomplishing them. And, frequently, goals and objectives have not achieved the consensus of either governing bodies or implementers.

Professional Development

For each different goal and objective mandated for instruction, a modicum of expertise in either subject matter or instructional strategies (often both) is expected or required. Evaluation of teaching must take into account the opportunities that teachers have to learn to know and do what they are expected to know and do. Frequently, teachers do not have the opportunity, either in their preservice education or in renewal programs inservice, to become secure enough in the substance and/or process of new requirements to assure that new goals and objectives will be adequately achieved.

A current prime example of the need for such opportunities is in Public Law 94-142, which requires, to a large extent, mainstreaming the handicapped into regular classrooms. Many teachers have not had opportunities to learn the special skills required to work effectively with students who come to them possessing a broad range of handicaps. They arc, therefore, in a poor position to demonstrate proficiency and to achieve success with such students.

Human Support Services

Specialization within the professions and within almost all other occupations has become a way of life in the society. As the goals and objectives of schooling have proliferated, as the knowledge explosion in the disciplines has intensified, and as understanding about human growth and development and how humans learn has increased, a need has arisen for a great range of special expertise to support and extend the teaching function.

Student characteristics also appear to have changed or to have become more diversified—for example, bilingual, multicultural and multiethnic, assertive, independent (or at least recognized to be so)—and call for a broader range of professional understanding of a cultural, sociological, and psychological nature. Part of the diversification is doubtless a result of the school's arriving at a situation in which larger and larger percentages of students are in school over a longer time (approximately 75% in 1978 stayed to secondary school graduation compared to only 48% 35 years ago). Other factors requiring the expertise of specialists are the changes in today's students in terms of social, ethical, and sexual mores, differences in the kinds of home and family support systems for youth, and the effects of mass media and other technological developments on the ways in which students view their world and respond to it.

All these factors require that to accomplish the increased range of goals and objectives, a variety of human support services—social, psychological, medical, and others—need to be at the command of teachers. Evaluation of teacher performance that does not take in account the availability, sufficiency, and efficiency of such may attribute less than success to teachers when the deficiencies are in other human support services.

Time and Numbers of Students

Over a long period it has been suggested by many in the profession that if teachers had "time enough and few enough," a preponderance of the serious problems of schooling would be greatly diminished. This is much more than a platitude, and there is increasing evidence that this admonition needs to be taken with great seriousness.

Time. Long ago the title of a monograph of the National Education Association recommended "Time to Teach." In the 1950s the Bay City Teacher Aide studies showed that large percentages of teachers' time (up to 40% or more) was spent in noninstructional activities, many of them clerical or manual, which contributed little or nothing to promoting student learning. More recent findings, notably those of the Beginning Teacher Evaluation Study and the work of Wiley and Harnischfeger (1975), confirm that more "time on task," particularly in the basic-skills areas, results in increased learning—at least as learning is assessed by cognitive measures. There is also evidence from a variety of sources that too little time is available in relation to the large number of goals and objectives mandated for schooling. Of that available, much continues to be consumed by required noninstructional activities, interruptions, getting ready to work, cleaning up, and the like.

In terms of total time available, some studies have shown that, with the number of subjects to be taught and other mandated responsibilities to be discharged, the typical teacher with the typical number of students in an elementary self-contained classroom would have no more than a couple of minutes each day to work with an individual student on a learning activity such as arithmetic. Efforts at providing more flexible time formats for particular instructional purposes in programs of higher education are also indicative of the relationship between time and the successful accomplishment of instructional objectives at that level.

With no increased time allotted for schooling in most places, and with the increased array of responsibilities that have been mandated to the schools, there must be less time for each. It then follows that, if time is a significant contributor to promoting important goals and objectives of learning, the ability of teachers to contribute at the highest level to achieving those goals and objectives should be considered in the light of whether there is time enough. Since time available varies widely within as well as among institutional settings, this variation needs to be taken into account as teachers are evaluated.

Number of Students. The controversy that has continued over many decades as to whether smaller classes contribute to improved instruction and student learning is well-known and amply documented, although not always accurately. In spite of the fact that carefully controlled studies in the 1950s showed "smaller is better" for a variety of instructional activities, these findings were either ignored, distorted, or discredited for political or other reasons. Two recent analyses by Glass and Smith (Notes 4 and 5) of a large number of studies, both of the educational process and student learning outcomes at elementary and secondary levels, clearly and persuasively confirm what earlier studies showed: Smaller classes are conducive to promoting a broad range of educational purposes. Advantages accrue the most when class sizes are well below 20.

A large proportion of teachers in the elementary and secondary schools of America work with classes that run well above 20. In the larger cities, where student learning problems are considered the most severe, classes tend to be the largest. In higher institutions the numbers of students that professors must deal with range from small discussion groups to classes of several hundred.

From the most recent, definitive findings it seems clear that one important determinant of success in teaching is the number of students that teachers must deal with each day. Therefore, the evaluation of teaching and teachers must take into account the numbers of students assigned to each teacher.

Materials, Media, and Facilities

In recent years, it has become increasingly clear that different instructional objectives require different kinds of print and nonprint stimuli. Yet stories abound of classrooms in poorer school systems, or poorer neighborhoods within systems, that lack such basic materials as up-to-date textbooks or enough books for all students, let alone a variety of other print materials, films, laboratory equipment for experimentation, raw materials for crafts, and the like. One need only visit classrooms in different school systems or within systems to be aware of the disparity among them in the availability of material, media, and the suitability of facilities.

Although provisions for software and hardware alone may not be major determinants of whether teachers are able to accomplish the goals and objectives of the schools, they certainly affect goal achievement. Therefore, teacher evaluation needs to be conducted in the context of the availability, quality, and appropriateness of the physical conditions, equipment, and materials provided to the instructional setting.

Organizational Structure and Process of the School

How the school is organized and arrangements for how instructional processes are to be conducted represent a significant contextual climate, which needs to be taken into account in judging the success of teaching and teachers. Structures that affect teachers' potential for success include the organization of schools by grades or levels, or interdisciplinary arrangements in higher education, how the services of specialist personnel are provided (e.g., do they work with teachers to help them better serve students, or do they work directly with students, or both?), and accounting and reporting systems and procedures.

The organization for administering individual school units as well as some aspects of the arrangements for instruction within classrooms are frequently mandated by authorities outside the classroom. Even the materials provided sometimes dictate classroom organization. For example, a decision by a curriculum director or department chairperson that a particular instructional system will be used in all classrooms mandates an arrangement for instruction from which a teacher may not veer but which may not be compatible with a teacher's specific objectives or teaching style.

In a recent field study of the effects of class size (Filbey et al., Note 6), teachers reported that when class sizes were reduced, among those things that deterred them from making the most of this increased potential for improving instruction and learning were mandated curriculum series, fixed daily schedules, and emphasis by the school principal on orderliness, quiet, and written work (so students would "always have something they are supposed to be doing").

The ecological theory of teaching project, cited earlier, has identified two constructs for studying teaching that take into account structure within the classroom, *activity structure* and *participation structure*. Activity structure is represented by the rules and routines within the classroom that govern how the work activities are controlled and carried out, for example, grouping for reading or lining up to get art supplies. Participation structure is defined as the way students respond to rules and routines and are involved in carrying them out and the interactions that take place between teacher and students and among students in the conduct of work activities. Sometimes these two structures are established and controlled by the classroom teacher. Sometimes they are not. Their effects on teaching and teacher performance under both conditions must be taken into account as teachers are evaluated.

School Leadership and Evaluation Skills of Supervisors

Leadership is receiving renewed attention as a key focus for influencing change that will lead to school improvement. Recent examples of this are in the findings of Goodlad (1979) and the Carnegie study on the relationship between secondary education and higher education. Among other things, these studies point to the significant role of leadership at the building level in implementing programs and activities that promote innovation and curricular improvement. Teacher evaluation needs to take into account the quality of leadership teachers are provided for accomplishing the goals and objectives of the schools.

If leadership roles at the building level are important for innovation and improvement, they are also crucial in evaluating teaching and teachers for at least two other reasons. First, it is the principal (or his/her representative in a school-building leadership position) who most often has the major or sole responsibility for conducting the evaluation of teaching and teachers. Second, it is also the principal or his/her representative who makes, or whose recommendations are a major basis for making, decisions and who takes actions as a result of evaluation activities.

Principals and others who carry out evaluation activities and make, or largely influence, the decisions based on such activities should have intense preparation in evaluation theory and process, the commitment to make it a priority, the attitude to make it fair and objective, and the time and resources to discharge the responsibility in a creditable manner. Evaluation of teachers must take into account the important contextual elements related to those who evaluate: the preparedness, willingness, and opportunity to conduct this complex activity at the highest level of proficiency and to make the wisest, fairest, and most constructive judgments possible based on the findings.

Decision-Making Power of Teachers

Professionals are ostensibly labelled as such and licensed in particular professions because they possess high levels of expertise as certified by licensing authorities and degree-granting institutions. One unique characteristic of senior professions is that they have the leeway to exercise a high level of professional judgment. In this respect there is a distinct difference between the control of education and the exercise of professional authority and judgment. The control of education is, and rightly so, within the purview of

the duly elected or otherwise delegated governing bodies and includes determining and allocating resources for schooling and organizing and managing
the schools and colleges. On the other hand, the authority for exercising the
appropriate professional expertise and judgment for accomplishing particular instructional purposes with students of particular backgrounds and needs
ought to be mainly within the purview of the professional teacher.

When they have decision-making power, teachers are in the best position
to select the most appropriate ways of organizing classrooms, selecting
among instructional strategies and materials, and conducting processes for
evaluating student learning progress. When such power is absent, teachers
who work most closely with students are often unable to adjust instructional
programs to meet individual needs of which only the teacher may be aware.
This is particularly true when the power to make decisions about instructional matters is removed from classrooms or instructional departments to
central office headquarters—where mandates on what and how to teach
come from such remote sources as state education departments, boards of
trustees, and state legislatures—or where teaching assistants lead small
discussion sections of large survey courses but have little or no voice in the
overall conduct of the course.

Teacher evaluation must take into account the leeway provided teachers
to make decisions, based on their professional expertise, in (1) developing
specific objectives based on the broader goals set by the citizenry, (2)
selecting instructional strategies and materials, and (3) selecting, applying,
and interpreting programs and processes for evaluating student learning
progress.

Climate of Professional Worth and Contribution

A contextual factor in teaching that is more felt than observed is increasingly referred to as "efficacy," the sense of success. Recent studies of teacher
stress and teacher "burn-out" have turned attention to the effect of a sense of
success on success itself. It appears from research to date that efficacy can be
an important contributor to success. Although all the factors that contribute
to a sense of efficacy have not been identified, one implication of recent
studies is that the institutions that employ teachers need in some way to
create an organizational climate that causes professionals to sense that what
they do is important, valued, and respected. In addition, the institutions
need to recognize and publicly acclaim successful acts, which acclamation
tends to lead to more successful acts.

Teaching success, then, depends at least in part on how successful the
teacher sees himself/herself; this sense, in turn, depends to a considerable
degree on how the employing institution recognizes, supports, and applauds
success. Teacher evaluation should take into account the institution's com-

mitment to and behavior in creating a climate that is conducive to a high degree of efficacy among its professional staff.

Working Conditions, Human Services, and Security Benefits

Like students who may be in a poor frame of mind to learn if they begin the school day without breakfast and in uncomfortable classrooms, teachers who arrive at school insecure about health protection and financial security for their families and who must work in poorly lighted, poorly ventilated, cramped conditions are in a poor condition to demonstrate their highest levels of proficiency. A sense of security about health, financial welfare, and preparation for the future are essential for optimum functioning in all occupations. Since the basic material rewards (salaries) of teachers do not compare well to other professions and are also low compared to some other occupations with fewer requirements for preparation, the human service and security benefits become even more significant to teachers.

The idea of teaching as a missionary occupation, if it ever did have any validity, is no longer a viable rationale for expecting teachers to accept a lower standard of living and less security for the future than other segments of the population. Expectations for high motivation, mental state, and proficiency among teachers to conduct the best professional practice known must take into account what the system does to alleviate personal insecurities and to provide pleasant and conducive working conditions.

Community Characteristics, Priorities for Schooling, and Financial Ability, Effort, and Resources

Over the long term it has probably been, and continues to be, the local social order that has created and sustained the kinds of schools characteristic of various communities within the society. It is in this sense that community characteristics are viewed here as importantly influencing much of what the school is and does, including the performance of teachers.

Over a long period, relationships have been drawn between the characteristics of a community's citizenry and the kind (quality) of schools it maintains. Higher educational levels, greater percentages of professionals, and higher income levels in a population have all typically been accompanied by "better" schools, whether better is measured by more preparation of the school staffs, more adequate facilities and equipment, more innovative instructional processes, or greater achievement of the students.

Such characteristics as more education among the populace, not surprisingly, tend to be accompanied by greater community wealth (as measured by property values), which, in turn, is accompanied by a higher priority given to education among other services a community provides. The higher priority is then reflected in greater financial effort and, consequently, higher expenditure per student for schooling.

The higher expenditure per student purchases, per given numbers of students, more teachers—who are likely to have more preparation, more inservice opportunities, more planning time, and few enough students to employ the best known instructional strategies for diagnosing individual learning problems and providing individualized remediation for solving the problems.

A pedagogical sage of the middle half of this century has used the analog of the steam engine to describe this phenomenon. The late Paul Mort of Columbia University concluded from long years of research on the relationship of cost to quality in education that many communities do not provide enough resources for schools "to get the water warm in the boiler" let alone to generate enough steam to produce education of quality. The potential for success of teachers is directly linked to the characteristics of the total community in which they function and needs to be taken into account as teacher evaluation plans are developed.

SUMMARY AND CONCLUSIONS

Teacher evaluation, it has been argued here, must be considered in the context of community characteristics, resources, and effort for schooling, in the context of the total school system climate and organizational arrangements, in the context of the way in which the school unit and its leadership function, in the context of the time, human, and material resources and autonomy provided the classroom teacher, and in the context of the characteristics of the students themselves. Unless all of these factors are considered as mediators in judging the performance of teachers, whatever judgments (favorable or unfavorable) are made may be attributed to teachers when the compelling forces underlying teacher performance reside in places quite apart from the transactions that take place between teacher and student.

Context for the purpose of this discussion was conceived in the broadest sense to include characteristics of the community and their effect on teachers' ability to demonstrate proficiency. The decision to consider context broadly was based, in part, on a philosophical bent of this writer related to the query of George S. Counts a half century ago about whether the schools could create a new social order. The suggestion by Counts that the schools might make such a large impact on human behavior that the social order would be largely altered as a result has not fully materialized. And it is questionable whether it is practicable to conceive the school's role so broadly. On the other hand, if one has much faith in the power of education, one must believe that, as humans become better educated, they will make better decisions and, eventually, larger contributions to improvement of the social order.

REFERENCE NOTES

1. Rivlin, A. M. *Systematic thinking for social action*. Washington, DC: The Brookings Institution, 1971.
2. Bussis, A. M. *Collaboration for what?* Presented at the annual meeting of the American Educational Research Association, Boston, April 1980.
3. Dawson, M. B., W. J. Tikunoff, and B. A. Ward. *Toward an ecological theory of teaching*. San Francisco: Far West Laboratory for Educational Research and Development, 1978.
4. Glass, G. V. and M. L. Smith. *Meta-analysis of research on the relationship of class-size and achievement*. San Francisco: Far West Laboratory for Educational Research and Development, 1978.
5. Glass, G. V. and M. L. Smith. *Relationship of class-size to classroom processes, teacher satisfaction, and pupil affect: A meta analysis*. San Francisco: Far West Laboratory for Educational Research and Development, 1979.
6. Filbey, N., L. Cohen, G. McCutcheon, and D. Kyle. *What happens in smaller classes: A summary report of a field study*. San Francisco: Far West Laboratory for Educational Research and Development, 1980.

REFERENCES

Callahan, R. E. (1962) *Education and the Cult of Efficiency*. Chicago: University of Chicago Press.

Glass, G. V (1973) "Statistical and measurement problems in implementing the Stull Act," in N. L. Gage (ed.) *Mandated Evaluation of Educators: A Conference on California's Stull Act*. Washington, DC: Capitol Publications.

Goodlad, J. I. (1979) "Can our schools get better?" *Phi Delta Kappan*, 60: 342–347.

Harnischfeger, A. and D. E. Wiley (1976) "Teaching-learning processes in elementary school: A synoptic view." *Curriculum Inquiry*, 6: 5–43.

Joyce, B. and M. Weil (1972) *Models of Teaching*. Englewood Cliffs, NJ: Prentice-Hall.

McKenna, B. H. (1973) "A context for teacher evaluation." *National Elementary Principal*, 52 (5): 18–23.

PART II

Sources of Evidence

Many procedures are available for collecting data about a teacher's effectiveness, including interviews, testing of teachers, peer review of teaching materials and other documentary evidence, classroom visitation, student ratings of their instructors, student achievement, teacher out of class activities and other indirect evidence, and the teachers' self-assessments.

Two fundamental kinds of teacher interviews are examined in Chapter 4, the teacher selection interview and the teacher appraisal interview. Suggestions are provided for designing and conducting both types.

The recent revelation that many prospective and actual teachers in elementary and secondary schools perform poorly in basic tool subjects has prompted many states and school districts to institute competency tests for teachers. These trends are discussed in Chapter 5, together with a description of some of the approaches and instruments currently used to ascertain teacher mastery of subject matter primarily, but not exclusively, at the precollege level.

The need for peer review of those aspects of teaching that can best be judged by faculty is pointed out in Chapter 6. Identified are the kinds of documentary evidence most appropriate for peer review and the principles of judgment that improve the validity and fairness of decisions about teaching merit. A form for use in peer review is also included.

Classroom observation techniques are identified in Chapter 7. The strengths and weaknesses of various observation methods are discussed. Practical and technical considerations in the use of classroom observations are described.

Just as classroom observations are the dominant method of teacher evaluation in elementary and secondary schools, student rating of instructors is the method most widely used in colleges. Student rating is also the evaluation method most researched during the last decade. Chapter 8 provides a review of this research and covers the design, construction, administration, and reporting procedures for student rating forms.

The view that teaching competency can be measured effectively by the level of student learning has been attacked by many educators. Chapter 9 contains a discussion of this controversy and offers a set of criteria and techniques for the fair use of student achievement in both the formative and summative roles of teacher evaluation.

Also controversial is a host of indirect indicators sometimes used to evaluate teaching. Three types of these proxy measures, labelled professional, presage, and personal in Chapter 10, are seen to have a place in teacher evaluation by making explicit the several domains involved in teaching.

A summary of methods, instruments, and procedures for incorporating faculty self-assessment into the evaluation of teachers is presented in Chapter 11, the final chapter in Part II. Five major aids for self-evaluation are considered: self-rating forms, self-reports, self-study materials, observation of colleagues' teaching, and videotape/audiotape feedback of one's own teaching. The discussion of each aid includes a description of the basic technique, its options, examples of materials available, and general guidelines for use.

CHAPTER 4

TEACHER INTERVIEWS

DONALD L. HAEFELE
The Ohio State University

A variety of methods exist that can be of use in the evaluation of teachers. One cornerstone of an effective system of teacher evaluation is the teacher interview. As an approach to teacher evaluation, the teacher interview serves two important functions. First, it is the most significant phase of the process used in the selection of teachers at the elementary, secondary, and higher education levels. In addition, the teacher interview is the principal method of conveying a performance appraisal to the employed teacher. These two types of personal interviews, the selection interview and the appraisal interview, are important components in the acquisition and development of teachers.

THE TEACHER SELECTION INTERVIEW

There is ample evidence that in the 1980s the surplus of applicants for positions in public schools and higher education will continue ("Want to be a teacher?" 1978). This continuing trend is both a blessing and a burden to education officials who are responsible for filling a few vacancies. Assuming that administrators conduct an active recruiting program, many of the applicants will probably be highly qualified candidates "on paper." Confronted with several solid prospective candidates for a vacancy, the task of selecting from among them the one most likely to meet with success can be formidable. It is ironic that the opportunity to become more selective is accompanied by the need to invest more effort to screen the many applicants. Without a systematically ordered plan to guide the selection process, however, a candidate hired today could be a casualty by midyear. Haphazard selection procedures reduce the probability of success.

The Critical Requirements of the Vacancy

A systematic plan for teacher selection should initially focus on the teaching position. Before any applicants' materials are reviewed, the critical requirements for the specific teaching vacancy should be spelled out in detail. When a candidate is hired, it is assumed or predicted that this person will be successful. If the interviewer looks only for some general traits (e.g., interest in teaching, past success with undergraduate advisement) and ignores the critical requirements of the vacancy, that is, the responsibilities and demands associated with it, the chances of success for a new teacher or instructor may be significantly decreased. To isolate the critical requirements, an important question to ask is, "Can a person lacking quality A or B be effective in this teaching situation?" If clarity of instruction is one of the critical requirements, the question may become, "Can a teacher who lacks clarity of instruction be effective in this teaching situation?"

Many school systems and institutions of higher education harbor unique conditions which can lead to the failure of the candidate if essential selection procedures are ignored, such as (1) identification of the critical requirements of the vacant position; (2) identification of each candidate's experience, training, and competencies; and (3) achievement of the best match between one candidate's attributes and the critical requirements of the vacant position. If, for example, the vacant position is in an inner-city public school with a predominantly black population, the school would want to employ a person who not only can teach comfortably in that situation but who also understands black culture and how to employ it advantageously in teaching. These three conditions are some of the critical requirements for this particular position. Another situation may require a teacher who can work effectively with gifted students or with students who have very low self-concepts.

If a school does not know what kind of employee competencies it is looking for and is, therefore, unable to communicate accurately the vacancy requirements to the candidates, the selection interview becomes undirected and vague. The subsequently employed candidate may be misled, and the candidate's potential for success in the job may be seriously reduced. This situation could occur, for example, for the recently employed instructor in the English Department who thought her teaching load and related assignments would be moderate the first year on the job. Instead, she was unexpectedly assigned to teach four different courses per term, placed on three committees with substantial workloads, and told that she must publish a minimum of three scholarly papers per year to retain her job. This instructor could easily become a midyear casualty. Had the requirements for this vacancy been identified and clearly communicated to the applicant, she might have negotiated for a more reasonable workload, not have accepted the position, or accepted it with the understanding that some tasks will be performed better than others.

This problem is not entirely the fault of the interviewing team. It is also a responsibility of the candidates to ascertain from the selection committee an explicit description of the critical requirements for the position. Selection is a two-sided process, in which (1) the committee attempts to determine how well the candidates meet the critical requirements and (2) the candidates attempt to determine how well the job requirements fit their experiences and professional demands.

The Application Screen

When a vacancy occurs, a selection committee is established to determine the critical requirements of the position, publicize the vacancy, and review all applications. Ideally, in elementary and secondary schools this committee includes a principal, one or more teachers from the school where the vacancy exists, perhaps another administrator from the district office, and a couple of teachers from other schools in the district. The committee would be trained to employ a set of criteria in the review of each applicant's folder, and each member would initially evaluate each folder independently. One criterion could be certification; another could be high ratings in student teaching from a principal, cooperating teacher, and college supervisor. The latter criterion emerged from Schalock's (1979) review of research in teacher selection, indicating that performance ratings for student teaching are reasonably good predictors of performance ratings in the first two years of teaching. In higher education, a selection or search committee is usually established consisting of the department chairperson and a few faculty members. In reviewing applicants' folders, this committee might look for high ratings from undergraduate classes taught by the candidate as one of several criteria or indicators of teaching performance.

In elementary, secondary, and higher education, a set of standardized criteria, or characteristics, that are capable of being rated on a scale and that also permit commentary are very valuable for evaluating each applicant's folder. Selection team members could be trained through rating a common set of fabricated folders, followed by discussion of how individual member's ratings compared. If high interrater agreement is established and determined to be stable, each folder could be reviewed by one or at most two team members. This would reduce some of the workload when there are many applicants. The author has observed the application of this rather rigorous approach to screening applicants' folders at the public school level. This standardized process is not typical of how all school districts operate, however. Although it may appear to be an objective process that determines the best four or five candidates in teaching potential, no solid evidence exists to support this view. In many school districts, an elementary or secondary personnel office administrator reviews folders and recommends the best candidates for interviews.

Applications for elementary and secondary school vacancies typically include an application form, evidence of certification, a college transcript, references, a résumé, and student teaching evaluations from the principal, cooperating teacher, and college supervisor. Scholastic Aptitude Test scores of teacher graduates have declined, in recent years, faster than the much-reported decline in the scores of students as a whole. This trend has prompted many school district officials to include tests of verbal and quantitative skills as an integral part of the application process. In addition, many school districts require written compositions from applicants. Usually each applicant is required to respond to a question such as, "Choose a topic within your subject area and briefly describe how you would teach a unit on that topic with elementary or high school students. Be sure to describe provisions for individual differences." At the college level as well, candidates are sometimes asked to prepare a statement on a topic of particular relevance or interest to the selection committee. All of these sources of information are subsequently available for use in the selection interview to probe ideas, to stir discussion, and, ultimately, to arrive at a decision about which one of several screened candidates will be offered a teaching position.

Schalock's (1979) review of research in teacher selection revealed that teacher attributes such as knowledge about teaching, performance on ability tests, personality traits, and other proxy measures of effectiveness bear little or no relationship to the criterion of student attainment. The only screening source that currently has an established relationship to observed classroom performance is student teaching performance. Information about the prior college teaching performance of candidates for positions in higher education might also furnish a more accurate prediction of subsequent performance with undergraduate and graduate students than proxy measures such as grade point average or research experience.

It is important to note that questions should not be included in the application form or in a subsequent interview that ask for information that can be used to discriminate unlawfully among candidates from legally protected racial, sex, or ethnic groups. In many states (e.g., Ohio and New York), unlawful inquiries include questions or statements such as the following: Are you known as Mr., Mrs., Miss, or Ms? Are you married? Single? Divorced? Separated? Name or other information about spouse. Are you able to reproduce, or do you advocate any form of birth control or family planning? Have you ever been arrested? Please affix photograph. Did you receive an honorable discharge from military service? What is your national origin? Do you have any handicaps? Employers are not prevented from asking questions that they need to ask to fill positions with qualified people. Information may not be sought before hiring that would permit a person to be

labelled or pigeonholed in one of the categories that have been used historically to exclude qualified persons.

Reliability and Validity

The principal goal of the selection interview is to determine which
screened candidate possesses the professional experience and qualities that
match the critical requirements for the vacant teaching position. Lack of
reliability is, unfortunately, a hallmark of many selection interviews. As
Shouksmith (1968) stated, "Often this unreliability is produced when we ask
the interview to do too much, to discriminate more finely than it is capable of
doing" (p. 4). To maximize agreement among interviewers and to achieve
greater accuracy in the assessment of interviewees, the interview should
focus only on a few broad categories and decisions (e.g., good-bad, hire-no
hire, innovative-conventional). This process becomes more systematic
when the critical requirements for the position are rank ordered and when
more time is devoted to a few (four or five) of the most important requirements rather than when a little time is devoted to all of them.

Reliability can also be improved by permitting the interviewee to have
several opportunities to respond to questions. The arrangement of two or
more interview sessions with different interviewers allows a range of opportunities for the candidate to be reviewed. This approach is more typical of
higher education interviews, in which the candidate usually meets with
several groups of faculty and administrators during an entire day's visit.
Elementary and secondary school selection committees infrequently engage
in this practice. Even within small school systems, several candidates may
be interviewed in one day, each for an average time of less than one hour. In
many elementary and secondary school systems, applications and related
materials are screened at the district office. The most outstanding candidate
is then interviewed at the school site by the principal, with the hiring decision left in the principal's hands. When the employment decision resides
with one person, and teachers and others are excluded from the process,
reliability can become a problem. Even though this process has often met
with success, acceptance of and a personal investment in the new teacher by
the faculty and staff of the school are maximized when the decision is
shared. Teachers are equally, if not more, capable of determining how well
the candidate's professional experience and qualities meet the needs of their
school and the particular teaching position than are many school administrators.

Since the selection interview focuses on determining how good a teacher
each candidate is, validity of the interview could be enhanced by asking each

of the final candidates to teach a class that corresponds to the vacant position. Candidates for positions in higher education are increasingly asked to deliver a scholarly presentation before the faculty and other graduate students during their visit. This approach has merit. It permits the selection committee and others to view the interviewee's teaching methods and capacity to interact effectively with a group of students. Inasmuch as all candidates would be exposed to the same standardized conditions, this "teaching sample" would furnish opportunities for the subsequent interview to focus on actual teaching behavior in addition to documenting prior teaching performance. Thus, if critical requirements for the teaching vacancy include the ability to (1) organize for teaching, (2) teach with clarity and enthusiasm, (3) sustain the attention of the class, and (4) engage the students in learning activities, some estimation of these teaching behaviors can be achieved through a standardized teaching situation. As Schalock (1979) noted, these behaviors are only "proxy measures" of teacher effectiveness and are not necessarily related to student attainment. However, if performance rather than effectiveness is the criterion, the "teaching sample" approach allows comparisons among candidates and furnishes concrete evidence for discussion in the interview. Employment of a standardized observation form or schedule for the teaching sample is important. Subjectivity is always a part of rating a performance. However, if the members of the selection team are trained to use an observation form, average ratings for each candidate can supply useful comparative data.

Nondirective and Directive Approaches to Questioning

Most writers on the subject agree that the interview should be a pleasant experience for the candidate, with the candidate doing most of the talking—perhaps as much as 80% or 90%. The interview might begin with small talk if a candidate appears very tense initially. Transition to the interview proper may be accomplished by furnishing an overview of the interview, emphasizing a need to know the candidate more personally and to determine the candidate's particular qualities that relate to the teaching vacancy.

Writers and prominent consultants to business and industry (Fear, 1978; Maier, 1976; Shouksmith, 1968) stress the value gained from interviews in which the interviewer assumes a nondirective, reflective role. In this role, the interviewer does little talking and attempts to keep the candidate talking by statements and gestures that demonstrate understanding and acceptance of the candidate's ideas. An example of the nondirective approach is furnished in the following interviewer's reaction to a candidate's statement.

Candidate: As you can see, my grades in methods and other education courses are not very high. However, when it came to student teaching, I put all my energy into it. It seemed like I'd gone into a totally different world. Teaching kids was so real and meaningful for me. I began to see what I needed to know in order to teach well. Much of what I needed was not covered in the education courses. My evaluations by the cooperating teacher, the principal, and my college supervisor were very good. My student teaching experience convinced me I could do a good job in teaching.

Interviewer: I think I know what you mean. In other words, you felt the education courses weren't very effective because you had no immediate opportunity to apply your knowledge and skills with children. This isn't an uncommon reaction. But the student teaching brought things together for you, and you found you could be effective in helping kids learn.

The interviewer indicated acceptance of the candidate's behavior and, in addition, demonstrated an understanding of what the candidate said by reflecting the candidate's ideas.

Although the nondirective approach may be nonthreatening and effective when used by a highly skilled interviewer, direct questioning can reflect these same qualities. An example of the application of both nondirective and directive approaches to the candidate's response to the critical requirement of discipline may be useful here. A direct approach might include a question like the following, "How would you deal with one or more persistently disruptive students?" In contrast, the nondirective approach to the requirement might be phrased like this, "Discipline in the schools continues to be viewed as an important national issue. Perhaps you could share some of your ideas or experiences in this area." If the response to the latter statement fails to produce a specific response, a follow-up directive question, less abrupt than the one above, might be, "Please take a few minutes to describe for us your view of an effective classroom discipline plan." This question implies the additional need to connect specific strategies to some philosophical base.

A critical requirement for a higher education position might call for a person who can teach undergraduate as well as graduate level courses. A direct approach would be to ask, "How would you feel about teaching courses in history to undergraduates?" A more nondirective statement would be, "I see you have had experience in teaching undergraduates. Perhaps you could describe some of your experiences for us."

Some writers classify the directive approach to probing the candidate's qualifications for the teaching position as a standardized interview. Questions that are posed in the directive approach to interviewing are usually established in advance and are presented to each candidate. A number of school districts that employ this approach find that it furnishes a common basis for comparing candidates who seek the same position. Interviewers who employ the nondirective approach may also have some preestablished questions to present to each candidate, which emerge from an examination of the candidate's background and experiences.

Nondirective approaches to questioning typically seek more expansive responses and, in a more subtle fashion, attempt to elicit the same information that may be derived through more direct questioning. The freedom to pursue the flow of ideas and thought generated by the candidate in the nondirective interview sometimes prevents consideration of all the critical requirements. In contrast, direct questioning has the advantages that it does not disguise intent, takes less time, and usually allows the interviewers to obtain responses to all the questions. Some may wish to experiment with both approaches in the selection interview situation.

A Standardized Approach

An interview approach that reflects an extreme, inflexible interpretation of a directive, standardized interview method is the Teacher Perceiver Interview (TPI; Haefele, 1978). The TPI consists of 60 open-ended questions, many of them presented as simulated problems. For example, the TPI interviewer may read the following problem situation to a candidate, "John tells you that Robert's schoolwork has suddenly slid from good to poor because of problems at home." Following presentation of each situation or question, the candidate is required to describe what action the teacher should take and to supply reasons for that action. No verbal interaction between the interviewee and the interviewer is permitted. The interviewer may only repeat the question related to the particular incident. Questions and simulated situations presented on the TPI purportedly assess noncognitive traits, such as goal or mission strength, responsiveness to students, satisfaction through others' achievements, ability to motivate students, innovative ideas, and inner drive toward completeness. Responses to each of the 60 questions are rated as 0 (failed) or 1 (passed). The TPI is a test in which it is assumed that right and wrong answers exist. All responses are rated by a trained TPI interviewer.

Several advantages mentioned by TPI trainers and some users are ease of administration, standardization of questions and test conditions, and objectivity. But there are also several disadvantages. A TPI workshop leader, in a published article (Muller, 1978), noted that an infinite number of potentially acceptable or unacceptable responses exist for each question. The responsibility for assigning a pass or fail to each response from the candidate places an imposing burden on the interviewer. Unquestioned faith in a TPI score is encouraged by TPI trainers, and some school administrators have misused the TPI data by selecting new teachers simply on the basis of a high TPI score. The cost of training raters, up to $1350, is another disadvantage associated with the TPI. Still another disadvantage of the TPI frequently voiced by candidates is the impersonal atmosphere that permeates this interview technique. In the TPI situation, the candidate typically assumes a guarded or defensive stance and carefully screens responses to an impassive interviewer. How ironic that this impersonal process is designed to identify candidates who embody warmth, empathy, rapport, openness, and creativity. Because the questions are fixed, there is no assurance that the questions will elicit information that relates to the critical requirements of the vacant position.

A significant criticism of the TPI and similar measures (e.g., National Teacher Examination) is the total absence of published research indicating the degree to which performance on these measures can predict more effective and less effective teachers. The question that must be addressed is "Can they furnish desirable information that is valid, accurate, and unobtainable through the personal interview?" Research is necessary to determine if the TPI, National Teacher Examination, or other measures can supplement the selection interview and, in particular, to ascertain if they have any predictive power. Prediction is what the selection interview process is all about.

Verbal and Nonverbal Cuing

Because the principal function of the selection interview is to obtain information from the candidate that will assist the selection team in judging each candidate's qualifications for the teaching position, the interviewer should avoid imparting explicit or implied evaluations or verbal and nonverbal cues that influence or bias the *direction of responses* by the candidate. Verbal cuing of the candidate is illustrated in this statement:

> Mr. Blake, students in our intermediate psychology course are typically assigned a significant amount of library research each quarter. We feel such assignments are very helpful in expanding the students' knowledge of research and important journals. Don't you agree?

This blatant cuing indicates Mr. Blake should take a positive stance regarding this course requirement as one step in landing the position. If the interviewer wishes to avoid influencing the candidate's response, a more open-ended question might be:

> Mr. Blake, what is your opinion regarding the assignment of library research to students in an intermediate psychology course?

Of course, the tone of the questioning and the nonverbal behavior of the interviewer should not impart cues that direct the response. Another example of verbal bias in questioning is:

Ms. Taylor, what is your opinion about the busing for desegregation program that uproots children from their neighborhood schools and ships them several miles across town to a school that is located in a high crime area?

Again, the wording of the question obtrusively cues the candidate, importuning a response that opposes busing for desegregation. A more impartial question that avoids bias is:

What is your view on the desegregating of schools?

Reactions to a candidate's statement should not be followed by influencing comments from the interviewer such as, "That's how I feel about basal readers too," or "That really doesn't agree with what we know about how kids learn to read, does it?" A less leading statement is, "Your comment about organization for reading is interesting; please tell me more about it." This latter response is also more likely to keep the candidate talking.

The nonverbal behavior of the interviewer(s) is another of the subtle ways in which the direction of the response and the responsiveness of the candidate can be influenced; in fact, Mehrabian (1972) concluded that nonverbal behavior is more potent and revealing than speech. Nonverbal behaviors can communicate a challenge to a candidate's statement or position as forcefully as verbal confrontation or can lead a candidate in a desired direction.

Some significant nonverbal behaviors by an interviewer that can indicate a positive attitude toward the candidate's response include frequent smiling, continued eye contact, leaning bodily toward the candidate, moderate to high degree of open-arm position, facing the candidate directly, and physical closeness to the candidate. In contrast, infrequent smiles, low eye contact, a very relaxed body posture, leaning bodily away from the candidate, a crossed (folded) arm position, shoulders and legs turned away from the candidate, and increased physical distance from the candidate are nonverbal behaviors that singly or in combination are frequently interpreted as negative (or nonpositive) indicators.

Interviewers are sometimes unaware that they are emitting these nonverbal cues. Disguising one's lack of positive regard for a candidate's response, when it exists, is not easy. Sensitivity to nonverbal cues varies among interviewees, and some cues are more obvious indicators than others (e.g., smiles and eye contact). Application of them should vary with the individual situation. Increased use of any or all of the positive cues may be particularly desirable when a candidate is nervous or tense in the initial minutes of the interview.

Because the degree to which the candidate's professional preparation and experience fit the critical requirements is the principal interest, a warm atmosphere should permeate the interview to obtain maximum information about the candidate. Both directive and/or nondirective approaches integrated with appropriate verbal and nonverbal behaviors can effectively influence the candidate to address the basic critical requirements and to furnish the necessary information. Interviews that adhere to the basic principles briefly outlined above will, as Shouksmith (1968) claimed, make the candidates feel that they have had a "pleasant conversation."

THE TEACHER APPRAISAL INTERVIEW

Although the teacher appraisal interview is generally perceived as a way in which an evaluator communicates progress in teaching performance to the teacher, it may serve several specific functions or objectives, such as warning that improvement in teaching is needed, establishing teaching performance standards for the coming year, motivating teaching performance, assessing the degree to which teaching performance standards have been achieved, recognizing superior teaching performance, and determining what the evaluator or others can do to sustain or improve teaching performance. Naturally, all of these objectives would not be applicable in each appraisal interview. For example, an interview convened to recognize superior teaching would be quite different in content and direction from one convened to motivate improved teaching performance. The superior teacher would not receive a warning that improvement in teaching is needed, but would receive recognition for outstanding performance. However, the teacher whose performance is in need of marked improvement would require support to motivate further performance.

Essential Conditions for Effective Appraisal Interviews

An important condition for an effective appraisal interview is an agreement between the teachers and the evaluator about the goals of teacher evaluation and how the interview relates to these goals. Before any data gathering on teaching is undertaken, the teacher and the evaluator should collectively identify and describe what data will be obtained and how they will be gathered. In many school districts and in some institutions of higher education, the types of information that may be collected and the collection methods are negotiated and incorporated into contracts. An outcome of this negotiated arrangement is a standardization of the instrument (often an observation form), which offers some control of evaluator bias. That is, the categories and kinds of information that may be included in the evaluation are restricted.

Some readers may question the value of an appraisal interview limited to information gathered through a standardized form. Restricted consideration of a limited set of characteristics of teaching may suggest a perception of teachers as interchangeable parts, rather than as individualized professionals characterized by different strengths, weaknesses, and capabilities. To counteract this perception, teachers are often asked to furnish a self-appraisal of teaching on a standardized form, which is subsequently compared with the evaluator's appraisal during the interview.

Another basic condition for the conduct of effective appraisal interviews is a clear understanding of what the observation and related instructional data mean. For example, low student evaluations in interpersonal relationships received by an instructor who teaches classes that include 70 or more students might be anticipated yet unrepresentative of relationships in small classes. Most sources of teaching information consist of several brief samples of behavior that are assumed to be representative of teaching performance over 10 or more months of instruction. When one or two observations a year (not unusual in many situations) or a survey of students' attitudes from one or two courses constitute the appraisal data, the evaluator is not on very firm ground for decision making, particularly for contract renewal decisions. When the sample of teaching performance is inadequate, the evaluator must recognize this and resist interpreting it as representative.

What information is conveyed to the teacher and how it is communicated are other significant considerations. In general, the evaluator should communicate the appraisal to the teacher in a nonthreatening manner. Teachers typically welcome appraisal interviews that focus on teaching improvement rather than on fault-finding, particularly when the information is meaningful and useful to the teacher. It is common knowledge that human beings perform best when there is ample trust and encouragement. Sometimes the teacher is furnished with a copy of the evaluator's appraisal before the interview. This is a practice favored by many teachers. Presentation of an unexpectedly negative appraisal in the interview can place a teacher at a serious disadvantage. The evaluator will have had time to prepare, whereas the teachers may enter unsure of where they stand.

Perhaps the most important condition for a mutually beneficial appraisal interview is the evaluator's competence. It is generally assumed that all evaluators are gifted in assessing the quality of teaching information and in conducting effective appraisal interviews. Evaluation of teaching and appraisal interviewing are significant aspects of an administrative role (e.g., principal or department chairperson). However, administrators are not highly trained as evaluators and interviewers, if they are trained at all. Many administrators assume evaluation responsibilities for a brief period during the year and fail to perceive evaluation as an extension of their continuing interrelationships with teachers. The appraisal interview is not something that is simply plugged in at a certain time. To be effective, the appraisal interview must be viewed as a continuation of professional and personal relationships between the teacher and the evaluator. A competent evaluator is an instructional leader, who continuously interacts with the teachers, convening several interviews throughout the year and working with each teacher to achieve instructional goals.

Too often when an instructional deficiency is judged to occur, it is assumed that the teacher has the problem and that the evaluator can fairly judge the teacher and/or issue advice about how to remedy the problem. The deficiency may, however, reside with the evaluator. For example, an evaluator who places emphasis on report deadlines and paperwork and invests little effort in establishing relationships with the instructional staff will often react negatively to a teacher who may be adequate in teaching performance but frequently late with reports. In another situation, an evaluator may favor orderly, tidy classrooms and disregard the quality of teacher-student involvement. The conditions deemed important by the evaluator in each of the above situations have little to do with teaching performance or effectiveness. They reflect an evaluator's bias, which may negatively influence the evaluation of the teacher and the subsequent appraisal interview. To evaluate teachers and to conduct effective appraisal interviews, it is vitally important that evaluators understand how their values affect their judgments of teaching competence.

Two Illustrative Cases

Inadequacy and misinterpretation of evaluation information can damage the evaluator-teacher relationship. For example, the evaluator may present the following comments to a first-year teacher who has received an unsatisfactory appraisal:

> Carol, you've had a rough year. I must admit that there are several teachers in this system who, like you, have also found it difficult to teach slow learners.

Some empathy for Carol's situation is expressed by the evaluator, but the implication of the statement is that the perceived problem is Carol's and not unique to the school system. Carol may believe the appraisal has not represented her situation accurately and react negatively by stating:

I feel I have been treated unfairly! I have four classes of slow learners and I have to pack up each period and move to a different room four times a day to meet each class. By the time I reach the classroom, the students are running around the room, throwing erasers and chalk and sometimes even fighting! It takes 15 minutes just to calm them down. Nobody has offered any assistance—teachers or administrators. I don't feel this teaching problem is all my fault.

Having been assigned some responsibility for Carol's unsatisfactory performance, the evaluator who is committed to using information to enhance teaching performance would welcome this undisclosed information and try to use it in a constructive way. The evaluator might react to Carol by stating:

In other words, Carol, you feel you have been placed in a very difficult teaching situation and that this appraisal doesn't present your situation accurately. I can understand your reaction. You've mentioned a major factor we seemed to have overlooked.

In this situation, the evaluator does not attempt to obtain compliance with the appraisal. More significantly, the evaluator recognizes that relevant information about Carol's teaching situation has been overlooked. The teacher is more likely to view this kind of interview as worthwhile and feel the evaluator is concerned about the problem situation and wishes to help rather than as an interview in which the evaluator refused to listen to her comments.

Because a significant objective of the appraisal interview is to determine what the evaluator or others can do to improve teaching performance, after reviewing the poor teaching situation Carol experienced, the evaluator might offer assistance through a statement such as:

Carol, you have been unintentionally placed in a difficult teaching situation. I'm sorry to say we can't rearrange teaching assignments at this time of the year. However, what do you think we, including other teachers and administrators, can do to help you with this problem?

The evaluator not only accepts substantial accountability for Carol's unsatisfactory performance but also indicates that a cooperatively developed plan might alleviate this problem. One possible solution to this problem was worked out by Carol, the evaluator, and another teacher. The evaluator agreed to meet two of Carol's classes as they enter her classroom. A more experienced teacher volunteered to cover the other two classes until Carol arrives. They would have the students seated and ready when Carol enters the classroom. Final determination of this plan rested with Carol, the teacher. She was committed to it because she had a personal stake in its creation.

This problem suggests how the inadequacy of evaluation information can reveal a distorted profile of a teacher and seriously impair the evaluator-teacher relationship in the appraisal interview. In addition, it is clear that an evaluator who has blind faith in the accuracy of limited information and who becomes defensive when challenged by the teacher will lose the opportunity to employ intrinsic or teacher-motivated remedial options and build strong teacher-evaluator relationships. An externally imposed remedial plan will usually be less acceptable and, ultimately, less effective than a teacher-motivated plan.

Thus far, some considerations or conditions that may be of use in the establishment and conduct of effective appraisal interviews have been examined. The above example, involving Carol, focused on, among other things, one of the objectives of appraisal interviews, determining what the evaluator and others can do in the interview to improve teaching performance. It may be profitable to examine another function of the appraisal interview, namely, warning that improvement is needed.

It is John's first year of employment as a mathematics teacher. A tenure review appraisal interview is scheduled to consider a serious teaching problem that John is experiencing. Information from several sources (students, peers, administrators) indicates that John regularly uses some inappropriate teaching methods with his students. In the interview, the evaluator informs John that ridicule and sarcasm seem to be instructional processes that he employs daily. The evaluator notes one observed incident when an obviously anxious student failed to respond promptly to a question and John said:

Why do you even bother to take this course if you're too dumb to do the assigned work?

John says that he has little patience with students who will not work hard. Although he is well-prepared for class and knows his subject well, it is clear that this problem rests with John.

In this situation, the evaluator does not have to defend the evaluation. John's comments indicate general agreement with this evaluation, although he failed to note in his self-evaluation that he uses such teaching approaches. The evaluator states that this teaching behavior is unacceptable. Two approaches are now available. A plan for remediation of this teaching problem could be suggested by the evaluator. Another route to remediation would be to encourage John to suggest a plan that substitutes positive procedures for the negative ones and motivates student effort. If John is amenable to working with the evaluator and perhaps with other teachers to improve his instruction substantially, particularly his perception of teacher-student relationships, an acceptable plan could be adopted. If John fails to generate a plan that clearly demonstrates a desire to alter significantly his teaching approach, the evaluator has to take charge, suggest specific steps that John will have to follow, and convince him to implement them. The evaluator must clearly indicate what John must do to change his teaching behavior and that his contract will not be renewed if he fails to do so.

If it is determined in the discussion that John dislikes teaching, the evaluator could suggest that John explore alternative areas of work that will permit application of his abilities in mathematics. This may be the kindest suggestion of all and one option that John may not have considered. The evaluator should be aware that counseling someone out of teaching and into alternative lines of employment stretches the typical scope of the appraisal interview. Other resource people may subsequently be involved in this career exploration phase.

Some Do's and Don't's

All the particulars associated with appraisal interviewing cannot be considered within this section. The following summary of major points may be useful to the reader.

(1) Conduct more than one appraisal interview a year. Year-end summation appraisal interviews should be avoided, particularly when they are negative and allow no opportunity for correction.

(2) Convene goal-setting interviews early in the year. Establish additional interviews during the year to monitor progress toward goals.

(3) Involve, whenever possible, different evaluators in appraisal interviews during the year.

(4) Involve teachers in the design and testing of the evaluative criteria that form the basis for the appraisal interview.

(5) Furnish evaluators with ample training in appraisal interviewing. Simulated data and transcripts of interviews are useful as training aids.

(6) Recognize that often only limited and sometimes biased data are available for making judgments about the quality of teaching.

(7) Establish the evaluator's responsibility for the achievement of teaching goals.

(8) Consider only one significant problem at each interview, even though several may have been observed.

(9) Share the creation and development of remedial instructional plans with the teacher.

(10) Avoid a fault-finding evaluation posture, which assumes that the teacher is solely accountable for a disclosed problem.

(11) Avoid an appraisal interview approach that places the teacher in a defensive posture. To be helpful, the evaluator needs the confidence of the teacher.

Additional suggestions for conducting interviews may be found in Figure 3 in Chapter 12. For further useful information related to selection and appraisal interviews, see Bolton (1973), Fear (1978), Maier (1976), Mehrabian (1972), Schalock (1979), Shouksmith (1968), and Thomas (1979).

REFERENCES

Bolton, D. L. (1973) *Selection and evaluation of teachers*. Berkeley, CA: McCutchan.

Fear, F. A. (1978) *The evaluation interview*. New York: McGraw-Hill.

Haefele, D. L. (1978) "The teacher perceiver interview: How valid?" *Phi Delta Kappan*, 59: 683–684.

Maier, N. R. (1976) *The appraisal interview: Three basic approaches*. La Jolla, CA: University Associates.

Mehrabian, A. (1972) *Nonverbal communication*. Chicago: Aldine-Atherton.

Muller, G. D. (1978) "In defense of the teacher perceiver." *Phi Delta Kappan*, 59: 684–685.

Schalock, D. (1979) "Research on teacher selection." *Review of Research in Education*, 7: 364–417.

Shouksmith, G. (1968) *Assessment through interviewing*. New York: Pergamon.

Thomas, M. D. (1979) *Performance evaluation of educational personnel*. Bloomington, IN: Phi Delta Kappa Educational Foundation.

Want to be a teacher? Don't try it 'til 1985. (1978) *Phi Delta Kappan*, 59: 725.

CHAPTER 5

TEACHER COMMAND OF SUBJECT MATTER

WILLIAM U. HARRIS
Educational Testing Service

This chapter explores some of the problems involved in determining the extent of a teacher's knowledge of subject matter. It cites questions, discusses trends that are emerging at state and local levels, and highlights some of the approaches, instruments, and methods currently employed to ascertain teacher mastery of subject matter, primarily, but not exclusively, at the elementary and secondary school levels. As used here, the phrase "teacher command of subject matter" is intended to include that knowledge of basic skills deemed necessary by the teacher-training institution as a prerequisite to admittance to the teacher-training curriculum and that knowledge of the substantive field, as well as of teaching techniques and methodologies, that is required for a degree in education and/or initial licensing.

The educational establishment in the United States is a complex and awesome institution, which is called on to perform an enormous array of functions. More than 70 million children are now under the tutelage of more than 2 million teachers in 150,000 schools of varying levels across the country. Not included in these figures are the more than 15 million students enrolled in more than 3,000 institutions of higher education. Ironically, the increasing and ready availability of education to American youth, which has been championed as the hallmark of a truly democratic society, has not only propelled education into public view but has also brought it under siege as never before. There are, no doubt, many reasons why the integrity of American education is now in jeopardy; however, few if any reasons rival the decline in pupil achievement (as evidenced by scores on standardized tests) for igniting the call for accountability by the educational establishment. Alarmed by a steady drop in the scores of students at the elementary-secondary level on such tests as the Scholastic Aptitude Test (SAT) and those of the National Assessment of Educational Progress and by the revelation that many college students and prospective teachers perform poorly in basic tool subjects (readin', 'ritin', and 'rithmetic), the public is speculating that, if students demonstrate deficiencies in their learning, the teachers who dispense that learning must be deficient. These factors, coupled with the reality that a major portion of property taxes is used for administering an educational system whose product is possibly out of kilter with the expenses needed to run the enterprise, have increased the call for accountability. (For example, in 1971–1972 the per-pupil expenditure in the United States for students in K-12 was $926; by 1976–1977 the figure had escalated to $1,561. The mean SAT-Verbal score for high school seniors was 453 in 1971–1972 and the mean SAT-Mathematical score that year for the same group was 484. By 1976–1977 the mean SAT-Verbal score had declined to 429 and the mean SAT-Mathematical score to 470.)

One of the outcomes of this call for accountability has been the movement toward minimum competency testing for students, which began in 1975–1976 in two or three states. Within a few short years, the movement has swept the country. Currently more than 35 states have either adopted minimum competency testing programs or are exploring the feasibility of doing so. Because of the growing belief that many teachers, particularly the recent graduates, evidence the same deficiencies observed in their students, more state and local boards are also being pressured to be more accountable for the teachers they hire. This includes, of course, ascertaining that teachers have command over the subject matter that they are preparing to dispense.

VIEWS ON TESTING TEACHERS

It has been said that "education is the engine of social progress and intelligence is its fuel." It has also been said, sarcastically, that "those who can, do; those who can't, teach." These two ideas provide the substance for the changing attitudes of the public about American education; whereas American educational institutions are seen as primary tools for social change and have been called on to serve a variety of functions, from enhancing the melting pot concept for various social and ethnic groups earlier in the century to solving the discipline and drug problems today, the rank-and-file members of the profession are seen as showing signs of running low on the "fuel" that makes the engine run.

In a recent article that spoke to this point, W. Timothy Weaver offered evidence that the fuel, or the academic caliber of prospective teachers, is comparatively low. When studying the college entrance examinations of freshmen who were entering 19 different fields, he found that education majors ranked 17th in mathematics and 14th in English. Mr. Weaver commented,

If it is a reasonable expectation that new teachers ought to be able to read and write sentences, recognizing common words, add, subtract and multiply numbers, with at least average proficiency, then discovery that such skills are not average and have diminished would be cause for alarm. The education profession must be able to make the claim that its members are competent in the basics they are teaching, because it is a reasonable presumption that such competencies are necessary for effective teaching [1979: 30].

Views of the Public

Those parents, educators, and lay people who have been critical of American education apparently do presume that such competencies are essential for effective teaching and that those who dispense the knowledge or develop literacy must themselves be knowledgeable and/or literate. In the 11th annual Gallup Poll of the Public's Attitudes Toward the Public Schools conducted in May 1979 (Gallup, 1980), the majority of those polled felt that education is worse today than in earlier times. Included in this survey were two questions about the testing of teachers:

In addition to meeting college requirements for a teacher's certificate, should those who want to become teachers also be required to pass a state board examination to prove their knowledge in the subject(s) they will teach before they are hired? After they are hired, do you think teachers should be tested every few years to see if they are keeping up to date with developments in their field [1980: 39]?

There was widespread approval for such examinations, with 85% of those polled answering "Yes, they should" to both questions. Teachers in the public's ideal school, as described in this poll, would be required to pass state board examinations not only before they were hired but also at regular intervals thereafter.

Views of Professional Associations

The number of professional associations that represent teachers, or to which persons in the field of education can belong, is overwhelming to say the least. An association serves virtually every level, discipline, and interest in the field. Some have been more prominent and forthright than others in responding to the public demand for accountability. Two of the largest and most prominent associations are the National Education Association (NEA) and the American Federation of Teachers (AFT). The NEA, the larger of the two, represents 1.7 million persons who are actively engaged in, or on leave from, professional work. In a recent outline of its views on teacher education and standards, the NEA (1980) identified 10 areas of knowledge and skills that it believes to be critical to the performance of educators in the profession. Among them are the following:

(1) a working familiarity with psychometrics, tests, and testing and competence to evaluate and use contemporary diagnostic instruments
(2) a general education that includes exposure to the various academic disciplines making up the curriculum of the school
(3) written and spoken mastery of the English language
(4) highly developed communication skills, including effective speaking, writing, and use of communications technology
(5) thorough and comprehensive understanding of developmental psychology and the psychology of learning.

The NEA proclaims that teacher education is more than courses, that it involves cognitive, theoretical, and abstract thinking. It recommends that the process of licensing be rigorous, but it asserts that evaluation of the proficiency of teachers and prospective teachers must be derived from a wide variety of related data gathered over a long period of time. Apparently the "wide variety of related data" excludes the results of standardized tests, because the NEA has taken a strong stance against their use, especially for certifying teachers. According to the NEA's position "A broad range of multiple determiners should be used, including professional judgments of the candidate's instructors, samples of candidate's work, and evaluation of their working relationships with students and teachers" (p. 7).

The AFT, unlike the NEA, is a labor union. Affiliated with the AFL-CIO, it represents approximately 500,000 teachers, guidance counselors, and paraprofessionals in collective bargaining. Like that of the larger association, the AFT philosophy toward the proficiency of inservice teachers tends toward the establishment of rigorous standards for evaluating teachers. However, the two organizations disagree about the place of tests of cognitive knowledge in the licensing of prospective teachers. The AFT position is reflected in a resolution passed at its 1979 annual convention (American Federation of Teachers, Note 1):

ENTRANCE EXAMINATIONS

WHEREAS, written examinations for the purpose of qualifying beginning teachers are useful to test literacy and a fundamental knowledge of subject matter and educational principles, and

WHEREAS, these examinations must be field-tested to assure that they reflect both the content areas and pedagogical knowledge necessary for effective teaching;

RESOLVED, that teachers, through their union, have significant involvement in test review and selection, and

RESOLVED, that AFT will oppose the use of examinations for decisions related to retention, salary, or tenure, and

RESOLVED, that American Federation of Teachers supports the use of an examination to qualify new teachers as part of a process which includes a full teacher education degree program and which tests the level of literacy, knowledge of subject matter, and pedagogy.

Professional associations that represent the interests of those in higher education include the American Association of Colleges for Teacher Education, the Association of Teacher Educators, the Association for Continuing Professional Education, and the National Council for Accreditation of Teacher Education. To the author's knowledge, these and others not mentioned have been mute on the use of tests in the licensing and renewal process.

Other Views

In addition to the organizations already mentioned, others have expressed views on the testing of teachers. For example, there are those who speak acceptingly of tests as uniform measures of the same mental tasks expressed on a scale common to all who take them. The tests are seen as "leveling" or "democratizing" agents, which cut across local institutional differences and give certification officers the opportunity to assess teachers' abilities on a common yardstick.

Others are less sanguine about teacher testing. For example, David S. Seeley (1979) stated that "the link between student accountability and teacher accountability is no doubt what makes many educators so fearful about the competency movement" (p. 248). Despite the fact that he feels that efforts to hold back the movement will not prevail and that the public is aware that ignorance is dangerous and that too many students are reaching adulthood with dangerously low levels of knowledge, he considers teacher testing a bad idea:

> The main problem is that no one has come up with a test that can predict who will make a good teacher . . . the most that tests can be expected to do is screen out those whose general educational background is too weak, or those teachers who do not know their subject matter well enough to teach it. Once you get beyond the minimal use of tests, there is no escape from the need for human judgment followed by very careful monitoring of performance [1979: 251].

Acknowledging that the academic caliber of teacher trainees is comparatively low, the Council for Basic Education (1979) questioned whether the probable percentage of functional illiterates among this country's school teachers is high enough to warrant legislation to require testing of teachers:

> We have been properly appalled by recent horror stories [about teachers]; we can tell some of our own. But common sense constrains us to read or tell them as sensational, not as representative of more than two million teachers. In our view, minimum competency testing of teachers can serve to single out the most egregiously incompetent—and to antagonize or insult the great majority [1979: 4].

Del Schalock (1979), a researcher with the Oregon State System of Higher Education, noted that the logic of teacher preparation calls for prospective teachers to be knowledgeable both of content to be taught and of the principles and procedures to be used in conveying that content to others. However, he acknowledged that this logic is not borne out either by the quantity of research done on teacher effectiveness (surprisingly little) or by the results that have been achieved. Research results have revealed the following:

> While knowledge of content to be taught and knowledge of methods used in teaching content to be taught to others obviously are necessary for success in teaching, it appears that knowledge alone is not sufficient to measure success [1979: 22].

CURRENT PRACTICES OF TEACHER TESTING

National Testing Program

Although several different teacher testing programs are in use at the state and local levels, only one program has a national label: the National Teacher Examinations (NTE). These tests are administered for the NTE Policy Council by the Educational Testing Service. The NTE program (National Teacher Examinations Policy Council, Note 2), inaugurated in 1940 by the American Council on Education, was turned over to Educational Testing Service, a nonprofit educational organization, in 1950. In 1979, the Educational Testing Service turned over policy direction for the NTE to the NTE Policy Council. Although the program was originally developed to coordinate the testing of teacher applicants for a number of cooperating city school systems, its services were quickly extended to individual candidates and to institutions preparing teachers. Services are now provided to state departments of education and licensing commissions as a source of objective data for statewide studies of teacher education and as part of the process of certification.

Approximately 75,000 candidates take the tests annually. Test content, which is updated periodically by committees of specialists, has been validated against the content of teacher education programs in several locations to monitor the effectiveness of the NTE as measures of achievement in teacher education.

The NTE provide measures of academic achievement in three domains of teacher preparation: general education, professional education, and areas of specialization. Scores on the tests are currently used by licensing and certification agencies in 24 states, by 307 colleges and universities, and by 311 school districts.

The NTE battery consists of the Common Examinations and 26 Area Examinations. The former consist of a test in Professional Education and three in General Education (Written English Expression; Social Studies, Literature, and the Fine Arts; and Science and Mathematics). They cover material that is typically required for all students in teacher education. The Area Examinations focus primarily on the content of a specialty field or major in undergraduate teacher education. All NTE tests consist of four- or five-choice questions.

State Testing Programs

Several states (sometimes initiated by the Department of Education and sometimes by legislation) have begun to embrace a certification process that involves testing as a prerequisite for initial certification. For example, Vlaanderen (Note 3) cites the following:

To qualify for an initial certificate as a teacher in a school district an applicant must, in addition to other requirements, satisfactorily pass an English and mathematics proficiency examination to include at least arithmetic, grammar, sentence structure and reading [Arizona H.B. 2034, January 10, 1979].

Beginning July 1, 1980, each certificate issued shall be valid for a period not to exceed 5 years and each applicant for initial certification shall demonstrate, on a comprehensive written examination and through such other procedures as may be specified by the state board, mastery of those minimum essential generic and specialization competencies and other criteria as shall be adopted into rules by the state board [Florida CB/SB 549, June 1978].

No teacher shall be regularly employed by a school board or paid from the public funds unless such teacher holds a certificate in full force in accordance with the rules of certification laid down by the State Board of Education, which rules shall include a requirement that every teacher seeking initial certification on or after July one, nineteen hundred eighty, take a professional teacher's examination prescribed by the Board [Virginia H1723].

These examples from various states are indicative of the kinds of educational matters that are receiving attention in many legislative chambers across the country. As much as any other indicators, they reflect the attitude that schools are failing to meet the intellectual demands and training needs of American citizens. As a means of compensating for the perceived failure of the educational establishment, some educators and legislators have turned to the most readily accessible remedy they can find: the standardized paper/pencil test. This is not the only remedy that exists (others are discussed with much reverence in various factions of the educational community). But some feel that remedies other than tests have not proven to be more effective, more accessible, more comprehensive, or more cost effective.

E. S. Nothern (1980) reported on a survey of superintendents and commissioners of education in all 50 of the United States which revealed that 10 states now require some form of competency testing for prospective teachers. Included in Nothern's count were states that currently use externally produced examinations as a prerequisite for certification, as well as some that require state-specific instruments. For example, at the writing of this article North Carolina, South Carolina, Louisiana, Mississippi, and West Virginia used the NTE for certification. Since the article appeared, Arkansas and Virginia have adopted an NTE requirement. Of other states that use tests, Nothern indicated that Tennessee used California Achievement Tests to evaluate prospective teachers, and in Washington each teacher preparatory institution is responsible for developing its own instruments.

Some states have found it preferable and advantageous for the tests to be locally specified and developed. Two states, Georgia and Florida, have initiated locally specified and developed certification measures. Two others, North Carolina and South Carolina, have taken giant steps toward exploring homegrown tests. Listed below are some of the tenets of these states' testing programs or plans for such.

Georgia Teacher Area Criterion Referenced Tests. In 1972 the Georgia State Board of Education started to design a new certification program (Georgia Department of Education, Note 4). One of the major goals of the program was to develop criterion-referenced tests[1] for teacher certification, which would assess an individual's knowledge of the content of a teaching field. Through a contract with National Evaluation Systems, Inc., of Amherst, Massachusetts, the State Board has developed and is currently administering 17 tests for 32 teaching fields. The tests, which take approximately three hours to complete, were developed because "there is a need to assess teachers so that certification is based on demonstrated performance, assuring that educational personnel have the competencies essential to facilitate the intellectual, social, emotional and physical growth of learners" (p. 10). The tests are required of three classes of persons: those seeking initial certification at the baccalaureate or master's level; those seeking a six-year teaching certificate who were admitted to a six-year program after July 1, 1978; and certified teachers in elementary grades 1–8, English, mathematics, broad-field social studies, and science who had not completed conversion requirements for the middle grades' (4–8) endorsement by September 1, 1978.

Florida Generic Competencies. Under state law CS/SB 549, called the Teacher Competency Bill, Florida abolished automatic certification of teachers and enforced an evaluation of these persons every five years (Office of Preservice Teacher Education, Note 5). In addition, it requires candidates for teaching positions in the state, beginning in 1980, to pass a competency test and to complete a one-year internship before being awarded a teaching certificate. The competency test, currently under development, will measure 23 essential teacher competencies that Florida has determined to be minimally essential for entry into teaching. Plans call for the examination to be an all-day, comprehensive written evaluation, with a criterion-referenced portion organized into at least four subtests: reading, writing, mathematics, and professional. The professional subtest will assess examinees' familiarity with and ability to use the knowledge base related to (1) developing students' physical, social, and academic skills; (2) organizing and presenting content skills; (3) managing the classroom; and (4) evaluating student progress and diagnosing learning needs.

North Carolina Quality Assurance Program. In October 1978, the State Board of Education joined the Board of Governors of the University of North Carolina in adopting a resolution that supports a "systematic, continuous and extended approach to quality assurance in the initial programs of preparation and continuing conditions of service for professional personnel" (Note 6, p. 1). This resolution provides the framework for a long-range "stem to stern" evaluation program that begins with admission to an institution of higher education and extends throughout the individual's preservice program and professional service. Until this comprehensive program is actually implemented, North Carolina will continue to require that all persons presenting themselves for initial teacher certification in the state take the National Teacher Examinations. Essential elements of the program include the following:

(1) comprehensive evaluation and assessment of requirements for entrance to institutions of higher education
(2) development and implementation of a preteacher education screening procedure, which will examine the basic skills required of all teachers and which will serve as a prerequisite for admission to professional teacher education programs
(3) establishment of a program of coordination between institutions of higher

education and public schools that will enhance the clarification of competencies that should be included in professional and academic programs

(4) development of a mechanism that will assure strong supervision of student teaching experiences through close coordination of campus-based and field-based program activities (This program would involve the state education agency, institutions of higher education, local education agencies, and successful classroom teachers.)

(5) development, validation, and implementation of a system of criterion-referenced tests covering the various disciplines and program areas, which would serve as a part of the final preservice evaluation and which would be a prerequisite for initial certification

(6) development and implementation of an evaluation and educational support system to assess the professional performance of all individuals granted initial three-year certifications as a prerequisite to continuing certification. This system would also function as a means of evaluating the effectiveness of teacher education programs, and the results of the evaluation would, consequently, help to improve these programs

(7) establishment of several pilot centers to develop and evaluate the competency-based approach to certification, the organization and function of the partnership between institutions of higher education and cooperating school systems, and the validity of the evaluation instruments and systems developed to implement this proposed program of quality assurance.

South Carolina. In May 1979 the General Assembly of South Carolina passed Bill S.528 (Note 7), which provides for, among other things, the creation of a basic skills examination for prospective teachers and the development or selection of a testing program to be called the "South Carolina Teaching Examinations." The basic skills examination, covering reading, writing, and mathematics, will be used to determine students' suitability for admittance to undergraduate teacher education programs, beginning with the 1981–1982 school year. The examination will be designed so that results can be reported to students and their institutions in a profile that highlights student strengths and weaknesses.

The South Carolina Teaching Examinations will be developed, or selected, not later than July 1981 for areas in which NTE Area Examinations are not available. They will measure competencies in the cognitive teaching areas considered essential for initial job assignments in typical elementary and secondary schools in the state and will also include a minimum number of questions on common or general knowledge.

Another provision of Bill S.528 is that each new teacher who qualifies will be given a provisional certificate, which will remain in effect for one year. During that year the teacher will be evaluated at least three times. Upon successful completion of the provisional year, teachers will be fully certified and may be employed by any South Carolina school district for a maximum of four one-year contracts, or they may be given one annual contract followed by a continuing contract.

Local District Testing Programs

In addition to the hundreds of local districts using the NTE, several others test teachers in other ways.

Dallas, Texas. Perhaps the most widely publicized testing program administered by local school districts is the one operated by the Dallas (Texas) Independent School District. In 1978 the district administered the Wesman Personnel Classification Test to all teacher applicants, to some experienced teachers, and to some newly hired administrators. Dallas chose the Wesman for screening teacher competence because it measures the verbal and mathematic competencies that the district felt were essential and because the test can be administered and scored before a candidate signs a contract for a teaching position. The Wesman, with a time limit of 28 minutes, consists of 60 multiple-choice questions, 40 verbal analogies, and 20 mathematical questions that test command of basic arithmetical skills and processes as well as general facility in the use of numerical skills. Used by many businesses and industries to predict success in work of a nonphysical nature, it is considered a measure of power rather than of speed. The program gained notoriety because 36% of the applicants, 50% of the teachers hired in 1977, and 54% of the involved administrators failed to attain the cut-off score set by the district (Mitchell, 1979).

Montgomery County, Maryland. Concerned that their students' test scores were falling below the national norms in English mechanics and about the possible correlation between this fact and a combination of the decreasing amount of time devoted to the teaching of grammar, spelling, and usage and the decreased emphasis in this area by the institutions training English teachers, the Montgomery County Public Schools in 1972–1973 incorporated the Mechanics of Writing Test, published by Cooperative Tests and Services of Educational Testing Service, into its selection process for English teachers. This program was followed by a study of the predictive efficiency of the test and its effects on the selection of English teachers and the teaching of English mechanics. The test, which was found to be a good predictor of teaching success of English mechanics, is comprised of two parts: Part I requires that candidates identify misspelled words in a group; Part II presents sentences that contain problems in capitalization and punctuation and asks candidates to find the error.

Prince George's County, Maryland. Since 1975 all teachers hired in the Prince George's County District have been required to take the New Purdue Placement Test in English, published by Houghton-Mifflin. The test, which requires 65 minutes, consists of seven parts: Punctuation, Grammatical Classification, Recognition of Grammatical Errors, Sentence Structure, Reading, Vocabulary, and Spelling. The purpose of the test is to sample knowledge of what is called "good English." In addition to this examination, new teachers in the county are required to take and pass a locally produced mathematics test.

Torrington, Connecticut. Although specific details are absent, all prospective teachers for positions in the Torrington schools are required to pass a battery of tests as part of the selection process. Each is required to write an essay of up to 500 words on an educational topic, take a 10-word spelling test, and pass a 20-sentence grammar test.

Houston, Texas. The Houston (Texas) Independent School District currently uses the Selection Research Incorporated Test, which is distributed by SRI, Lincoln, Nebraska.

Other Tests

In addition to the national, state, and local instruments mentioned thus far, several other standardized measures are used at the preservice and inservice levels. The tests listed below are by no means exhaustive, but they are illustrative of what exists.

Multiple-Choice Items for a Test of Teacher Competence in Educational Measurement. The items that comprise this test were selected, after tryout and analysis, by 11 specialists in the teaching of measurement courses for teachers (National Council on Measurement in Education, Note 8). Assembled under the guidance of the council's Committee on Development of a Test of Measurement Competence for Teachers, the items are grouped by content topic, for example, History of Testing, Test Selection, Item Writing, Validity, Use of Tests. This test covers knowledge of terms, knowledge of facts, explanations of interpretations, and applications of numerical problems. In the interest of simplicity of presentation and uniformity, only multiple-choice items are included. One of the special merits claimed for this collection of items is that they were selected as "good items" by specialists in measurement education, those who know the value of testing the quality of items analytically and of revising or rejecting those that show up poorly.

Curry-Geis Syllabication Skills Test. The Curry-Geis Syllabication Skills Tests (Curry and Geis, Note 9) are designed to measure the proficiency of college students in the application of syllabication skills. Specifically, these tests were designed to measure the performance level of college students enrolled in basic reading methods courses. The theory supporting the development of these tests is that anyone with the responsibility for teaching a given set of skills should understand and be proficient in the application of these skills in order to provide effective instruction. Two forms, A and B, each composed of 100 multiple-choice items, were constructed and standardized as parallel tests. Each item consists of a word followed by four options, one of which is the correct syllabication. The student's task is to select the correct option. Time limits are not significant to the results of these tests; however, the suggested time for completion is 40 minutes.

Illinois Tests in the Teaching of English (ITTE). These tests (Evans and Jacobs, 1972), published first in 1969 and revised in 1972, are designed to measure how well preservice and inservice high school English teachers have achieved certain professionally established objectives, based on criteria developed in the form of guidelines and standards by educational specialists and practicing teachers. The ITTE were developed in cooperation with more than 20 universities and colleges. The battery consists of four competency tests: Knowledge of Language, Attitude and Knowledge in Written Composition, Knowledge of Literature, and Knowledge of the Teaching of English.

Inventory of Teacher Knowledge of Reading. The Inventory of Teacher Knowledge of Reading (Artley and Hardon, 1975) was designed with several purposes in mind: (1) to provide clues to reading supervisors or directors of inservice programs to topics or items of information about which teachers are in need of professional understanding, (2) to provide researchers interested in teacher variables and their effect on pupil performance an instrument that deals with the professional information variable, (3) to denote changes taking place in inservice groups as a result of instruction, and (4) to supply information about the understanding levels of their students to teachers of preservice reading methods courses or programs. The inventory measures an individual's understanding of reading in terms of the items included on the seven subtests that make up the instrument. It is not an indicator of the extent to which the teacher will use the understanding in the classroom. The inventory is said to have "sufficient reliability" to justify the uses for which it was intended. Norms are not provided for this instrument, since the developer did not intend that it be used for comparative purposes.

SUMMARY

The much-publicized decline in student performance, as evidenced by standardized measures, has resulted in aroused suspicions about the viability of teacher training programs, has called into question the caliber of persons graduating from those programs, and has intensified the public's concern about the need for the nation's total educational establishment to become more accountable for its personnel and products. Although all segments of the American educational establishment have been subject to and, to varying degrees, implicated in the decline, those segments with responsibilities for credentialling and hiring (state departments of education and school districts) have seemingly received the brunt of the public ire.

In response to public demands, these agencies have taken both remedial and preventive steps aimed at improving the corps of teachers. The remedial measures include instituting formative, as well as summative, evaluation processes, which allow for the detection of weaknesses and which provide inservice opportunities that will help remove deficiencies. The preventive measures include the increasing use of competency measures and a decreasing use of the approved program approach as a means of determining a teacher's cognitive strength. Because competency measures are so tangible, so accessible, and felt by many segments of the public to be objective, the evidence seems to point not only to their continued use but also to an increased use of paper/pencil standardized measures in the process of credentialling and selecting new teachers.

NOTE

1. A criterion-referenced test is one that references an individual's performance to a criterion of proficiency. This is contrasted to a norm-referenced test, on which an individual's performance is referenced to that of a norm group.

REFERENCE NOTES

1. American Federation of Teachers, AFL-CIO (1979) *Convention Resolutions, 1979*. Washington, DC: Author.
2. National Teacher Examinations Policy Council (1979) *Guidelines for Using the National Teacher Examinations*. Princeton, NJ: Educational Testing Service.
3. Vlaanderen, R. (1979) *Trends in Competency-Based Teacher Certification*. Denver: Education Commission of the States.
4. Georgia Department of Education (1979) *Registration Bulletin 1979–80—Georgia Teacher Certification Testing Program*. Atlanta: Author
5. Office of Preservice Teacher Education (1979) *The Florida Teacher Certification Exam*. Tallahassee: Florida Department of Education.
6. *Concurring Resolution—Quality Assurance for Professional Personal* (1978) Raleigh: The Board of Governors of the University of North Carolina and the State Board of Education.
7. *Bill S.528*. A bill introduced by the South Carolina Education Committee, May 29, 1979.
8. National Council on Measurement in Education (1962) *Multiple-Choice Items for a Test of Teacher Competence in Educational Measurement*. Washington, DC: Author.
9. Curry, R. L. and L. Geis (1976) *Curry-Geis Syllabication Skills Test Teacher's Manual*. Norman: University of Oklahoma.

REFERENCES

Artley, A. S. and V. B. Hardon (1975) *Inventory of Teacher Knowledge of Reading*. Columbia, MO: Lucas.
Council for Basic Education (1978) "Testing teachers." *Basic Education*, 24(2): 3–6.
Evans, W. H. and P. H. Jacobs (1972) *Illinois Tests in the Teaching of English*. Carbondale: Southern Illinois University Press.
Gallup, G. H. (1979) "The eleventh annual Gallup Poll of the public's attitudes toward the public schools." *Phi Delta Kappan*, 61: 33–45.
Mitchell, R. (1979) "Testing the teachers: The Dallas experiment." *School Leader*, 8: 20–23.

"National Education Association outlines views on teacher education and standards. *Teacher Education Reports*, 2: 6–8.

Nothern, E. F. (1980) "The trend toward competency testing of teachers." *Phi Delta Kappan*, 61: 359.

Schalock, D. (forthcoming) "Research on teacher education." *Review of Research in Education.*

Seeley, D. S. (1979) "Reducing the confrontation over teacher accountability." *Phi Delta Kappan*, 61: 248–251.

Weaver, W. T. (1979) "In search of quality: The need for talent teaching." *Phi Delta Kappan*, 61: 29–46.

CHAPTER 6

PEER REVIEW

Documentary Evidence in the Evaluation of Teaching

GRACE FRENCH-LAZOVIK
University of Pittsburgh

The evaluation of a "professor as teacher" requires that evidence be examined in the peer review process, just as has traditionally occurred in the evaluation of the "professor as research scholar." So deeply rooted as to be almost universal in American colleges and universities, peer review is the procedure by which a faculty member's work is judged by peers in all matters of academic and disciplinary decision—appointment, promotion, the granting of tenure, the selection of manuscripts for publication, the approval of research grants. Its essential function is to guarantee that members of an academic community have control over their own standards, their own membership, and the future course of their disciplines. Although peer review has been widely used in the evaluation of research scholarship, its crucial role in evaluating teaching has been largely ignored (Batista, 1976, Martin, Note 1). Continued neglect in the peer review process of the evidence bearing on certain aspects of teaching could bring disturbing consequences in the decades ahead. Specifically, there is a growing tendency at colleges and universities, when they begin to recognize that they have not adequately attended to the teaching function in academic decisions, to use students' evaluations of teaching as the *only* source of data about teaching merit. Developments in evaluation methodology during the decade of the 1970s, especially in the methodology of measurement, have resulted in

Author's Note: All of the author's work has been related to college teaching, and the procedures suggested in this chapter stem from that work. Perhaps those readers who have worked at the elementary or secondary level can determine whether the chapter has any relevance for those levels as well.

73

considerable improvement in the quality of data obtained from students' evaluations of teaching on many campuses. The greater confidence that can now be placed in these measures often leads academic administrators to believe that other data on teaching quality are not needed. There are indeed aspects of teaching for which the students are the most appropriate judges, but other aspects of teaching can be judged only by peers knowledgeable in the discipline being taught. It is these latter dimensions of teaching that are most often neglected in the peer review process.

Any discussion of teaching merit must first acknowledge the distinctly different purposes that evaluation serves. Current literature identifies evaluation for the purpose of helping a teacher improve as *formative* evaluation. Its requirements as to the type of data needed, the procedures used in collecting data, the policies governing its results, and the frequency and timing of its occurrence are markedly different from the requirements for *summative* evaluation, which serves the purpose of decision making. (See French-Lazovik, Note 2, for a discussion of the implications of these purposes in evaluating teaching.) Of overriding importance in summative evaluation is the requirement that the data used be as reliable and free of bias as possible, so that they can contribute to fair decisions.

Also essential to the examination of its role is a sharp differentiation of peer review based on the examination of documentary evidence from classroom visitation by peers. Research has clearly indicated that, although discussion of teaching among colleagues following visitation can contribute to formative evaluation, peer ratings based on visitation are so lacking in reliability that they are useless for summative purposes. This is true even when visitation is carried out in a very systematic way. In a study by Centra (1975), 54 teachers were evaluated on the basis of two classroom visits by each of three different colleagues; 94% of all ratings were in the top two categories of a five-point scale. Data from other sources, in addition to common sense, suggest that there are more variations in teaching quality among these 54 teachers than indicated by 94% of the ratings. This degree of positive bias not only discourages the placing of confidence in such assessments but also prevents reliable measurement, which depends in part on the discrimination of differences in performance among individuals, rather than the assignment of the same score to everyone.

The essential reason that peer review is needed in the evaluation of college teaching rests on two fundamental principles of psychological measurement. When human judgment is used as a basis for measurement, it must be based on careful observation or examination of evidence; in addition, those rendering judgments must have appropriate background against which to compare their observations. The judgments about teaching that peers should make are those that require a thorough knowledge of the discipline, that is, the substance of teaching, what is taught, its accuracy, currency, sophistication, depth, and the level of learning it fosters. The evaluation of these characteristics of teaching must be based on the examination of documentary evidence.

Faculty peers are uniquely qualified to judge the substance of teaching because faculty possess two distinctive requirements for the judgment task: (1) their knowledge of the discipline being taught provides the background against which comparison can occur and (2) their long training in the evaluation of evidence enables them to weigh what is revealed through documentation.

The assumption that just any process of peer review will improve the validity of evaluations of college teaching is untrue. Improved validity depends heavily on what questions are addressed by the review, what documentation is provided to the reviewers, what principles are followed in selecting peer judges, and what procedures govern the conduct of the review process.

DOCUMENTATION

Collection of Data

In the same manner as data are prepared on a candidate's research performance, so data on teaching to be examined in peer review should be contained in the candidate's dossier. Current practice in most colleges and universities places the responsibility for the completeness and currency of the dossier directly on the individual faculty member. In some colleges, faculty now keep their dossiers in their offices, with the dean retaining only minimal files on the dates of official actions and salary changes. Enabling faculty to add material on a continuous basis, this policy also includes the requirement that dossiers can be called for at any time for review.

The guiding principle for assembling data is that they should be as factual and as objective as possible. To provide a context for evaluating teaching, the dossier should contain a brief and factual description of each course taught, its objectives, its enrollment, its credit hours, its role in the curriculum (introductory course, requirement for majors, honors course, service course to other departments, etc.), a statement of any special problems associated with teaching it, and a description of the grading policy used (e.g., grading contracts, content-referenced grading, or norm-referenced grading, including the basis of the norms). With these materials as general background, the peer reviewers, knowledgeable in the discipline, can examine the additional documentation specific to each question to be judged.

Questions Addressed in the Review

The task of a peer review committee in judging teaching merit has sometimes been conceived to be a matter of arriving at a single, overall judgment
of quality, but experience has shown that when only a single, global question
is asked, it is subject to sources of bias that attenuate its validity (Guthrie,
Note 3). To improve the validity of judgments on the global question of
teaching merit, subquestions should be addressed in regard to the undergraduate courses taught by any faculty member about whom an academic decision is to be made. I would like to suggest five subquestions that are general
enough to apply to undergraduate teaching in many disciplines. Though they
are not appropriate for courses in the performing arts or for graduate academic teaching, they may apply to some first-level graduate or professional
areas in which teaching is similar to that in undergraduate courses. Because
their degree of appropriateness depends on the discipline, it should be emphasized that they are meant to be suggestive, not prescriptive.

1. What is the quality of the materials used in teaching? Appropriate
documentation for this question would include course outline, syllabus,
reading list, text used, study guide, description of nonprint materials, handouts, problem sets, and assignments. Inspection of these documents should
focus on questions such as, Are these materials current? Do they represent the
best work in the field? Do they represent superficial or thorough coverage of
the course content? Does the course plan provide opportunities for students
to practice the behaviors specified in the course goals? For example, if one
goal of a course in college algebra is to enable students to solve algebraic
problems, are problem assignments provided?

2. What kinds of intellectual tasks were set by the teacher for the students
(or did the teacher succeed in getting students to set for themselves), and
how did the students perform? Here, dossier materials should include copies
of graded examinations, examples of graded research papers, examples of
the teacher's feedback to students on written work, a copy of the final grade
distribution, descriptions of student performances (e.g., class presentations), and examples of completed assignments. Examination of these documents enables peer reviewers to look at the level of intellectual performance
achieved by the students. What kind of work was given an A? a B? a C? Did
the students learn what the department curriculum expected them to learn
from this course? How adequately did the tests or assignments represent the
kinds of student performance specified in the course objectives? Were tests
all true-false items, or did they demand higher intellectual functions?

This question takes on additional significance at institutions where student evaluations of teaching are considered in academic decisions. Despite
the mountain of evidence that favorable student evaluations cannot be
bought by giving easy grades (Abrami et al., 1980; Stumpf and Freedman,

1979; Voeks and French, 1960), some faculty persist in believing this myth. This factor and possibly others, such as a desire to help students avoid losing financial aid or athletic eligibility because of low grades, might contribute to grade inflation, and the peer review process can examine whether grading has been especially lenient as compared to that in the department as a whole, as well as whether it accords with the teacher's stated grading policy.

3. How knowledgeable is this faculty member in the subjects taught? Few would disagree that good teaching depends on a teacher's knowledge of the subject. Attention to evidence of knowledge is customary in hiring a new Ph.D. as an assistant professor, but it may be even more important in the case of tenured faculty. What Guthrie (Note 3) described years ago is still true today: "Every man who has spent many years on a college campus knows many cases of a good teacher who has not kept up with his subject and becomes a tragic figure in his later years" (p. 8). In recent decades, much more of the undergraduate teaching in American colleges is done in academic settings that provide little or no time for scholarship, and a concern for those faculty is now emerging. "How are they to maintain currency in disciplinary (and in many cases interdisciplinary) subject matter?" (Kormondy, 1980: p. 365). Surely the evaluation of teaching must attend to whether teachers have kept in thoughtful contact with developments in their fields.

The evidence here is necessarily somewhat different from that required for the other questions. Even if the faculty member is a publishing scholar, his or her particular area of research may be far removed from undergraduate course content. In addition, the scholarship necessary to good teaching may not result in publication. Thus, peer reviewers need to rely on observations that occur on a daily basis: colleague discussions of ideas and new developments, interactions about curriculum matters or choice of texts, and attendance at meetings, colloquia, and lectures. The ongoing activities of an intellectual community provide ample opportunities for faculty to develop informed opinions as to the substantive knowledge of a colleague in the same department.

4. Has this faculty member assumed responsibilities related to the department's or university's teaching mission? The dossier materials should contain a record of service on departmental curriculum committees, special committees on teaching problems (e.g., on grading policies, admission standards, honors program), or advisory boards of teaching support services. Peer reviewers can then examine whether the involvement of the faculty member has been appropriate to his or her academic level. Eckert (1950) has provided the focus for questions here: "Does [this faculty member] recognize problems that hinder good teaching in his institution and does he take a responsible part in trying to solve them? Or does he look upon

teaching as a kind of unfortunate adjunct to his scholarly career, its duties to be discharged with the minimum expenditure of effort?" (p. 66). If all members of the faculty were like this individual, what would the college be like? Has he or she become a departmental citizen in regard to teaching responsibilities?

5. To what extent is this faculty member striving for excellence in teaching? Each professor should include in the dossier a factual statement of what activities he or she has engaged in to improve teaching. Examples of student questionnaires used formatively, examples of changes made on the basis of feedback, as well as any record of activities directed toward vitalizing the teaching of his or her courses ought to be available in the dossier materials. Peer reviewers can ascertain whether the professor has sought feedback about teaching quality, explored alternative teaching methods, made changes in a course over time. Has he or she sought aid in trying new teaching ideas, developed special teaching materials, or participated in co-operative efforts whose principal purpose was upgrading teaching quality?

In order to provide a convenient way for peer reviewers to carry out their judgment task, these five questions are presented in Figure 1 in the form of a questionnaire. (For a different peer review rating form, see Miller, 1972, p. 31.) This questionnaire might also serve other purposes if a copy of it were given to all faculty members, for it would not only inform them about the aspects of their teaching to be evaluated but also alert them to the documentation they should provide in their dossiers.

Additional guidelines as to what *cannot* be placed in dossiers are needed. Some authors have suggested the inclusion of lecture notes (Centra, 1979; McIntyre, Note 4), descriptions of teaching style, (McIntyre, Note 4), and self-evaluations stressing self-perceived strengths and weakness (Arreola, Note 5). (Self-evaluation should be differentiated from self-report, the objective reporting of activities that have occurred.) These data can be useful for formative evaluation, but they simply do not have the requisite reliability for summative decisions. (See Blackburn and Clark, 1975, for data on the reliability of self-assessments.) Despite the fact that the threat of summative evaluation is considerably lessened for faculty who believe that their self-evaluations will be considered, the more defensible course is to rely on data that are as objective as possible. It is especially important that the *results* of individual, faculty-made student evaluation forms not be included in the dossier, for it is possible to construct questions and to give instructions that will guarantee favorable responses. When no effort is made to control rating bias, then ratings do not have the psychometric properties necessary to provide the basis for fair decisions.

(text continued on p. 82)

SUGGESTED FORM FOR PEER REVIEW OF UNDERGRADUATE TEACHING BASED ON DOSSIER MATERIALS

QUESTION	DOSSIER MATERIALS	SUGGESTED FOCUS IN EXAMINING DOSSIER MATERIALS
1. What is the quality of materials used in teaching?	Course outline Syllabus Reading list Text used Study guide Description of non-print materials Hand-outs Problem sets Assignments	Are these materials current? Do they represent the best work in the field? Are they adequate and appropriate to course goals? Do they represent superficial or thorough coverage of course content?

Peer Reviewer's Rating   Low |____|____|____|____|____| Very High

Comments _____

_____

_____

Figure 1. Suggested form for peer review of undergraduate teaching based on dossier materials.

QUESTION	DOSSIER MATERIALS	SUGGESTED FOCUS IN EXAMINING DOSSIER MATERIALS
2. What kind of intellectual tasks were set by the teacher for the students (or did the teacher succeed in getting students to set for them-selves), and how did the students perform?	Copies of graded examinations Examples of graded research papers Examples of teacher's feedback to students on written work Grade distribution Descriptions of student per-formances, e.g. class pre-sentation, etc. Examples of completed assign-ments	What was the level of intellectual performance achieved by the students? What kind of work was given an A? a B? a C? Did the students learn what the department cur-riculum expected for this course? How adequately do the tests or assignments rep-resent the kinds of student performance spe-cified in the course objectives?

Peer Reviewer's Rating Low _____:___:___:___:___ Very High

Comments _____

QUESTION	DOSSIER MATERIALS	SUGGESTED FOCUS IN EXAMINING DOSSIER MATERIALS
3. How knowledgeable is this faculty member in subjects taught?	Evidence in teaching materials Record of attendance at regional or national meetings Record of colloquia or lectures given	Has the instructor kept in thoughtful contact with developments in his or her field? Is there evidence of acquaintance with the ideas and findings of other scholars? (This question addresses the scholarship neces-sary to good teaching. It is not concerned with scholarly research publication.)

Peer Reviewer's Rating Low _____:___:___:___:___ Very High

Comments _____

Figure 1 (continued)

QUESTION	DOSSIER MATERIALS	SUGGESTED FOCUS IN EXAMINING DOSSIER MATERIALS
4. Has this faculty member assumed responsibilities related to the department's or University's teaching mission?	Record of service on department curriculum committee, honors program, advising board of teaching support service, special committees (e.g. to examine grading policies, admission standards, etc.) Description of activities in supervising graduate students learning to teach. Evidence of design of new courses.	Has he or she become a departmental or college citizen in regard to teaching responsibilities? Does this faculty member recognize problems that hinder good teaching and does he or she take a responsible part in trying to solve them? Is the involvement of the faculty member appropriate to his or her academic level? (e.g., assistant professors may sometimes become over-involved to the detriment of their scholarly and teaching activities.)

Peer Reviewer's Rating   Low ___:___:___:___:___:___ Very High

Comments _____

| 5. To what extent is this faculty member trying to achieve excellence in teaching? | Factual statement of what activities the faculty member has engaged in to improve his or her teaching. Examples of questionnaires used for formative purposes. Examples of changes made on the basis of feedback. | Has he or she sought feedback about teaching quality, explored alternative teaching methods, made changes to increase student learning? Has he or she sought aid in trying new teaching ideas? Has he or she developed special teaching materials or participated in cooperative efforts aimed at upgrading teaching quality? |

Peer Reviewer's Rating   Low ___:___:___:___:___:___ Very High

Comments _____

Peer Reviewer's Signature _____

G. F. Lazovik, University of Pittsburgh

Figure 1 (continued)

When peer review of the substance of teaching has been completed, the resulting evaluation can be placed beside systematically obtained students' evaluations of teaching, which focus on how successful the teacher is in the classroom. These two kinds of evaluations, taken together, provide the necessary indicators of the degree of success that a candidate has achieved in becoming a first-rate teacher.

THE REVIEW PROCESS

Problems of Bias in Peer Review

Even when appropriate questions are addressed and adequate documentation is provided, the process of peer review is open to considerable criticism if it is not very carefully structured. Lewis's (1975) data provide abundant evidence of the extent to which peer judgments of merit can be contaminated by extraneous and nonprofessional criteria. Other writers (Batista, 1976; Polishook, Note 6; Stumpf, 1980) have also identified problems in the review process, including the following: too close friendships between the candidate and the judges, too few judges, judges lacking sufficient knowledge in the candidate's field, judges in competition with the candidate, lack of anonymity of judges, lack of independence in the judgment process permitting some peers to act as advocates or adversaries, and failure of peer review committees to provide reasons for negative decisions. Shipka (Note 7) forecast a most undesirable consequence of these problems when he said:

> Understandably, advocates of peer review will say that the recommendations of peer committees reflect conscientious academic judgments, not the whims of the members. Given the *modus operandi* of peer committees, however, it is not easy to prove this claim. Such committees usually meet in executive session, keep perfunctory minutes if any, and state no rationale for their recommendations. It seems to me that committees which operate this way are on a collision course with the courts which will observe that such procedures make it impossible for colleges and universities to provide satisfactory evidence that personnel decisions are non-discriminating. I anticipate that judicial scrutiny will circumscribe the loose procedures of peer committees to protect the rights of those under review [p. 41].

It is important to notice, however, that the author of this dire prediction did not suggest that the peer review process be abandoned. His implication is similar to that expressed by Polishook (Note 6):

It is true that the due process inherent in [giving] reasons [for a negative action] may be inconsistent with the *tradition* of peer judgment, with the way it has been exercised in the past. I believe we must be prepared, in defense of tradition, to change any part of the process that we now find objectionable. The respect we have developed in recent centuries for the rights of the individual must be acknowledged and accommodated in higher education. Above all, due process is not inconsistent with peer judgment itself [p. 39].

Nor is it necessary to wait for the courts to prescribe, for there are safeguards already in use by some that ought to be considered wherever peer review is used.

Frequency of Peer Review

As faculty become less mobile, there is an increasing need for systematic peer review at regular intervals as a means of preserving standards. On the other hand, one finds in the literature, especially on collective bargaining in colleges, references to the "right" of faculty to periodic review. Some colleges are now instituting plans in which untenured faculty are reviewed every two years, tenured faculty every five years. Where such plans are used, evaluations should be staggered as much as possible, so that only one-fourth to one-third of the members of a given department or division are being reviewed each year. The reason for this arrangement is that good evaluation is time-consuming, requiring careful reading of all the material in a dossier (and of all manuscripts and publications when research is being judged); if too much is undertaken at one time, care and thoroughness are bound to suffer. Poorly done evaluation not only harms individual faculty but also exposes an institution to serious risks, not the least of which are legal challenges.

Number of Reviewers

A basic requirement when ratings are used in measurement entails the pooling of judgments by several raters on each of the separate characteristics judged. Essential to the interpretation of such ratings is a determination of the degree of consensus evidenced among the judges, for rater agreement is one of the conditions upon which reliability rests. The general rule is that the number of judges should be no less than three, since that number gives a minimal notion of whether consensus exists in a specific evaluation. It is well-known that rating reliability improves as the number of raters increases, so more than three raters are desirable where possible. There is, however, a point of diminishing returns, for peer ratings that point is somewhere in the neighborhood of six or seven raters. The actual number chosen will depend on many factors, such as the size of the department involved, the size of the college or university, and the method of selecting reviewers. It must be remembered that three or four well-qualified peer judges will produce a sounder evaluation than six less qualified judges, or even than three well-qualified and four poorly qualified ones.

Selection of Peer Reviewers

One of the most crucial points of control in trying to eliminate sources of bias in the review process lies in the method by which peer reviewers are chosen, and this in turn depends, at least to some degree, on where in the academic decision chain peer review occurs. It is most frequently found at two different levels and, in a particular college, may be used at either one or both of them. The first level is the basic administrative unit at which a recommendation for promotion or tenure is initiated (department or division). Here, peer review provides data to be combined with data from other sources in arriving at a recommendation for tenure or promotion or, if these are not involved, a periodic review to be given to the faculty member for formative purposes. The second level is the postdepartment review of recommendations for promotion or tenure, usually conducted for or with a dean. At each of these levels, peer review may be accomplished by a standing committee or by an ad hoc committee, either of which may be appointed, elected, partially appointed/partially elected, or appointed from a nominated or elected group. (For an unusual method of reviewer selection by computer, see Centra's, 1979, description of procedures used at Kansas State University.) There are even colleges where any faculty member may contribute an evaluation of any other faculty member. This method provides no safeguards whatever and should be discouraged, not only for that reason but also because it tends to engender suspicion and hostility among faculty members.

Next most vulnerable to criticism is the appointed, standing peer review committee, for it fails to provide equal safeguards to all the candidates under review. The faculty member whose field is best represented in the group or who has one or more close friends on the committee will certainly be viewed as having received different treatment from others. Even when the standing committee is an elected one, relieving the dean or the department chairperson of possible charges of bias in making appointments, the same criticisms apply. Equal protection of all is not possible with standing committees for peer review. Only ad hoc committees provide the possibility of insuring that the reviewers are all adequately knowledgeable in the candidate's field and that the committee is not stacked with the candidate's close friends. However, the use of ad hoc committees necessitates the clear specification of a rule by which each committee is to be chosen.

Some Models of Peer Review at the Postdepartmental Level

In a previous publication, this author described the Guthrian model of peer review, used by the late Edwin R. Guthrie when he was Dean of the Graduate School, and later Academic Vice President, at the University of Washington. His procedures were so carefully worked out that they provide a useful illustration of how rules for peer review can work. The following description is taken from that publication (French-Lazovik, 1976):

Whenever a faculty member was a candidate for promotion or tenure, Dean Guthrie requested him or her to nominate five colleagues who could serve as evaluators. They could be from the faculty member's own department or from a related department, but the essential requirement was that each evaluator be conversant with the field of the person to be judged. From the five, the Dean chose three and added three more of his own choice. Within this structure, he tried to insure that no rater was in competition for rank or salary with the person evaluated (thus, only tenured faculty served on committees) and that there were at least two members on the committee from outside the department of the candidate, but in a related field. The six constituted a secret committee that never met. No member knew who the other members were nor did he know whether he had been nominated by the ratee or chosen by the Dean to serve on the committee. *He was asked not to reveal his appointment to anyone*, and instructed that this was a matter of academic integrity. Each rater was supplied with a set of materials that the ratee had provided to the Dean. The task of each rater was to arrive at a totally independent judgment on the specified characteristics and to write a general statement about the candidate. Each member returned his or her signed ratings directly to the Dean, and the six judgments were pooled for each characteristic rated.

The principles underlying this set of procedures included these:

1. The person being evaluated had some choice, with the Dean, of his evaluators.

2. Because more faculty were nominated than were chosen, the candidate could not be sure which of his or her nominees had been appointed and thus could not identify any individual as definitely on the committee. This provided a measure of protection for the anonymity of the raters.

3. The secret committee prevented one rater from trying to influence the others. No one could act as an advocate or an adversary.

4. Each rater was forced to rely on his own judgments—not those of others.

5. The knowledge that the Dean, and only the Dean, saw the signed evaluations promoted a good deal of care on the part of the evaluators.

6. The pooling of a set of independent judgments gave maximum reliability—better than a jointly agreed upon judgment.

7. The extra-departmental members acted as a corrective for occasional intradepartmental biases [pp. 5–6].

Guthrie used peer review as a postdepartmental check on the recommendations that came to him. When the reviewers' ratings had been pooled and their individual statements typed, he called in the candidate and showed him or her the results, not revealing, of course, any identifying information about the raters. An essential of the Guthrian model is that the dean be a person whose integrity is respected by the faculty.

At another large university, each department elects representatives to a standing committee, the number depending on the size of the department. From this elected group of more than 50, peer review committees of 5 are appointed by the committee itself for each review. The members of the elected committee are known to the faculty, but which 5 serve on any one subcommittee is not revealed, thus preserving the anonymity of the judges in individual cases.

A third model, used by Dean Jerome L. Rosenberg of the Faculty of Arts and Sciences, University of Pittsburgh, incorporates elements of both of the above models. A large elected committee chooses three of its members and the Dean adds three faculty of his choice to form six-member ad hoc committees, again without the candidate's knowledge of the membership.

Not meant to be representative of the wide variation that exists in large universities, these models are presented for the purpose of illustrating efforts to eliminate some of the known sources of bias in the peer review process. Two elements common to these three models deserve attention. The first is that each distributes the responsibility for the selection of reviewers to at least two sources. Thus, the potential that the bias that may be operating in one source can be counterbalanced by the other exists in each model. The second common feature is that each model includes some mechanism for protecting the identities of the peer judges from the person judged while at the same time identifying each reviewer's responses to the dean. The dual purposes of encouraging frank and honest judgments while discouraging carelessness or inadequately considered opinion are both served by such procedures.

The question of anonymity of peer reviewers has sometimes occasioned objections based on the notion that anonymity provides a cloak for discriminatory practices. It is well-known, however, that judgments made without the protection of anonymity have neither the reliability nor the validity of ratings made with the guarantee that the rater will remain anonymous to the person being rated. As is the case with letters of recommendation, when peer evaluators' identities are accessible to the candidate, a noticeable leniency appears and "peers [are] prepared to say only nice things if they [say] anything at all," (Shipka, Note 7, p. 42). Even the National Science Foundation (National Science Board, Note 8), after a careful examination of its procedures for peer review of requests for research grants, concluded that the anonymity of its reviewers must be protected. It did point out, however, that the text of the reviewers' comments should be available to the grant applicant. The solution to the objection to anonymity is not to abandon it and, thereby, to destroy the value of peer review, but to follow procedures for selecting reviewers and for conducting the review that are generally accepted by faculty as fair.

Peer Review at the Departmental or Divisional Level

The variation found in peer review procedures used at the departmental level (or in small colleges at the divisional level) is so great as to defy categorization, and perhaps the only admonition that can be made is that attention should be given to the principles that have already been mentioned in structuring peer review procedures. It is not an uncommon practice in departments that members of each rank are judged by those of higher ranks. A prudent caution to ensure that a thorough examination of evidence occurs entails assigning to a subgroup of three or four the responsibility for a more intensive review than most faculty members will undertake. I recently encountered a department where the candidate for tenure and the department chairperson sit down together and agree on one faculty member to be appointed to a three-member review team. The candidate nominates two others and, if he or she chooses, specifies as many as two who should not be chosen. From the two nominated, the chairperson selects one and adds one of his or her choice, avoiding those vetoed by the candidate. Each member of the selected three then reads and evaluates all of the candidate's dossier materials and also prepares a report to the full group of faculty whose ranks are higher than the person under consideration. At the meeting where the reports are presented and discussed, a recommendation to be sent to the dean is formulated and voted upon. This model incorporates some of the safeguards in Guthrie's model but adds the possibility of veto. A carefully limited number of vetoes by the candidate may help eliminate unsuspected sources of bias.

The thrust of this chapter has been to point out the need to evaluate aspects of teaching that can be judged only by peers knowledgeable in the discipline taught and to suggest the kinds of data and the principles of judgment that can improve the validity and fairness of decisions regarding teaching merit. Peer review of the substance of teaching based on documentary evidence and employing procedures that attend to eliminating known sources of bias should result in fewer challenges of its fairness. It should also produce judgments that are more defensible than those typically rendered at present.

REFERENCE NOTES

1. Martin, M. A. (1978) *Peer Input in Evaluating Teaching Effectiveness: A Review of the Literature*. Unpublished manuscript. (Available from author, Research for Better Schools, 444 N. 3rd St., Philadelphia, PA 19123.)

2. French-Lazovik, G. (1976) *Evaluation of College Teaching: Guidelines for Summative and Formative Procedures*. Washington, DC: Association of American Colleges.

3. Guthrie, E. R. (1954) *Evaluation of Teaching: A Progress Report*. Seattle: University of Washington.

4. McIntyre, C. (1977) "Evaluation of college teachers (*Criteria*, No. 6)." Ann Arbor: University of Michigan, Center for Research on Learning and Teaching.

5. Arreola, R. A. (1979) *Essential Components of a Faculty Evaluation System*. Unpublished manuscript, Florida State University.

6. Polishook, I. H. (1977) "Peer judgment and due process," in A. Levenstein (ed.), *Collective Bargaining and the Future of Higher Education: Proceedings of the 5th Annual Conference*. New York: City University of New York, Baruch College, National Center for the Study of Collective Bargaining in Higher Education.

7. Shipka, T. A. (1977) "Is peer review viable today?" in A. Levenstein (ed.), *Collective Bargaining and the Future of Higher Education: Proceedings of the 5th Annual Conference*. New York: City University of New York, Baruch College, National Center for the Study of Collective Bargaining in Higher Education.

8. National Science Board (1977) Resolution N.S.B. 77–150. Washington, DC: National Science Foundation (March 30).

REFERENCES

Abrami, P. C., W. J. Dickens, R. P. Perry, and L. Leventhal (1980) "Do teacher standards for assigning grades affect student evaluations of instruction?" *Journal of Educational Psychology*, 72: 107–118.

Batista, E. E. (1976) "The place of colleague evaluation in the appraisal of college teaching." *Research in Higher Education*, 4: 257–271.

Blackburn, R. T. and M. J. Clark (1975) "An assessment of faculty performance: Some correlates between administrators, colleagues, students, and self-ratings." *Sociology of Education*, 48: 242–256.

Centra, J. A. (1979) *Determining Faculty Effectiveness*. San Francisco: Jossey-Bass.

———— (1975) "Colleagues as raters of classroom instruction." *Journal of Higher Education*, 46: 327–337.

Eckert, R. E. (1950) "Ways of evaluating college teaching." *School and Society,* 71: 65–69.

Kormondy, E. J. (1980) "Currency in subject matter." *Science,* 207: 365.

Lewis, L. S. (1975) *Scaling the Ivory Tower: Merit and Its Limits in Academic Careers.* Baltimore: Johns Hopkins University Press.

Miller, R. I. (1972) *Evaluating Faculty Performance.* San Francisco: Jossey-Bass.

Stumpf, S. A. and R. D. Freedman (1979) "Expected grade covariation with student ratings of instruction: Individual versus class effects." *Journal of Educational Psychology,* 71: 293–302.

Stumpf, W. E. (1980) " 'Peer' review." *Science,* 207: 822.

Voeks, V. N. and G. M. French (1960) "Are student-ratings of teachers affected by grades?" *Journal of Higher Education,* 31: 330–334.

CHAPTER 7

CLASSROOM OBSERVATION

CAROLYN M. EVERTSON
The University of Texas at Austin

FREDA M. HOLLEY
Austin Independent School District

Classroom observation can be valuable for personnel evaluation. Although methods of conducting classroom observations vary and implementation has its own special conditions, observations can provide information that may not be acquired through other kinds of inquiry. Other methods of measuring teacher competencies and student learning are also important, but classroom observation gives us a view of the climate, rapport, interaction, and functioning of the classroom available from no other source. Help in understanding and ultimately in improving instruction can come from seeing just how events take place in the classroom. As a means to this end, classroom observation is a useful tool in providing the most immediate form of contact with important events.

Classroom observation can also be a valuable tool for research and for program evaluation. In the context of research, the dynamics of the classroom, of teaching and learning, cannot be fully understood without the validation that classroom observation yields. In the context of program evaluation, it is important to determine whether a program of instruction is being employed as prescribed by the designers and whether that prescribed program is appropriate for the particular classroom. Such information needs can be met through classroom observation. However, the focus of this chapter is on classroom observations for teacher evaluation and improvement. We consider suggestions for implementing an observation system, what to observe, methods of observation, and the reliability and validity of observation.

It is not our purpose to provide here a definitive treatment of observation systems or instruments, but to suggest how observation can be appropriately and effectively used for teacher evaluation. We will pay special attention to problems that must be met, limitations that must be taken into account, and expectations that must be avoided. We will also briefly explain and discuss some formats that have been used for observation and some problems of systematic observation in general to acquaint the user with the possibilities of systematic observation (as realized in the various formats) and the non-special factors that can limit those possibilities.

This chapter is organized into three sections to facilitate use by practitioners. The first section is addressed to the evaluator, the person charged with conducting and using observation for evaluation purposes. The second section is addressed to the designer of school or college evaluation systems, including requirements for observation. The third section discusses, for the dedicated, technical considerations about observation instruments and systems.

OBSERVATION IN PRACTICE

The evaluator wishing to conduct observations effectively faces a number of problems. The first and most serious of these is dealing with the concerns of the individual to be evaluated. Only when these personal concerns are sufficiently attended to can the evaluator go on to concerns about conducting the evaluations so that they will be responsive to the purposes established for the evaluation.

Establishing a Climate for Observation

Below are examples of two kinds of evaluators.

James Gregory, Department Chairperson, walked into the classroom of a first-year instructor five minutes after class began, took his seat in the back of the classroom with a pad and pencil prominently in evidence, and watched as the instructor froze. After several minutes, the instructor managed to collect himself and to proceed shakily with his lesson. After about 20 minutes, James Gregory rose and left the room. The instructor was left in the classroom to deal with the pity obvious on the face of his students. (For an illustration of a similar situation, see Figure 1.)

Carla Ramirez, Department Chairperson, met with the six instructors in her department in early September and reviewed the evaluation form that she would be required to submit on each instructor in the spring. Then they examined six possible observation instruments and discussed which would give the most information in relation to the questions on the evaluation form. Finally, they agreed on two of the observation instruments as best suited to their situation. Dr. Ramirez duplicated both instruments and provided copies

"*Just pretend we're not here, Ms. Robinson . . .*"

Figure 1. No one ever said teaching was going to be easy. © 1979 by David Sipress. Reprinted by permission.

to each instructor. She asked the help of a colleague and then the permission of several teachers in another department to try out the observation instruments in their classrooms before using them with the instructors in her department. When she was satisfied that her observations and those of a colleague were yielding the same type of statements about each classroom they observed, she was ready to begin her observations. Before the first observation of each instructor, she scheduled a time for the observation and then spent about 15 minutes with the individual covering the types of things with which she would be particularly concerned. On the day of the observation, she arrived well before the bell and took her place in the back of the room. She remained for the entire class period, and, before leaving, she made an appointment for a time when she and the instructor could get together to discuss the observation. During that conference, she and the instructor agreed that the next observation would be unscheduled and would take place some time later in the month.

It should be obvious that the second evaluator will eventually have received a better idea than the first evaluator of the instructional skills and classroom climate that are generally typical of the instructor observed. Moreover, the second evaluator will have a much better relationship from which to begin working with the instructor on any areas requiring improvement.

The essentials of good human relations that must be attended to first in any evaluation situation are assuring (1) that the individual to be observed is fully informed about the purpose and nature of the observation, (2) that the entire process is conducted as unobtrusively as possible and with as little disruption of the normal routine as possible, and (3) that good communication is maintained throughout the evaluation process.

Effective Use

In the above examples, the better evaluator, in cooperation with the teachers to be observed, made a careful choice of the observation instrument to be used. This is actually the first step in the effective use of observation. After all, the evaluator is concerned, first, that the observation conducted yield accurate insights into the matters of concern to the evaluator and, second, that the data obtained in the classroom be typical both of the observation period and of periods other than the particular time observed. Therefore, the choice of the observation instrument is critical. Sources of observation instruments (which can also serve as guides for designing an instrument) include *Mirrors for Behavior* (Simon and Boyer, Note 1), *Learning To Look* (Stallings, 1977), *Evaluating Teacher Performance* (Kowalski, Note 2), and *Evaluating Classroom Instruction: A Sourcebook of Instruments* (Borich and Madden, 1977).

When the observation system has been chosen, the evaluator should be sure that the system is well-understood. Practice with use will assist in that process. The instrument is a selective, specially designed and organized way of looking at the classroom, and the observer must learn to look at the classroom in the way defined by the instrument if it is to be used effectively and is to capture the data desired. Categories to be used in observation systems should be carefully defined and decisions must be made in advance as to how to record events that do not clearly fit any of the categories. The observer can translate the phenomena of the classroom into the categories or concepts employed by the instrument only with the knowledge of how to operationalize those categories and to give them meanings in terms of the concrete phenomena of the classroom. The more abstract the categories, the greater is the need for operational definitions.

Appropriate selection of the time and length of observation can ensure that the sample of behavior recorded is appropriate. However, the classroom does not present the same appearance day in and day out. The observer cannot be sure that the behavior observed in a given classroom on a given day is typical or representative of what normally occurs in the classroom. This presents an obvious problem for the reliability and validity of observation systems. If observation is being used as a means for understanding the classroom or assessing what happens within it, then it is necessary to be sure that the data are representative. This problem becomes particularly serious in the context of classroom observation for the evaluation of teachers.

This problem can be examined from another point of view. When a classroom is observed on a given day, the observer cannot be sure that the observation will contain the information desired. It may have been that for some particular reason the behavior that the observer wished to see was not exhibited on that day. That day may have been atypical.

This problem—whether one characterizes it in terms of the representative quality of the observational data or in terms of the value of the information gathered—is aggravated the more one limits the sample of behavior that is observed. Thus, although classroom observation on any scale is expensive and time-consuming, one should provide as much observation time as possible. In addition, it is important to ensure that the observed behavior is a representative sample, and this obviously has implications for the amount and scheduling of observation time. One can clearly not hope to gain a representative sample of teacher and student behavior by observing only 5 or 10 minutes. But the concern for obtaining a representative sample has even clearer implications with respect to the selection of the times at which to observe. If one is interested in assessing teachers with respect to the improvement of teaching skills, then one must select observation times in which one can reasonably expect such skills to be evidenced and which are not characterized by extraordinary conditions or constraints. For example, a class meeting devoted to diagnostic testing is probably not a fruitful time to observe a teacher develop a class lesson. Observations are also affected by the time of day, the subject being taught, the calendar of holidays and special events, and a number of other temporal factors.

It is not reasonable to expect classroom observation (particularly under these circumstances) to carry the entire burden of teacher evaluation, and such a role is certainly not being suggested here. Classroom observation is only one, albeit a very important, source of relevant information for teacher evaluation and must be supplemented by other sources of information, such as outcome measures. Thus, the problem of obtaining an accurate picture of teacher behavior can be mitigated by using other sources of relevant information, which serve as an important check on the data gathered by observation, enhancing the likelihood of achieving a fair assessment of teacher performance.

Distinguishing when intensive observation and follow-up are necessary is also a needed evaluator skill. Because the evaluator has so many observations to perform, it is usually necessary to distinguish between those in which a teacher is in critical need of help and those in which a simplified observation may be sufficient to suggest further development areas that might be of some benefit. Making wise decisions about how best to expend the time available for observation is critical.

The evaluator must usually work actively to look past external characteristics to strengthen objectivity in doing observations. Adherence to formal systems helps a great deal, but awareness of how easily parent or staff comments can influence what is seen is also needed. Indeed, the literature is full of documentation of factors that can influence ratings, such as attractiveness, age, sex, ethnicity, height, and weight.

The evaluator must also be sensitive to the values, needs, and functioning of the institution, if observation is to meet its specific objectives and yet be a tenable and manageable operation. This can be done with careful forethought and planning, guided by some awareness of the ways in which the institutional context can obstruct the successful use of the observation instrument. The disruptive impact of observation on the institution and of the institution upon observation can be mitigated.

The evaluator should have a faculty meeting early in the year in which observations are to occur to explain how they will be conducted, to share any forms or guidelines to be used, and to share openly the full intent and purpose of the observations. Some research suggests that when the evaluator has the liberty to do so, joint planning of the events to be observed and of the form to be used may contribute to instructional improvement.

In addition to the general meeting, it is helpful to meet with each teacher to discuss any particular concerns that either the evaluator or the teacher may have about the observation, perhaps at the time when the observations are scheduled. Many teachers have great fears about being observed; even very good teachers may be unnerved at the prospects.

The integration of multiple sources of observation data is also a problem faced by the evaluator. To the extent that the evaluator works actively to communicate with others doing observations, this problem may be reduced. When the evaluator is using a team approach to evaluation, the other members of the team need to be trained. A carefully planned sequence of training with the other team members results in better practice.

DESIGNING OBSERVATION SYSTEMS

Constraints

School or college administrators can support their personnel in attempts to improve instruction through observation by providing well-designed evaluation systems with observation components. "Well-designed" signifies systems that fully recognize constraints. Anyone proposing to design observation systems for use in teacher evaluation should be as well aware of the constraints upon the practice of observation in schools and colleges as they are of the technical problems associated with observation systems. Some of these constraints are discussed below.

Time. At best, an observation of a teacher for evaluation purposes is likely to occur two to five times and have a duration of not more than one hour. Often, observations of 5 to 10 minutes are the standard. Perhaps as a result, there is a fairly consistent failure to find relationships between ratings of teacher performance and other external measures of competence (Carter, Note 3) and a rather general feeling that the reason lies as much in the unreliability of these ratings as elsewhere (Andrews et al., 1980). Typically, the administrator responsible for evaluation is ultimately accountable for evaluations of from 10 to perhaps 100 teachers. In most schools, not every teacher is evaluated every year, but at least one-third of the staff probably is. Evaluation, however, is only one of an array of critical areas demanding the administrator's attention. The behavior problems of students or the demands of the central office may both have higher priority for the administrator. In today's school, the administrator also faces the difficulties of managing multiple special programs, including special education, bilingual education, and Title I programs for the educationally disadvantaged. Additional time is demanded for the supervision and evaluation of special personnel such as custodians, aides, clerical personnel, a nurse, and perhaps a home visitor or other outreach personnel. When all these demands are added up, the typical administrator finds that the day-to-day crises of management will divert attention from routine classroom visits, however important they may be. The constraint on time also holds for the college administrator as well. Deans typically have supervisory responsibilities for numerous faculty members distributed in several departments, special academic programs, various committees, and so on. In addition, the typical college dean cannot avoid being involved in other college or university functions. Though the content may be different, the college administrator can be equally besieged with management concerns that limit the amount of time available for observation.

Another person who typically conducts classroom observations for purposes either of evaluation or instructional improvement is the instructional specialist, supervisor, or coordinator. In the case of schools, this is often a school district staff member with responsibility for a given subject area, although in recent years some special programs have made such staff available on a local school basis. In general, however, this is another person with a complex role and a large span of responsibility. In many cases this person is responsible for the supervision of even more teachers than is the principal. Language arts supervisors, for example, may have several hundred teachers to work with, spread out over many buildings.

Focus and Selection. According to Holley (Note 4), only 19% of the formally documented teacher evaluation systems used competency-based ratings with any type of expanded behavior descriptors, that is, a fuller explication of what each point on the scale means, or what the scale itself means. In practice, this means that most observers have little, if any, direction about what to look for in observations. Thus, most observers are probably trying to gather information that will be useful to them in filling out rating forms containing vague generalities covering everything from personal characteristics to knowledge of subject matter. In doing observations, they are faced with the panorama of the classroom without much of a guideline about critical factors to observe.

In addition, in most cases an observation component is not designed for evaluating sixth-grade math teachers at a given school, for example, but rather is designed for a district-wide evaluation system. The organizational and bureaucratic implications of this cannot be ignored. Here bureaucratic needs can have a detrimental impact on observation needs. To direct an observer in what to watch for in the performance of a kindergarten teacher, a junior high drama teacher, or a high school physics teacher using an observation system that is also useful at the district level in describing the performance of all teachers presents a considerable challenge. Although some general findings coming out of the research on teaching suggest some teacher behaviors that span this spectrum of performance, much of this research has yet to find its way into practical use in the design of evaluation systems. Thus, the need for a single observation instrument may mean less congruence between the variables of the instrument and the relevant classroom phenomena at some schooling levels. In addition, although it may be desirable from a bureaucratic standpoint to have a single instrument in the observation component, it can be politically difficult to require its use. The use of more than one observation instrument may satisfy needs for relevance, with greater sensitivity to differences in educational practice throughout the district and convenience on the part of the observers. On the other hand, it also leads to problems in assessing the observation results as a step to reaching a final judgment. With the use of more than one instrument, no single procedure can be employed for interpreting the observation results.

Integration/Coordination. When observations are conducted by persons other than the principal evaluator, whether they be peers, assistant administrators, or instructional specialists, the principal evaluator is usually responsible for coordinating the observation activity and integrating data into a coherent picture of the teacher's performance. Problems can arise in this cooperative effort for several reasons—communication breakdowns, value and attitudinal differences, and so on. Some principal evaluators try to handle these problems and forestall others by requiring that the other observers always have a preobservation conference with the principal evaluator in order to learn of any concerns that the observers may have. Since the problems often center around philosophical differences that may exist among the observers, however, there is often no easy solution to the differences that arise.

Aggregation and Communication of Data. Usually persons being observed for evaluation purposes want immediate feedback. It is difficult to accept a delay while tallies are being added and divided. Moreover, they want specific language that they can react to or take action on. The truth also is that many observers find it difficult or undesirable to manage any data processing. Although hand calculators have made this a far more realistic possibility than in the past, experience suggests that heavily number-dependent systems may have limited success in the school setting.

Politics. For the most part, classroom observations are not conducted in quiet and obscurity, but in the fishbowl of school management. The observer is constantly aware that the comments put into writing can be challenged by the person being observed. Taking schools as an example, if the observation is considerably at odds with feelings that parents have about their child's experiences or with the experiences of observers from the central office, justification is likely to be demanded. Thus, the employment of an observation component in a teacher appraisal system most likely reflects the need for justification or accountability. Evaluators and observers want instruments that yield data that can serve without much difficulty in their accounts of the accuracy and rationality of their observations and judgments based upon those observations. Instruments that yield data that cannot be easily interpreted do not meet this need very well. Instruments which employ only or primarily high-inference measures present a greater problem in this respect than low-inference measures.

System needs can also generate factors influencing the employment of an observation component. Care must be taken to ensure that the concern to generate rapport and team spirit among teachers and administrators, whether at the school or college level, does not affect the objectivity of observation by indirectly encouraging observers (when they are a part of the system) to record only favorable data.

Law. Although affecting extraordinarily few teachers being observed, termination is a shadow always present in the evaluation process. Every administrator and teacher is aware that any written observation may be a potential piece of evidence. Many teacher organizations or unions regularly employ staff or attorneys who are on call to advise teachers about their rights and about any infringements that observation or evaluation may represent. Thus, the language and data collected by the observer must be able to stand heavy scrutiny. For this reason, caution is extremely important in observation.

Training. The problem of training observers to see the classroom in terms of the instrument they are to use arises with the use of any observation system. The very nature of a structured observation guided by certain objectives introduces some degree of distance between the observer and the natural perspective of the participants: the teacher and the students. The severity of this problem varies with the observation format. In the case of some formats, this training problem is directly related to the amount of information yielded by the instrument. Instruments of this kind frequently face the user with a trade-off between information and training demands; if the user is unwilling or unable to devote much effort to training, some information will be lost.

The training of observers to use an observation system successfully also involves the coding or recording of what is seen. The observer must first learn to see the classroom through the terms of the instrument, but, second, must learn to code or record what is seen according to a method required by the instrument. Here again, the severity of the training problem depends upon the instrument. Elaborate category systems require a large amount of training before the observer can successfully, consistently, and reliably code classroom events in the manner required (Stallings, 1977; Simon and Boyer, Note 1). Rating, field notes, checklist, and narrative systems require less training in this regard, being simpler methods of recording classroom data, but may require the categorizing of events before they are recorded.

Historically, as the understanding of the classroom grew, researchers began to ask more complicated questions and, correspondingly, to demand more complicated information from their instruments. In response, observation instruments became more complex and imposed new demands upon the observers employing them. Using these instruments effectively required fairly elaborate training on the part of the observer, and an observer training program became a common (and necessary) feature of research programs employing sophisticated observation systems. An elaborate training program, however, does not appear feasible when classroom observation is used for teacher evaluation.

Practicality demands that the observers be either principals, supervisors, teachers, or other administrators, none of whom can be reasonably expected to participate in an elaborate, lengthy training program. Since teacher evaluation is a necessary (and ubiquitous) feature of all educational establishments, practicality and economics demand that the observers be participants in the educational process and that an observation system be devised that does not require elaborate training of the observers. This places a constraint on the complexity of the observation system.

Moreover, fairly high rates of turnover in administrators create a complex training situation in which fairly individualized training is requisite. Few school systems have the kind of staff development program that fosters such training. The greater the complexity of the proposed observation system, the more this constraint acts against implementation.

Features

Designs for observation systems that reflect these constraints are likely to feature the following:

1. Observation requirements and purposes are clearly specified. The evaluation form may, in fact, have a place where the number of observations conducted must be specified and signed by both evaluator and evaluatee. Mandatory time-lengths may also be set. In particular, the role of observation and the overall purpose it serves in a total evaluation system are specified.

2. Observation instruments are made mandatory, or multicopy forms are provided. Mandatory forms simplify training needs but constrain the selection of the most appropriate instrument for the purpose desired. Multicopy forms facilitate communication.

3. Observers and their role in relation to the overall evaluation are specified. Recipients of written copies of the observation forms are also specified. If, for example, department heads are to make observations that will play a role in the ultimate evaluation ratings completed by the evaluator, the evaluatee should be fully informed about this in advance. Similarly, if peer observations are done to assist the instructor and will not be used in the final ratings, this should also be clarified.

4. Training is ample and cyclical. Training is necessary to familiarize evaluators with the system and to teach observation skills. It should reduce inconsistency in judgments and promote the reliability of recordings. In addition, training must be cyclical because there is regular turnover in personnel responsible for evaluation and because attendance is unlikely to be perfect. Efforts must be made to keep those who miss training abreast of other staff.

TECHNICAL CONSIDERATIONS

The Classroom and the Problems It Presents for Observation

One of the first tasks that faces the user of any observation system is the selection of those aspects, among the large number of happenings in the classroom, that it is important to observe. This selection has to confront not only the number of such happenings but also their complexity. The classroom presents the observer not simply with behavior, but with structured behavior. The behavior of the teacher and the students is interdependent and interrelated in complicated ways. A further problem for observation is created by the extreme density of the phenomena, that is, a great deal happens in a short time. One study (Jackson, Note 5) showed that the elementary teacher may engage in as many as 1,000 interpersonal interchanges each day.

Although these properties of the classroom—the wealth, complexity, and pace of the phenomena—create problems for successful classroom observation, they do not make it impossible. Any observation is governed by objectives defined by the purpose of the evaluation and the information needed; not all events or behavior are equally relevant. Therefore, all classroom observation is selective, a selectivity that can go all the way to the extreme of focusing upon only one behavioral item. For example, Harrington (1955) employed an observation scheme that recorded teacher smiles during the observation period and ignored everything else.

The complexity and pace of classroom events mean that classrooms must be observed very carefully. To pick out the phenomena relevant to the objectives in a regular, systematic way, the observer must enter the classroom with a careful, well-defined sense of what he/she is looking for. In the absence of this, the observer is likely only to get a confused representation of the classroom, which may disguise more than it reveals.

Successful Observation

Two things are essential for successful observation: (1) a systematic approach and (2) reliable and valid instruments. A systematic approach alone is not sufficient and is ultimately worthless if the instrument does not have an acceptable degree of reliability and validity.

A systematic approach is characterized by (1) a careful focus on the items of interest by means of the terms of the instrument and (2) a methodical way of attending to classroom events. The terms of the instrument must be given an operational or behavioral meaning. If sufficient care is not devoted to defining and operationalizing the terms of the instrument, it will fail to focus clearly upon the items of interest. However, some important variables, such as "setting variables," are nonbehavioral. For example, the number of students in the room, the number of blackboards, and the presence of an observer are all setting variables.

Methods of Recording

Various methods have been employed for gathering data in the classroom, all of which have their relative advantages and disadvantages.

Frequency/Count Systems. Several types of systems record the frequency, number, or presence of certain behaviors or events (Rosenshine and Furst, 1973). Those designed to record a behavior, event, or interactional sequence each time it occurs are *category systems*. The object of a category system is to classify each behavioral item of interest into one and only one category, where the categories are defined as independent and mutually exclusive. Categories are designated in advance, limited in number, and represent classifications on a given dimension, such as teacher-pupil interaction or the nature of teacher questioning. Systems that record an item only once if it occurs within a certain time period, regardless of how many times it occurs, are *sign systems*. Since sign systems do not require the recording of each instance of an item, but only the presence of an item over a given period of time, it is possible for the observer to pay attention to a greater number of items than when using a category system. Checklists, containing a list of items that the observer is to focus upon, can be either category or sign systems.

Rating Systems. Rating systems ask the observer to rate, usually at the end of an observational session or period, the degree to which a certain variable was present. They are sometimes used to assess the frequency and intensity of certain behaviors. With these systems, the observer estimates the degrees and frequencies of classroom events. Although rating systems can be used as frequency/count systems, their strength is in providing information about high-inference items, such as the degree of teacher warmth, which require a greater amount of interpretation on the part of the observer, in contrast with the low-inference variables, such as the number of times that the teacher smiled, usually associated with category or sign systems (Rosenshine and Furst, 1973).

Narrative Systems. A narrative approach to classroom observation is substantially different from frequency/count and rating systems. Category, sign, and rating systems yield a representation of the classroom one step removed from classroom phenomena as they actually occur. The narrative method, on the other hand, depicts classroom phenomena in the manner in which they occurred; it describes the phenomena in the natural terms of the classroom itself. When employing the narrative methods, although the use of some technical terms may be useful and desirable, the observer for the most part simply describes in more or less ordinary terms what happens in the classroom. For example, whereas the narrative method would record that the teacher asked a student how he felt about his brothers and sisters, the category system might code that as an instance of an "open-ended, high task-ambiguity" question.

The anecdote, a brief narrative description, usually of a biographical incident, has perhaps been the most frequently used kind of narrative system for observation in the natural as well as the social sciences. As a brief narration, it is limited with respect to the amount of data that it can record and is most useful as a means of recording episodes of limited scope.

However, it should be noted that despite this limitation, observers who are economical, precise, and focused can use anecdotes very efficiently. One cannot expect too much information from anecdotes, but they can be used to provide concrete instances that illustrate an already identified, general problem.

Interpretive notes are similar to anecdotes with respect to the scope of the events observed, but differ by a greater emphasis upon interpretation as opposed to mere objective description. With the inclusion of interpretation and generalization, this form of narrative record is particularly useful when there is a concern for the larger significance of events that are relatively limited in scope. However, there are two problems that can emerge when this form of narrative record is used. First, when interpretation enters the picture, the stability of observations across observers is threatened. Whenever observers are asked to interpret, rather than simply to describe, subjective elements become a factor and render observer agreement less likely. Second, due to the de-emphasis of simple objective description, field notes usually do not permit a return to the original observational data for reinterpretation. There is usually not enough objective data recorded to permit reinterpretation.

Specimen records differ from anecdotes and interpretive notes with respect to both purpose and coverage. In a specimen record, behavior (usually of a single individual) is described continuously over a relatively brief interval with the deliberate intention of avoiding selectivity and theoretical reflections. The purpose of the specimen record is not so much to characterize an incident, as in the anecdote, or to interpret events in an effort to get to their larger significance. The purpose is simply to record everything that the individual does and everything that happens to that individual in a limited time. Depending upon the time interval selected, specimen records can be very lengthy. Barker and Wright (1951) discovered, for example, that it required 420 printed pages to recount the events that transpired with respect to a boy in a single day, from 7:00 am to 8:33 pm. Although specimen records are particularly useful in discovering behavior patterns, their focus upon only one individual limits their value for classroom research and the evaluation of teaching.

The complete descriptive narrative resulted from the concern to exploit as much as possible the advantages of the narrative methods. In contrast to "partial" narratives, such as anecdotes and brief narratives in general, the purpose of the complete descriptive narrative is to render a "complete" record of the significant classroom phenomena in a given observational period. In addition to rectifying the rather limited viewpoint and correspondingly limited capabilities of the anecdote as a narrative form, the complete descriptive narrative has the further advantage of supplying a kind of complete record of classroom phenomena, which can serve as an adequate basis for any number of reanalyses governed by different questions. Narrative observation systems of this kind have been used very effectively to add to our understanding of the functioning of the classroom. They are particularly effective—achieving a great deal of explanatory power—when used jointly with more quantitatively oriented instruments. The disadvantages of this approach are similar to those for recording in other narrative formats.

The narrative methods have several advantages over the other methods of recording. First, there is the value of its natural approach, which allows an understanding of the classroom in terms that are easily communicated to participants. Second is its holistic perspective. Category systems, for example, generally yield only the amounts of designated teacher behavior and usually abstract it from the particular contexts in which this behavior is embedded. However, the contexts in which particular kinds of teacher behavior occur are very important. For example, it is important to know not simply *how much* teacher probing occurs, but *when* it occurs and in *what* situations. If teacher behavior is abstracted from the context in which it occurs, understanding of teacher behavior may be limited. Category systems, in recording only the frequency of designated types of behavior, thus leave an important gap that must be filled. Narrative systems, on the other hand, are able to preserve the original sequencing of behavior and the contexts in which it occurs, offering a much less selective and more holistic perspective on classroom phenomena. The importance of this perspective for the evaluation of teaching cannot be emphasized too much. Teachers and students do not simply behave in the classroom; they behave in response to the classroom environment, and any evaluation that fails to take account of this will be somewhat inadequate. (See Chapter 3 for further elaboration of this view.) Some limitations of this approach lie in the fact that several interpretations may be made of the same events. If certain events do not appear in the narrative record, it may be for one of two reasons: (1) they did not occur or (2) observers failed to record them because they were looking at other events.

It has been pointed out that the observers must be trained to see the classroom in terms of the instrument. In the case of category and sign systems (and even rating systems), this can require quite a bit of training. Narrative recording also requires carefully trained professional staff and facility with language and written composition (Clements and Evertson, Note 6), but the problem is not so severe. Although the narrative approach, too, may use some abstract notions and thus may require some operationalizing, it is generally less removed from the natural (and most obvious) perspective on the classroom. With the possibility of employing relatively ordinary terms, as opposed to technical, narrowly defined categories, the narrative format has the further advantage of making it easier to obtain agreement among observers about the use of the instrument, which is an important factor in its overall reliability.

Finally, the authors would like to make it clear that they are not concerned to prescribe the use of a particular observation format to the exclusion of any others. The various formats have strengths and weaknesses, depending also upon factors too numerous to be discussed here. The authors would only like to recommend that potential users of observation instruments be sensitive to the needs and circumstances of their situations, which may recommend the use of one format (or combination of formats) as opposed to others.

Reliability and Validity

Once an observation system has been constructed in accordance with stated objectives, the next question that arises is, does it do what it is supposed to do? How well does it meet the objectives? The issues involved in answering these two questions fall into two categories, reliability and validity. Evaluators must be sensitive to the need for an acceptable degree of reliability and validity for an observation component in a teacher appraisal system.

The reliability of an instrument refers to "the extent to which measures give consistent results" (Selltiz et al., 1976, p. 161). In other words, it refers to the degree of measurement error. Reliability is an important concern for two reasons. First, reliability is a precondition of the success of the instrument in measuring what it is supposed to measure, that is, it is a prerequisite of the validity of the instrument. If an observation instrument does not possess a good degree of reliability, then it is not likely to have much validity. Ensuring reliability is thus a first step to achieving any kind of validity. Second, unless an instrument measures a variable relatively consistently, there is little hope of determining by means of that instrument whether changes in that variable are the result of other variables or are merely the reflection of the unreliability of the instrument.

Unreliability arises when two measurements of the same phenomenon (or group of phenomena) tend to differ too much (i.e., when there is too much measurement error). There are three respects in which an instrument can lack reliability: (1) the phenomenon (or phenomena) is (or are) unstable, (2) the observers disagree about what occurs, or (3) the instrument itself lacks consistency in the measurement of this particular phenomenon (or phenomena; Medley and Mitzel, 1963). One can help to ensure reliability in these areas by having a sufficient number of observation occasions, a sufficient number of well-trained observers, and a large number (as large as is practically feasible) of indicators of the trait to be measured.

A high degree of reliability in an instrument does not guarantee a high degree of validity. For example, one could imagine an instrument attempting to measure intelligence by having children throw stones as far as they could (Nunnally, 1967). There might be a very high correlation between how far stones were thrown on one occasion and how far they were thrown on another. But this hardly constitutes a valid measure of intelligence. Whereas the reliability issue concerns whether the instrument yields consistent measures, the validity issue asks whether the instrument does what it is intended to do.

Central to the issue of validity is the relationship between the instrument and its properties and that which the instrument is designed to measure. Three types of validity have been distinguished.

Content validity refers to the appropriateness of the items on the measuring instrument to the trait to be measured. A given instrument has content validity if the items represent a logical sampling of items from the universe of items that can be presumed to indicate the trait to be measured; ensuring content validity amounts to ensuring that the content of the instrument is logically relevant to the characteristic to be measured. Although content validity is fairly easy to assess, relying upon the professional judgment of the researcher and not requiring any statistical procedures, it is not a very powerful measure of the validity of an instrument.

The predictive validity of an instrument refers to the degree to which that instrument predicts some other variable. In the educational context, there is much interest in identifying teacher and student behavior that is predictive of achievement and in designing observation instruments that yield data most predictive of achievement.

Construct validity is often employed to measure a trait or construct, such as teacher warmth, that is not directly observable. A variety of data is collected to test the claim that the trait being measured by the instrument is indeed what is intended and not something else.

Regardless of the type of validity, the most relevant judgments, empirical data, and procedures of analysis depend upon the values of the interpreters and the counter-hypotheses they advance (Cronbach, 1980).

Foremost among the factors that affect the validity of observation instruments are the possible reactive effects of respondents, such that classes which are observed are different from classes which are not. It is certainly a reasonable assumption that the knowledge that they are being observed can alter the behavior of teachers and students. But any attempt to determine what the reactive effects might be would most likely have to rely upon observation in which the respondents were unaware that they were being observed. This situation confronts the ethical problem of nonvoluntary participation. So it is difficult to see how reactive effects can be determined to any precise degree. However, the successful application of research findings gathered in correlational studies to the experimental context suggests that reactive effects may not significantly affect external validity. In any case, it is certainly possible, if care is taken, to minimize the impact of the observer.

CONCLUDING THOUGHT

Can classroom observation measure effective teaching with a reasonable degree of reliability and validity? With respect to reliability, the very successful use of observation in classroom research leaves no doubts about that. With respect to validity, a full answer cannot be given without considering the state of our knowledge of effective teaching. Notwithstanding a well-known but somewhat dated pessimistic appraisal, classroom research has recently made progress in identifying process variables that are good indicators of effective teaching as measured by achievement. A picture of what effective teaching looks like in the classroom is beginning to emerge, and the assessment of teachers by means of observation can now be regarded as a meaningful activity.

Perhaps the most striking result of recent classroom research, however, is the realization of the need for a multivariate approach when assessing teacher competency. Effective teaching in the classroom is not a simple affair, and it cannot be measured by attending to a single variable or narrow range of variables, such as "teacher behavior." Classroom observation for teacher evaluation all too frequently degenerates into "teacher observation." However, teaching is an interactive process involving teachers, students, and classroom environmental variables; one cannot hope to measure teaching by attending to a single component of this dynamic process. Neither can teaching be reduced to simply a teacher-student interaction, for this betrays ignorance of the environmental context in which that interaction takes place. Recent classroom research (Brophy and Evertson, 1978) has indicated the importance of context; for every behavior, whether of teachers or students, an environmental context plays a crucial role in the formation of that behavior. To focus exclusively upon the behavior of the teacher ignores the fact that teacher behavior does not occur in a vacuum, but is in response to classroom environmental demands. This means that "effective teaching," taken abstractly, may have no single behavioral translation, for effective teaching is always teaching in a particular context or environment. Thus, the assessment of teacher competency must not be guided by a fixed, abstract class of teacher behaviors but by contextually meaningful teacher behavior. If the competency of teachers is to be assessed, their ability to behave appropriately, to respond to environmental conditions in a way that facilitates teaching, must also be assessed.

Teachers have perhaps always known experientially the importance of classroom environmental features for teaching and learning, but classroom research has only fairly recently turned to teacher behavior directed toward structuring those features in terms of the notions of classroom management and organization. Inquiry into classroom management and organization, though possessing only a relatively short history, has demonstrated its importance for effective teaching. That research suggests that successful classroom management and organization may be the primary enabling conditions of effective teaching. Any observation instrument intended to evaluate teachers must take account of these variables if it is to have any validity.

REFERENCE NOTES

1. Simon, A. and E.C. Boyer (1967) *Mirrors for Behavior: An Anthology of Classroom Observation Instruments* (6 vols.). Philadelphia: Research for Better Schools.
2. Kowalski, J.D.S. (1978) *Evaluating Teacher Performance*. Arlington, VA: Educational Research Service.
3. Carter, W. (1979) *An Interpretative Analysis of the Teacher Selection and Evaluation Process* (Pub. No. RE 79-804-61-05). Dallas: Dallas Independent School District.
4. Holley, F. (1979) "Teacher testing, teacher evaluation, and research on teaching: Converging fields?" Presented at the annual meeting of the American Educational Research Association, San Francisco.
5. Jackson, D.W. (1965) "Teacher-pupil communication in the elementary classroom: An observational study." Presented at the annual meeting of the American Educational Research Association, Chicago.
6. Clements, B.S. and C.M. Evertson (1980) "Developing an effective research team for classroom observation (R&D Report No. 6103)." Austin: University of Texas, R&D Center for Teacher Education.

REFERENCES

Andrews, J.W., C.R. Blackmon, and J.A. Mackey (1980) "Preservice performance and the national teacher exam." *Phi Delta Kappan,* 61: 358–359.

Barker, R.G. and H.F. Wright (1951) *One Boy's Day: A Specimen Record of Behavior*. New York: Harper & Row.

Borich, G.D. and S.K. Madden (1977) *Evaluating Classroom Instruction: A Sourcebook of Instruments*. Reading, MA: Addison-Wesley.

Brophy, J.E. and C.M. Evertson (1978) "Context variables in teaching." *Educational Psychologist,* 12: 310–316.

Cronbach, L.J. (1980) "Validity on parole: How can we go straight?" *New Directions for Testing and Measurement,* 5: 99–108.

Harrington, G. M. (1955) "Smiling as a measure of teacher effectiveness." *Journal of Educational Research*, 48: 715–717.

Medley, D. M. and H. E. Mitzel (1963) "Measuring classroom behavior by systematic observation," in N. L. Gage (ed.), *Handbook of Research on Teaching*. Skokie, IL: Rand McNally.

Nunnally, J. C. (1967) *Psychometric Theory*. New York: McGraw-Hill.

Rosenshine, B. and N. Furst (1973) "The use of direct observation to study teaching," in R. M. W. Travers (ed.), *Second Handbook of Research on Teaching*. Skokie, IL: Rand McNally.

Selltiz, C., L. S. Wrightsman, and S. W. Cook (1976) *Research Methods in Social Relations*. New York: Holt, Rinehart & Winston.

Stallings, J. (1977) *Learning To Look*. Belmont, CA: Wadsworth.

CHAPTER 8

STUDENT RATINGS OF INSTRUCTION

LAWRENCE M. ALEAMONI

University of Arizona

The origin of student ratings can be traced to the time of Socrates, when they were gathered informally and unsystematically. Since then, faculty have solicited, chastized, and ignored them, whereas students and administrators have requested, used, misinterpreted, and misused them. Faculty, students, and administrators have all claimed, at one time or another, that the ratings are both reliable, valid, and useful and unreliable, invalid, and useless.

In spite of their agitated history, student ratings are increasingly being used by faculty, students, and administrators for formative and summative decisions about instructional effectiveness. In fact, student ratings tend to be the only tangible source of instructional evaluation information in the majority of colleges and universities, both here and abroad (Thorne et al., Note 1; O'Connell and Smartt, Note 2). This is a disturbing state of affairs, given the level of faculty dissatisfaction with student ratings. Such dissatisfaction could be allayed, however, if faculty were made aware of the extensive research on student ratings and presented with rationale for developing a comprehensive system to improve and reward instructional effectiveness. This chapter concentrates on student ratings, one of the components of a comprehensive instructional evaluation system.

The types of student ratings covered in this chapter range from formally developed questionnaires printed on optically scanned answer sheets to informally put-together forms tailor-made by an instructor for his/her class. The questions might require a limited response, extensive discussion, or some combination of the two on the part of the students.

The rationale for gathering student ratings can be found in the following arguments:

Author's Note: Most of the research and use of the student rating forms has occurred at the college and the university level. Generalizations to other educational and noneducational levels will be left to the discretion of the reader.

110

1. Students are the main source of information about (a) the accomplishment of important educational goals, such as the development of motivation for continued learning, and (b) areas of rapport, degrees of communication, and the existence of problems between instructors and students. This information can help instructors as well as educational researchers describe and define the learning environment more concretely and objectively than they could through other types of measurement.

2. If one assumes that course elements such as the instructor, textbook, homework, course content, method of instruction, student interest, student attention, and general student attitude toward the course all serve to change student behavior in a specified direction and that they constitute effective instruction, then students are the most logical evaluators of the quality and effectiveness of and satisfaction with those course elements, since they are the only ones who are directly and extensively exposed to them. Such evaluations, unlike visits from outside evaluators, do not intrude into the class and are made by those with a genuine interest in the instructor's success.

3. Student ratings provide a means of communicating between students and instructor, which, in large institutions, may not exist in other forms. Such communication may lead to the kind of involvement by student and instructor in the teaching-learning process that raises the whole level of instruction. The institution may also be stimulated by such ratings to consider its overall goals and values.

4. Students' demands for information about particular instructors and courses for use by other students in selecting courses and instructors and/or to encourage instructional improvement can be provided through systematic student evaluation. Such evaluation might increase the chances that excellence in instruction will be recognized and rewarded.

RESEARCH

Faculty have several concerns about the appropriateness of using student ratings of instructor and instruction at all. Research spanning a 56-year period addresses these concerns. The concerns along with the relevant research are presented below:

1. Students cannot make consistent judgments about the instructor and instruction because of their immaturity, lack of experience, and capriciousness. Evidence dating back to 1924, according to Guthrie (Note 3), indicates just the opposite. The stability of student ratings from one year to the next resulted in substantial correlations in the range of .87 to .89. More recent literature on the subject, cited by Costin et al. (1971), and studies by

Gillmore (Note 4) and Hogan (1973) indicated that the correlation between student ratings of the same instructors and courses ranged from .70 to .87.

2. Only colleagues with excellent publication records and expertise are qualified both to teach and to evaluate their peers' instruction. There is a widely held belief (Borgatta, 1970; Deming, 1972) that good instruction and good research are so closely allied that it is unnecessary to evaluate them independently. Research is divided on this point. Positive correlations between research productivity and teaching effectiveness have been found by Maslow and Zimmerman (1956), McDaniel and Feldhusen (1970), McGrath (1962), Riley et al. (1950), and Stallings and Singhal (Note 5). In contrast, Aleamoni and Yimer (1973), Guthrie (1949, Note 3), Hayes (1971), Linsky and Straus (1975), and Voeks (1962) found no significant relationship between instructors' research productivity and students' ratings of their teaching effectiveness. One study (Aleamoni and Yimer, 1973) also reported no significant relationship between instructors' research productivity and colleagues' ratings of their teaching effectiveness.

3. Most student rating schemes are nothing more than a popularity contest, with the warm, friendly, humorous instructor emerging as the winner every time. Studies conducted by Aleamoni and Spencer (1973), while developing and utilizing the Illinois Course Evaluation Questionnaire (CEQ) subscales, indicated that no single subscale (e.g., Method of Instruction) completely overlapped the other subscales. This result means that an instructor who received a high rating on the Instructor subscale (made up of items like "The instructor seemed to be interested in students as persons.") would not be guaranteed high ratings on the other four subscales (General Course Attitude, Method of Instruction, Course Content, and Interest and Attention). In reviewing both written and objective student comments, Aleamoni (1976a) found that students frankly praised instructors for their warm, friendly, humorous manner in the classroom, but if their courses were not well-organized or their methods of stimulating students to learn were poor, the students equally frankly criticized them in those areas. This evidence, in addition to that presented by Costin et al. (1971), Frey (1978), Grush and Costin (1975), Perry et al. (1979), and Ware and Williams (1977), indicates that students are discriminating judges.

4. Students are not able to make accurate judgments until they have been away from the course, and possibly away from the university, for several years. It is very difficult to obtain a comparative and representative sample in longitudinal follow-up studies. The sampling problem is further compounded by the fact that almost all student attitudinal data relating to a course or instructor are gathered anonymously. Most studies in this area, therefore, have relied on surveys of alumni and/or graduating seniors. Earlier studies by Drucker and Remmers (1951) showed that alumni who had been out of school 5 to 10 years rated instructors much the same as students currently

enrolled. More recent evidence by Aleamoni and Yimer (Note 6), Marsh (1977), Marsh and Overall (1979), and McKeachie et al. (1978) further substantiated the earlier findings.

5. Student rating forms are both unreliable and invalid. Well-developed instruments and procedures for their administration can yield high internal consistency reliabilities. Costin et al. (1971) reported such reliabilities to be in the .90 range. Aleamoni (1978a) reported reliabilities ranging from .81 to .94 for items and from .88 to .98 for subscales of the CEQ. It should be noted, however, that wherever student rating forms are not carefully constructed with the aid of professionals, as in the case of most student- and faculty-generated forms (Everly and Aleamoni, 1972), the reliabilities may be so low as to negate completely the evaluation effect and its results.

Validity is much more difficult to assess than reliability. Most student rating forms have been validated by the judgment of experts that the items and subscales measure important aspects of instruction (Costin et al., 1971). These subjectively determined dimensions of instructional setting and process have also been validated using statistical tools, such as factor analysis (Aleamoni and Hexner, 1980). Further evidence of validity comes from studies, in which student ratings are correlated with other indicators of teacher competence, such as peer (colleague) ratings, expert judges' ratings, graduating seniors' and alumni ratings, and student learning. The 14 studies cited by Aleamoni and Hexner (1980) in which student ratings were compared to (1) colleague rating, (2) expert judges' ratings, (3) graduating seniors' and alumni ratings, and (4) student learning measures all indicated the existence of moderate to high positive correlations, which can be considered as providing additional evidence of validity. This is in contrast to two studies (Bendig, 1953; Rodin and Rodin, 1972) that found a negative relationship between student achievement and instructor rating. The latter study has been soundly criticized for its methodology by several researchers (Frey, 1973; Gessner, 1973; Menges, 1973; Centra, Note 7).

6. Extraneous variables or conditions that faculty think can affect student ratings are listed below.

The Size of the Class. Faculty members frequently suggest that instructors of large classes may receive lower ratings because students generally prefer small classes, which permit more student-instructor interaction. Although this belief is supported to some extent by the results of eight studies cited by Aleamoni and Hexner (1980), other investigations do not support it. For example Aleamoni and Hexner (1980) cited seven other studies that found no relationship between class size and student ratings. Some investigators have also reported curvilinear relationships between class size and student ratings (Gage, 1961; Kohlan, 1973; Lovell and Haner, 1955; Marsh et al., 1979; Pohlmann, 1975; Wood et al., 1974).

Sex of the Student and the Instructor. Conflicting results have been obtained when relating the sex of the student to student evaluations of instruction. Aleamoni and Thomas (Note 8), Doyle and Whitely (1974), Goodhartz (1948), and Isaacson et al. (1964) reported no difference between faculty ratings made by male and female students. In addition, Costin et al. (1971) cited seven studies that reported no differences in overall ratings of instructors made by male and female students or in the ratings received by male and female instructors. Conversely, Bendig (1952) found female students to be more critical of male instructors than their male counterparts; more recently Walker (1969) found that female students rated female instructors significantly higher than they rated male instructors. In addition, Aleamoni and Hexner (1980) cited five studies that reported female students rate instructors higher on some subscales of instructor evaluation forms than do male students.

The Time of Day the Course was Offered. The limited amount of research in this area (Guthrie, Note 3; Yongkittikul et al., Note 9) indicates that the time of day the course is offered does not influence student ratings.

Whether the Student was Taking the Course as a Requirement or as an Elective. Several investigators have found that students who are required to take a course tend to rate it lower than students who elect to take it (Pohlmann, 1975; Cohen and Humphreys, Note 10; Gilmore and Brandenburg, Note 11). This finding is supported by Gage (1961) and Lovell and Haner (1955), who found that instructors of elective courses were rated significantly higher than instructors of required courses. In contrast, Heilman and Armentrout (1936) and Hildebrand et al. (Note 12) reported no difference between students' ratings of required courses and elective courses.

Whether the Student was a Major or a Nonmajor. The limited amount of research in this area (Null and Nicholson, 1972; Rayder, 1968; Aleamoni and Thomas, Note 8; Cohen and Humphreys, Note 10) indicates that there are no significant differences and no significant relationships between student ratings whether they were majors or minors.

The Level of the Course (Freshman, Sophomore, Junior, Senior, Graduate). Aleamoni and Hexner (1980) cited eight investigators who reported no significant relationship between student status (e.g., freshman, sophomore, etc.) and ratings assigned to instructors. However, they also cited 18 other investigators who reported that graduate students and/or upper division students tended to rate instructors more favorably than did lower division students.

The Rank of the Instructor (Instructor, Assistant Professor, Associate Professor, Professor). Some investigators reported that instructors of higher rank received higher student ratings (Clark and Keller, 1954; Downie 1952;

Gage, 1961; Walker, 1969; Guthrie, Note 3); however, others reported no significant relationship between instructor rank and student ratings (Aleamoni and Graham, 1974; Aleamoni and Yimer, 1973; Linsky and Straus, 1975; Aleamoni and Thomas, Note 8; Singhal, Note 13). Conflicting results have also been found when comparing teaching experience to student ratings. Rayder (1968) reported a negative relationship, whereas Heilman and Armentrout (1936) found no significant relationship.

7. The grades or marks students receive in the course are highly correlated with their ratings of the course and the instructor. Considerable controversy has centered around the relationship between student ratings and their actual or expected course grades, the general feeling being that students tend to rate courses and instructors more highly when they expect or receive good grades. Correlational studies have reported widely inconsistent grade-rating relationships. Some 22 studies have reported zero relationships (Aleamoni and Hexner, 1980). Another 28 studies have reported significant positive relationships (Aleamoni and Hexner, 1980). In most instances, however, these relationships were relatively weak, as indicated by the fact that the median correlation was approximately .14, with the mean and standard deviation being .18 and .16, respectively.

A widely publicized study by Rodin and Rodin (1972) reported a high negative relationship between student performance on examinations and their ratings of graduate teaching assistants. These results have been contested on methodological grounds by Rodin et al. (1975). Subsequent replications of the study using regular faculty rather than teaching assistants and using more sophisticated rating forms have resulted in a positive rather than a negative relationship (Frey, 1973; Gessner, 1973; Sullivan and Skanes, 1974).

8. How can student ratings possibly be used to improve instruction? Studies by Braunstein et al. (1973), Centra (1973), and Miller (1971) were inconclusive with respect to the effect of feedback at midterm to instructors whose instruction was again evaluated at the end of the term. However, Marsh et al. (1975), Overall and Marsh (1979), and Sherman (1978) reported more favorable ratings from and improved learning by students by the end of the term. In order to determine if a combination of a printed report of the results and personal consultations would be superior to providing only a printed report of results, Aleamoni (1978b) and McKeachie (1979) found that instructors significantly improved their ratings when personal consultations were provided.

All this research points out several advantages and disadvantages of student ratings. Gathering student ratings can provide the instructor with first-hand information on the accomplishment of particular educational goals and on the level of satisfaction with and influence of various course elements. Such information can be used by the instructor to enrich and improve the course as well as to document instructional effectiveness for administrative purposes.

Students can benefit through an improved teaching and learning situation as well as from having access to information about particular instructors and courses. Administrators (deans and department heads) also benefit through an improved teaching and learning situation as well as a more accurate representation of student judgments.

The disadvantages of gathering student ratings primarily result from how they are interpreted and used. Without normative (or comparative) information, a faculty member might place inappropriate emphasis on selected student responses. If the results are published, the biases of the editor(s) might misrepresent the meaning of the ratings to both students and faculty. If administrators use the ratings for summative and punitive purposes only, the faculty will be unfairly represented.

DESIGN AND CONSTRUCTION OF THE STUDENT RATING FORM

Whenever an individual, group, or institution decides to use student ratings, it assumes that its needs and situation are so unique that it has to generate its own form. Such an assumption is frequently the result of a very simplistic determination of the purpose of the gathered information. Very little thought is given to how such information can be used by the faculty member to improve the teaching-learning situation. Even less thought is given to how such information can be appropriately used by administrators to encourage and reward faculty improvement efforts.

Of primary importance in the development and/or selection of a student rating instrument is the purpose for which it is to be used. Is the purpose primarily to provide formative evaluation information, which will be used by the faculty member to modify and improve the instructional process? Is the purpose, instead, primarily to provide summative evaluation information, which will be used by colleagues, administrators, and students for decisions about promotion, tenure, merit increases, and course selection? Or is the purpose to provide both formative and summative evaluation information?

Student rating questionnaires have been constructed by students, faculty, administrators and/or committees. By and large the questionnaires constructed in this way have not had the benefit of advice and consultation with experts in questionnaire design, resulting in a highly questionable product. Such questionnaires usually reflect the thinking and biases of one or two individuals with regard to meaningful criteria of instructional effectiveness and, therefore, are not useful for all instructors and courses.

DO NOT WRITE YOUR NAME

Course Improvement Questionnaire

1. At present, 12 1/2% of the class time is spent in review, 12 1/2% in taking and going over tests, and 75% of the time in regular instruction. Is this balance in emphasis about right?＿＿＿ (If you answered no, please specify the balance you'd prefer.)

2. Do you usually write down the answer to a learning exercise before looking at the answer?＿＿＿ (yes or no)

3. About how often are you unable to understand why the answers to the learning exercises are correct?＿＿＿ (Note: this question is not asking if you answered the questions correctly, but rather how often you couldn't understand why the answer given was correct.)

4. How helpful would it be if, in the answer to each learning exercise, a reference was given to the page(s) in the book or to a portion of the lecture in which the relevant concepts are discussed?
   a) Would be very helpful to me.
   b) Would not be very helpful to me.

5. Assuming the same total content covered is the same, would you prefer:
   a) fewer objectives that are broader in scope.
   b) more objectives that are more specific.
   c) about the same number of objectives we now have.

6. The number of learning exercises provided for each objective is usually:
   a) too few (wish there were more):   b) too many: c) about the right number.

7. How do you feel about the use of several different forms of each quiz?

8. Some of the regular instruction (A) goes over concepts in the book or over related ideas; other time is spent (B) discussing through handouts, material or examples of the concepts as found in applied work. Do you approve of the present balance between the two instructional acts?＿＿＿ If no, please indicate which activity (A or B) you prefer receive more attention.

9. Have you gone to see any of the three instructors for help outside of class time?＿＿＿ If yes, did you feel he/she was willing to spend sufficient time to help you with your difficulty?

10. Is there something you wanted to get out of this course in statistics that has not yet materialized?＿＿＿ If yes, please describe what it is.

11. Please indicate any other suggestions you have for the improvement of this course.

Figure 1. Example of a rating form for a particular course and instructor.

Types of Student Rating Forms

The least generalizable type of rating form is the one made up by a particular instructor for a particular course. Figure 1 is an example of such a form. The results of such questionnaires are considered to be highly valid and useful for the instructor, since they are usually concerned with unique organizational aspects of the course.

A more generalizable type of rating form is one made up by a particular instructor selecting items from a pool of items made up for his/her institution. One of the earliest examples of such a pool is the Purdue Cafeteria System, which provides a 200-item catalog. Instructors select their items, which are then computer-printed on an optically scanned answer sheet along with five standard general items. Normative data are provided only for the five general items.

A third type of rating form has a standard section of items applicable to almost all courses and instructors with additional optional item sections that allow the instructor to select supplementary (or more diagnostic) items from the institutional pool. (Figure 2 is an example of such a questionnaire.) The pool of items is usually categorized and presented in a catalog form. Figures 3 and 4 give samples from such catalogs. Normative data are provided only for the standard items and their composite subscales.

For a fourth type of rating format, multiple standard forms are available. The instructors' only choice here is the type of form, not the items. The University of Washington, for example, provides five forms to their faculty, one for small lecture/discussion sections, one for large lecture courses, and so on. The University of Arizona College of Nursing provides three forms to their faculty: one for clinical instructor evaluation, one for seminar instructor evaluation, and one for individual lecturer evaluation.

Finally, the fifth type of rating form is one used for all instructors and courses with no provision for additional items selected by the instructor. Such forms are typically sponsored by the student government association, resulting in a campus-wide publication of the results. Figure 5 is an example of such a questionnaire.

If an institution is determined to generate its own form, then it should involve individuals with expertise in questionnaire design and analysis at the outset. This also helps avoid questionnaires with too narrow applications and poorly defined responses. Figure 6 illustrates a form with poorly defined responses that was developed by a specific department for its own purposes.

Types of Items

A logical consequence of determining the purpose of the student rating instrument is to decide on the types of items it should contain. The types of items can be classified in terms of their content, level of inference, and type of response called for.

When deciding on the content of the items, one should determine which elements of the course, of the instruction, and of the learning are to be addressed. Questions constructed for the course area should address its organization, structure, objectives, difficulty, pace, relevance, content, usefulness, and so on. Questions constructed for the instruction area should address instructor characteristics, instructor skill, clarity of presentation, instructor rapport, method of presentation, student interaction, and so on. Finally, questions constructed for the learning area should address student satisfaction, student perceived competency, student desire to continue study in the field, and so on.

If the purpose of gathering student ratings is to produce measures that require considerable inference from what is seen or heard in the classroom to the labelling of the behavior, then higher inference measures are needed. These measures are obtained as ratings of the instructor on scales such as "partial-fair," "autocratic-democratic," or "dull-stimulating" (Rosenshine, 1970). Such measures are appropriate when making summative (final and global) decisions about the instructor and/or the instruction. If, on the other hand, the purpose is to produce measures that require the rater to classify teaching behaviors according to relatively objective categories, then low-inference measures are needed. These measures are obtained as frequency ratings of the instructor on scales such as "gesturing," "variation in voice," "asking questions," or "praise and encouragement." Such measures are appropriate when making formative (specific diagnostic) decisions about the instructor and instruction.

Ratings on high-inference items are particularly useful in exploring new ideas, and they have generally yielded higher correlations with instructor effects than the more specific, or low-inference, behavioral measures. But the information in low-inference measures is easier to use in instructional improvement programs because it is easier to translate into specific behaviors (Rosenshine, 1970).

The rater's initial judgment of the worth of a questionnaire results from the format of the items and their responses. How serious and honest the rater will be in responding to the items, how accurately the rater's responses reflect true feelings and attitudes, and how meaningful the ratings will be to the instructor, and so on, all depend upon the appropriateness of the item and response formats. The use of open-ended (free-response) items usually produces a colorful array of responses in "the student's own words" but provides very little "representative" (consensus) information for the instructor to use in formative evaluation. Instructors, however, seek such responses because they like to read comments to which they can attach their own

(text continued on p. 126)

ARIZONA COURSE/INSTRUCTOR EVALUATION QUESTIONNAIRE (CIEQ) (FORM 76)

OFFICE OF INSTRUCTIONAL RESEARCH AND DEVELOPMENT, UNIVERSITY OF ARIZONA © LAWRENCE M. ALEAMONI, 1975

MARKING INSTRUCTIONS

MARK:

AS IF YOU AGREE STRONGLY WITH THE ITEM

A IF YOU AGREE MODERATELY WITH THE ITEM

D IF YOU DISAGREE MODERATELY WITH THE ITEM

DS IF YOU DISAGREE STRONGLY WITH THE ITEM

MARK ONLY ONE RESPONSE PER ITEM USING PENCIL ONLY

ERASE CHANGED ANSWERS CLEANLY AND COMPLETELY.

SAMPLE MARK

AS A D DS

STUDENT INFORMATION

ARE YOU A: FRESHMAN SOPHOMORE JUNIOR SENIOR GRADUATE OTHER

ARE YOU TAKING THIS COURSE FOR PASS/FAIL: YES NO

ARE YOU TAKING THIS COURSE AS A: REQUIRED ELECTIVE

ARE YOU A: MALE FEMALE

YOUR EXPECTED GRADE IN THIS COURSE IS: A B C D E

THIS COURSE IS WITHIN YOUR: MAJOR MINOR OTHER

SEMESTER: FALL SPRING SUMMER

COURSE INFORMATION

RATE EACH OF THE FOLLOWING

COURSE CONTENT: EXCELLENT VERY GOOD GOOD FAIR POOR VERY POOR

MAJOR INSTRUCTOR: EXCELLENT VERY GOOD GOOD FAIR POOR VERY POOR

COURSE IN GENERAL: EXCELLENT VERY GOOD GOOD FAIR POOR VERY POOR

CODING INFORMATION

COURSE CODE

0 1 2 3 4 5 6 7 8 9

0 1 2 3 4 5 6 7 8 9

0 1 2 3 4 5 6 7 8 9

0 1 2 3 4 5 6 7 8 9

0 1 2 3 4 5 6 7 8 9

SPECIAL CODE

0 1 2 3 4 5 6 7 8 9

0 1 2 3 4 5 6 7 8 9

0 1 2 3 4 5 6 7 8 9

0 1 2 3 4 5 6 7 8 9

0 1 2 3 4 5 6 7 8 9

0 1 2 3 4 5 6 7 8 9

0 1 2 3 4 5 6 7 8 9

0 1 2 3 4 5 6 7 8 9

0 1 2 3 4 5 6 7 8 9

(Number)

(Name)

STANDARD ITEM SECTION

1	It was a very worthwhile course.	AS A D DS
2	I would take another course that was taught this way.	AS A D DS
3	The instructor seemed to be interested in students as individuals.	AS A D DS
4	The course material was too difficult.	AS A D DS
5	It was easy to remain attentive.	AS A D DS
6	NOT much was gained by taking this course.	AS A D DS

OPTIONAL ITEMS

SECTION I		SECTION II	
22	AS A D DS	43	A B C D E
23	AS A D DS	44	A B C D E
24	AS A D DS	45	A B C D E
25	AS A D DS	46	A B C D E
26	AS A D DS	47	A B C D E
27	AS A D DS	48	A B C D E

Figure 2. Example of a university/college-generated standard rating form.

PLEASE PRINT.
THE MAJOR INSTRUCTOR OF THIS COURSE IS _____
THE NAME AND NUMBER OF THIS COURSE IS _____

7	I would have preferred another method of teaching in this course.	AS A D DS	28	AS A D DS	49	A B C D E F
8	The course material seemed worthwhile.	AS A D DS	29	AS A D DS	50	A B C D E F
9	The instructor did NOT synthesize, integrate or summarize effectively.	AS A D DS	30	AS A D DS	51	A B C D E F
10	The course was quite interesting.	AS A D DS	31	AS A D DS	52	A B C D E F
11	The instructor encouraged development of new viewpoints and appreciations.	AS A D DS	32	AS A D DS	53	A B C D E F
12	I learn more when other teaching methods are used.	AS A D DS	33	AS A D DS	54	A B C D E F
13	Some things were NOT explained very well.	AS A D DS	34	AS A D DS	55	A B C D E F
14	The instructor demonstrated a thorough knowledge of the subject matter.	AS A D DS	35	AS A D DS	56	A B C D E F
15	This was one of my poorest courses.	AS A D DS	36	AS A D DS	57	A B C D E F
16	The course content was excellent.	AS A D DS	37	AS A D DS	58	A B C D E F
17	Some days I was NOT very interested in this course.	AS A D DS	38	AS A D DS	59	A B C D E F
18	I think that the course was taught quite well.	AS A D DS	39	AS A D DS	60	A B C D E F
19	The course was quite boring.	AS A D DS	40	AS A D DS	61	A B C D E F
20	The instructor seemed to consider teaching as a chore or routine activity.	AS A D DS	41	AS A D DS	62	A B C D E F
21	Overall, the course was good.	AS A D DS	42	AS A D DS	63	A B C D E F

PLEASE FILL OUT THE OTHER SIDE

79/9235-C

Figure 2 (continued)

121

SIRS SUPPLEMENTARY AND DIAGNOSTIC ITEMS

Instructors often desire to gather information, or ask questions, on topics not covered by the items on the SIRS FORM or to examine student response to course characteristics more exhaustively. This supplement provides the instructor with items to achieve these purposes. Each item was developed as a part of the SIRS project and is in a format that is consistent with the standard items on the SIRS FORM. Therefore, the items can be used with the spaces made available for optional items.

These additional items are categorized into several sections. Each of the first six sections corresponds to one of the five SIRS Composite Profile indices or to the laboratory and recitation section. The remaining items are concerned with topics not included on the SIRS FORM but pertaining to other aspects of the learning situation—Grading and Examinations, Relevance of Course, Classroom Supplements and Audiovisual Aids.

INSTRUCTOR INVOLVEMENT

The instructor was generally prepared for lectures.
The instructor was friendly and relaxed in front of the class.
The instructor over-emphasized minor points.
The instructor frequently digressed from the subject matter of the course.

The instructor's voice was clear and understandable.
The instructor presented material in a clear and logical manner.
The instructor showed mastery of the subject matter.
The instructor clarified complex sections of the text.

The instructor imparted essential material that was not in the text.
The instructor was able to relate information in his field to other fields.
The instructor adapted the course to your level of comprehension.
The instructor recognized individual differences in the ability of students.

Figure 3. Sample of the Michigan State University SIRS supplementary and diagnostic items.

INTRODUCTION

The following pages contain a lengthy but by no means exhaustive collection of possible course and instructor evaluation items. These items have been somewhat arbitrarily divided into 20 categories on the basis of their content. All items are written so as to be responded to in an agree strongly to disagree strongly format.

This catalog represents an effort by the staff of the Office of Instructional Research and Development to provide instructors with a collection of items from which they may choose a relevant subset for use in their own classes, either as optional items with the standard CIEQ items or by themselves.

TABLE OF CONTENTS

Item Categories

Figure 4. Sample of the University of Arizona CIEQ optional item catalog.

ASUA COURSE EVALUATION QUESTIONNAIRE

INSTRUCTIONS: 1. If you **strongly agree** with the item 2. If you **agree** moderately with the item
3. If you **disagree** moderately with the item 4. If you **strongly disagree** with the item

1. 1-Freshman 2-Sophomore 3-Junior 4-Senior 5-Grad

2. Your expected grade in course is 1-A 2-B 3-C 4-D 5-E

3. This course is within your 1-Major 2-Minor 3-Other

4. Course content 1-Excellent 2-Very Good 3-Good 4-Fair 5-Poor

5. Major Instructor 1-Excellent 2-Very Good 3-Good 4-Fair 5-Poor

6. Course in general 1-Excellent 2-Very Good 3-Good 4-Fair 5-Poor

7. The instructor made objectives of course clear to students.

8. The instructor was willing to discuss points of view other than his own.

9. The instructor clearly explained course material

10. The instructor summarized or stressed major points which were of assistance in learning.

11. The instructor provided student with opportunity to apply learned experiences to demonstrate understanding.

12. The instructor gave helpful feedback in commenting on exams or papers.

13. The instructor was found to be flexible and willing to change his approach to meet the needs of individual students.

14. The tests were fair in their level of difficulty.

Figure 5. Example of a student-generated campus-wide rating form.

The questionnaire items, each with a rating scale from 1 to 5:

No.	Statement	1	2	3	4	5
15.	The tests gave me an adequate opportunity to show what I learned.					
16.	I understood and knew in advance the kinds of tests that I was to be given.					
17.	The tests were graded fairly and objectively.					
18.	The instructor provided an opportunity for the students to discuss the tests at a later time.					
19.	My interest in the subject area has been stimulated by this course.					
20.	The instructor is unavailable or unwilling to help or advise students outside of class.					
21.	The instructor does not display particular interest in teaching the course.					
22.	The instructor has displayed an excellent knowledge of the subject matter.					
23.	The information presented is timely and up-to-date.					
24.	I would rate my instructor in general (all-round) teaching ability as one of the best instructors.					
25.	The time was wasted most frequently by dwelling on insignificant, irrelevant material.					
26.	The pace or rate at which the instructor covered the material during the semester was just about right.					
27.	In general, I would rate the assigned readings as fair.					
28.	In general, I would rate the textbook(s) as excellent.					
29.	I would have preferred another method of teaching in this course.					

THE MAJOR INSTRUCTOR OF THIS COURSE IS _____

NAME AND NUMBER OF THIS COURSE IS _____

Figure 5 (continued)

IV. Student Activity and Participation

1. How would you describe the classroom participation of class members?

1	2	3	4	5
Insufficient		About right		Excessive; interfered with covering course material

2. To what extent did you learn from other class members?

Other class members proved to be an essential & effective component of the learning process	Only occasionally did I derive stimulation and insights from other class members	Other class members generally exerated a negative and inhibiting influence on the learning process

3. COMMENTS ELABORATING ON YOUR ANSWERS OR ON OTHER ASPECTS OF STUDENT ACTIVITY OR PARTICIPATION ON THE COURSE:

Figure 6. A section of a course and instructor evaluation form constructed by a department.

interpretations. The use of closed-ended (limited response) items, on the other hand, can provide accurate counts on the types of responses to each item. The most satisfying approach, to both instructors and students, is to use some combination of closed-ended and open-ended responses.

The type of closed-ended responses to use is largely determined by the type of question being asked. If care is not taken to match the appropriate responses to each question, then incongruous and unreliable responses will result. For example, an item stated as, "Was the instructor enthusiastic?" dictates a yes/no response; if it is stated as, "The instructor was enthusiastic," a response along an agree strongly/disagree strongly continuum is dictated. Neutral or "don't know" responses should be used only when they represent necessary options; otherwise they will be used by those respondents who do have an opinion but are somewhat reluctant to indicate it. If a continuum response format is used with only the end points anchored (e.g., excellent 1 2 3 4 5 6 very poor), it tends to produce unreliable responses. It is important that each response point along the continuum be identified. In general, the agree strongly/disagree strongly continuum is appropriate whenever an item is stated either positively or negatively. Another type of response scale that can be used is one that requires elaborate behavioral descriptions along the continuum. Such scales are called behaviorally anchored rating scales (Reardon and Waters, 1979). If items require varying responses, those responses should be defined; if possible, the items with common responses should be grouped together.

Selection of the Items

One alternative to generating a questionnaire is to survey what is available from other institutions or individuals and to use those in part or their entirety. Many institutions have, in addition to their own generated and tested forms, catalogs of additional optional items that have also been tested. Of course, using this approach may still result in a questionnaire of questionable value if the other institution did not avoid the pitfalls cited above. Another alternative is a commercially developed questionnaire. Such forms usually avoid the pitfalls cited above but still have to be carefully matched to the needs of the using institution. This means that a careful content analysis of the questionnaire and items needs to take place before adaptation. Figure 7 is an example of such a questionnaire.

If one has generated or obtained a pool of items rather than adopting an entire instrument, then a careful selection of the appropriate items must take place. Such a selection can be based on a logical and/or empirical analysis of the items. A logical analysis requires the developers of the form to make subjective judgments in selecting appropriate items, whereas an empirical analysis requires that studies be conducted to determine the usability of the items.

The final step in the design and construction of the items and the questionnaire is the organization of the items in the questionnaire. One has to decide how the items are to be grouped and labelled, how they should be organized for easy reading and answering, and how and where the responses should be recorded. If there is a logical or chronological flow to the questions, then their organization on the form should reflect that. If there are only a few negative questions, then one or two should appear very early in the questionnaire to avoid positive response set mistakes. It is advisable to have negatively stated items in the questionnaire, but only if they can be stated negatively in a logical manner. Most questionnaire items can be grouped into subscales. If the original grouping was done on a logical basis, then an empirical analysis using a statistical technique such as factor analysis should be used to insure that the grouped items do, in fact, represent a common scale.

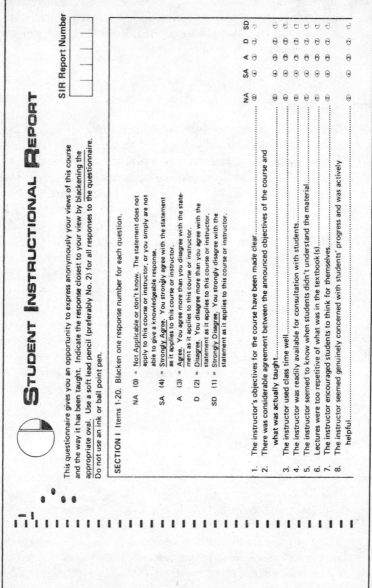

Figure 7. Example of a commercially developed rating form. (Reprinted by permission of Educational Testing Service.)

128

9. The instructor made helpful comments on papers or exams........

10. The instructor raised challenging questions or problems for discussion........

11. In this class I felt free to ask questions or express my opinions........

12. The instructor was well-prepared for each class........

13. The instructor told students how they would be evaluated in the course........

14. The instructor summarized or emphasized major points in lectures or discussions........

15. My interest in the subject area has been stimulated by this course........

16. The scope of the course has been too limited; not enough material has been covered........

17. Examinations reflected the important aspects of the course........

18. I have been putting a good deal of effort into this course........

19. The instructor was open to other viewpoints........

20. In my opinion, the instructor has accomplished (is accomplishing) his or her objectives for the course........

SECTION II Items 21-31. Blacken one response number for each question.

21. For my preparation and ability, the level of difficulty of this course was:

① Very elementary   ④ Somewhat difficult
② Somewhat elementary   ⑤ Very difficult
③ About right

22. The work load for this course in relation to other courses of equal credit was:

① Much lighter   ④ Heavier
② Lighter   ⑤ Much heavier
③ About the same

23. For me, the pace at which the instructor covered the material during the term was:

① Very slow   ④ Somewhat fast
② Somewhat slow   ⑤ Very fast
③ Just about right

24. To what extent did the instructor use examples or illustrations to help clarify the material?

① Frequently   ④ Seldom
② Occasionally   ⑤ Never

Questionnaire continued on the other side.

572MRC77P300X
283562

FORM NO. 5887

Figure 7 (continued)

129

ADMINISTRATION OF THE STUDENT RATING FORMS

If possible, the responsibility for managing and directing a campus-wide program of administering student ratings should be placed in the hands of instructional development, evaluation, or testing personnel. Otherwise, the responsibility should be assumed by the office of the chief academic officer of the institution. One should avoid placing such responsibility either in the hands of students or faculty in individual departments or colleges, because its application would be restricted and the possibility of a lasting program would be reduced.

The method of administering and gathering student responses can determine the quality of the resulting data. It is advisable to administer the ratings in a formalized manner in the classroom by providing a standard set of instructions and enough time to complete all the items. If the questionnaire is administered in an informal manner, without a standard set of instructions and a designated time to fill it out, the students tend not to take it seriously and possibly do not bother to turn it in. Furthermore, if the students are permitted to take the questionnaires home to fill them out and return them at the next class meeting, very few questionnaires will be returned.

If the instructors are to administer their own questionnaires, then they should read a standard set of instructions, select a student to gather them when completed and deposit them in the campus mail, and then leave the room. Students tend not to be as candid and frank in their responses if they feel that the instructor will see them at the end of that class period or, in some cases, before the course has ended. The exception to this rule is when instructors have informed their students that their responses will be used in a formative way to improve the current course.

Representatives of the student government association could administer the student rating questionnaires if the faculty and department and/or college administrators were willing or requested them to do it. The students administering the questionnaires should read a standard set of instructions and request that the instructor leave during the administration. The student organization could use the campus newspaper to announce when the questionnaires are going to be used and how they will be administered.

If an administrator decides to designate one of his/her staff to administer the student rating questionnaire, then the same procedure should be followed as suggested above. This option should be avoided unless there is no other way to insure a common administration of the questionnaires. Faculty and students tend to feel threatened if they know that an administrator is controlling and directing the administration of the questionnaires.

The amount of time it takes to administer a questionnaire in the classroom may represent only a portion of the actual time required to complete the process of using student ratings. The printing of the forms, mailing information to faculty, printing of directions, distribution of forms and directions to faculty, distribution of forms to students, and the gathering and returning of the completed forms all enter into the total time computation for administering the forms. Cost considerations can be related both to the time required of personnel and to the actual expenses in producing and providing materials (pencils, answer sheets, etc.) for the administration of the questionnaires.

When the questionnaire is administered the students should have all of the necessary materials. Students should generally fill out the forms in their regular classroom near the end of a particular class session. Above all, the students must be left with the impression that their frank and honest comments are desired and not that this is their chance to "get back at" the instructor. If students get the impression that the instructor is not really interested in their responses, they will not respond seriously. If the students feel the instructor is going to see their responses before final grades are in, they will respond more positively and write very few comments. This is especially true if the students are asked to identify themselves on the questionnaire. If the questionnaire is administered immediately before, during, or after the final examination (or any other meaningful examination), the students tend to respond in an inconsistent manner. If students are allowed to discuss the course and instructor while filling out the questionnaires, then biases will enter into their ratings.

DETERMINING THE RELIABILITY AND VALIDITY OF THE RATINGS

The problem of determining the reliability and validity of student ratings is not always addressed in the plethora of questionnaires that have been developed. If, however, the data from such questionnaires are to be used for both improvement and decision making, then it is imperative that such evidence be obtained.

Reliability may be defined in two ways. The first describes the instrument's capability of producing stable student responses from one time to another in a given course. The second describes the consistency (or degree of agreement) among the respondees. Since most student rating questionnaires ask students to respond to different aspects of the instructional setting (e.g., instructor, instruction, textbook, homework), the reliability of the items and the subscales should be the major concern. If one cannot demonstrate that the items and subscales of a particular questionnaire can yield stable student responses, then the data and resulting evaluations may be meaningless.

One method of calculating an instrument's stability reliability is to administer a given questionnaire to the same group of students on two consecutive days and then to correlate the two sets of scores. The magnitude of the correlation (which ranges from -1.00 to 1.00) indicates the degree to which the students' scores on the first day tended to match their scores on the second day. Since the opportunity or the time to administer the same questionnaire more than one time occurs very seldom, the most common method of estimating the stability reliability is to take the item scores for a given group of students and to divide them into halves by placing all odd-numbered items in one category and all even-numbered items in the other. Each student then has two scores, which are correlated. The magnitude of the correlation indicates the degree to which their scores on one half of the questionnaire tended to match their scores on the other half.

If the questionnaire contains highly reliable items and subscales, then one needs to determine how consistent the student responses are. One method commonly used is that of interrater reliability, in which the degree of agreement among students in a particular class is determined. The higher the agreement, the more consistent the student ratings are for a given instructor and course.

A third method is to determine the degree of stability of course and instructor ratings for similar but unique groups of students. This might be called the reliability of the course and/or instructor. This method of calculating a stability reliability involves gathering student course ratings for a given instructor and/or student instructor ratings for a given course. The student course and/or instructor ratings are then correlated to determine the degree of stability of instructor and/or course ratings.

Once the reliability problem has been resolved, then attention should be focused on the validity of student ratings. Logical validation is concerned with the question "What does the questionnaire measure?" and empirical validation is concerned with the question "To what extent does the questionnaire measure what it is intended to measure?" A logical validation requires judgment on the content validity of the questionnaire. This is usually accomplished by carefully constructing the instrument so that it contains items and subscales that will yield measures in the areas that are considered appropriate by an individual or group of experts in the field under consideration.

Empirical validation procedures require the use of criterion measures against which student ratings may be compared. Validity studies normally report the magnitude of the correlation between criterion measures and student ratings. The rule of thumb here is the higher the correlation, the better the validity.

HOW RESULTS ARE REPORTED

The method of reporting the results of student ratings is one of the most important aspects of the program. If the results are not reported in an appropriate, accurate, and timely manner, then the usefulness of the questionnaire will be seriously compromised. One of the first decisions to be made is whether the questionnaire data are to be tabulated and summarized or simply returned to the instructor in their original form. If the questionnaires are returned to the instructor as is, instructors tend to concentrate on either the negative or positive feedback, with little attention paid to the representativeness of that feedback. In order to help instructors interpret their results, they should be provided with a method of tabulating and summarizing their own results. This could be accomplished with a brief handout outlining the procedures to be followed.

If the questionnaire responses are to be tabulated and summarized before being returned to the instructor, then the following procedures should be considered:

(1) The item responses should be weighted (that is, given numerical values) in order to calculate descriptive statistics and the descriptive statistics should be reported.
(2) The results should be reported by item and subscale, if appropriate.
(3) The results should be summarized by class section, department, college, and so on.

When items are presented with defined response scales, such as agree strongly, agree, disagree, and disagree strongly, they should be weighted to reflect direction and ideal response when the results are tabulated and summarized. For example, if the above response scale were weighted 4, 3, 2, 1, respectively, it would indicate that the item was positively stated with the ideal response being agree strongly. With such a weighting, it is possible to calculate a mean and standard deviation for each item for a given class of students describing their average rating and how similar or dissimilar their responses were. With such a weighting scheme and the resulting means and standard deviations, the results can then be reported for both items and subscales and can also be summarized and reported by class section, course, selected courses, courses within a department, courses within a college, and courses within the university.

An important aspect of any system of reporting student rating results is who will or should actually see the results. If the administration of the questionnaires is completely voluntary on the part of the faculty members, then they are the only ones who should receive the results. They could, however, be provided with the option of releasing copies of their results to other interested parties. If this is done, it should be in such a manner that the instructor feels no pressure to release results but needs only to sign a formal release form.

If the administration of the questionnaire is mandatory, then all faculty members should be aware of who is to receive copies of their results and how frequently. Students' written comments should not be reported to administrators and/or student organizations, since those comments tend to be susceptible to widely discrepant subjective interpretations by the reader.

If the faculty and/or administration has entered into an agreement with the campus student organization to publish the results of the student ratings, they should try to insure a fair and accurate reporting of the results. Such results are usually reported in a book divided by discipline or content area. Student published books are usually promoted as course and instructor guides for prospective student enrollees as well as vehicles to encourage instructional improvement. Unfortunately, due to the overzealousness of some student editors and the vendettas of others, such publications have generated antagonistic relationships between the rated faculty and student editors.

One vehicle that can be used to disseminate student ratings of faculty to a wider segment of the student body is the student newspaper. The most effective way to present such results is to do it in a positive manner. For example, only the names and/or course numbers of the most highly rated are reported; the others are not mentioned. Figure 8 is an example of how this has been done. Whoever is responsible for publishing student ratings for mass consumption should remember that accentuating the positive results in better acceptance, continued participation, and potential instructional improvement on the part of the participating faculty members. Any attempt to be "cute" or to "get an instructor" usually results in short-lived systems with serious negative repercussions.

HOW RESULTS ARE INTERPRETED AND USED

How accurately and meaningfully the results of student ratings are interpreted and used depends on the type of information provided to the participating faculty member and other interested parties. The research on student ratings has revealed a definite positive response bias, which needs to be addressed when interpreting and using the results. That is, if students are asked to respond to questions using a four-point scale of agree strongly, agree, disagree, and disagree strongly, the responses tend to be distributed as follows for positively stated items:

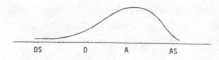

The use of comparative (normative) data when reporting results can serve to counteract the positive response bias, resulting in a more accurate and meaningful interpretation of the ratings. For example, comparative data gathered on freshmen level courses in the Political Science Department allow the instructors to determine how they and their courses are perceived in relation to the rest of the courses in the department. When such comparative data are not available, the instructor will be interpreting and using results in a void with very little substantiation for the resulting conclusions and actions taken. Once established on a representative number of courses, the normative data base should not change appreciably from year to year. Additional courses can be added to the normative data base without significantly changing the distribution and comparative judgments. For some of the sources of invalidity identified as nontrivial by research studies, such as class level and required-elective status, comparative data stratified by course level and required-elective status will provide meaningful interpretations of the results. Aleamoni (Note 14) includes particular examples.

Qualitative judgments can also be provided to the instructor by identifying course mean intervals in the comparative data, which can be defined as representing levels of excellence or needed improvement. For example, the comparative data for the freshmen level courses in the Political Science Department consisting of course means on student rating questionnaires could be divided into 10 equal portions. Each portion could be defined as representing a 10% interval of rated courses with a defined minimum and maximum course mean. These 10 intervals could then be defined as follows:

(1) Any course mean falling in the lowest 10%, 20%, or 30% interval is defined as "poor" and indicates that improvement is definitely necessary.
(2) Any course mean falling in the 40%, 50%, 60%, or 70% interval is defined as "average" and indicates that some improvement is necessary.
(3) Any course mean falling in the upper 80%, 90%, or 100% interval is defined as "very good" and indicates that very little, if any improvement is necessary.

This information could be provided to each participating instructor in a computerized format along with the appropriate interpretive materials. An example of such interpretative material is given in Figure 9.

Once faculty members are provided with both comparative and interpretive materials, they can then use them to interpret the results. The comparative interpretations result from the normative data provided, and the subjective interpretations result from reflections on what had taken place in the classroom that could be related to the comparative interpretations. Using this procedure in addition to a careful reading of the students' written comments (if available), each instructor should be able to generate diagnostic interpretations of instructional strengths and weaknesses in the course. If an instructor has results on two or more similar sections, then he/she may compare the

(text continued on p. 140)

AN INCOMPLETE LIST OF EXCELLENT TEACHERS

Teaching faculty who consistently have been rated high by students completing Advisor forms are listed below. Probably less than half of the faculty have used the Advisor form, so that this list is incomplete and does not include all of the excellent teachers on campus. Those that have not had students evaluate their classes had no chance to be included, nor did those that had their classes evaluated in some way other than through the use of the Advisor form.

METHOD OF PREPARATION

The list is based on Advisor forms filled in by students during the last three semesters (Fall, '70; Spring, '71; Fall, '71). It should be noted that only those instructors who gave out Advisor forms at least once during this time period, and who released the data for publication, could possibly be included in the list.

In the case of teaching assistants, only last semester's data were used, since few teaching assistants teach the same course for more than a year.

Only the numerical data from the Advisor forms were used. Each instructor included in the list was, on at least one occasion, rated in the top 30 percent of all instructors whose students filled in Advisor forms. In addition, those who used the Advisor forms more than once in the three-semester period had to score consistently high in order to remain on the list. In most cases, the decision was fairly clear-cut, but in borderline cases a partially subjective decision had to be made. In all cases, considerable attention was paid to the number of students responding and the proportion of enrolled students responding.

ORIGIN

This list was prepared by Terry Crooks, Research Assistant in the Course Development Division of the Office of Instructional Resources, with the assistance of members of both the Course Development and the Measurement and Research Divisions of that Office. The list came into being as a result of the demise of the Advisor, and it is hoped that it can fulfill some of the functions of the Advisor.

More detailed information on how the list was compiled may be obtained by contacting Terry Crooks at the Office of Instructional Resources, 205 South Goodwin (3-3370).

INTERPRETATION OF LIST

Instructors' names are listed under the alphabetical part of the course name, with the specific courses which were included in the rating of each instructor indicated by the course numbers which follow the instructor's name.

The symbols used in the list have the following meanings.

    T.A.—Teaching Assistant.

    F12—Faculty rated on teaching in 100 and 200 level courses.

    F34—Faculty rated on teaching in 300, 400, and 500 level courses.

    —The instructor has been consistently outstanding.

    #—The listing is based on very limited data.

    ( )—The instructor was not rated as highly in this particular course (i.e., on the basis of the results from this course alone, he would not be included in the list).

Figure 8. Example of how students can publicize their ratings.

136

		Course
ACCOUNTANCY		
T.A.	* Mautz, C.	101
	Wilson, D.	108
F12	* Mautz, R.	221
	McKeown, J.	108
	Neumann, F.	101, 201
	Skadden, D.	274
F34	* Fess, P.	372
	Mautz, R.	371
	Perry, H.	377, 378
	Schoenfeld, H.	366, 462
ADVERTISING		
F34	* Jugenheimer, D.	309,
	* Leckenby, J.	381, 388
AERO. & ASTRO. ENGINEERING		
F12	* Prussing, J.	254
	Van Tassell, W.	213
F34	* Bennett, J.	391
	Prussing, J.	305
	Sivier, K.	391
	Van Tassell, W.	493
AGRICULTURE		
F12	* Dahl, D.	214
	Evans, J.	214
AGRICULTURAL ECONOMICS		
F12	* Knaus, N.	303
	Sraus, N.	303
F34	* Spitze, R.	305
	Van Arsdall, R.	324
AGRONOMY		
F34	* Boast, C.	308
	Miller, L.	322
AIR FORCE AEROSPACE STUDIES		
F12	Reid, A.	241, 242
ANIMAL SCIENCE		
F12	* Frayley, D.	201
	Homan, R.	103
	Romans, J.	204, 205

	* Burns, H.	367, 402, 468
	* Dee, J.	384
	Millar, J.	357
	Resek, R.	411, 476
	Shupp, F.	402
	Spernale, C.	301, 401, 421
	Wells, P.	301
F34	* Williamson, H.	460, 470, 477
	Yavey, T.	367
EDUCATIONAL ADMINISTRATION		
F34	* Burnham, R.	462, 470
	Raubinger, F.	440, 460
	Sergiovanni, T.	438, 461, 463
EDUCATIONAL PSYCHOLOGY		
T.A.	* Selter, T.	236
F34	* Aleamoni, L.	490
	Anderson, R.	313
	Askins, L.	311
	Delaney, D.	311
	Husting, T.	390
	Long, T.	312, 424
	McGuire, D.	343
	Menges, R.	311
	Simpson, R.	413, 414, (311)
	Tatsuoka, M.	196, 497
ELECTRICAL ENGINEERING		
F12	* Brooks, M.	262
	Fairman, F.	294
F34	* Anner, G.	360, 344
	Streetman, B.	344
ELEMENTARY EDUCATION		
F12	* Lerch, H.	222
	Denny, T.	459
F34	* Katz, L.	334, 434
	Lerch, L.	332
	Powell, W.	336
	* Shoreamar, P.	332
ENGLISH		

	Kersch, T.	206
HIGHER EDUCATION		
F34	* Broudy, H.	490
	O'Banion, T.	442, 477
HINDI		
F12	* Subbarao, K.	201
F34	* Subbarao, K.	303
HISTORY		
F12	* Beattie, M.	181
	Drake, P.	275
	Heinrich, W.	274
	Hoxeter, D.	262
	Ransel, D.	219
	Solberg, W.	298
	Sutton, R.	298
F34	* Arnstein, W.	341
	Bernard, P.	309
	Drake, P.	378
	Eastman, L.	390
	Foster, F.	333, 403
	Heinrich, W.	374, 406, 453
	Jaher, F.	363, 384, 458
	Schroeder, P.	318, 319
	Solberg, W.	371
	Sumler, D.	313, 314
	Trexler, R.	305
	* Wechsler, H.	391
HISTORY AND PHILOSOPHY OF EDUCATION		
F34	* Broudy, H.	408
	Ennis, R.	301, 407, 490
	Karier, C.	302
	Peshkin, A.	303
	* Violas, P.	302, 402, 490
HOME ECONOMICS		
T.A.	* Klein, B.	125
F12	* Johnson, E.	132, 133
F34	* Anderson, J.	375

PHYSICAL EDUCATION		
F12	* Dannehl, W.	139, 173, 204
	Deutsch, H.	111
	Patrick, G.	110, 134, 146,
	* Pirnat, J.	147, 148
		110,
	* Razor, P.	105, 124, 132,
	Starey, V.	
	Trimble, R.	193, 166
F34	* Ziegler, E.	402
PHYSICS		
F12	* Lazarus, D.	150, 151
	O'Halloran, T.	106
	Wortis, M.	102
F34	* Chang, S.	483
	Eisenstein, B.	321, 322
	Frauenfelder, H.	382
	Sullivan, J.	400
	Williams, W.	383
PHYSIOLOGY		
F12	* Harris, J.	234
F34	* Ducoff, H.	331
PLANT PATHOLOGY		
F12	* Linn, M.	204
F34	* Gerdemann, J.	304
POLITICAL SCIENCE		
F12	* Byers, R.	191
	Gold, L.	150
	Iverson, J.	184
F34	* Piacotte, J.	312
	Byars, R.	342, 343
PORTUGESE		
F34	* Preto-Rodas, R.	407
PSYCHOLOGY		
F12	* Bjou, S.	216
	* Hake, D.	230
	Hill, K.	216

Figure 8 (continued)

UNIVERSITY OF ARIZONA Office of Instructional Research & Development (IRAD)
1325 E. Speedway, Tucson, Arizona 85721   Telephone: (602) 626-4488

INTERPRETATION OF THE ARIZONA CIEQ (FORM 76) QUESTIONNAIRE RESULTS

Enclosed are the results of the CIEQ (Form 76) questionnaire which you administered in your class last semester. You will note that the student responses in the student and course information sections are presented in proportions at the top of the computer print-out indicating student responses to the questions of class status, pass/fail, required-elective, sex, expected grade, major-minor, and how the students rated the content, the instructor, and the course as a whole.

The standard item information is presented next on the print-out. Each of the 21 items could have been answered either agree strongly, agree, disagree, or disagree strongly (coded AS, A, D, DS). The proportion of responses under each category of the scale (including OMITS) is presented as well as the most favorable response (BEST), the average (MEAN) of the responses to each item (which can range from 1.00-4.00 and is always such that a higher mean indicates a more favorable response) and the standard deviation (S.D.). YOur course averages are compared to the 5189 course averages obtained at the University of Arizona during the period of 1975-1978. How your course compares to these 5189 courses is presented under decile (DECL) where a decile of 9 is highest and 0 is lowest. Deciles can be interpreted in the following manner:

0 indicates that your course falls in the lowest 10% of the ratings obtained
1 indicates that there are 10% to 19% who received a lower rating
2 indicates that there are 20% to 29% who received a lower rating
and so on through 9.

For these items, a decile of from three to six can be considered average. The deciles are also "profiled" by means of the asterisks for easier interpretation.

138

The items are grouped in terms of their content into five subscores, and a total score, which is the sum of all items. These appear at the bottom of the computer print-out and are compared to other classes via deciles in the same manner as are the individual items. A decile of four or five can be considered average for the subscores and the total score. Your course has been compared to five different norm groups for the subscores. The norm groups can be interpreted as follows:

RANK	compares your course to all courses of U of A instructors at your rank
LEVEL	compares your course to all U of A courses at your course level (i.e., freshman, sophomore, junior, senior, graduate)
INSTI	compares your course to the 5189 U of A courses
COLL	compares your course to all U of A courses in the same college
OVERALL	compares your course to 5189 U of A plus 14,374 outside courses
DEPT	compares your course to other U of A courses in the same division or department.

Please note that a NONE is printed if you have not specified your rank or course level, or there are insufficient data to provide norms at this time. The subscore names and the items which are combined to form each are as follows:

General Course Attitude	Items 1, 6, 15, 21
Method of Instruction	Items 2, 7, 12, 18
Course Content	Items 4, 8, 13, 16
Interest and Attention	Items 5, 10, 17, 19
Instructor	Items 3, 9, 11, 14, 20.

THE SUBSCORE RESULTS CAN INDICATE THE AREAS OF STRENGTHS AND WEAKNESSES IN THE COURSE. ONCE AN AREA OF WEAKNESS HAS BEEN IDENTIFIED BY A SUBSCORE (e.g., A DECILE OF 2 ON THE INSTRUCTOR SUBSCORE), THEN LOOKING AT THE ITEM RESULTS MAKING UP THAT SUBSCORE CAN HELP YOU TO FOCUS ON THE MORE SPECIFIC PROBLEM AREAS. IF THE RELIABILITY (REL) OF ANY SUBSCORE FALLS BELOW .65, THE NORM DECILE SHOULD BE INTERPRETED WITH CAUTION. SEE INTERPRETATION GUIDE FOR MORE DETAILED INFORMATION.

Any questions regarding the objective items, the computer print-out, the norming, or the interpretation of results should be directed to the IRAD office. If you desire a personal consultation and/or interpretation of your results, please call the number above.

Figure 9. Example of interpretative material provided with the Arizona Course/Instructor Evaluation Questionnaire.

ratings of one section to those of another section to determine what instructional behaviors may have led to the higher comparative ratings in one section.

If a faculty member is not able to generate any diagnostic interpretations, then he/she may need to talk with the department head, dean, or instructional development person about the results. This assumes, of course, that any of these individuals knows how to interpret the results. Finding that this approach still does not adequately identify the source of instructional difficulty, the instructor may want to consider other procedures (such as the use of additional diagnostic optional items, classroom visitation, videotaping, etc.) in future evaluations.

After identifying their instructional strengths and weaknesses, instructors can use the information to plan an improvement strategy. In some instances the strategy may simply require minor modifications in the course or teaching method. In other instances the strategy may require a substantial commitment of time and resources on the part of both the faculty member and the department.

If faculty members decide to submit copies of their student evaluation results to their department head or dean for rank, pay, and tenure considerations, then all of the appropriate interpretive materials should also be provided. Deans and department heads should be made aware of the necessity of using the comparative data to interpret the results rather than relying on the more subjective and highly unreliable written and oral comments of students. Ideally such results should be considered by a small (three-person) departmental review committee using several other assessments of instructional effectiveness such as self-evaluation, quality of student learning, and peer evaluation of content (Aleamoni, 1976b).

DETERMINING THE EFFECTIVENESS OF STUDENT RATINGS

A question that naturally arises in developing systems of student ratings of instruction and instructors is "Can student ratings of instruction and instructor be useful in improving college teaching once they are made available to the instructor?" Although there has been a great deal of anecdotal evidence from instructors and researchers to suggest that student evaluations do have a positive effect, very few studies are available that deal with that effect on college-level instruction. McKeachie (1979) felt that the most impressive results were those reported by Overall and Marsh (1979). They found that instructors who received feedback from student ratings at midterm not only received more favorable ratings at the end of the year but their students also scored higher on an achievement test and on a measure of motivation for further learning and application of the material learned, when compared with a control group of instructors. In a study at the University of Arizona, Aleamoni (1978b) investigated the effect on faculty performance of a combination of feedback of ratings and personal consultations. This approach proved to be superior to simply providing a printed report of the results. McKeachie and Lin (Note 15) obtained similar results.

In his review of studies on the validity of student ratings in achieving cognitive, attitudinal, and motivational goals, McKeachie (1979) concluded that, taken as a whole, the results indicate that the highly rated instructors and courses result in higher student achievement of cognitive, attitudinal, and motivational goals. More research, however, needs to be conducted in these areas.

Instructors would be willing to devote the time and resources necessary to achieving excellence in teaching if they felt that such efforts would be appropriately rewarded. However, the limited research available (McKeachie, 1979; Thorne et al., Note 1; Aleamoni, Note 16; Centra, Note 17) indicates that very little, if any, weight is applied to evidence of teaching effectiveness in promotion and tenure decisions. Where such evidence is used, it tends to be based on anecdotal or testimonial information or student ratings. Very few systems have been developed to provide systematic, objective, and comprehensive instructional evaluation. Where such systems have been developed, the satisfaction on the part of the participant faculty and administrators appears to be very high (O'Connell and Smartt, Note 2; Harrell, Note 18). It, therefore, seems logical to encourage the development of comprehensive systems of instructional evaluation that have guidance for improvement and reward for success as their two major outcomes. When student ratings are introduced as a component of such systems, then faculty acceptance of their use will be greatly enhanced.

REFERENCE NOTES

1. Thorne, G. S., C. S. Scott, and J. J. Beaird (1976) *Assessing faculty performance: Final project report*. Monmouth: Oregon State System of Higher Education, Teaching Research Division.
2. O'Connell, W. R., Jr., and S. S. Smartt (1979) *Improving faculty evaluation: A trial in strategy* (A Report of the SREB Faculty Evaluation Project). Atlanta: Southern Regional Education Board.
3. Guthrie, E. R. (1954) *The evaluation of teaching: A progress report*. Seattle: University of Washington.

4. Gillmore, G. M. (1973) *Estimates of reliability coefficients for items and subscales of the Illinois Course Evaluation Questionnaire* (Research Report No. 341). Urbana: University of Illinois, Office of Instructional Resources, Measurement and Research Division.

5. Stallings, W. M. and S. Singhal (1968) *Some observations on the relationships between productivity and student evaluations of courses and teaching* (Research Report No. 274). Urbana: University of Illinois, Office of Instructional Resources, Measurement and Research Division.

6. Aleamoni, L. M. and M. Yimer (1974) *Graduating senior ratings relationship to colleague rating, student rating, research productivity and academic rank in rating instructional effectiveness* (Research Report No. 352). Urbana: University of Illinois, Office of Instructional Resources, Measurement and Research Division.

7. Centra, J. A. (1973) "The student as godfather? The impact of student ratings on academia," in A. L. Sockloff (ed.), *Proceedings of the first invitational conference on faculty effectiveness as evaluated by students.* Philadelphia: Temple University, Measurement and Research Center.

8. Aleamoni, L. M. and G. S. Thomas (1977) *Is the instructor's rating of the class related to the class' rating of the instructor?* (Research Report No. 1). Tucson: University of Arizona, Office of Instructional Research and Development.

9. Yongkittikul, C., G. M. Gillmore, and D. C. Brandenburg (1974) *Does the time of course meeting affect course ratings by students?* (Research Report No. 346). Urbana: University of Illinois, Office of Instructional Resources, Measurement and Research Division.

10. Cohen, J. and L. G. Humphreys (1960) *Memorandum to faculty.* Unpublished manuscript, University of Illinois, Department of Psychology.

11. Gillmore, G. M. and D. C. Brandenburg (1974) *Would the proportion of students taking a class as a requirement affect the student rating of the course?* (Research Report No. 347). Urbana: University of Illinois, Office of Instructional Resources, Measurement and Research Division.

12. Hildebrand, M., R. C. Wilson, and E. R. Dienst (1971) *Evaluating university teaching.* Berkeley: University of California, Center for Research and Development in Higher Education.

13. Singhal, S. (1968) *Illinois course evaluation questionnaire items by rank of instructor, sex of the instructor, and sex of the student* (Research Report No. 282). Urbana: University of Illinois, Office of Instructional Resources, Measurement and Research Division.

14. Aleamoni, L. M. (1979) *Arizona Course/Instructor Evaluation Questionnaire: Results interpretation manual, form 76.* Tucson: University of Arizona, Office of Instructional Research and Development.

15. McKeachie, W. J. and Y. G. Lin (1975) *Use of standard ratings in evaluation of college teaching* (NIE, Grant NO-6-00-3-0110). Ann Arbor: University of Michigan, Department of Psychology.

16. Aleamoni, L. M. (1978) *Report on the investigation of the criteria and guidelines used by various departments and colleges at the University of Arizona for promotion and tenure decisions* (Research Memorandum No. 4). Tucson: University of Arizona, Office of Instructional Research and Development.

17. Centra, J. A. (1977) *How universities evaluate faculty performance: A survey of department heads* (GREB No. 75-5bR). Princeton, NJ: Educational Testing Service.

18. Harrell, R. A. (1979) *The development of a comprehensive faculty evaluation system.* Presented at the annual meeting of the National Council on Measurement in Education, San Francisco, April.

REFERENCES

Aleamoni, L. M. (1978a) "Development and factorial validation of the Arizona Course/ Instructor Evaluation Questionnaire." *Educational and Psychological Measurement*, 38: 1063–1067.

_____(1978b) "The usefulness of student evaluations in improving college teaching." *Instructional Science*, 7: 95–105.

_____(1976a) "Typical faculty concerns about student evaluation of instruction." *National Association of Colleges and Teachers of Agriculture Journal*, 20(1): 16–21.

_____(1976b) "Proposed system for rewarding and improving instructional effectiveness." *College and University*, 51: 330–338.

_____and M. H. Graham (1974) "The relationship between CEQ ratings and instructor's rank, class size and course level." *Journal of Educational Measurement*, 11: 189–202.

Aleamoni, L. M. and P. Z. Hexner (1980) "A review of the research on student evaluation and a report on the effect of different sets of instructions on student course and instructor evaluation." *Instructional Science*, 9: 67–84.

Aleamoni, L. M. and R. E. Spencer (1973) "The Illinois Course Evaluation Questionnaire: A description of its development and a report of some of its results." *Educational and Psychological Measurement*, 33: 669–684.

Aleamoni, L. M. and M. Yimer (1973) " An investigation of the relationship between colleague rating, student rating, research productivity, and academic rank in rating instructional effectiveness." *Journal of Educational Psychology* 64: 274–277.

Bendig, A. W. (1953) "Relation of level of course achievement of students, instructor and course ratings in introductory psychology." *Educational and Psychological Measurement*, 13: 437–488.

_____(1952) "A preliminary study of the effect of academic level, sex, and course variables on student rating of psychology instructors." *Journal of Psychology*, 34: 21–26.

Borgatta, E. F. (1970) "Student ratings of faculty." *American Association of University Professors Bulletin*, 56: 6–7.

Braunstein, D. N., G. A. Klein, and M. Pachla (1973) "Feedback, expectancy and shifts in student ratings of college faculty." *Journal of Applied Psychology*, 58: 254–258.

Centra, J. A. (1973) "Effectiveness of student feedback in modifying college instruction." *Journal of Educational Psychology*, 65: 395–401.

Clark, K. E. and R. J. Keller (1954) "Student ratings of college teaching," in R. A. Eckert (ed.), *A University Looks at Its Program*. Minneapolis: University of Minnesota Press.

Costin, F., W. T. Greenough, and R. J. Menges (1971) "Student ratings of college teaching: Reliability, validity, and usefulness." *Review of Educational Research*, 41: 511–535.

Deming, W. E. (1972) "Memorandum on teaching." *American Statistician*, 26: 47.

Downie, N. W. (1952) "Student evaluation of faculty." *Journal of Higher Education*, 23: 495–496; 503.

Doyle, K. O. and S. E. Whitely (1974) "Student ratings as criteria for effective teaching." *American Educational Research Journal*, 11: 259–274.

Drucker, A. J. and H. H. Remmers (1951) "Do alumni and students differ in their attitudes toward instructors?" *Journal of Educational Psychology*, 42: 129–143.

Everly, J. C. and L. M. Aleamoni (1972) "The rise and fall of the advisor . . . students attempt to evaluate their instructors." *Journal of the National Association of Colleges and Teachers of Agriculture*, 16(2): 43–45.

Frey, P. W. (1978) "A two-dimensional analysis of student ratings of instruction." *Research in Higher Education,* 9: 69–91.

———(1973) "Student ratings of teaching: Validity of several rating factors." *Science,* 182: 83–85.

Gage, N. L. (1961) "The appraisal of college teaching." *Journal of Higher Education,* 32: 17–22.

Gessner, P. K. (1973) "Evaluation of instruction." *Science,* 180: 566–569.

Goodhartz, A. S. (1948) "Student attitudes and opinions relating to teaching at Brooklyn College." *School and Society,* 68: 345–349.

Grush, J. E. and F. Costin (1975) "The student as consumer of the teaching process." *American Educational Research Journal,* 12: 55–66.

Guthrie, E. R. (1949) "The evaluation of teaching." *Educational Record,* 30: 109–115.

Hayes, J. R. (1971)"Research, teaching and faculty fate." *Science,* 172: 227–230.

Heilman, J. D. and W. D. Armentrout (1936) "The rating of college teachers on ten traits by their students." *Journal of Educational Psychology,* 27:197–216.

Hogan, T. P. (1973) "Similarity of student ratings across instructors, courses and time." *Research in Higher Education,* 1: 149–154.

Isaacson, R. L., W. J. McKeachie, J. E. Milholland, Y. G. Lin, M. Hofeller, J. W. Baerwaldt, and K. L. Zinn (1964) "Dimensions of student evaluations of teaching." *Journal of Educational Psychology,* 55: 344–351.

Kohlan, R. G. (1973) "A comparison of faculty evaluations early and late in the course." *Journal of Higher Education,* 44: 587–595.

Linsky, A. S. and M. A. Straus (1975) "Student evaluations, research productivity and eminence of college faculty." *Journal of Higher Education,* 46: 89–102.

Lovell, G. D. and C. F. Haner (1955) "Forced-choice applied to college faculty rating." *Educational and Psychological Measurement,* 15: 291–304.

Marsh, H. W. (1977) "The validity of students' evaluations: Classroom evaluations of instructors independently nominated as best and worst teachers by graduating seniors." *American Educational Research Journal,* 14: 441–447.

———H. Fleiner, and C. S. Thomas (1975) "Validity and usefulness of student evaluations of instructional quality." *Journal of Educational Psychology,* 67: 833–839.

Marsh, H. W. and J. U. Overall (1979) "Long-term stability of students' evaluations: A note on Feldman's 'Consistency and variability among college students in rating their teachers and courses.'"*Research in Higher Education,* 10: 139–147.

Marsh, H. W., J. U. Overall, and S. P. Kesler (1979) "Class size, students' evaluations, and instructional effectiveness." *American Educational Research Journal,* 16: 57–69.

Maslow, A. H. and W. Zimmerman (1956) "College teaching ability, scholarly activity and personality." *Journal of Educational Psychology,* 47: 185–189.

McDaniel, E. D. and J. F. Feldhusen (1970) "Relationships between faculty ratings and indexes of service and scholarship." *Proceedings of the 78th Annual Convention of the American Psychological Association,* 5: 619–620.

McGrath, E. J. (1962) "Characteristics of outstanding college teachers." *Journal of Higher Education,* 33: 148.

McKeachie, W. J. (1979) "Student ratings of faculty: A reprise." *Academe,* 65: 384–397.

———Y. G. Lin and C. N. Mendelson (1978) "A small study assessing teacher effectiveness: Does learning last?" *Contemporary Educational Psychology,* 3: 352–357.

Menges, R. J. (1973) "The new reporters: Students rate instruction," in C. R. Pace (ed.), *New Directions in Higher Education: Evaluating Learning and Teaching*. San Francisco: Jossey-Bass.

Miller, M. T. (1971) "Instructor attitudes toward, and their use of, student ratings of teachers." *Journal of Educational Psychology*, 62: 235 –239.

Null, E. J. and E. W. Nicholson (1972) "Personal variables of students and their perception of university instructors." *College Student Journal*, 6: 6 –9.

Overall, J. U. and H. W. Marsh (1979) "Midterm feedback from students: Its relationship to instructional improvement and students' cognitive and affective outcomes." *Journal of Educational Psychology*, 71: 856 –865.

Perry, R. P., P. C. Abrami, and L. Leventhal (1979) "Educational seduction: The effect of instructor expressiveness and lecture content on student ratings and achievement." *Journal of Educational Psychology*, 71:107 –116.

Pohlmann, J. T. (1975) "A multivariate analysis of selected class characteristics and student ratings of instruction." *Multivariate Behavioral Research*, 10(1): 81 –91.

Rayder, N. F. (1968) "College student ratings of instructors." *Journal of Experimental Education*, 37: 76 –81

Reardon, M. and L. K. Waters (1979) "Leniency and halo in student ratings of college instructors: A comparison of three rating procedures with implications for scale validity." *Educational and Psychological Measurement*, 39: 159 –162.

Riley, J. W., B. F. Ryan, and M. Lipschitz (1950) *The Student Looks at His Teacher*. New Brunswick, NJ: Rutgers University Press.

Rodin, M., P. W. Frey, and P. K. Gessner (1975) "Student evaluation." *Science*, 187: 555 –559.

Rodin, M. and B. Rodin (1972) "Student evaluations of teachers." *Science*, 177: 1164 –1166.

Rosenshine, B. (1970) "Enthusiastic teaching: A research review." *School Review*, 78: 499 – 514.

Sherman, T. M. (1978) "The effects of student formative evaluation of instruction on teacher behavior." *Journal of Educational Technology Systems*, 6: 209 –217.

Sullivan, A. M. and G. R. Skanes (1974) "Validity of student evaluation of teaching and the characteristics of successful instructors." *Journal of Educational Psychology*, 66: 584 – 590.

Voeks, V. W. (1962) "Publications and teaching effectiveness." *Journal of Higher Education*, 33: 212.

Walker, B. D. (1969) "An investigation of selected variables relative to the manner in which a population of junior college students evaluate their teachers." *Dissertation Abstracts*, 29(9-B): 3474.

Ware, J. E. and R. G. Williams (1977) "Discriminate analysis of student ratings as a means of identifying lecturers who differ in enthusiasm or information giving." *Educational and Psychological Measurement*, 37: 627 –639.

Wood, K., A. S. Linsky and M. A. Straus (1974) "Class size and student evaluations of faculty." *Journal of Higher Education* 45: 524 –534.

CHAPTER 9

STUDENT ACHIEVEMENT AS A MEASURE OF TEACHER COMPETENCE

JASON MILLMAN
Cornell University

This chapter explores students' performance on achievement tests as a measure of teacher competence. Achievement tests is used broadly to refer to a variety of measures of what students have achieved. Classroom examinations and quizzes, homework assignments, and questions asked during instruction are all indicators of student achievement. The word *tests* is in no way limited to commercially available, standardized tests. Indeed, the point of view taken in this chapter is that many standardized achievement tests administered to students have relatively little value in assessing the teaching competence of individual teachers.

The appropriateness of student test results for evaluating teachers is being hotly debated. The National Education Association, largest of the teacher unions, is calling for an end to standardized testing and opposes "the use of any measures of student progress to evaluate teacher competence" (Quinto and McKenna, Note 1). Many teacher contracts specifically exclude evaluation of teachers on the basis of students' test scores. On the other hand, there is a growing emphasis on holding the schools responsible for what and how well students learn. In public schools in New Jersey and New York, for examples, it will soon be required that acceptable proportions of the students pass statewide competency examinations or the schools will face stiff penalties. At the college level, approval of teacher education programs in Florida will soon depend upon whether 80% of the graduates can pass certain tests.

The treatment followed in this chapter derives from the following propositions.

1. Using student achievement as a measure of teacher competence rests on the assumption that an important function of teaching is to enhance student learning. Student achievement has no role in teacher evaluation when the teacher is seen solely as a classroom manager.

2. Many factors affect student achievement, including the teacher's performance, the particular measures of achievement being used, and the characteristics of the students.

3. Students differ markedly in their level of past achievement, ability, and willingness and opportunity to learn. Thus, any valid and equitable measure of teacher competence requires that these individual differences among students be taken into account.

4. Teacher evaluation can be used either for improving instruction (formative evaluation) or for making decisions about teacher status (summative evaluation). Knowledge about student achievement, appropriately obtained, can be useful for either purpose. Because formative and summative teacher evaluations using student achievement measures are so different with respect to purpose, degree of controversy, and method, they are treated separately in this chapter.

USE OF STUDENT ACHIEVEMENT FOR FORMATIVE TEACHER EVALUATION

If one believes that one goal of teaching is to enhance learning, that is, to help students acquire facts, understand concepts, and achieve skills, and if one also believes that learning occurs, in part, as the result of a teacher's effort, then the improvement of teaching is most apt to occur when connections can be made between teaching and learning. For this purpose, it is important to know how the teacher is helping to produce learning, and this knowledge requires measures of both teaching and learning. Thus, evaluating the quality of instruction and improving instruction depend on knowing what is learned. It follows that if teachers have an accurate portrayal of the facts, concepts, and skills that the students have mastered, they can make more efficient and effective use of their instructional time by targeting their instruction to areas in which further learning is most desired.

Criteria of Good Achievement Measures for Formative Evaluation

Measures of achievement that accurately portray student learning are free from teacher bias, diagnostic, reliable, and broadly conceived.

Free from teacher bias. The teacher can engage in unconscious practices that limit the validity of the information from the test. One bias apt to occur on essay type examinations is for teachers to read between the lines and to assume that the student knows more than is actually demonstrated. The effect of this bias is that the teacher concludes that instruction has been more successful than it actually is.

A more subtle bias occurs when the teacher words questions in ways that are more limited than the instructional objective calls for. Thus, a particular skill might be assessed in exactly the same way on the test as in class or in a textbook question. It is important to know if students can answer questions when they are asked in the format and wording as practiced, but it can also be misleading to conclude from the results of this kind of test alone that the broader objective has been met. As a simple example, suppose an arithmetic teacher is teaching the basic addition facts and always presents the problems in a vertical arrangement. A valid measure of knowledge of the ability to solve such arithmetic problems would include questions laid out horizontally, such as $8 + 3 = $ _____ .

Diagnostic. Just as a doctor who is told only that the patient does not feel well is handicapped in suggesting appropriate treatment, so is the teacher who does not know specifically what the students know and do not know handicapped in suggesting remediation. It is not enough, for purposes of formative evaluation, that the teacher receives an overall indication of the achievement level of the students. It is only through diagnostic information that pinpoints the students' greatest strengths and weaknesses that the teacher is able to modify instruction most effectively.

Reliable. Anyone who has constructed tests knows that questions can be made easier or harder by any of several means. Examples that the author has used successfully to illustrate this point are shown in Figure 1. Although both questions measure the same content, the relative land sizes of the continents, invariably most of the students tested can answer the first question completely correctly, whereas only a minority of students have such success with the second question. The second question is much harder because the student must make much finer discriminations. In similar fash-

---

Directions:

For each question, place a 1 to the left of the continent with the largest area; a 3 to the left of the continent with the smallest area.

1) _____ Africa   2) _____ Antarctica

   _____ Asia   _____ Europe

   _____ Australia   _____ South America

Figure 1. Two questions that differ greatly in their difficulty.

ion, instructors could devise a test covering the course material on which most students would score very high and, similarly, could also construct an examination on the same material on which the class average would be very low.

More than one item on a topic is needed to have an accurate grasp of the students' achievement. If only question 1 in Figure 1 had been used, the instructor might feel very comfortable about meeting the instructional objective, whereas if only question 2 had been used, the opposite conclusion might have been reached. One item is not reliable enough. To learn if the students have achieved what was intended, several questions that get at the skill, knowledge, or concept in a variety of ways are particularly informative.

Broadly conceived. When the purpose of testing is to improve teaching rather than to grade students, it is appropriate to measure objectives other than those of the course. The measurement of skills prerequisite to the course can alert the teacher to needed remedial instruction and to reasons for poor performance on measures of the current instructional objectives. Also, measurement of objectives toward which future instruction is to be directed can inform the teacher of what the students already know and do not know and can suggest appropriate emphases that various topics should receive. Finally, instruction can have unintended effects, both positive and negative, and broadly conceived assessment can help uncover unanticipated outcomes.

One implication of tests that are free from bias, diagnostic, reliable, and broadly conceived is that much more testing is needed. Testing free from bias requires, in part, use of many different ways to measure a competence, diagnostic testing requires many items that can point up specific weaknesses, reliable testing requires many items measuring each skill, and broadly conceived testing requires measuring many different objectives. All this testing might seem too much of a burden for the teacher who already feels that class time is inadequate for instruction. Fortunately, when the purpose of testing is to improve instruction rather than to assign grades to students, methods are available for reducing in-class testing time while retaining the required amount of assessment.

Methods of Data Collection

For most teachers, the purpose of measuring student achievement is to assign grades. For this purpose, it is important that many testlike conditions are met. Students should know what they will be tested on, the questions should measure the course objectives, and all class members should respond to the same set of questions. The last-named condition is important to insure that the scores are comparable. If, for example, one student is given an easier examination than another and receives a higher score, the teacher cannot be sure that the better performance was due to a higher level of achievement or to an easier test. The student being given the harder test is being treated unfairly.

For purposes of evaluating instruction and measuring teacher effectiveness, however, these conditions can be relaxed. Fairness to students is not the concern, since individual judgments and decisions about students (such as the grade that the student will receive) do not have to be made to evaluate instruction. Teachers can employ data-gathering techniques other than traditional testing to secure information about student learning.

Curriculum embedded tasks. Student achievement can be assessed as part of the everyday instruction. Evidence of student learning can be obtained from completed homework and in-class assignments, answers to questions posed by the teacher, questions asked of the teacher, and students' self-appraisal of their learning accomplishments and difficulties. Good teachers attend to these sources of information about their ability to get the material across. Teachers might even be more conscious of the information available in these ways and plan for their collection more systematically.

Matrix sampling. In the traditional method of testing, all students are asked the same questions. The top half of Figure 2 shows how the 36 students in a class are all administered the same questions (numbers 1, 4, 7, and so forth). Since more questions could be asked than there is time for the students to provide answers, the students are only asked a portion of the possible questions. In this example, only every third question is administered.

In a matrix sampling test plan, sometimes called item-by-person testing, each student still receives only one fraction of the questions, but not all students are administered the same questions. As illustrated in the bottom half of Figure 2, because only one-third of the students respond to any one question, student answers to three times as many questions are available. In matrix sampling plans, relatively less information is provided about many more items. The instructor can obtain information on many different kinds of questions without requiring any one student to spend an inordinately large amount of time responding to questions. Greater information for formative evaluation is likely to be obtained by looking at the results for many questions, especially if several concepts or skills are being covered, than can be learned from having an entire class answer the same questions. The larger the number of students in the course, the more likely that the teacher can benefit from matrix sampling.

It is possible to combine traditional and matrix sampling strategies on any one testing occasion. A teacher might give a unit test consisting of, for example, 20 questions on the material covered. These 20 questions would be

Traditional Test Plan

Students	Questions												
	1	2	3	4	5	6	7	8	9	10	11	12	etc.
1	x			x			x			x			
2	x			x			x			x			
3	x			x			x			x			
4	x			x			x			x			
5	x			x			x			x			
6	x			x			x			x			etc.
7	x			x			x			x			
8	x			x			x			x			
.	.			.			.			.			
.	.			.			.			.			
.	.			.			.			.			
34	x			x			x			x			
35	x			x			x			x			
36	x			x			x			x			etc.

Matrix Sampling Test Plan

Students	Questions												
	1	2	3	4	5	6	7	8	9	10	11	12	etc.
1	x			x			x			x			
2		x			x			x			x		
3			x			x			x			x	
4	x			x			x			x			
5		x			x			x			x		
6			x			x			x			x	etc.
7	x			x			x			x			
8		x			x			x			x		
.	.	.	.	.	.	.	.	.	.	.	.	.	
.	.	.	.	.	.	.	.	.	.	.	.	.	
.	.	.	.	.	.	.	.	.	.	.	.	.	
34	x			x			x			x			
35		x			x			x			x		
36			x			x			x			x	etc.

Figure 2. A comparison of traditional and matrix sampling test plans.

the same for all the students. In addition, different students might receive three or four different questions about the next unit, which are not scored as part of the graded examination. The data about these extra items, no one of which is answered by all the students in the class, can be helpful to the teacher in planning for the next unit. Alternatively, the extra items could probe how far the students could transfer their learning to situations about which they were not specifically provided instruction, or the items could probe for unintended instructional effects.

Because students respond to different items, the students should be able to read the questions on their own. Matrix sampling is not appropriate for very young children unless a common set of oral directions will suffice for several versions of the test questions, as is the case with the California State Assessment Program at the primary grade levels.

For further information about matrix sampling, see Sirotnik (1974) and Shoemaker (1973).

Teaching Performance Tests

Student achievement measures other than performance on course examinations can be used to assess teacher competence for purposes of formative evaluation. Teachers can give instruction on a single or limited number of objectives, a work sample, and then assess how well the students learned. If the students could master the objective(s), the teaching is considered successful; otherwise, improvement is needed. Such work samples differ from micro-teaching (see Chapter 11) in that in micro-teaching the focus of the assessment is on what the teacher does, whereas in the present context, the measure of teaching effectiveness is student performance.

Teaching performance tests represent a highly controlled version of work samples. Popham (1971) provided an early description of the rationale, development, and validation of teacher performance tests. Examples of their use with college faculty and with teacher training programs can be found in Sesney (Note 2) and in Popham (1974). They work as follows.

First, teachers are provided with a minilesson, written material about a particular subject that they will be asked to teach. Frequently, the subject is one with which students are unfamiliar, so that student mastery of the material can be credited to the teacher's efforts rather than to the previous knowledge of the students. The material includes a statement of the instructional objective, examples of the kinds of questions that the students are expected to be able to answer, and enough information about the subject so that the teachers themselves would be able to answer the questions. To avoid inadvertently teaching to the specific questions being used to assess learning, it is best if the teachers do not see the actual questions to be used before instruction. An example of a minilesson is reproduced in Figure 3.

Second, the teachers are given sufficient time to plan their teaching strategy. The teachers are not told how to teach. Their goal is to maximize student learning using whatever methods they feel will work best under the circumstances.

Third, the teachers then instruct groups of students (or colleagues) for a specified time. The length of time given is a function of the scope and complexity of the objectives and the ability of the learners.

Fourth, at the conclusion of the instruction, students are tested with items similar to, but not identical with, those examples made available previously to the instructor. The degree to which the students can answer the questions provides a measure of teaching effectiveness.

Teacher performance tests have several limitations. Some objections to them center on the general belief that student outcomes are inappropriate measures of teaching effectiveness. This view will be discussed more fully in the next section of the chapter, use of student achievement for summative teacher evaluation, where the concern is more prevalent than it is in the present context of teacher improvement.

A second objection is that the teaching activity is too superficial. Teachers, the argument goes, instruct classes over a long time; teaching is not limited to achieving single objectives on what could be obscure or trivial material. One response to this criticism is to ask whether a teacher who is unsuccessful with a minilesson will be able to function expertly with an entire course.

Another objection is a technical one. The author (Note 3) has assembled some data that show that teaching performance tests are unreliable. That is, a teacher may do well on one lesson and not nearly so well on another lesson. Unreliability is a very serious concern if the results of the test are to be used to evaluate teachers for summative purposes; the concern is less when the improvement of teaching is the focus of the test.

Finally, merely knowing how students do on the tests does not necessarily lead to improved teaching. It is for this reason that advocates of teaching performance tests suggest that the instructor receive additional feedback, either from the learners (who could be colleagues participating in the exercise), from observers, or through written suggestions for teaching the minilessons.

USE OF STUDENT ACHIEVEMENT FOR SUMMATIVE TEACHER EVALUATION

Summative evaluation is more controversial than formative evaluation. More is at stake. It is not surprising, therefore, that the appropriateness of using student achievement data for evaluating teachers comes under closer

Sensitivity of Words:
Descriptiveness of Adjectives

Statement of the Instructional Task. Critical to an ability to read prose with full appreciation and to write most forms of literature is an understanding of how adjectives can be skillfully used as modifiers. They can be used to paint vivid, mental pictures or in a flabby and ineffective way which does little to enhance the nouns they modify.

Your task is to teach the pupils to distinguish between two general types of adjectives. There are adjectives which are primarily descriptive and which refer to qualities perceived directly by the senses—qualities that can be seen, heard, tasted, felt or smelled. These adjectives are descriptive in a fairly specific way. For example, "John has *blue* eyes.", or, "That is a *heavy* box." There are some differences in the way each of us perceives *blue* eyes or *heavy* boxes, but we have been given a specific quality and we react with a mental image within fairly prescribed limits. We shall call such adjectives, "specific adjectives."

There are other adjectives which are far more general and subjective, requiring inferences and judgments and generally not containing specific sense-related description. Such words as *happy, sad, harsh,* and *friendly* fall into this category. Although it is true that we can see, for example, a happy person, happy is not a specific adjective. For one reason, simple sense-related description (twinkling eyes, smiling expression, etc.) is not provided and each of us must imagine for himself what a happy person looks like. Second, happy goes beyond mere description and implies a whole set of circumstances about the happy person—his state of mind, for example, as well as his physical appearance.

Obviously, there is no sharp distinction between these two types of adjectives. Nevertheless, it is possible to classify an adjective as belonging at one end or the other of a continuum according to the degree to which a specifically defined mental image is generated by the use of the adjective.

Consider the following two descriptions:

> The deserted barn was dark with dirty, cobwebby rafters. The floor was creaky underfoot and an owl gave a loud hoot somewhere outside. The barn was scary.

Note: Figure 3 continues on next page

In the first example, adjectives have been provided to communicate a fairly specific image to the reader. The words may indeed mean the same thing as, "The barn was scary." However, *scary* is far too nebulous and general an adjective to be counted on to communicate a sharp picture. In contrast, the mental images of readers evoked by the adjective, *loud*, are much mor alike. A a loud hoot and a deserted barn pin down the nature of the hoot and barn far more than a scary barn would.

A habit of overgeneralizing is one of the most frequent and serious weaknesses in student writing; it makes such prose tiresome to read. We need to train pupils to write accounts that will be as clear and real to the reader as possible. Awareness of the role and use of adjectives should be a step in this direction.

Your specific instructional objective is:

> *Given sentences containing an underlined adjective, the pupil will designate which sentences contain specific adjectives by circling a letter* S *placed before the sentence.*

Test Directions. (To be read aloud by the person giving the test and to appear on the test sheet as well.) "Each sentence has an underlined adjective. Circle the letter *S* next to those sentences which contain specific adjectives. Remember, circle the *S* only next to those sentences containing specific adjectives."

Sample Items and Answers. (To be read aloud by the person giving the test and to appear on the test sheet as well.)

S 1. Jill used a <u>red</u> crayon.

S 2. Tom is a <u>friendly</u> person.

S 3. I had a <u>nice</u> time.

Answers: 1. *S* circled; 2. *S* not circled; 3. *S* not circled.

Suggested Time Limit for Instructions. 15 minutes

Posttests. Eight items comparable to those above. In addition, each child will be asked to rate how interesting the lesson was.

Figure 3. Example of a minilesson. Reproduced with permission, Instructional Appraisal Services, Comprehensive Kit Grades 4-6, 1972.

scrutiny when the purpose of the evaluation is summative. The major arguments for and against using student achievement data for the summative evaluation of teachers are presented first. Next, criteria are offered for the fair assessment of teachers when student achievement data are used. Finally, examples of how the criteria can be met are provided.

Arguments For and Against Student Achievement Data in Teacher Evaluation

The advocates of any form of summative teacher evaluation argue that decisions about promotion and retention can be improved by objective and equitable assessments of teachers. Student achievement data are seen by many as one such source of information about teacher effectiveness. These data are considered particularly relevant by those who view the primary role of teaching to be improved student learning. Gains in student achievement are a direct measure of student learning. Other indicators of teaching effectiveness, such as teacher behavior in the classroom, student ratings, and the like, are seen as, at best, a proxy for the "real" criterion of teaching success, namely, student learning.

The proponents of the use of student achievement data in teacher evaluation strengthen their case by noting that the other data sources are not very good proxies. Several reviews (e.g., Kulik and McKeachie, 1975) of studies on the relationship between what a teacher does in the classroom and student learning have concluded that teacher classroom behavior is a poor predictor of student learning. Cohen (Note 4) reviewed 41 independent studies that related scores on student rating forms and measures of student achievement in 68 separate multisection courses and found a mean correlation of .43, which can be interpreted as a definite, but moderate, correlation between the two measures. In sum, research has shown that student learning information does not duplicate the information obtained by other indicators of teacher effectiveness. And, the argument continues, since student learning is viewed as the true test of a teacher's effectiveness, such a direct measure is more apt to be valid than the proxies.

Some people, of course, object to any evaluation of individuals, and since student achievement represents one way to evaluate teachers, they believe that it should not be used. However, large numbers of people, many of whom are in the teaching profession, do not object to summative teacher evaluation, but they do object to the use of student achievement data for that purpose. Their objection rests primarily on the ground that, since too many confounding factors affect student learning besides the teacher's performance, achievement measures should not be used.

Three types of confounding factors have most often been mentioned, all of which have the characteristic that they are frequently beyond the teacher's control. Student learning is seen to depend upon the students' characteristics, the instructional materials and setting, and the achievement tests used.

Students differ widely in many ways that affect learning. Some are smarter than others, some have more prior knowledge about the course content, some exert more effort, and some have greater aptitude in the specific learning area. As one teacher puts it, "There is no way to motivate a certain number of kids. They put forth absolutely no effort. I will not be held accountable for teaching an unteachable student" (Denny, Note 5). Is it fair, the opponents of student achievement data for summative evaluation ask more generally, to penalize a teacher whose students are less able, less experienced, and less motivated than those in other classes?

The context of teaching is an important determiner of teacher effectiveness (see Chapter 3). In some situations, teachers have little control over where and how the course is to be taught. Many claim that noisy or overcrowded rooms and early morning or evening classes are not conducive to efficient student learning. Some teachers have textbooks assigned to them or are restricted in other ways in the content and method of teaching.

The measures of learning, the achievement tests themselves, may not be of the teacher's making, or sample only a small and unrepresentative set of the instructional goals. Consequently, the student learnings resulting from the teacher's efforts may not be adequately assessed by the test.

In short, the opponents claim that student achievement is a flawed indicator of teacher competence. The best teacher in the world would not fare very well if faced with slow learners, unmotivated students, a poor learning environment, and an achievement measure out of harmony with the teacher's goals.

Criteria for Fair and Accurate Assessment of Teachers

All measurement contains error. No method of teacher evaluation will ever be completely free from bias and other sources of invalidity. Nevertheless, it is possible to minimize these unwanted contaminants. The following criteria, if met, go a long way toward improving student achievement indicators of teacher effectiveness.

Amenable to instruction. The indicator should measure those learnings most likely to be affected by classroom instruction. Tests that measure more general intellectual abilities and out-of-school learnings are inappropriate as indicators of teaching effectiveness. We do not subscribe to the view of those who judge teacher and school quality by results of college entrance examinations, by the number of National Merit semifinalists, which is determined by scholastic aptitude tests, or by scores on general intelligence and ability tests.

Valid in content. The test content should reflect the curriculum, that is, the knowledges and skills measured by the test should match the instructional objectives of the course. One of the difficulties of using commercially available, standardized achievement tests and minimum competency or statewide assessment tests is that they may not measure the teacher's instructional objectives. The differences in content being assessed by these tests are surprisingly large, even among instruments supposedly measuring the same skills (Walker et al., Note 6). Only from a careful inspection of the test questions can the user be sure that the test references those knowledges and skills included in the instructional program.

Mismatches between test content and instructional objectives can also occur even when the instructors themselves construct the achievement measures. Hard-to-measure skills often get slighted; easy-to-measure skills often are overrepresented on the tests. Miller et al. (1978) provide instruction on how to construct test questions that tap higher levels of thinking.

Reliable. Judgments of a teacher should be based on several tests, if possible, and not on just one. Student learning should be assessed for several of the teacher's classes or for more than just one year. Although for convenience we speak of the test as though there is only one, the reliability of the judgments would be enhanced if results were available from more than one test administered at different times during the course or year.

Since the entire class contributes achievement data, judgments about teacher effectiveness determined from student achievement data are usually more reliable than a judgment about any one student's degree of learning. The mean of many scores is more reliable than a single score.

Equitable. Assuming that the results of a common test are used to evaluate teachers, it is important that the test is equally fair for all teachers. One practice that promotes equitable treatment in this regard is describing in detail the knowledges and skills to be tested, so that each teacher will know what will be tested. If, for example, several instructors are teaching different sections of the same class or teaching several classes at the same grade level, and if a common final examination is constructed by one of the teachers, that teacher has a decided advantage over the others. The teacher constructing the test is not apt to include questions measuring content that the teacher did not cover in class. Also, the teacher may unconsciously emphasize in class specific content and test formats that find their way into the test. By making explicit exactly what students are expected to know and not know, there is much less danger that any one teacher will be unfairly disadvantaged.

Another practice that promotes equitable treatment is for all teachers to refrain from giving practice on the specific questions that appear on the test. Otherwise, the test scores become a measure of familiarity with the questions and answers for students in some classes rather than a measure of the achievement that the test is designed to measure.

Further, if the test involves essay questions or other subjectively scored questions, pains should be taken to limit bias in the scoring process. Bias-reducing practices include involvement of all the teachers in the grading, agreement on a scoring key, scoring each question twice with different graders, having each teacher grade papers from all classes, and making the identity of the student unknown to the graders.

Comparable. Quantities acquire meaning largely through comparisons with other quantities. A typing rate of 90 words per minute is impressive because few individuals acquire such rates. Without a basis of comparison, achievement gains are difficult to interpret. Is an improvement from 12 to 31 on a test from the beginning to the end of the year or course commendable?

Lack of comparability can occur for many reasons. The teaching contexts, the students being taught, and the tests being used may be very different from teacher to teacher. In an ideal situation for assessing teacher competence, the teaching situations are very similar, the students are assigned randomly to the classes or course sections, and a common measure of achievement is used. But these ideal conditions seldom occur. However, statistical procedures can increase comparability, and such procedures are discussed next.

Adjusting Student Achievement Scores

Procedures for converting student achievement data into judgments about teacher effectiveness are considered in this section. Some of the following remarks, especially those for the situation in which several teachers are being compared, are appropriate for other evaluative data, such as student ratings, as well as for achievement information. In the discussion, the criteria for fair and accurate assessment are assumed to have been met, except that the teaching situations and the student characteristics may be different. Indeed, much that is discussed below represents attempts to adjust for these differences.

It is assumed, however, that a common measure is used. That is, all students take the same achievement test or respond to the same student rating form, or, more generally, all teachers are judged on the same indicator. One exception is to use professionally developed tests whose different forms have been equated. However, the relevance of the content of such tests for judging teacher effectiveness must be considered carefully.

Three cases are considered. In the first situation, only a single teacher is being evaluated. Next is the case in which several teachers are being evaluated on a common measure, and an adjustment for differences in student characteristics among the classes is desired. Finally, a procedure is described for handling the case in which differences among classrooms, in addition to differences in student characteristics, are to be controlled.

One teacher. In this case, data from only one teacher are assumed to be available. It is nearly impossible to interpret meaningfully, for summative teacher evaluation, a class average. An average score of 80% may be very good if the test contained difficult questions and the students were slow learners. On the other hand, an able student body averaging 80% on an easy test is not a noteworthy accomplishment.

Even if the test is standardized and percentile rank norms are available, meaningful interpretation of the results is difficult. Suppose that the median percentile rank score of the students in the class was 39; is that good or bad? It is true that in the norm group, only 39% of the students scored below the typical student in the teacher's class, but if the students in the class were slower than average, the students' performances might be very good indeed. (It is inappropriate first to average the test scores of the students in a class and then to look up in a norm table a percentile rank. A percentile rank for a class average does not have the same value as the average percentile rank for a class of students.)

The situation improves slightly if test data are available from two points in time, such as at the beginning and at the end of the year or course. When such data are available, one is tempted to compare the median percentile ranks at the two testing occasions as a measure of teacher effectiveness. For example, if the percentile ranks at the beginning and end of the year were 39 and 45, respectively, one might want to conclude that since the typical student ranked higher among the norm group at the end of the year than at the beginning, the teacher was doing a better than average job of teaching.

Before a change in the median percentile at the two points can be interpreted as a measure of teacher effectiveness, at the very least the following conditions must be met: (1) the test is a fair measure of what the teacher is expected to teach, (2) the norm tables were constructed from tests given at the same two times as the test was given to the teacher's class, (3) the same students were used in calculating the beginning and end median percentiles for the teacher (that is, the weaker students that may have moved or dropped out of the class were counted in neither the first nor the second calculation), and (4) the students were not assigned to the teacher because of their low performance on the first test (that is, the first test was not used as a screening device for entrance into the teacher's class). The reason for the last concern is that the average score is expected to regress toward the mean. That is, when students are selected for a class or course because they had extreme scores, their performance on a subsequent test is expected not to be so extreme, even in the absence of instruction.

If the achievement test has no norms, some small measure of interpretability can be obtained, if conditions (1), (3), and (4) are met, by forming the fraction

$$\frac{(\text{Mean Test Score Time 2}) - (\text{Mean Test Score Time 1})}{(\text{Maximum Possible Test Score}) - (\text{Mean Test Score Time 1})}.$$

The fraction represents the proportion of the total gain that the class could have made on the test that was actually accomplished from time 1 to time 2.

Several classes (adjustment for student characteristics). Suppose that several teachers are either teaching the same grade in a school district or teaching the same college course that has a large enrollment. Assuming again that the criteria for fair assessment have been met (except for possible differences in characteristics among the students in several classes), it is possible to adjust the test scores to estimate what they would be if each student in a teacher's class had the same values on the characteristics being measured as the average value of all the students in the classes being compared.

The technique suggested is called the analysis of covariance. Although the calculations are tedious, many computer packages can perform them at a very modest cost. What is required for all the students are both their scores on a common achievement measure (not converted to some transformed scores like percentile ranks) and their scores on one or more common measures collected before or at the start of the year or course. The latter measures are called covariates. They should be measures of student characteristics that are expected to relate to their final achievement in the course. Scores on a standardized achievement or aptitude test, grades in a previous course, or other possible indicators of student ability or motivation are appropriate as covariates.

The common achievement measure acquired at the end of the year or course that is being adjusted statistically is called the dependent, or criterion, variable. The grade earned in the course is not recommended as the criterion. Grades are usually based on many factors, so that a grade of B, for example, in one teacher's class may not designate the same achievement as a grade of B in another teacher's class. For that reason, we recommend the score on a common achievement test or, better still, the average score from two or more common achievement tests.

The analysis of covariance predicts for every student the score that the student is expected to earn on the criterion based upon the student's score on the covariate(s). For example, high-ability students are predicted to earn higher scores on the criterion than low-ability students. Teachers having students who, in general, perform better than expected are judged to be stronger teachers than those whose students, in general, perform less well than expected on the common criterion. The analysis provides only relative judgments about teaching effectiveness. All teachers might be quite competent; nevertheless, some will be rated below average.

TABLE 1   Results of an Analysis of Covariance in Which the Final
Examination Scores of Students in Nine Discussion Sections
are Adjusted for Section Differences in Scholastic Aptitude

Discussion Section	Teacher	Class Size	Mean (SAT)	Mean (Final)	Deviation Final from Wt. Aver.	Deviation Adjusted for SAT
1	A	9	1144	37.9	−0.8	−0.6
2	A	11	1147	39.0	0.3	0.5
3	B and A	12	1191	38.6	−0.1	−0.7
4	B and C	12	1138	37.7	−1.0	−0.7
5	C	10	1147	37.6	−1.1	−0.9
6	C	11	1200	42.3	3.5	2.8
7	D	14	1119	36.8	−1.9	−1.2
8	E	13	1228	40.1	1.4	0.1
9	E	11	1108	38.8	0.1	1.0
	Weighted Average:		1159	38.7	0.0	0.0

Table 1 shows the results of a computer analysis of the final examination
scores earned by students in an introductory course at an eastern university.
That term the course had nine discussion sections, each taught by one, or a
pair, of five instructors. The College Board's Scholastic Aptitude Test (SAT)
was the covariate; the dependent variable was the score on the common final
examination. The average SAT scores and the average scores on the final
examination showed some variation among the sections.

Consider the data for sections 8 and 9, both taught by teacher E. The
average score on the final for section 8 was 40.1, or 1.4 points higher than
the overall course average of 38.7. Because students in section 8 had a
relatively high average (1228) on the covariate, the students were predicted
to do relatively well on the final examination. Thus, the deviation of 1.4 was
adjusted downward to .1. That is, the section average of 40.1 is just one-
tenth of a point higher than predicted. In section 9, the students had relatively low SAT scores yet managed to score about average on the final (38.8
versus 38.7). This average performance on the final, accomplished in spite
of the handicap of relatively low SAT scores, produced an adjusted final
examination average one point higher than predicted. To summarize, although section 8 had a higher average score on the final than section 9, the
effectiveness of teacher E was judged somewhat greater in section 9 (1.0)
than in section 8 (.1).

With the possible exception of section 6, the performance of students in
all the sections was very close to that predicted from their aptitude scores. It
is not surprising that differences among instructors were small, since they
met only once a week for an hour. Most of the material covered on the final

examination was presented in large group lectures and in the textbook and other readings.

Like any technique, analysis of covariance is not immune to possible bias. Even if all the conditions of fair assessment are met, except for differences in student characteristics, the results of analysis of covariance would still not be completely unbiased. The measures, both the covariate(s) and the criterion, are unreliable to some extent. Also, undoubtedly the students in the classes differed initially in many ways, and one or two covariates cannot measure all those differences. The effect of the unreliability of the measures used and the less-than-complete measurement of all the factors on which the classes differ prior to instruction is to underadjust the criterion scores. Thus, a teacher with more able and more motivated students may be judged somewhat more favorably than an equally competent teacher with less able and less motivated students. Nevertheless, this bias may be small, especially if the students in the several classes being compared were not very different at the start of the course or year. Analysis of covariance is a helpful technique to adjust the differences in class averages on a common achievement measure for initial classroom inequalities in student characteristics.

Several classes (adjustment for classroom variables). Again let us suppose that we have several classrooms and a common measure of teaching effectiveness such as the average rating that a teacher receives on the questionnaire item, "Rate the overall teaching effectiveness of this teacher." In addition, let us also assume the existence of one or more variables that describe a characteristic of the classroom as a whole such as class size, whether the course was required, grade level or class year, and so forth. (It should be mentioned that it is possible to treat as a classroom variable the class average of student characteristics, such as average score on an ability measure or percentage of students in the class majoring in a given discipline.)

The classroom variables selected should have three attributes. First, they should be related to the values on the common criterion measure; otherwise, no adjustments will be made. Second, they should not be affected by the teacher's effectiveness; otherwise, by controlling the variable, one adjusts away meaningful teacher differences. By measuring classroom variables at the beginning of the year or course, one protects against using a variable contaminated with teacher competence. Third, the variable must be different for the classes being compared; that is, it must be a variable. Thus, if 14 fifth-grade school teachers in a district were being evaluated, grade level could not be a classroom variable.

Previous research has shown that social science teachers receive higher student ratings than physical science teachers. Whether that factor is used as a predictor depends upon whether you believe that the difference in the ratings given to teachers in these two general fields is due to the nature of the course content or to the differing quality of the teachers. If you believe the former, you would use the factor to adjust the student ratings, because it would not be fair to compare teachers some of whom are teaching courses whose content makes it harder to earn higher ratings. On the other hand, if you believe that the differences in ratings between physical science and social science teachers merely reflect true differences in their teaching effectiveness, you would not want to adjust the average ratings for the field the course is in, because in that case you would be controlling the very factor that you want to measure, differences in teaching ability.

The technique that one uses to adjust for classroom variables is called multiple regression analysis. The predictors are the independent variables, and the criterion measure, such as average rating for the class, is the dependent variable. The analysis has as many "cases" as there are classrooms to compare and thus differs from analysis of covariance, in which the number of cases is the number of students in all the classes. Like analysis of covariance, programs for calculating multiple regression analysis are widely available at computer centers, and the costs are small.

Multiple regression analysis also provides an expected value for each class on the common criterion measure. The difference between the actual value and the expected value is the measure of teacher effectiveness. Teachers for whom the actual values are greater than the expected values are judged as relatively more effective than teachers for whom the actual values are less than the expected values.

As part of a workshop on teacher evaluation conducted by the author, 91 college instructors administered a student rating form that asked their students to rate them on overall teaching ability using a 4-point scale. A multiple regression analysis was performed using four classroom variables as predictors. Results for teachers 1 and 91 only are shown in Table 2. Although the first teacher received a slightly higher average rating than the last teacher (2.76 versus 2.71), the first teacher's effectiveness value, measured by the difference between the actual and expected values, is lower than that of the last teacher. The first teacher was teaching a smaller class that differed from the class of the last teacher in other ways that suggested that the first teacher would be expected to receive a much higher rating than the last teacher. Because the last teacher, in spite of the handicaps, actually received

TABLE 2   Multiple Regression Analysis of Teaching Ability Ratings

Teacher	Actual Rating	Expected Rating	Difference
1	2.76	2.87	−.13
91	2.71	2.56	+.50

almost the same rating as the first teacher, the last teacher was judged as more effective on the student rating criterion measure.

One drawback of multiple regression analysis is that the potential exists to capitalize significantly on random error and, as a result, to draw erroneous conclusions. Such error is most likely to occur when only a few classrooms are involved in the analysis or when the number of classroom variables is large relative to the number of classrooms available.

SUMMARY

For many people, measures of student achievement are both the most direct evidence of effective teaching and the evidence most prone to misinterpretation. Separately for the formative and summative uses of teacher evaluation, this chapter has alerted the reader to the promises and dangers of this measure of teacher competence and has offered suggestions for maximizing the former and minimizing the latter.

REFERENCE NOTES

1. Quinto, F. and B. McKenna (1977) *Alternatives to standardized testing*. Washington, DC: National Education Association.
2. Sesney, J. W. (1972) *The development of teaching proficiency tests at the university level*. Ph.D. dissertation, University of Utah.
3. Millman, J. (1973) *Psychometric characteristics of performance tests of teaching effectiveness*. Presented at the annual meeting of the American Educational Research Association, New Orleans, February.
4. Cohen, P. A. *A meta-analysis of the relationship between student ratings of instruction and student achievement*. Ph.D. dissertation, University of Michigan.
5. Quoted in T. Denny (1978) *Some still do: River Acres, Texas* (Report No. 3). Kalamazoo: Western Michigan University, Evaluation Center.
6. Walker, C. B., et al. (1979) *CSE criterion-referenced test handbook*. Los Angeles: University of California, Center for the Study of Evaluation.

REFERENCES

Kulik, J. A. and W. J. McKeachie, (1975) "The evaluation of teachers in higher education." *Review of Research in Education*, 3: 210–240.
Miller, H. G., R. G. Williams, and T. M. Haladyna, (1978) *Beyond Facts: Objective Ways To Measure Thinking*. Englewood Cliffs, NJ: Educational Technology.
Popham, W. J. (1974) "Minilessons as criterion variables for evaluating competency-based teacher education programs." *Performance-Based Teacher Education*, 3: 5–6.

———— (1971) "Performance tests of teaching proficiency: Rationale, development, and validation." *American Educational Research Journal,* 8: 105–117.

Shoemaker, D. M. (1973) *Principles and Procedures of Multiple Matrix Sampling.* Cambridge, MA: Ballinger.

Sirotnik, K. A. (1974) "Introduction to matrix sampling for the practitioner," in W. J. Popham (ed.), *Evaluation in Education: Current Applications.* Berkeley, CA: McCutchan.

CHAPTER 10

BEYOND CLASSROOM WALLS
Indirect Measures of Teacher Competence

JEAN A. KING
Tulane University

A common metaphor in educational writing compares a teacher to a gardener. Like gardeners working in greenhouses, teachers nurture growing things, watching carefully over their tender charges, adjusting conditions to provide for optimal growth, clipping back leaves and buds that grow in an improper direction, and so on—an idealistic image, perhaps, but a workable one.

The metaphor also provides a useful starting point for considering the use of indirect measures in the evaluation of teachers. In evaluating a gardener, the most direct and ultimate criterion is obvious: either the seedlings prosper and bloom, bringing abundance to the greenhouse and success to the gardener, or the plants wither in the soil, the greenhouse is barren, and the gardener fails at the one test that counts. The fact that the same gardener handles a roto-tiller with ease, serves as president of the local gardeners' union, and earns straight A's in courses on biodynamic farming simply does not excuse repeated failures in the plot. If the plants do not thrive, it does not matter, finally, if the tools used are clean and well cared for, if the compost added is wonderfully rich, or even if U.S. Department of Agriculture soil tests suggest that the growing conditions are the best to be found. Apart from the success of the crop, none of the variables listed above is either necessary or sufficient to determine the competence of the gardener.

Determining the competence of teachers in one sense parallels the case of the gardener. Many would say, in this era of accountability, that the one and only indicator of teaching effectiveness should be a direct measure, the ultimate growth and improvement of students. Without growth, regardless of the conditions under which the instruction occurs, the teacher is viewed a failure. But, as anyone who has taught will readily see, the teacher's case is not that simple, and, for a number of reasons, the gardener metaphor is finally inadequate to apply to the complexities of teacher evaluation. For one thing, the goals of education are far more complicated and difficult to agree upon than those of a garden. A second weakness in the metaphor is the classic difficulty of measuring growth in an educational sense. Whereas a gardener can detect small signs of growth immediately, a teacher often cannot. Third, unlike plants, students are not unmoving beings who react passively to their surroundings, but are, rather, active participants in the process of education. A further weakness of the metaphor is that, unlike the controlled atmosphere of a greenhouse, the context of learning is often beyond the teacher's control, and forces before which the teacher is helpless affect students, classrooms, and schools in ways that impede learning.

Others can surely think of additional inadequacies in the metaphor, but one point is clear. The evaluation of teachers will be insufficient if the sole criterion of success is the final achievement of students. It is for this reason that indirect measures of teacher competence, used with an awareness of their inherent limits and deficiencies, are not only appropriate but also of value in teacher evaluation.

VARIABLES INVOLVED IN DETERMINING TEACHER COMPETENCE

Figure 1 presents five sets of variables that can be involved in determining teacher competence, roughly placed on a continuum from direct to indirect measurement. The product variables are the most direct measures of teaching competence because they involve actual measurement of student growth. Indeed, as was suggested earlier, the strict gardening view of teaching would hold that the final products are all that matter in such evaluations.

Next are the process variables, more proximate indicators of teaching competence, including measures of in-class behaviors and activities (see Chapters 7 and 8), as well as assessments of teacher-produced instructional materials (see Chapter 6). The traditional importance of studying process and product variables in the evaluation of teachers is evident, and until recently few would have questioned the theoretical propriety of evaluating teachers on the activities and outcomes of their classrooms. But the measurement of product and process variables, although most direct, often proves difficult in practical settings, and other variables must often play a part in the evaluation of teaching competence.

One such set of variables involves professional activities, that is, non-classroom work that marks the teacher as a member of a school staff and of the teaching profession. As a staff member, a teacher might chaperone dances, do hall duty, hold fund drives, or work on curriculum committees. The commitment of the teacher as a professional might include participation in professional organizations at the local, state, or national level, attendance

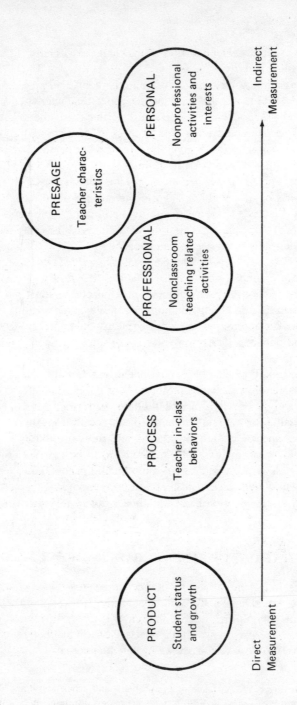

Figure 1. Variables involved in determining teacher competence.

at inservice or continuing education courses, and, especially at the college level, publishing activity.

Encompassed in the next set of variables, here labelled presage variables after Mitzel (1960), are the traditional teacher characteristics variables, some of which are more directly related to teaching than others. In this early summary of research on teacher effectiveness, Mitzel pointed to four categories of such variables in common use: "(a) teacher personality attributes, (b) characteristics of teachers in training, (c) teacher knowledge and achievement, and (d) in-service teacher status characteristics" (p. 1484). The "preoperational" variable categories given in a more recent work by Borich (1977) include teacher personality, aptitude/achievement, attitude, and experience. Other presage variables, sometimes called "employee" variables, include teachers' credentials and popularity.

The last set of variables includes personal activities of two types: community work, for example, active involvement in the Red Cross, American Civil Liberties Union, or a church; and more purely personal pursuits, for example, cello lessons, daily running, vegetable gardening, or part-time employment. The appropriateness of these additional nonteaching measures in evaluation depends clearly on what is considered "good" and what is considered "teaching."[1]

As McNeil and Popham (1973) have noted, indirect measures of the type described above allow the value preferences of the individual and the local community to operate. This can be limiting; in former days presage and personal variables bearing little relation to instruction, for example, teacher dress codes, expected church attendance, and rules forbidding teachers to smoke, drink, or (in the case of women) even to be married, sometimes determined who would be in the classroom. In all fairness, however, it must be noted that until quite recently direct measurement of student gain was just not feasible, and evaluation had little choice but to rely on such indirect measures.

THE LIMITATIONS OF RESEARCH ON INDIRECT MEASURES

Given the longstanding use of indirect measures in the evaluation of teachers, one would hope and assume that research has supported this practice. Unfortunately, this has not been the case. In a lengthy review of almost 200 studies on the personality and characteristics of teachers, Getzels and Jackson (1963) came to the discouraging conclusion that

> Despite the critical importance of the problem and a half-century of prodigious research effort, very little is known for certain about the nature and measurement of teacher personality, or about the relation between teacher

personality and teaching effectiveness. The regrettable fact is that many of the studies so far have not produced significant results [p. 574].

They pointed to three persistent obstacles facing researchers in this area: (1) the problem of defining "personality," (2) the problem of choosing appropriate instruments for measuring it, and (3) the problem of identifying and measuring the criterion (pp. 574–575). These obstacles continue to affect research on teacher characteristics and other presage variables.

The most elaborate project to date has been the Teacher Characteristics Study, a collection of approximately 100 separate studies over a period of six years, involving more than 6,000 teachers, in 1,700 schools and 450 school systems across the country (Ryans, Note 1). In the terms of Figure 1, the study worked to relate significant process and presage variables to each other. The study had three general objectives:

(1) To identify, analyze, and describe some of the patterns of teachers' classroom behavior and teachers' attitudes, viewpoints, and intellectual and emotional qualities. (2) To isolate and combine into scales significant correlates . . . of some of the major dimensions of teacher behavior—scales which might be used in evaluating and predicting important teacher characteristics. (3) To compare the characteristics of various groups of teachers when they had been classified according to such conditions as age, experience, sex, size of school, cultural climate of the community, and the like [p. 369].

It is worth noting, however, that the correlates of teacher classroom behavior calculated for various groups (by age, sex, extent of teaching experience, marital status, etc.) *are* simply correlates; although they relate variables, they do not demonstrate causation. The fact that older teachers as a group differed from younger teachers in certain ways (they scored lower on all variables except "systematic and businesslike classroom behavior" and "learning-centered, traditional educational viewpoints") does not necessarily mean that getting older will lead to predictable behaviors or attitudes in teaching. More important, the relation of any of these variables to actual student growth is uncertain because, although such growth is not entirely ignored, the study places its emphasis elsewhere. Although the points it makes are made well, by examining the correlation between presage and process variables, the Teacher Characteristics Study focuses on the middle of the direct-to-indirect continuum and can, therefore, say little about the relation between teacher characteristics and student growth.

A theoretical limitation of research on indirect measures was noted over 20 years ago by Mitzel (1960), who wrote that

For sample presage variables

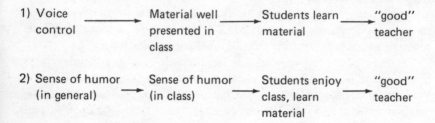

1) Voice control ⟶ Material well presented in class ⟶ Students learn material ⟶ "good" teacher

2) Sense of humor (in general) ⟶ Sense of humor (in class) ⟶ Students enjoy class, learn material ⟶ "good" teacher

For professional or personal variables

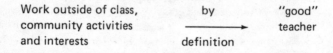

Work outside of class, community activities and interests ⟶ by definition ⟶ "good" teacher

OR

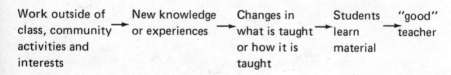

Work outside of class, community activities and interests ⟶ New knowledge or experiences ⟶ Changes in what is taught or how it is taught ⟶ Students learn material ⟶ "good" teacher

Figure 2. Assumptions underlying research on indirect measures.

Presage criteria, so-called here because of their origin in guessed predictions, are from a logical standpoint completely removed from the goals of education . . . In a sense they are pseudo criteria, for their relevance depends upon an *assumed* or conjectured relationship to other criteria, either process or product [p. 1484].

The assumptions implicit in research on indirect measures—professional and personal as well as presage—are presented in Figure 2. The required leaps of faith suggest why empirical research on these variables is conceptually problematic. For the presage, teacher-as-a-person variables, an assumption links a teacher's personality traits, knowledge, or attitudes to certain behaviors in the classroom. These, in turn, are assumed to facilitate students' learning. Not that all variables in this category are equally important to the final criterion; some, like knowledge of subject matter and voice control, are necessary minimally for success; as Hildebrand (1973) noted, as in bathing and doing dishes, their neglect is noticed. If, for example, a teacher lacks the requisite diction and volume to present a subject so that all can comprehend what is said, student growth in the end may be impossible, regardless of what else the teacher does. Research on this point is not appropriate because the results would be predetermined; a tightrope walker without balance is bound to fall.

Other variables, like sense of humor, are not necessary in the same way—we have all known effective teachers who made few jokes—but they somehow seem supportive of the learning process. A teacher who jokes in class may create an atmosphere more conducive to learning than one who does not joke. However, given the tenuous chain of assumptions linking this characteristic and student growth, and given what we now know about the multidimensional arena called a classroom, expectations that these variables will relate significantly to effective teaching seem unrealistic.

Figure 2 also presents the assumptions involved in researching professional and personal indirect variables. Again, the likelihood of empirical research showing that these variables affect student growth seems small. Depending on how teaching is defined, these indirect variables can be viewed in one of two ways. On the one hand, a teacher doing work outside of class may, by definition, be rated good (or bad). Some would say that participation in professional organizations makes a teacher good simply because good teachers must be part of the professional community. Others, however, would not want to condemn teachers who do nothing beyond the tasks required in their contract and would not label teachers inadequate because they worked at Woolworth's in the evenings. In either case, research would not alter such opinions.

A second way to view professional and personal variables is to assume that work of whatever type outside the classroom somehow encourages positive changes in or provides support for certain process variables, thus leading to enhanced student growth. A teacher who develops a new curriculum may implement the change and somehow convey newfound enthusiasm to students.Or, by having a life outside the classroom, a teacher who has a hobby—water-skiing, sewing, or collecting helmets—may avoid the burnout that other teachers experience. But even assuming that it is true theoretically, to demonstrate this chain of events empirically would be monumental.

Upon reflection, no one should be surprised that research to date has been inconclusive. As Ryans (Note 1) suggested and Medley (1973) reminded us, there is no single set of skills, attitudes, interests, and abilities that all good teachers have and that all poor teachers lack. Effective teaching means different things for different students at different times, and research that has sought to discover one set of characteristics for effective teachers has doomed itself to failure.

POSSIBLE ROLES FOR INDIRECT MEASURES

Evaluations that include indirect measures of teacher competence have three inherent weaknesses. First, some teachers reject out of hand any definition of teaching that goes beyond classroom activities or contractual requirements. The development of teacher militance makes even the suggestion of supplementary requirements for teachers a potential grievance. In addition, some characteristics, like age, cannot be changed. A second weakness is that indirect measures have not been even minimally validated by research, and their use is therefore based more on custom and intuition than on knowledge. As McNeil and Popham (1973) pointed out, indirect measures may predict "retention in a teaching position," rather than instructional effectiveness (p. 233).

Related to the second is a third weakness; even the theoretical validation of indirect measures presents some difficulties.One way to validate the use of any measure is to consider the three general attributes of criteria for teacher competency presented in McNeil and Popham (1973). The first of these is the reliability or consistency of a measure. The second is a neutral orientation, that is, the ability of a measure to be used successfully by people with a variety of different instructional viewpoints. The final attribute is its having an assignment indicator, an ability to yield "information about the types of instructional situations in which a given teacher functions best" (p. 238).

Applying these attributes to the three types of indirect variables— professional, presage, and personal—suggests that the use of these measures in teacher evaluation requires careful consideration. First, the reliability of certain measures may present a problem; although information on professional and personal variables may be reliably collected, personality variables are sometimes difficult to measure. The second attribute, a neutral orientation, presents another problem for indirect measures, although not in a usual sense. Because they do not involve observation in the classroom, indirect measures are neutral in McNeil and Popham's sense. However, because they measure nonclassroom aspects of a teacher's life, indirect measures in another sense are not neutral, but are, instead, biased toward a view of teaching that reaches far beyond a single classroom. As for yielding information about where a given teacher might function best—the third general attribute—professional and personal variables may appear useful but should be of secondary importance because they concern activities outside the classroom. As these arguments suggest, people who oppose the use of indirect measures in evaluating teacher competence have reasons to support their position.

The fact that these reasons exist, however, is not sufficient argument for ignoring or dismissing indirect measures of teacher competence. Despite the limitations given above, their use can be validated conceptually by considering two of the six additional attributes that McNeil and Popham (1973) suggested for discriminating among criterion measures. These two attributes, differentiation among teachers and adaptation to teachers' goal preferences, suggest the value of including data from indirect measures in teacher evaluation.

McNeil and Popham gave as one attribute of a good criterion measure its ability to discriminate among teachers. Indirect measures can easily differentiate among teachers, not in the way that more direct measures can, by showing whose students learn more, but rather in a preconceived, conceptual way. Given a broad definition of teaching that includes nonclassroom activities, teachers can be distinguished on the basis of what they know, what they are like, and how they choose to spend their time outside of class.

This strength of indirect measures leads to the second attribute of a good criterion measure, the adaptation to teachers' goal preferences. If teachers look at their overall abilities and activities (being, of course, careful not to ignore their effectiveness in the classroom) they may then choose areas in which to improve themselves. Faculty development will thus be encouraged, and teachers will continue to learn while they teach. Given these criteria, indirect measures have a viable role in the evaluation of teachers because they can effectively discriminate among teachers while adapting to teachers' goal preferences.

The question that then arises is how to use such measures in real life. The criteria just mentioned suggest two possible uses for indirect measures. First, because they do not directly address instructional concerns, they are not immediately appropriate for improving instruction. They may, however, be appropriate for decisions of hiring and firing because they help to discriminate among teachers. In many job interviews, little beyond transcripts, recommendations, and applications is available to administrators, and hiring decisions have traditionally relied almost totally on presage and professional variables (see Chapter 4). The same has frequently been the case in retention decisions, although the move toward the use of more direct process and product variables in teacher evaluation may now begin to add new validity to such decisions (see Chapters 7–9). Whether retention decisions should be entirely based on process and product measures is, for now, a moot point. In any case, the use of indirect measures in such decisions must be tied to a predetermined definition of good teaching accepted by the faculty and administration for a given school and community. As Gephart (1979) has pointed out, "Evaluation of teaching rests heavily on the values in a given setting. If it is to be a productive activity, those structuring values must be made known to all people involved" (p. 3). Where such a definition of values exists—and the process of definition itself can be worthwhile—indirect measures can play an important role in evaluating teaching competence.

In addition to their use in personnel decisions, indirect measures can also play a viable part in self-evaluation and professional growth by adapting to teachers' goal preferences. Making teachers aware of their professional profile can allow them to make conscious decisions about their role in education both inside and outside of the classroom. There are, after all, many different ways to be a competent teacher. The procedure could be as simple as completing a form similar to the outline of Figure 1, with data provided in each category. Looking at such a form, a teacher might see, for example, that he has done a great deal of professional work within the school, but nothing at all in the community. Or a teacher might realize that she has learned nothing new in her subject area since completing her most recent certification courses. Whether this makes a difference will depend on the teacher, the variable, and the school; cooperation and the possibility of and a desire to change are requirements in this process. But given these, the explicit use of indirect measures in teacher evaluation can be a positive way to allow for individual goal differences among teachers, schools, and even educational levels.

This use of indirect measures already occurs to some extent. At the college level, for example, the publish-or-perish ethic with its requisite professional duties has for years placed emphasis on professional variables, although sometimes to the exclusion of process and product variables. At the elementary and secondary levels, more often, emphasis on professional activities at the school, for example, sponsoring clubs, serving in the P.T.A., or participating in inservice workshops, has demonstrated a commitment to teaching or to working with students.

The key to the use of indirect measures in evaluation is the consent of the evaluated. Teachers must be willing to look for ways to change their professional profile, including what they are and what they are doing outside the class, as well as more direct measures of what life is like in their classroom. If they reject this concept, indirect measures can have no place in their evaluation.

Are teachers willing to be evaluated using indirect measures? I think so and offer three reasons to support a view that, to some, may seem overly idealistic. First, teachers are accustomed to such measures. Historically their use is commonplace. Second, most teachers are more concerned with becoming better at what they do than with just getting by in their work. Few teachers want to be mediocre, and the possibility of continual improvement in some areas should be welcome to the teacher looking for ways to improve. Third, it seems to me that even the most militant teachers would be hesitant to be evaluated solely on process and product measures, given the current reality of evaluation in the schools. Indirect measures can represent positive input into an evaluation process that has the potential to become too cut-and-dried. Although indirect measures cannot replace more direct measures, they can provide supplementary information about a teacher's effectiveness.

There is a wonderful educator's fable that details the trials of a young man named Nathan who wants to become a teacher (Nagle, 1977). The wisest, most respected counselor in the land tells Nathan that to become a teacher he must first overcome three obstacles: the Sea of Children, the Mountain of Paperwork, and the Country of Duties and Commitments. Undaunted, Nathan sets out to face these challenges and, after much memorizing of names, writing of objectives, correcting of papers, and duties of myriad types, he returns wearily to the counselor to ask if he is now worthy of the title Teacher.

> "Why, Nathan," began the counselor, "you have been a teacher all along."
> Nathan protested, "But I have not stimulated any minds. I have not guided anyone down the road to knowledge. I have not had any time to teach."
> "Oh, you say you want to TEACH! I thought you said you wanted to be a TEACHER. Well, that is an entirely different story" [p. 19].

As the wise counselor knows and Nathan sadly learns, doing the work of a teacher is not always the same thing as teaching. The professional activities demanded of teachers, and even many activities performed in the classroom, may not seem to affect the growth of students directly. Evaluation schemes that look only at the most direct criteria may ignore or belittle the often exhausting demands of being a teacher. Indirect measures such as those discussed above are needed because they take these and other demands into account.

This is not to say, however, that indirect measures can or should *replace* more direct measures. Evaluation of teaching competence must ultimately look at the outgoing students, regardless of how teaching is defined. Even if indirect measures are used, this must never be forgotten. But the more research on teaching that is done, the more it is becoming evident that there is no single way to be a good teacher. Teaching is a multivariate process within which goodness is often relative. To return to the metaphor that began this chapter, schools are not, finally, like greenhouses or gardens. Because they are social institutions, schools need teachers who are aware of personal and professional goals outside of the classroom as well as within. The value of indirect measures in teacher evaluation is that they make as explicit as possible the several domains of activities involved in teaching. Whether they are used in personnel decisions or in self-evaluation for professional growth, indirect measures suggest an appropriately multidimensional model for teacher evaluation. Because they can provide valuable information unavailable from more direct sources, indirect measures may prove invaluable.

NOTE

1. It must be noted that at the base line are certain contractual and humane considerations. A teacher who repeatedly misses first period, who makes no attempt to prepare or present lessons, or who beats students should not be evaluated positively regardless of what else he or she is doing within or outside the school. That this will necessarily exclude some people who have much to offer is sometimes lamentable, but unavoidable.

REFERENCE NOTE

1. Ryans, D. G. (1960) *Characteristics of teachers, their description, comparison, and appraisal.* Washington, DC: American Council on Education.

REFERENCES

Borich, G. D. (1977) *The Appraisal of Teaching: Concepts and Process.* Reading, MA: Addison-Wesley.
Gephart, W. J. (1979) "Practical applications of research on personnel evaluation (editorial)." *Practical Applications of Research,* 2(2): 1; 3.

Getzels, J. W. and P. W. Jackson (1963) "The teacher's personality and characteristics," pp. 506–582 in N. L. Gage (ed.), *Handbook of Research on Teaching*. Skokie, IL: Rand McNally.

Hildebrand, M. (1973) "The character and skills of the effective professor." *Journal of Higher Education*, 44: 41–50.

McNeil, J. D. and W. J. Popham (1973) "The assessment of teacher competence," pp. 218–244 in R. M. W. Travers (ed.), *Second Handbook of Research on Teaching*. Skokie, IL: Rand McNally.

Medley, D. M. (1973) "Closing the gap between research in teacher effectiveness and the teacher education curriculum." *Journal of Research and Development in Education*, 7: 39–46.

Mitzel, H. E. (1960) "Teacher effectiveness," pp. 1481–1486 in C. W. Harris (ed.), *Encyclopedia of Educational Research*. New York: Macmillan.

Nagle, T. L. (ca. 1977) "An American educator's fable." *American Educator*.

CHAPTER 11

FACULTY SELF-EVALUATION

J. GREGORY CARROLL

University of Pennsylvania

To some of us, the term *self-evaluation* may seem a contradiction. After all, faculty evaluation conjures up images of promotion and tenure committees, deans' offices, school boards, and union contracts. Evaluations are typically conceived as external measures imposed on faculty, as grades assigned us by our supervisors, by our peers, and even by our students. If the aim of evaluation is cost-benefit accountability, then the term *self-evaluation* begins to sound as suspect as the proverbial free lunch. In fact, Seldin (1975) points out that many authors of faculty evaluation systems have omitted self-evaluation from their discussions entirely. To this author, such an omission reveals a misconception about an important aim of faculty evaluation.

Surely one basic aim of faculty evaluation should be the study and improvement of teaching. It is in pursuit of this aim that various forms of self-evaluation contribute significantly to an overall evaluation strategy. Presumably because of limited objectivity, self-evaluation is not widely employed in considerations of contract renewal, promotion, and tenure (Astin and Lee, 1967; Seldin, 1975). One's objectivity can rightfully be questioned when one's own teaching career hangs in the balance. Although self-evaluation can contribute useful data for administrative decisions by providing additional information and perspectives that may be unavailable from other sources, its greatest value continues to be for self-understanding and instructional improvement. In particular, self-evaluation techniques often provide the individual instructor with insights into and explanations and interpretations of data from other sources.

In this chapter, self-evaluation is defined as making judgments about one's own teaching. In making such judgments, instructors can appropriately use any of the evaluation techniques outlined in other chapters of this handbook, for example, student ratings, colleague ratings, and measures of student achievement. This chapter avoids detailed discussion of the data sources described in other chapters and focuses instead on the unique sources of data available through self-evaluation. The intent is to emphasize the techniques designed purely for self-evaluation, without diminishing the importance of other kinds of evaluation techniques. In addition, the discussion in this chapter is oriented primarily toward assessing the quality of one's teaching. The implications for subsequently improving one's teaching are not discussed in detail here, since this is the topic of Chapter 13.

Five major aids for self-evaluation are considered: self-rating forms, self-reports, self-study materials, observation of colleagues' teaching, and videotape/audiotape feedback of one's own teaching. For each aid there is a discussion of the basic technique, its options, examples of materials available, and general guidelines for use.

SELF-RATING FORMS

Research on the validity of self-ratings of instruction is quite limited, especially in comparison to the research on student ratings of instruction. Empirical studies have generally demonstrated that self-ratings show little agreement with ratings of students, colleagues, or administrators (Centra, 1972). Clark and Blackburn (Note 1) and Centra (1973) reported correlations of approximately .20 between self-ratings and student ratings. Similarly, the correlation between self-ratings and colleague ratings was .28 (Clark and Blackburn, Note 1). On the other hand, correlations of approximately .70 have been reported between student ratings and colleague ratings (Maslow and Zimmerman, 1956; Blackburn and Clark, 1975; Murray, Note 2). Doyle and Crichton (1978) found that self-rankings yielded greater agreement with student and colleague observations than did self-ratings, probably because the instructors were forced to discriminate more closely when ranking themselves against other faculty members than when rating themselves.

Self-ratings appear to be most helpful for comparisons with and interpretations of other sources of data, such as student ratings, student achievement, classroom observations, and videotape feedback. For example, instructors have been shown to achieve significant improvement in subsequent student ratings after a moderate discrepancy has been identified between initial student ratings and the instructors' own self-ratings (Pambookian, 1974, 1976). Instructors whose initial self-ratings were moderately favorable, and somewhat higher than their student ratings, were those most likely to show gains in subsequent student ratings. Thus, self-ratings appear to facilitate the use of student feedback to the extent that they identify unexpected discrepancies. In this way, self-ratings can serve to clarify one's concepts of teaching and can encourage further examination and evaluation of teaching performance.

In summary, the present research on self-ratings shows that they have little agreement with the observations of student, colleague, and administrator raters. Recent research indicates that self-assessments may show greater agreement with observations from others when they are cast in terms of ranking one's own performance against one's colleagues. Self-ratings are particularly effective when they serve to identify for the instructor certain unexpected discrepancies with other ratings.

A sample form of faculty self-rating is reproduced in Figure 1. This particular form is concise and broadly applicable to diverse settings and disciplines. It is free of troublesome educational jargon, and it can be easily adapted with the inclusion of additional items at the bottom of the page. A drawback of this form is that the points along the seven-point scale are loosely defined, with little indication about what observable differences would distinguish a 3 from a 4. Also, the items require a relatively high level of inference, and it is not clear how they contribute to an overall, composite rating. Instructors would be well-advised to view this instrument as a starting point for self-assessment activities.

It is also possible to construct scales, in the form of rankings, in such a way that one's comparisons are made relative to the standards of other instructors. This type of measure is likely to reduce the degree of bias in self-ratings, but it does require that instructors become familiar with the standards of others and receptive to the notion of normative measures of their teaching skills. Such rankings may create greater anxiety than self-ratings do on the part of the instructor and could serve to alienate rather than stimulate further interest in self-evaluation. Thus, self-rankings might optimally be reserved for instructors who have already become accustomed to some form of self-evaluation.

To attenuate the inherent bias of self-rating forms, several researchers at the University of Illinois have developed a forced-choice questionnaire. The Instructor Self-Evaluation Form (ISEF) "forces" the respondents to rank each of the four statements in a given set according to the degree to which that statement describes their course. Thus, by forcing the rankings within each tetrad, relative strengths and weaknesses are ascertained. There are 11 sets of statements in all, and each set of four corresponds to the subscales of the form: (1) Adequacy of Classroom Procedures, (2) Enthusiasm for Teaching and Knowledge of Subject Matter, (3) Stimulation of Cognitive and Affective Gains in Students, and (4) Relations with Students. By summing the rankings of similar statements across the 11 tetrads, one derives a composite score for each of the four scales. The ISEF results indicate the instructor's relative assessment of these four factors of the course. (Further information on the ISEF technique and scoring procedures is available from the Measurement and Research Division, Office of Instructional Resources, University of Illinois, Urbana, IL 61801.)

SELF-APPRAISAL OF TEACHING

Teacher _____ Course _____

Term _____ Academic Year _____

Thoughtful self-evaluation can help improve teaching effectiveness. This questionnaire is designed for that purpose. You are asked to look at your own performance in teaching.

At your option, questions 12 and 13 may be added. Use the back of this form for any written comments you might want to express. These might record any unusual circumstances that relate to the course and to your teaching it.

Directions:

Rate yourself on each item, giving the highest scores for unusually effective performances. Place in the blank space before each statement the number that most nearly expresses your view:

Highest			Average			Lowest	Don't Know
7	6	5	4	3	2	1	X

_____ 1. Have the major objectives of your course been made clear?

_____ 2. How do you rate agreement between course objectives and lesson assignments?

_____ 3. Are class presentations well planned and organized?

_____ 4. Are important ideas clearly explained?

_____ 5. How would you judge your mastery of the course content?

_____ 6. Is class time well used?

_____ 7. Have you encouraged critical thinking and analysis?

_____ 8. Have you encouraged students to seek your help when necessary?

_____ 9. Have you encouraged relevant student involvement in the class?

_____ 10. How tolerant are you of student viewpoints that differ from your own?

_____ 11. Considering the previous 10 items, how would you rate your performance in this course as compared to others in the department who have taught the same course?

_____ 12.

_____ 13.

_____ Composite rating.

Figure 1. A self-rating form. (Source: Miller, 1972. Reproduced with permission from Jossey-Bass, Inc.)

Self-rating forms can also be readily converted from forms used to obtain student evaluations or colleague observations (see Chapter 8). For the sake of comparisons, it is important to devise self-rating forms that are closely parallel in content and format to those used by the other observers. This approach greatly facilitates the identification of discrepancies for the instructor's consideration, discrepancies that can provide critical insights and decisions about one's teaching.

SELF-REPORTS

Typically the self-report uses an open-ended format, which calls for concise answers to a number of questions related to instruction. It often takes the form of an activity report and may become part of a dossier for administrative purposes. The self-report usually serves as a source of much more extensive information than the rating scale.

Research is lacking on the use and the effects of self-reports as an evaluation technique for instructors. It seems evident, however, that this type of instrument can serve teachers periodically as a device for taking stock of their aims, accomplishments, and shortcomings. Self-reports can thereby facilitate the setting of priorities and the formulation of long-range professional plans. By posing questions specifically related to concepts and methods of teaching, these reports can convey and emphasize the importance of instructional processes for achieving both institutional and personal goals.

Self-reports are particularly useful for interpreting data from other sources. For example, data from two classes may, at first, appear quite similar in statistical terms. However, these data, such as student achievement scores or student ratings of instruction, might be interpreted quite differently given additional information available in self-reports. One course may be a crowded, lower-level, required course that has been oversubscribed by the registrar and has enrolled many students who need remediation. The other could be a small, upper-level elective with bright, motivated learners. In either event, the instructor's self-report can serve to focus and clarify the inferences to be drawn from other data.

The self-evaluation form presented in Figure 2 is used by the Faculty Committee of Greenfield Community College to obtain the instructor's assessment of instructional goals, methods, and philosophy. Open-ended questions relate to the instructor's strengths and weaknesses in content areas, as a classroom teacher, and in instructional methods. Self-evaluation is also sought of the instructor's goals with students and of the instructor's sources of frustration and gratification in working at the college. Finally, the self-report form requests information about teaching activities, courses taught, com-

(text continued on p. 191)

Rating Scale 2-20. Greenfield Community College Faculty Committee

Self Evaluation Form for the File of _____

Dear Colleague:

One means of up-grading professional effectiveness is self-evaluation. To facilitate the process we have devised the attached questionnaire, which we are asking you to fill out. Completing the questionnaire will be useful in two ways: First and foremost, it will get you to think about your own strengths and shortcomings. (You probably evaluate your own teaching continually, but the questionnaire should help you to do it in a more formal, perhaps more precise, way.) Second, it should add a dimension to the committee's understanding and appreciation of you as a teacher.

We would ask that you try to avoid two common pitfalls in your self-appraisal: First, do not let modesty keep you from being very explicit about your assets. Second, try to be equally candid about your shortcomings. As teachers and as students of particular disciplines we are well aware that individuals are less knowledgeable in some areas of a discipline than in others, just as they have both good days and bad days in the classroom. We also appreciate only too well that every teacher has certain methods and approaches with which he is very comfortable and adept, as well as those with which he is less proficient.

One final comment on the questionnaire: You will notice that it is divided into two parts. The first part, consisting of two sections deals with those areas having a direct bearing on the committee's work. The first section, that which deals with subject area and classroom approach, is obviously the most important. The second section, dealing with your overall G.C.C. activities and experiences, asks for additional information which we feel can be of real help to us. The second part of the questionnaire is entitled *Supplementary Information*, and this title was deliberately chosen. We are asking that you complete this part of the questionnaire only if you feel the information will contribute to our picture of you as a teacher and member of the G.C.C. community.

Sincerely,

The Faculty Committee

Figure 2. A self-report form. (Source: Genova et al., 1976. Reproduced with permission of the Greenfield Community College Faculty Committee.)

185

FACULTY QUESTIONNAIRE

Section I—Subject Area and Classroom Approach

1. Within your own discipline, which area or areas do you regard as your strongest?

2. Which area do you regard as your weakest?

Figure 2 (continued)

3. What is your greatest asset as a classroom teacher?

4. What is your greatest shortcoming as a classroom teacher?

Figure 2 (continued)

5. Do you feel that your discipline is best taught by a particular approach (method) and, if so, which approach and why do you feel it is the best?

6. As a teacher in a Community College, what is your goal with respect to your students?

Figure 2 (continued)

7. Describe what you have found most gratifying in your work at G.C.C.

8. Describe what you have found most disappointing or frustrating in your work at G.C.C.

Figure 2 (continued)

189

Section II—G.C.C. Experience

1. List under *A* the courses you are presently teaching and under *B* any other courses you have taught in the past at G.C.C.

A.

B.

2. List the Committees on which you have served or are now serving.

3. List any other activities you have engaged in at the College.

4. For how many years, including the 1970-71 school year, have you been teaching full-time at G.C.C.?

SUPPLEMENTARY INFORMATION

If you think it appropriate, kindly give us a brief biographical sketch of yourself. Include any and all information which you think might help us to help you, items such as educational and professional background, honors received, articles published, community activities, general interests, etc. You may use the back of this sheet or make attachments.

Greenfield Community College, Greenfield, MA 01301. Form 4.

Figure 2 (continued)

mittee work, length of service, a biographical sketch, education, professional experience, honors and awards, publications, and community activities.

This particular form lacks a clear statement of its specific uses by the Faculty Committee. It is not clear from the form itself what actions might be taken in light of this information. In seeking candid information, a self-report form should clarify its exact purposes, as well as the degree of confidentiality to be expected.

Two other factors essential for the successful implementation of the technique are the timing and the design of the reports. Scheduling the self-reports at regular intervals, such as every two years or in sequence with regular departmental reviews, helps generate faculty acceptance and cooperation. Once the precedent is well-established, the recurring process will become routine. Forms that are clear, straightforward, and brief are essential if the process is not to be regarded as a laborious and burdensome task.

Self-reports tend to yield a great deal more information about teaching than do rating scales, but often this information is more difficult to quantify. For this reason, self-reports are best used when there is an opportunity to review and criticize one's teaching in some detail. For example, self-reports would probably be more useful than ratings in discussions between teachers and their supervisors, once a feeling of trust has been well-established between them.

SELF-STUDY MATERIALS

In preparing for teaching careers, few faculty members in higher education have received formal training in educational psychology, pedagogy, or curriculum development. Unlike the preparation of primary and secondary school teachers, the graduate training of college faculty is usually devoted entirely to scholarship and research in the content of one's discipline, with little attention to the methods and processes of teaching. Graduate training may well include considerable teaching experience, but it rarely calls for a serious study of teaching or for close supervision by faculty. It is not surprising, therefore, that early in their careers many junior faculty members feel dissatisfied, uncertain, and defensive about their teaching. It is also fairly common for senior faculty members to come to a sudden realization of their limitations after years of experience and uneasiness. For these reasons, considerable attention has been paid to self-study materials for instructors in higher education. Of particular interest in this section are the materials available for individually assessing and analyzing one's teaching skills. Self-study programs designed for these purposes enable instructors to evaluate their individual teaching styles and then to investigate the alternative teaching techniques and materials that they consider most appropriate. Self-study materials are most often packaged in modules, so that instructors can select and sequence the skills they seek to develop.

One set of self-study materials has been developed at San Jose State University. It contains 13 modules on various skills, such as preparing lectures, conducting discussions, developing self-paced programs, and constructing tests. The set includes a Self-Appraisal Form for Faculty, which serves to identify the instructor's interests and priorities among the general categories and individual modules. Each module also includes specific items for self-assessment, in the form of a text and an accompanying workbook. Throughout each module, the instructor is directed to the workbook for exercises, problems, and applications. Feedback and explanations for each exercise are then provided in the instructional text. For example, the module on preparing lectures includes exercises on student participation in the lecture. The exercises are then reviewed and discussed by the authors in the text. In addition, several modules include videotapes of classroom episodes or filmstrips of sample materials for self-paced instructional programs.

The San Jose materials are currently being used by over 300 universities in the United States, according to the developers of the series. This includes extensive use of the materials as a resource for training graduate students involved in college teaching. The developers recommend that the materials are most effective when they are coordinated by professional faculty development personnel, who can provide the instructor using them with an opportunity for interaction and guidance. (Additional information is available from the Faculty and Instructional Development Office, Instructional Resources Center, San Jose State University, San Jose, CA 95192.)

By using modular, self-study materials, instructors can gain considerable insight into their teaching styles, philosophies, and limitations. They can also explore subjects that are of particular interest, according to a sequence that they can determine themselves. Self-study materials lend themselves particularly to working in consultation with a faculty development expert, who can provide additional suggestions, clarification, and critique.

OBSERVATION OF COLLEAGUES

A common technique for assessing one's own teaching is to observe colleagues and to make comparisons with oneself. Such observations can take on a number of different forms and approaches. Team teaching and interdisciplinary programs provide excellent opportunities for comparing teaching styles and for experimenting with new ideas. Participation in formal programs for faculty development offers another means for learning from the example of one's colleagues.

It is also advisable to form mutual arrangements with selected colleagues for periodic classroom observation and critique. Sweeney and Grasha (1978) reported a program in which faculty members agreed to form trios for regular observations of one another's classes. The trios were formed by matching college instructors from different disciplines, and the participants reported that they gained important insights about teaching both from observing and being observed. By participating in several cycles of observation and critique, the participants were able to implement and test many of their colleagues' suggestions in subsequent class sessions.

Finally, faculty colloquium sessions offer an additional opportunity for observing colleagues teaching. Here one can observe the teaching skills used in the context of presentations on current research projects. In fact, in virtually any discipline, occasional colloquium sessions could be devoted to innovative educational approaches, curriculum revisions, and educational evaluation projects.

Regardless of the setting in which one observes colleagues teaching, important lessons can be drawn by making comparisons to one's own methods and techniques. This is particularly true when there is a subsequent opportunity to discuss the observed teaching episode with that teacher, in order to clarify the teacher's reasons for choosing a particular strategy or employing a specific technique at a given time. As elaborated in the following section on self-observation, it is also important to limit and specify the types of observations that one wishes to focus on during a particular class session.

VIDEOTAPE/AUDIOTAPE FEEDBACK

One of the potentially most powerful forms of self-assessment is the opportunity "to see ourselves as others see us" through video and/or audio recordings. The use of electronic recording technology seems to have great intuitive appeal, yet it creates enormous anxiety for most self-viewers.

One of the greatest problems with videotape is that it often leaves instructors wondering exactly what it is that they are supposed to look for on the tape. Several techniques have been developed to help instructors see themselves more objectively, to alleviate some of their anxiety, and to clarify what it is that they seek to observe. The most prominent techniques are microteaching (Allen and Ryan, 1969), interpersonal process recall (Kagan, 1975), and interaction analysis (e.g., Flanders, 1970). Before these techniques are examined in detail, however, it is useful to consider a general model for self-confrontation in teacher education, as developed by Fuller and Manning (1973).

A Self-Confrontation Model

In their extensive review of the literature on videotape playback in teacher education, Fuller and Manning (1973) concluded that goal setting and focused feedback were key elements for achieving significant changes in teaching behavior:

> Change is said to require not only the presence of facilitative conditions such as acceptance and empathy, but also "confrontation," i.e., identification of a discrepancy between the person's view of reality and that of some observer. One possibility is that the teacher will not benefit from seeing her videotape alone since there is no confrontation, but will change only when focus is provided by a supervisor, a peer, or some instructions. The other possibility is that solitary playback is most beneficial on the assumption that it is a lower threat situation.

> The literature almost unanimously supports the view that confrontation, or at least some focus, is necessary. Feedback that is not accompanied by some focus has been found to change behavior little, if at all [p. 493].

Unless focused feedback is provided, instructors often become preoccupied with the more superficial and cosmetic aspects of teaching. An example of this tendency occurred several years ago while the author was conducting a study of a teacher training program for university teaching assistants. The teaching assistants serving as the control group had been instructed to view their videotape alone at their own convenience. One of the few instructors who actually did view her tape mentioned that she gained a great deal from the experience. When asked to be more specific, all she could report was that she never realized before how much time she spent twirling her hair.

In order to obtain focused feedback, instructors may wish to view videotapes with an experienced colleague, after they have agreed to common goals and the type of feedback that is sought. Alternatively, instructors may arrange for a review session with an expert trained in teaching methods and observational techniques. Often a rating scale or observational checklist can facilitate the review, assuming that the instructor and the focuser have an opportunity to discuss the form in advance of the videotaping and playback. For example, a set of Videotape Self-Review Guides has been developed by the Office of Instructional Resources at the University of Illinois (307 Engineering Hall, Urbana, IL 61801). Each rating guide is designed to focus attention on a specific set of skills, such as organization and suitability of content, clarity of presentation, ability to question, and rapport with students. Another set of instruments and procedures has been published by Kindsvatter and Wilen (1977). These materials describe the use of questions, motivating and supporting behaviors, entry and closure skills, lecturing, and discussion.

On the basis of the research that they reviewed, Fuller and Manning (1973) recommended a number of practical guidelines for effective use of videotape playback. Although the conclusions were admittedly tentative, they remain the most informed principles available from the research conducted to date. A brief summary of the guidelines is as follows:

1. The recording setting should be typical rather than unusual.
2. The playback setting should be psychologically safe (e.g., confidential).
3. There should be prior agreement on the goals and behaviors to be focused on.
4. Optimum results are most likely with instructors who
   a. are genuinely interested in participating
   b. have personal concerns or goals related to teaching
   c. are young and intelligent
   d. have relatively good self-esteem
   e. are open to change and have the capacity for it
   f. are able to describe some deficiencies before playback
   g. are able to identify discrepancies between observed and expected performance
5. The feedback provided should be
   a. clearly focused on discrepancies that are moderate, rather than large or small
   b. unambiguous, trustworthy, informative
   c. accepted by the instructor as accurate
   d. balanced in terms of identifying strengths and weaknesses
   e. presented in a context in which treatments are available for establishing new behaviors
6. The persons serving as focusers should
   a. have previously been videotaped themselves
   b. communicate authenticity, positive regard, and empathy
   c. negotiate the goals of the video playback
   d. confront the instructor with moderate discrepancies
   e. be nonjudgmental toward the instructor.

Another factor to consider in video playback is the optimum amount of time between recording and critique. Fuller and Manning (1973) reported that the research on immediate versus delayed playback has generally been inconclusive. By allowing some time, rather than by providing immediate feedback, one is likely to increase the instructor's objectivity somewhat, but at the risk of some losses in memory and insight about the particular teaching episode on tape.

Finally, one must consider the choice between videotape and audiotape recordings. Again, the limited research is largely inconclusive. Some speculations from Fuller and Manning (1973), however, indicate the trade-offs to be considered:

> Apparently, listening to one's voice is like being given a little shake, but self-viewing is like a teeth-rattling blow. Subjects seem better able to sort out and select from audio tape. When the behavior of interest is mostly contained in the verbal interaction (as it is in counseling), audio playback may be as useful, and perhaps more useful, than video playback. However, when behaviors of interest are only partially represented by sound (such as teacher interactions with small children), the visual cues provided by video playback are essential. In addition, video may activate the person more than audio. . . .
>
> Video is arousing, self-involving, and should be used for individual but not group playback. Watching one's self remains interesting. Watching others becomes boring.
>
> In teacher education, video and audio might be combined. Once the neophyte has taught, even briefly, in the actual classroom and seen her own videotape, her system is aroused, ready for learning. Perhaps at that point, audio tape could be used for long-term practice towards improvement in the simulated situation [p. 492].

Thus far, we have discussed a general approach for reviewing videotape and audiotape recordings of regular classroom teaching, using the help of one or more focusers. We now examine three alternative techniques for accomplishing self-confrontation: micro-teaching, interpersonal process recall, and interaction analysis. Each of these methods helps teachers attend to their observational task, so that they can better assess their teaching performance.

Microteaching

Microteaching is a method for the systematic practice and critique of directly observable teaching skills (Allen and Ryan, 1969). Its basic premise is that teaching can be analyzed and improved by focusing on its component skills, such as introduction, presentation, questioning, use of examples, and closure.

Microteaching is probably best known as a technique for the preservice training of primary and secondary school teacher candidates. In its original form, microteaching was devised as a method for introducing prospective teachers to classroom settings in which they could obtain frequent practice and feedback on basic teaching skills. The settings were controlled, safe ones in which the novice teachers could experiment and feel open to criticism without the degree of fear and anxiety associated with traditional forms of practice teaching. In recent years, microteaching has been applied more generally to preservice and inservice training at all educational levels.

The microteaching process consists of short episodes (5 to 10 minutes) of practice teaching with a group of students or peers. The lesson is recorded and played back immediately on videotape or audiotape. Once the playback is completed, the presenter and other participants discuss the skills practiced during the episode according to the criteria identified before the lesson began. For example, the 5-minute lesson may have been designed as the opening (or closing) of a 50-minute lecture/demonstration. Feedback and critique would then focus on skills of introduction (or closure). By repeating the cycle, participants have an opportunity to improve the same skill or to practice additional skills.

Although the microteaching approach does allay much of the anxiety associated with being observed and evaluated during the course of one's regular teaching, the setting is an artificial one, and the scope and quality of the feedback are limited by the expertise and compliance of the participants. An experienced discussant is often needed to draw out the underlying criticisms and tensions, particularly among peers who wish, above all, to avoid confrontation. The success of the technique also hinges on clear specification of, and agreement beforehand about, the kind of feedback that is solicited. The presenter and observers must explicitly agree about the skills to be observed and the type of feedback to be offered. In short, microteaching is a good technique for getting instructors started in the use of video/audio critique, but it is limited in terms of the artificial setting employed and the type of feedback conveyed.

Interpersonal Process Recall

A detailed methodology of self-confrontation through review and recall of videotaped encounters has been developed and tested by Kagan (1975) and his colleagues at Michigan State University. Interpersonal Process Recall (IPR) has been used as a general tool for interpersonal skills training and has been applied most often to the training of counselors and therapists. More recently, it has been applied to teacher training, and a pilot study is now in progress in which the approach has been adapted for training graduate students as university teaching assistants. The methods and results of this study will be available in a forthcoming doctoral dissertation (Way, Note 3).

Videotape review sessions ordinarily include at least two participants from the videotaped interaction, for example, physician and patient, teacher and student. In addition, a trained "inquirer" serves as a facilitator and learner in the videotape playback sessions. The role of the inquirer is that of a passive and unbiased investigator. The inquirer asks questions and is reluctant to advise, direct, or contradict the other participants.

The role of the inquirer is clearly analogous to that of the focuser described by Fuller and Manning (1973). However, the emphasis in the IPR approach is on reciprocal feedback between the instructor and several of his or her students. As described in the text, videotapes, and transcripts of the IPR manual (Kagan, 1975), the trained inquirer must be skillful in identifying areas of confrontation, keeping the discussion on track, and leading the participants toward self-discovery.

The purpose of the playback session is that the participants gain insights by sharing their recall of the thoughts and feelings exhibited on videotape. Participants share the reasons for their own behaviors or statements, as well as the effects that the behaviors or statements of others had on them. Analyzing and comparing the two sources of thoughts and feelings associated with the same recorded events can be a powerful and profound lesson for instructors (and students) at all levels of training and experience. Through this process, it is hoped that instructors and students can achieve a greater understanding of the effects of their behavior on one another.

Interaction Analysis

Objective schemes are available for categorizing and counting the interactions that take place in the classroom. The purpose of such interaction analyses is to describe the types of activities that characterize one's teaching.

The observer assigns the behaviors observed on tape to one of the available categories on an interaction analysis scale. The tallies in each category are then summed to describe the patterns of interaction that took place. Although some systems of interaction analysis are too complex and too cumbersome for instructor self-evaluation, many systems are simple enough to tabulate for one's own recorded tapes.

One of the best known systems for interaction analysis in education is the Flanders (1970) Interaction Analysis Categories, which consist of 10 categories of classroom behavior. The categories can be readily learned and adapted to virtually all levels of teaching. By tabulating the Flanders categories, instructors can determine how much time they spend on direct modes of teaching (e.g., lecturing, criticizing, giving directions) versus indirect modes (e.g., asking questions, giving encouragement, accepting feelings, using student ideas). In addition, they can calculate how much time is devoted to the instructor's comments, student comments, and silence. By tabulating the results in the form of a matrix, they can also determine which categories of behavior tend to follow other categories. For example, are teacher questions generally followed by silence, student responses, student questions, or more teacher questions? By repeating the observations over several taped classes, instructors can compare their interaction patterns over time. Comparisons can also be made with normative data reported in the literature (Flanders, 1970).

Numerous alternative systems are available for interaction analysis. Powell (Note 4), in particular, has developed a system that combines ratings and interaction categories to quantify student tasks, teaching skills, classroom atmosphere, and leadership. Detailed behavioral descriptions have been developed for each item of the scale, resulting in high levels of interrater reliability. Other systems have adapted interaction analysis techniques for specific content areas, such as adaptations of the Flanders categories for science teachers.

To summarize, videotape and audiotape playback offer a wealth of information for self-evaluation. They can be incorporated with microteaching techniques to provide frequent practice and feedback on discrete, observable skills. Using the IPR approach, these recordings can serve as the source of extensive analysis and discussion. In both techniques, focused feedback is critical to the impact of the approach. Instructors typically derive very little simply by reviewing their tapes in isolation. Finally, additional insights can be obtained by quantifying one's observations of classroom activities using interaction analysis.

CONCLUSION

Self-evaluation plays an essential role in an overall program of faculty evaluation. By providing additional data and perspectives on teaching, self-assessment can contribute to the inferences and conclusions drawn in administrative decisions about teaching. Moreover, self-evaluation can be instrumental in gaining greater faculty participation in the improvement of teaching.

Institutions with newly developing programs of faculty evaluation can use self-evaluation as a logical point of departure. Institutions with existing programs of faculty evaluation would do well to reexamine the role of self-assessment and to include it in their programs. In general, the techniques described here tend to sharpen the inferences to be drawn from other sources of data, and they encourage a serious and objective investigation of one's own teaching.

REFERENCE NOTES

1. Clark, M. J. and R. Blackburn (1971) Assessment of faculty performance: Some correlates between self, colleagues, students, and administrators. Ann Arbor: University of Michigan, Center for the Study of Higher Education.

2. Murray, H. G. (1972) *The validity of student ratings of teaching ability.* Presented at the annual meeting of the Canadian Psychological Association, Montreal.

3. Way, D. (1980) Personal communication.

4. Powell, J. C. (1978) *Guidebook to the Teaching Performance Survey.* Windsor, Canada: Effectiveness Training Institute.

REFERENCES

Allen, D. W. and K. Ryan (1969) *Microteaching.* Reading, MA: Addison-Wesley.

Astin, A. W. and C. B. T. Lee (1967) "Current practices in the evaluation and training of college teachers," in C. B. T. Lee (ed.), *Improving College Teaching.* Washington, DC: American Council on Education.

Blackburn, R. T. and M. J. Clark (1975) "An assessment of faculty performance: Some correlates between administrator, colleague, student, and self ratings." *Sociology of Education,* 48: 242–256.

Centra, J. A. (1973) "Self ratings of college teachers: A comparison with student ratings." *Journal of Educational Measurement,* 10: 287–295.

——— (1972) *Strategies for Improving College Teaching.* Washington, DC: American Association for Higher Education.

Doyle, K. O. and L. I. Crichton (1978) "Student, peer, and self evaluations of college instructors." *Journal of Educational Psychology,* 70: 815–826.

Flanders, N. A. (1970) *Analyzing Teaching Behavior.* Reading, MA: Addison-Wesley.

Fuller, F. F. and B. A. Manning (1973) "Self-confrontation reviewed: A conceptualization for video playback in teacher education." *Review of Educational Research,* 43: 469–528.

Genova, W. J., M. K. Madoff, R. Chin, and G. B. Thomas (1976) *Mutual Benefit Evaluation of Faculty and Administrators in Higher Education.* Cambridge, MA: Ballinger.

Kagan, N. (1975) *Interpersonal Process Recall: A Method of Influencing Human Interaction.* Mason, MI: Mason Media.

Kindsvatter, R. and W. W. Wilen (1977) "Improving classroom instruction: A self- and shared-analysis approach," in S. C. Scholl and S. C. Inglis (eds.), *Teaching in Higher Education: Readings for Faculty.* Columbus: Ohio Board of Regents.

Maslow, A. H. and W. Zimmerman (1956) "College teaching ability, scholarly activity, and personality." *Journal of Educational Psychology,* 47: 185–189.

Miller, R. I. (1972) *Evaluating Faculty Performance.* San Francisco: Jossey-Bass.

Pambookian, H. S. (1976) "Discrepancy between instructor and student evaluations of instruction: Effect on instructor." *Instructional Science,* 5: 63–75.

——— (1974) "Initial level of student evaluation of instruction as a source of influence on instructor change after feedback." *Journal of Educational Psychology,* 66: 52–56.

Seldin, P. (1975) *How Colleges Evaluate Professors.* Croton-on-Hudson, NY: Blythe-Pennington.

Sweeney, J. M. and A. F. Grasha (1978) "Improving teaching through faculty development triads." *Improving College and University Teaching Yearbook.* Corvallis: Oregon State University Press.

PART III

Systemic Uses of Evidence

Whereas the preceding section of this volume provided information about and suggestions for developing and using specific data-gathering procedures, Part III focuses on the use of these individual techniques in a systemwide teacher evaluation plan. The chapters are roughly ordered from descriptions of specific strategies to discussions of teacher evaluation in the larger contexts of politics, morality, and the law.

Chapter 12 contains a practical discussion of the assumptions, prerequisites, and procedures crucial to the effective implementation of contract plans. The emphasis is on teacher evaluation as a professional growth process directed toward the personal needs of the teacher as well as toward the achievement of the objectives of the educational organization. Examples illustrate the application of contract plans in school and college settings.

The next two chapters consider, respectively, formative and summative teacher evaluation systems. Methods by which teachers can use evaluation information to improve their future instruction are described in Chapter 13. The effectiveness of different approaches to using feedback for improving teaching is discussed. Factors that influence the effectiveness of an evaluation-based teacher development program are considered.

A strong point of view about summative teacher evaluation is presented in Chapter 14. The chapter begins with a discussion of the conditions that must be present in a school or college before a proper and effective teacher evaluation system can proceed. Appropriate and inappropriate methods for conducting summative teacher evaluation are identified. The chapter concludes with a discussion of some ethical constraints on teacher evaluation.

Conflicting demands and needs give a political character to teacher evaluation. Events leading to this conflict and the views and roles of participating groups are identified in two complementary chapters, 15 and 16. Strategies for dealing with conflicting views of evaluation are described and illustrated. Guidelines for implementing teacher evaluation systems, with particular attention to those proposed by teacher unions, are offered.

The final chapter, Chapter 17, contains a discussion of theoretical concepts of fairness that pertain to teacher evaluation systems and a review of legal and contractual facts about such systems. Standards for a fair and legal teacher evaluation system are suggested. A general model for a teacher evaluation system that relies on the preceding moral and legal discussion is presented.

CHAPTER 12

CONTRACT PLANS
A Professional Growth-Oriented Approach to Evaluating Teacher Performance

EDWARD F. IWANICKI
University of Connecticut

The movement toward increased accountability in education has led schools, colleges, and universities to develop or refine further their teacher appraisal systems. As educators search for more effective approaches to teacher evaluation, they soon find that the issue is not which approach is the most effective but, rather, which approach is the most effective for a specific purpose. Reviews of teacher evaluation techniques (McNeil and Popham, 1973; Haefele, 1980) indicate clearly that contract plans are an effective technique when the purpose of evaluation is to improve teacher performance through a professional development program tailored to the needs of the teacher. If the purpose of teacher evaluation is to rank or compare teachers, other techniques should be explored.

The contract plan approach is commonly viewed as a process in which the teacher and the evaluator cooperatively work through the following steps of the evaluation cycle:

(1) Teacher performance is reviewed.
(2) Priority areas for improvement are identified.
(3) An improvement plan containing performance objectives is developed for each priority area.
(4) The improvement plan is implemented and monitored.
(5) The impact of the improvement plan on teacher performance is evaluated.

The assumption underlying contract plans is that teachers are competent professionals seeking to strengthen or improve particular aspects of their performance through the professional growth process. As educational institutions, programs, and the needs of students change, it is necessary for teachers to participate in professional development activities that enable them to deal effectively with these changes.

Through the contract plan approach, teachers develop performance objectives, which serve as a basis for their evaluation. Often these objectives are not the sole basis for their evaluation. Usually teachers are evaluated not only on their performance as it relates to their objectives but also on their performance as it relates to the responsibilities stated in their job description. For example, a university professor addressed some very challenging objectives focusing on providing service to the community. This faculty member did an outstanding job in accomplishing these objectives, but failed to meet regularly scheduled classes while engaged in community service activities. When evaluated at the end of the year, this professor was commended for his outstanding community service, but, much to his displeasure, he was reprimanded for not being more conscientious in fulfilling his teaching responsibilities. To avoid such situations, it is very important that teachers clearly understand that their performance as it relates to their objectives is only one part of the overall teacher evaluation process.

TWO APPROACHES

Contract plans can be implemented either in a manner oriented toward the philosophy and assumptions of management by objectives (MBO) or toward those of clinical supervision, depending on how a teacher's performance objectives are determined. When the MBO approach developed in business and industry (Drucker, 1973; Odiorne, 1965) is used, priority objectives are set for the organization and its subunits through a review of the mission, purpose, and long-range goals of the organization. For example, a university could set some priority objectives for providing service to the public. Given this focus, schools and departments would set their own objectives for providing public service. Then, through the contract plan process, faculty members within these schools and departments would develop performance objectives for providing service to the public. Each teacher's performance objectives are, therefore, largely a function of the priority objectives set by the school organization.

Clinical supervision (Cogan, 1973; Goldhammer, 1969) evolved in education from the need to provide teachers with a highly personalized system of guidance and support in the professional development process. When the contract plans approach to teacher evaluation is oriented toward the philosophy and assumptions of clinical supervision, a staff member's performance is analyzed as it relates to his or her unique role in the school organization. Then, objectives are set to strengthen the teacher's performance as it relates to that role. During the process of developing these performance objectives, the personal needs of the teacher receive the most consideration.

Because these different approaches to contract plans exist, when performance objectives are set with teachers, a decision must be made as to whether these objectives should be directed toward the needs of the organization, the needs of the teacher, or both. From this author's experience, contract plans have not been successful in situations in which either a largely MBO-oriented or a largely clinical supervision-oriented approach has been implemented. In settings in which personal needs received priority in developing performance objectives, teachers have tended to be satisfied with their professional growth, but appreciable changes in the overall quality of the educational program have not been observed. Teachers were growing in so many diverse areas that a cumulative effect was not perceived.

Where MBO-oriented approaches have been implemented, teachers have tended to feel that they were being manipulated or coerced into developing objectives in areas defined by the administration. In some school systems, administrators have tried to alleviate this problem by asking staff to set at least one performance objective directed toward the priorities set by the administration. Then other objectives could be directed toward personal priorities. Teachers have tended to react to such a compromise negatively, as evidenced by comments such as, "After all, we know which objectives will receive the most weight in the final evaluation, those directed toward the administration's priorities."

Some may disagree with these observations and cite situations in which largely MBO-oriented or clinical supervision-oriented approaches to contract plans have produced positive results. This can and does happen in highly synergistic organizations. Here it is easier to decide whether personal or organizational needs should receive priority when performance objectives are being developed, because of the closer alignment of these needs in a synergistic setting. Sergiovanni (1974) provides an excellent discussion of the issues one needs to examine when assessing the level of synergy in a school organization as well as the implications of organizational synergy for the effective implementation of teacher evaluation programs.

However, the issue here is not which approach is better. If the purpose of teacher evaluation practices is to improve the quality of educational programs, they must contribute to the needs of the organization as well as to the needs of individuals within the organization. It is essential for schools to engage in systematic planning activities, as identified in MBO approaches. At the same time, schools should provide teachers with a personalized system of guidance and support in the professional development process, as advocated in clinical supervision.

SOME PREREQUISITES FOR EFFECTIVE IMPLEMENTATION

Contract plans cannot be designed and implemented effectively unless a firm foundation has been set for the teacher evaluation process. Proper planning and organization are crucial in securing the commitment of staff to the concepts and processes of teacher evaluation. It is human nature that we commit ourselves to processes that are effective as well as to processes in which we have a vested interest. Through appropriate planning a school system, college, or university increases its chances of developing a teacher evaluation program that is both effective and accepted by staff. Unless staff accept the fact that effective teacher evaluation is an integral part of their professional responsibility, it is most difficult to build a commitment to contract plans.

This advice to plan is often met with skepticism. Why plan when we can evaluate? After all, school organization X has a good teacher evaluation program. Why not implement this program in our setting? This orientation points to two problems. The first is what Odiorne (1974) calls the "activity trap," which depicts educators as conditioned to perceive their roles as activity-oriented rather than as a combination of planning and activity. Applied to teacher evaluation, the activity trap gives the act of evaluating teachers paramount importance and places less value on planning the evaluation process. Odiorne would contend that the low value placed on systematic planning is a limiting factor in the quest for quality teacher evaluation programs.

The second problem is the "transplant problem." Here, a school organization assumes that it does not need to plan its own teacher evaluation program, since it can acquire a quality evaluation program from another setting. When attempts are made to conduct such transplants, however, it is soon found that the differences in the administrative, staff, program, and material resources between the two settings make it impossible to implement the teacher evaluation program in the new setting without considerable modification. Usually the amounts of time and money needed to make such modifications are similar to, if not greater than, the resources that the organization would have expended if it had decided to plan its own teacher evaluation program. These comments about the transplant problem are not presented to discourage school systems from working together in the development of their teacher evaluation programs or from sharing worthwhile teacher evaluation techniques. Such activities can be very beneficial provided that a school system's decision to adopt particular processes or techniques is made because these approaches are consistent with its own plan for teacher evaluation.

Role of Philosophy, Goals, and Objectives

The philosophy, goals, and objectives of a school organization provide the foundation for planning an effective teacher evaluation program. Any evaluation of teacher performance must be made in light of what the school organization believes its mission to be and in light of the general educational purposes that it hopes to achieve. As a school organization begins to plan its teacher evaluation program, it should review its philosophy and goal statements to be sure that they truly reflect the priority educational concerns of the school community. Once a representative philosophy and goals statement is developed, it is important to operationalize the goals in measurable or observable terms through the development of program objectives. A representative statement of the philosophy, goals, and program objectives clearly conveys the outcomes the school organization hopes to achieve.

Developing Job Descriptions

Given this statement, job descriptions can be developed specifying the performance criteria expected of staff responsible for facilitating these outcomes. Job descriptions are essential to the contract plan approach, since they describe the behaviors expected of a teacher in a particular position. Because these behaviors are the criteria that will be used in evaluating a teacher's performance, they should be identified through a review of the competency areas that the literature has identified as crucial to teacher effectiveness within the program context in which the teacher is operating. Job descriptions should be specific enough to communicate clearly to teachers the criteria that will be used to evaluate their performance. A brief, globally stated job description tends to be more susceptible to varying interpretations and tends to create more ambiguity than a comprehensive and more specific job description. In the example below, the specific criteria (Enfield Connecticut Public Schools, Note 1) communicate more clearly to the teacher what is expected in the areas of colleague and parent interaction than the global criterion statement. It is much easier to identify areas in which improvement in performance is needed using the specific criteria than when using the global criterion statement:

Global Criterion Statement:
   The teacher interacts effectively with colleagues and parents.

Specific Criteria:
   The teacher
   (1) is willing to cooperate with coworkers by sharing ideas and methods of
      instruction

(2) exhibits ethical behavior toward fellow teachers and coworkers

(3) attends committee and faculty meetings

(4) seeks assistance, advice, and guidance as necessary from colleagues and/or specialists

(5) confers, when necessary and possible, with parents to foster a constructive parent-teacher relationship

(6) involves parents in class-related activities when appropriate [p. 44].

A major portion of the competencies presented in most job descriptions are relevant for all teachers. The remaining competencies are important for some teachers and not for others, depending on factors such as grade level, subject, and background of the students being taught. Since competencies may vary somewhat among teachers, it is important that teachers know specifically which competencies will be used to evaluate their performance. This issue is particularly relevant in higher education, where many universities have developed a broad statement of the responsibilities of teaching faculty. Many a promotion decision has been contested because a faculty member's responsibilities as they relate to this statement were not understood clearly.

Defining Accountability Relationships

Before contract plans can be implemented effectively, it is essential for teachers to know to whom they are accountable in the evaluation process. In defining these accountability relationships, many issues need to be considered, such as the role and responsibilities of the teacher, the professional background of the evaluators, and the available time of the evaluator. It is also essential for teachers to know who is primarily responsible for evaluating their performance and to understand clearly the role of any other persons involved in the evaluation process.

As organizational size and teacher specialization increase, these accountability relationships become more difficult to define. Since curriculum or subject matter expertise is a crucial ingredient in the teacher evaluation process, many schools are moving away from the traditional approach of placing the responsibility for evaluation solely in the hands of administrators. In these settings, department chairpersons, team leaders, and curriculum resource personnel are assuming a more active role in the teacher evaluation process.

Defining the Purposes of Evaluation

It is crucial that teachers understand the purposes for which they are being evaluated. Bolton (1973) has identified the following purposes for teacher evaluation:

(1) improvement of instruction
(2) rewarding superior performance
(3) modification of assignment
(4) protection of individuals and the organization
(5) validation of the selection process
(6) promotion of individual growth and self-evaluation [pp. 99–101].

Some studies (American Association of School Administrators, Note 2; Palmer et al., Note 3; Hickox and Rooney, Note 4) have indicated that the primary purpose of teacher evaluation has been the improvement of instruction. Some states, such as Connecticut, have passed legislation that states that "the primary purpose of teacher evaluation is the improvement of the student learning experience" (Connecticut State Department of Education, Note 5, p. 2). As a teacher evaluation program is developed, it is important to review the potential purposes of evaluation and to set priorities. The more these priorities focus on the improvement of teacher performance through the professional development process, the more appropriate is the contract plan approach.

Setting worthwhile purposes alone will not produce the desired results unless the leadership in the school organization makes a strong commitment to these purposes, both philosophically and through the allocation of the necessary resources to design and implement effective teacher evaluation procedures consistent with these purposes. Zimmerer and Stroh (1974) note that "the most essential element in achieving a workable performance appraisal system in any organization is the support and commitment of top managers" (p. 39).

The Enfield (Connecticut) Public Schools Teacher Evaluation Philosophy, Purposes, and Guiding Principles (Note 1, pp. 2–3), presented in Figure 1, is an example of how one school system defined its purposes for teacher evaluation and then built a commitment to these purposes. Here, purposes were developed for the teacher evaluation process consistent with the philosophy of the system. Then, a commitment to its purposes was built by stating guiding principles that insure that the teacher evaluation process will be conducted in a manner consistent with the purposes defined.

Summary

Contract plans cannot be designed and implemented effectively unless a firm foundation has been set for the teacher evaluation process. In building this foundation, the school organization must commit itself to the process of planning a teacher evaluation program consistent with its unique needs. Before these teacher evaluation activities can focus on the design of an approach to contract plans, the school, college, or university must address

Central to the teacher evaluation process in Enfield is the belief that "A teachers' role is to facilitate, stimulate, and guide the learning of students, other teachers, and community members." The teacher will be an active participant in each learning situation and will be concerned with the intellectual, social, and emotional progress of his/her students.

Given this belief as stated in the Philosophy and Goals of the Enfield Public Schools, as well as in Connecticut's Teacher Evaluation Law (Section 10-151b), the following purposes and guiding principles have been established for the teacher evaluation process:

PURPOSES for which teacher evaluation will be used are as follows:

1. To improve instruction.

2. To provide a positive learning experience for the student and teacher.

3. To encourage teacher creativity and experimentation in the learning process.

4. To provide a means by which the teacher will continually analyze and assess his or her professional strengths and weaknesses.

5. To provide a means through which the evaluator and evaluatee will cooperatively identify teacher strengths and weaknesses as well as approaches for reinforcing strengths and overcoming weaknesses.

6. In addition to the prior purposes, teacher evaluation information may be used by the administration to make recommendations concerning continued employment of personnel, the granting of continuing contracts, the granting of increments, and/or other recommendations to the Board of Education.

GUIDING PRINCIPLES for the teacher evaluation process.

1. A fundamental guiding principle is that all evaluations will be the result of a cooperative process where a positive atmosphere is maintained between evaluator and evaluatee in the assessment of teacher performance.

2. The evaluator and evaluatee will cooperatively develop the criteria which will serve as a basis for the teacher evaluation process.

3. Every reasonable effort will be made to ensure that the teacher knows:

    a) the person(s) responsible for his/her evaluation, and
    b) the process by which he/she will be evaluated.

4. The general responsibilities and specific tasks of the teacher's position will be comprehensively defined, and this definition will serve as a frame of reference for teacher evaluation.

5. Self-evaluation will be an aspect of the evaluation process, and teachers will be given the opportunity to evaluate themselves in positive and constructive ways.

6. Evaluation will be more diagnostic than judgmental.

7. The evaluation process will provide for clear, personalized, constructive feedback.

8. Evaluation will take into consideration influences on the learning environment such as material and professional resources as well as external influences on both teachers and students.

9. All evaluations will take place without any bias as to race, creed, religion, national origin, sex, age, or residency.

Figure 1. Enfield Public Schools' teacher evaluation philosophy, purposes, and guiding principles.

some crucial prerequisite issues. These issues, as well as the action one would take in dealing with them, are summarized below:

Issue	**Action**
What outcomes does the school organization hope to achieve?	Develop a representative statement of philosophy, goals, and program objectives.
To achieve these outcomes, what performance expectations does the school organization hold for teachers?	Develop teacher job descriptions.
Who will be responsible for the evaluation of teachers?	Define staff accountability relationships.
Why are teachers being evaluated?	Define the purposes of teacher evaluation.
How committed is the school organization to the design and implementation of an effective teacher evaluation program? What resources will be allocated for this purpose?	Develop a process for conveying to staff the level of commitment the organization is placing on teacher evaluation as well as the resources being made available to support this commitment.

Based on this author's experience, attempts to design and implement contract plan approaches successfully are affected by the extent to which these prerequisite issues are addressed properly.

BASIC STEPS

Approaches to contract plans (Redfern, 1980; Lewis, 1973; Armstrong, 1973) differ depending on the assumptions made about the roles of the teacher and the evaluator in the process. In some approaches, the teacher assumes more responsibility for identifying improvement areas and developing performance objectives than in others. The position taken in this chapter is that the evaluator should assume responsibility for orienting the teacher to the processes of identifying improvement areas and developing performance objectives. After being oriented to and guided through these processes, the teacher should assume increased responsibility in these areas. The procedures advocated are based on the following assumptions:

(1) Self-evaluation is an essential component of the contract plan approach.
(2) The evaluator is responsible for working with the teacher to develop those skills crucial to the effective self-evaluation of one's performance.

(3) As the contract plan approach evolves, the role of the evaluator should become less directive and focus more on guiding, supporting, and monitoring the professional growth of the teacher in a supervisory manner.

(4) Increased responsibility for the evaluation of performance should be assumed by the teacher.

Before proceeding, it is important to discuss these assumptions. From theory and practice, two issues are clear. First, professional growth is a function of the teacher's ability to recognize the need for and to assume the responsibility for growth. Second, given the high teacher-evaluator ratios in many school organizations, the evaluator does not have sufficient time during the conferencing process both to draw out those areas in which the teacher perceives a need for growth and to plan and build commitment to a program of professional growth, unless the teacher has conducted a thorough self-evaluation of his or her performance before the conference. The self-evaluation process has received considerable emphasis in the assumptions presented, since both the effectiveness and the efficiency of the conferencing process depend upon the teachers' ability to assess their performance, identify valid areas for improvement, and plan appropriate professional development activities.

This emphasis on self-evaluation and the increased responsibility of the teacher in the evaluation process should not be construed as a move to diminish the leadership role of the evaluator. As the teacher and the evaluator confer to discuss potential growth areas and professional development strategies, the teacher should be allowed to assume an active role as long as the directions being proposed are valid. To the extent that the teacher cannot assume such an active role or proposes directions that the evaluator does not perceive as valid, then the evaluator should assume a more dominant role. The role of the evaluator is to lead as the need arises. Otherwise, the teacher should assume responsibility. This orientation will be clarified further as the specific steps in the contract plan approach are discussed in subsequent sections. The steps are as follows:

(1) Teacher conducts self-evaluation and identifies areas in which a need for improvement is perceived.

(2) Teacher develops draft performance contract(s).

(3) Teacher and evaluator confer to discuss the teacher self-evaluation information, the draft performance contract(s), and the evaluator's perception of areas in which improvement is needed in an effort to reach agreement on the specifics of the performance contract(s) for the current evaluation cycle.

(4) Teacher and evaluator confer periodically to monitor progress toward the accomplishment of the objective(s) stated in the performance contract(s).

(5) Teacher and evaluator confer near the end of the evaluation cycle to assess the extent to which objectives have been accomplished as well as to discuss future directions for improvement, which could be included in the teacher's performance contract during the next evaluation cycle.

Teacher Conducts Self-Evaluation and Identifies Improvement Areas

Teachers should be oriented to self-evaluation techniques for identifying valid areas for improvement. Although a broad range of self-evaluation techniques are presented in the literature (Carroll, the previous chapter; Iwanicki and McEachern, Note 6), a commonly used approach is for teachers to review their performance as it relates to their job description. A quality job description can be converted quite easily into a self-evaluation form by asking the teacher to identify those areas in which most improvement is desired. For example, one school system organized its teacher job description into a self-evaluation form using the format presented in Table 1 (Enfield Connecticut Public Schools, Note 1, p. 5). In using this form, teachers were instructed to rate themselves on each item in which improvement was desired by drawing an arrow from their present position on the scale to the point they wished to reach. The resulting arrows served as visual indicators of the relative amount of improvement desired across the items comprising the self-evaluation form. A space was also provided for teachers to comment on their ratings.

After the teacher has completed a self-evaluation, priority areas for professional improvement must be identified. This is sometimes difficult. Priority improvement areas are identified on the basis of personal judgment, possibly supplemented by advice from peer teachers and supervisory staff. Some crucial factors to consider when identifying those areas in which a change in teacher behavior would be most beneficial are the following:

(1) time required to bring about the change
(2) personnel, material, and financial resources needed to bring about the change
(3) impact of the change on teacher performance in the classroom

TABLE 1   Self-Evaluation Form

	Needs Considerable Improvement	Needs Some Improvement	Satisfactory	Above Average	Superior
Encourages full pupil participation in the learning process	1	2	3	4	5
Comments:					

(4) impact of the change on pupil learning
(5) impact of the change on the accomplishment of priority school or departmental objectives.

Once priority areas for improvement have been identified, the teacher can proceed to develop a draft performance contract for each area.

Teacher Develops Draft Performance Contract(s)

A performance contract is a plan for describing, monitoring, and evaluating the professional development activities of a teacher. Before drafting a performance contract, teachers should be oriented to a format they can follow. In working with schools, this author has found the basic format below to be effective when developing performance contracts.

(1) *Performance objective:* a statement of (a) the area needing improvement, (b) the rationale for focusing on this area, and (c) the outcome or product the teacher hopes to accomplish in this area.
(2) *Plan of action:* a description and schedule of activities relevant to accomplishing the performance objective.
(3) *Special operational requirements:* the material and personnel resources needed to accomplish the performance objective.
(4) *Procedures for evaluation:* the procedures to be used to evaluate progress toward and achievement of the performance objective.

This format can be modified depending on the needs of the school organization. In the example presented in Figure 2, this school system found it more useful to omit the section on special operational requirements and to include a section for rationale. In developing forms, titles such as "Improvement Plan" or "Professional Development Plan" have been substituted for "Performance Contract," since teachers felt that "Performance Contract" connoted a process more legally than professionally oriented. Some teachers have commented that "Performance Contract" sounds too much like contract negotiations. The issue here is not what the form is called, but rather whether the form is effective in guiding teachers in the process of planning their improvement strategies.

When drafting a performance contract, some teachers experience difficulty in stating their objective due to confusion resulting from the different ways in which the term *objective* has been defined in education. It is important to explain to teachers that two complementary categories of objectives transcend the educational process, student performance objectives and teacher performance objectives. Student performance objectives describe

Teacher _____ Position _____

1. *Desired Outcomes*—What areas do you want to strengthen?

   I will provide learning experiences during this school year which will encourage more pupil participation in the area of Social Studies.

2. *Rationale*—Why do you want to strengthen this area?

   My teaching is too directive, not allowing for self-initiated study.

3. What is your *plan* of action?

   In three different units during the year, students will work on the following three activities to encourage pupil participation.

   a. Individual written reports of their choice.

   b. Student-Initiated panel discussions.

   c. Art bulletin board projects in their area of interest.

4. What are the *criteria for evaluation?*

   A log will be kept to determine whether or not each child has participated in these project as outlned. Examples of projects will be kept.

Figure 2. A sample performance contract. (Adapted from a form used by Enfield, Connecticut, Public Schools.)

the educational outcomes expected of the students. Teacher performance objectives describe what the teacher is going to do to facilitate those expected student outcomes. When a teacher performance objective is being drafted, the focus is placed on the activity that the teacher will pursue as well as its anticipated impact on students' behavior in the classroom. In some cases, the impact of the teacher's activities are assessed later by looking at their affect on student performance.

Since a performance contract is drafted for each professional improvement area, teachers often ask how many improvement areas should be addressed during a year. This number varies, depending on the complexity of the areas addressed and the particular professional development activities planned by the teacher. Some may draft only one contract, and others more than three. The average is two to three performance contracts. The issue is not how many, but rather how worthwhile.

In assessing the overall quality of the performance contract being developed, it is important for the teacher to consider the following questions:

(1) Does the performance contract identify specific outcomes which can be observed or measured?
(2) Does the performance contract identify the means and criteria by which the desired outcome(s) will be evaluated?
(3) Does the performance contract specify a projected date for accomplishment of the outcome(s)?
(4) Does the performance contract avoid contradiction with system, building, and/or departmental objectives?
(5) Is the performance contract realistic and challenging?
(6) Is the performance contract consistent with available and anticipated resources?
(7) Does the performance contract lead to strengthened professional competencies and/or improved student learning?

To this point, the teacher has conducted a self-evaluation, has identified priority improvement areas, and has drafted a performance contract for each priority area. This information is now discussed with the evaluator in what is commonly called the goal- or objective-setting conference, since the focus is on the teacher's performance objectives as stated in the contract.

Teacher and Evaluator Confer to Discuss and Finalize Performance Contract

The objective-setting conference is a critical step in the contract plan approach. The teacher and the evaluator meet to discuss the teacher's performance and to plan the teacher's future professional development activi-

1. Avoid the "boss complex." Help the teacher feel that the principal doesn't consider himself foremost as a member of the "administrative hierarchy."

2. Clarify the role of the principal and teacher in the evaluation setting.

3. Seek to establish that both the teacher and the principal should be primarily concerned with the educational welfare of the pupils rather than their own self-interest.

4. Be conscious that the evaluator's personality, as well as that of the evaluatee—good or bad, will have an influence upon achievable results in the conference.

5. Strive for unity in leadership effort and action among all administrators in the building.

6. Be willing to let the teacher express his feelings in the conference without risk of censure or reprisal even if they may be markedly different from those of the evaluator.

7. Provide for privacy.

8. Safeguard the confidential nature of any matter requiring it.

9. Avoid asking for opinions on the spot; allow time for consideration.

10. Strive for a climate of mutual respect.

11. Be prepared to take as well as to give.

12. Be honestly committed to the concept that teacher, principal, and supervisor are members of a team working for the best interests of a good educational program.

13. Take the initiative in encouraging the teacher to make constructive criticisms.

14. Provide opportunity for the discussion of school problems.

15. Invite suggestions; when made, try to do something about them.

16. Don't give the teacher the brush-off when problems are presented.

17. Try to be aware of what the teacher is doing in his classes; be conversant with general developments in his field of specialization. Leave the technical aspects to the supervisor.

18. Don't talk too much; don't let the teacher talk too little.

Figure 3. Some guidelines for orienting school principles to effective conferencing practices. (Source: Redfern, Note 7, pp. 45-46.) Permission granted by George B. Redfern.

---

ties. Both parties need to share their perceptions in an open, positive, and constructive manner. It is sometimes difficult to approach the process in such a trusting manner because of the image of evaluation and the evaluator that has been promulgated in education over the years. To overcome this image, both the teacher and the evaluator need to understand clearly the purpose of the conference as well as their roles and responsibilities during the conference. Figure 3 contains some guidelines, which are most helpful when orienting school principals, department chairpersons, or evaluators in any school organization to effective conferencing practices. With slight modification, these guidelines are also appropriate for orienting teachers to the responsibilities of the evaluator in the conferencing process.

During the objective-setting conference, the teacher and the evaluator are to reach agreement on those priority performance objectives to be addressed by the teacher during the evaluation cycle. Once these objectives are agreed upon, consensus should be reached about the other components of the performance contract, such as the activities that the teacher will pursue in relation to each objective and the procedures for monitoring progress toward as well as accomplishment of each objective. To guide this process, attention should focus on those seven questions presented earlier in the chapter for assessing the quality of performance contracts.

It is important to emphasize that, in schools in which contract plans have been planned and implemented properly, the objective setting conference is, with few exceptions, a positive experience for the teacher and the evaluator, during which they can discuss the teacher's performance and mutually agree upon the priority objectives to be pursued. As each performance contract is finalized, both the teacher and evaluator should

(1) understand the contract
(2) know who is responsible for each part of the contract
(3) know what results are expected
(4) know how these results will be evaluated.

If agreement cannot be reached about an aspect of the performance contract, the impasse can be resolved either formally or informally. Formal procedures consist of bringing the issue to the attention of a representative arbitration board. In practice, this approach has two weaknesses. First, the logistics involved in convening a meeting of this board make it difficult to resolve the impasse in a timely manner. Second, this board reviews the case presented by the teacher and the case presented by the evaluator and then renders a decision. A decision is made about the teacher's contract by persons who are not directly accountable for the teacher's performance. The evaluator, who is usually an administrator, is placed in the precarious position of being accountable for the teacher's performance, but lacking the authority to control whether a teacher improves his or her performance in an area perceived as crucial to the quality of the educational program. In settings in which the formal arbitration approach is used, evaluators tend to feel that their authority is undermined somewhat and, thus, take the road of least resistance in setting performance objectives with their teachers.

Informal procedures for resolving an impasse consist of a meeting of the teacher, the evaluator, and third parties selected by both. These third parties are persons familiar with the school setting as well as with the issues relevant to the problem. At this meeting, the situation is discussed, and the third parties share their views on the issue. Then the evaluator and the teacher confer to discuss the situation further and to decide which performance objectives should be pursued, as well as the manner in which they will be accomplished and evaluated.

The advantage of this process is that a third-party perspective is provided, but the teacher and the evaluator are forced to resolve the problem themselves through continued dialogue. This informal approach to resolving an impasse is strongly supported by the supervision literature as more effective in promoting teacher growth than the decision of an arbitration board. Even if a teacher may not agree with the final outcome of the informal process, the teacher will at least clearly understand why the evaluator wants a particular area addressed.

Monitoring Teacher Progress

The purpose of monitoring teacher progress is to provide a guidance and support system for teachers as they pursue the objectives specified in their performance contracts. In practice, teacher progress is monitored both on a formal and an informal basis. On a formal basis, the teacher and the evaluator confer at various times during the year to discuss the teacher's progress. Depending on the nature of the objectives set by the teacher, these conferences may be held in conjunction with an observation of the teacher's performance. At the conclusion of the formal conferences, a written report of the teacher's progress is prepared. Usually, two to three such formal conferences are held during the evaluation cycle. Informal conferences differ from formal conferences in that a written report is not prepared. Sufficient numbers of formal and informal conferences should be conducted to provide teachers with the assistance needed to achieve their objectives. Some teachers need more conferences than others, depending on the nature of their objectives and the amount of support and guidance needed.

Support can be provided by complimenting as well as by helping a teacher. Some evaluators feel that more conferences should be held with teachers experiencing difficulty in accomplishing their objectives than with those experiencing success. The literature on motivation does not support this practice. Teachers need a "pat on the back" to reinforce their positive efforts as much as they need help in those areas in which they are encountering difficulty.

As the teacher and the evaluator confer to discuss progress toward objectives, a performance contract can be modified. For instance, if a teacher's professional development activities are not producing the desired results, they can be revised. Also, if it becomes evident that the outcomes of an objective are unrealistic, they may be adjusted appropriately. Any mutually agreed upon changes in a performance contract should be made during a formal conference and recorded in the written conference report.

Final Evaluation of Teacher Performance

Near the end of the evaluation cycle, the teacher and the evaluator meet to assess the extent to which performance objectives have been accomplished. During this conference, it is important to discuss the teacher's as well as the evaluator's perceptions of the extent to which each objective has been achieved in light of the activities and evaluation procedures specified in the performance contract. At the conclusion of this conference, a written final evaluation report is prepared by the evaluator and shared with the teacher.

The final evaluation conference is also an opportune time to initiate the development of performance objectives for the next evaluation cycle. Some of these objectives could simply be a continuation or extension of those objectives already pursued by the teacher. Other objectives could address new priority improvement areas.

It is not always necessary for a teacher to accomplish all of his or her objectives to receive a positive or even an outstanding final evaluation. The evaluator and the teacher must review and discuss the efforts that the teacher has made to accomplish the objectives in light of the end product. It is conceivable that a teacher could have spent considerable effort in a very challenging area in which appreciable results have not been observed. This teacher could still receive a favorable evaluation. For example, perhaps a teacher has encountered major problems in implementing some new curriculum materials. Although this teacher devoted considerable time and effort to adapting these materials to the needs of the students, more time is needed to assess their true impact. In such cases, the evaluator could document and commend the teacher for the fine work exhibited as well as recommend that the teacher continue to pursue this objective during the next evaluation cycle.

This final decision as to whether a teacher has attempted to accomplish the objectives in a conscientious manner is difficult to make unless the evaluator has monitored the teacher's progress continuously. Such systematic monitoring is a prerequisite for making effective end-of-cycle decisions about a teacher's performance. In the event that the teacher does not agree with any aspect of the evaluator's final report, many schools have made provisions for the teacher to file a written self-evaluation of his or her performance as it relates to the objectives specified in the contract plan.

SUGGESTED STRATEGIES FOR IMPLEMENTATION

When planning the teacher evaluation process, it is important to involve all groups affected by the process. This can be accomplished by forming a steering committee composed of administrators, teachers, and representatives of the teacher bargaining group. It is better to involve the bargaining group in the development of the evaluation process rather than to negotiate the process later at the bargaining table. This steering committee is responsible for designing, implementing, and evaluating the contract plan approach used in the school. During the design phase, this committee deals with the prerequisites to the teacher evaluation process discussed earlier in this chapter as well as with coordinating and overseeing the development of the specific procedures to be followed in the contract plan approach. The product of the design phase should be a draft handbook or guide describing the rationale for the contract plan approach as well as the procedures to be followed by teachers and evaluators. It is important that these procedures are described clearly and that they are realistic given the time, personnel, and material resources available to both the teacher and the evaluator.

Once a draft handbook is prepared, the process described should be pilot-tested with a sample of volunteer teachers and evaluators. Usually teachers and evaluators are most willing to participate in this pilot testing. Pilot testing consists of (1) providing inservice training for teachers and evaluators as it pertains to the contract plan approach, (2) monitoring teacher and evaluator reactions to the approach, and (3) revising the approach where necessary.

After the contract plan approach is pilot-tested, the handbook should be revised where necessary. Using the revised handbook, the process can be introduced to all staff in the school organization through a series of inservice sessions. As the contract plan approach is being used, it should be evaluated continuously and modified as the need arises. Open forums, interviews, and questionnaires can be used to monitor how the process is being implemented and to assess its effects. Also, surveys are available for assessing teachers' perceptions over time as they relate to particular aspects of the contract plan approach. For example, the Teacher Evaluation Needs Identification Survey (Iwanicki, Note 8) is a 30-item instrument, which can be used to assess teachers' perceptions of the evaluation process as they relate to the eight factors; purposes of evaluation, evaluation for personal improvement, cooperative planning, accountability relationships, job descriptions, performance objectives, feedback, and self-evaluation. Also, the Teacher Perceptions of Supervisor-Teacher Conferences instrument (Blumberg and Amidon, 1965), as validated by Sirois and Gable (Note 9), can be used to assess teachers' perceptions of the conferencing process in terms of two factors, relationships and productivity.

Inservice Training

Problems encountered by schools attempting to implement contract plans are usually a function of limited and sometimes inappropriate inservice training. The implementation of new evaluation procedures is a change. Benne (1949) provided some issues to consider when initiating change, which have particular relevance to the teacher evaluation process. These issues are summarized below:

(1) *Change should be collaborative*—the change agent and the clients should collaborate on the planning and implementation of the proposed change as well as on the alleviation of pressures and anxiety resulting from the change.

(2) *Change should be educational*—the clients should gain the feeling that they are developing new and beneficial competencies. Furthermore, inservice training should focus not only on the development of new competencies but also on the integration of these competencies into the clients' total approach to the educational process.

(3) *Change should be experimental*—if the anticipated better approach is not successful, consideration can be given to the implementation of the prior or alternative new procedures.

(4) *Change should be task-oriented*—the change should be controlled by the requirements of the task at hand and its effective solution, rather than by the maintenance of the position, power, or prestige of the change agent or clients.

Although each of these issues is relevant to the implementation of teacher evaluation programs, the points dealing with the collaborative and educational aspects of change are crucial in designing inservice programs. Inservice programs need to be planned that (1) introduce staff to the teacher evaluation process, (2) train staff in skill areas relevant to the effective implementation of the process, and (3) afford staff the opportunity to voice and resolve their concerns about the process. When planning such programs, it is important to keep in mind that there is generally an inverse relationship between group size and the complexity of the outcomes desired (Harris, 1975). For example, a large group session is appropriate if the intent is to provide teachers with a knowledge of the teacher evaluation process. If the intent is to develop skills in writing performance contracts, small group activities are more effective. When implementing contract plans, it is beneficial for both teachers and evaluators to receive inservice training in self-evaluation techniques, writing performance contracts, and conferencing skills. Also, it is useful for evaluators to receive training in writing evaluation reports.

The Time Problem

When contract plans are being proposed, a question of this nature is often asked, "Given the time required, how can an administrator responsible for the evaluation of 20 teachers effectively implement the contract plan approach?" The first issue to examine in such a situation is whether a real time problem does exist, or whether the administrator does not wish to spend a major portion of time on evaluation. In some settings, it has been found that the administrator would have sufficient time to devote to evaluation if less time were spent on lower priority responsibilities. In other settings, usually with high teacher-evaluator ratios, sufficient time was not available to implement the contract plan approach in a conscientious manner with each teacher. Where sufficient time is not available, some schools have implemented the approach on a cyclic basis. In this situation, only a portion of the staff participates in the process on a formal basis each year. When not participating in the process on a formal basis, teachers still develop performance contracts with their evaluator and a final evaluation conference is still held at the end of the cycle, but fewer interim conferences and classroom observations are conducted than for teachers participating in the process on a formal basis. The major distinction between the formal and informal approaches is the intensity of the teacher-evaluator relationship. Schools adopting this approach have established a cycle in which a teacher participates in the formal process every second or third year. However, nontenured teachers or teachers whose performance is in question participate in the formal process every year.

Another approach to dealing with the time problem is to vary the evaluation cycle. Some evaluators feel that the objective-setting conference is the most time-consuming aspect of the process. Although they do not have sufficient time to meet with all teachers in the fall to develop performance contracts, they do have sufficient time to develop contracts with half of their teachers in the spring and with the other half of their teachers in the fall. Using this approach, half of the staff are evaluated on a fall-to-fall basis and the other half on a spring-to-spring basis.

CONCLUDING REMARKS

Although this chapter has focused on considerations in the effective design and implementation of contract plans, much has been written about the weaknesses of this approach (Teel, 1978; Snider, Note 10). The major strengths and weaknesses of contract plans are summarized in Figure 4. These strengths and weaknesses are more relative than absolute, depending upon the philosophy of the professional staff in the organization and the manner in which the contract plan approach is implemented. Some staff would oppose an evaluation process based on measurable objectives no matter how it was conceived, whereas staff in another organization would welcome this approach. Also, teachers might accept this approach if "measurable" could be interpreted as observable in the broad sense, whereas they would reject this approach if "measurable" meant only outcomes that could be measured using student achievement tests. Through the appropriate involvement of staff in the planning and implementation of the contract plan approach, as well as the proper allocation of time and resources, contract plans can and have been implemented that maximize the strengths and minimize the weaknesses that have been noted.

As we move into the 1980s, educational leaders are being pressured by the public to hold teachers more accountable for their performance. On the

Strengths

Promotes professional growth through correcting weaknesses and enhancing strengths.

Fosters a positive working relationship between the teacher and the evaluator.

Focuses on the unique professional growth needs of each teacher.

Clarifies performance expectations and sets explicit criteria for evaluation.

Integrates individual performance objectives with the goals and objectives of the school organization.

Weaknesses

Cannot be used to rank teachers.

Places too much emphasis on the attainment of measurable objectives.

Is not realistic in terms of the time and inservice resources available in most school settings.

Requires too much paper work.

Forces evaluators to make decisions about teacher performance in areas in which they are not qualified.

Figure 4. A summary of the strengths and weaknesses of contract plans.

other hand, professional teacher organizations are pressuring administrators to be more responsive to the professional growth needs of teachers. The contract plan approach to teacher evaluation has the potential for meeting both these needs, provided that teachers and administrators accept the challenge and responsibility for making it work effectively.

REFERENCE NOTES

1. Enfield Connecticut Public Schools (1979) *Evaluation handbook for professional staff*. Enfield, CT: Enfield Public Schools.
2. American Association of School Administrators (1972) *Evaluating teaching performance* (Circular No. 2). Washington, DC: Educational Research Service.
3. Palmer, T., D. Musella, and S. Lawton (1972) *Teacher evaluation: Current practices*. Toronto: Ontario Institute for Studies in Education, Department of Educational Administration.
4. Hickox, E. S. and T. Rooney (n.d.) *The shape of teacher evaluation: A survey of practices in the capitol district of New York*. Albany: Albany, New York, Regional Planning District of BOCES.
5. Connecticut State Department of Education (n.d.) *Guidelines for teacher evaluation*. Hartford: Connecticut State Department of Education.
6. Iwanicki, E. F. and L. McEachern (1980) *Teacher self-improvement: A promising approach to professional development in the decade of the '80s*. Unpublished manuscript, University of Connecticut.
7. Redfern, G. B. (1972) *How to evaluate teaching*. Columbus, Ohio: School Management Institute.
8. Iwanicki, E. F. (1980) *Development and validation of the teacher evaluation needs identification survey*. Unpublished manuscript, University of Connecticut.
9. Sirois, H. A. and R. K. Gable (1977) *A factor-analytic validity study of the Blumberg-Amidon Teacher Perceptions of Supervisor-Teacher Conferences instrument*. Presented at the annual meeting of the American Educational Research Association, New York.
10. Snider, R. C. (1975) *Is MBO the way to go? A teacher's guide to management by objectives*. Washington, DC: National Education Association, Instruction and Professional Development.

REFERENCES

Armstrong, H. R. (1973) "Performance evaluation." *National Elementary Principal*, 52(5): 51–55.

Benne, K. D. (1949) "Democratic ethics and social engineering." *Progressive Education*, 27(7): 204.

Blumberg, A. and E. Amidon (1965) "Teacher perceptions of supervision-teacher interaction." *Administrator's Notebook*, 14: 1–4..

Bolton, D. L. (1973) *Selection and Evaluation of Teachers*. Berkeley, CA: McCutchan.

Cogan, M. L. (1973) *Clinical Supervision*. Boston: Houghton-Mifflin.

Drucker, P. F. (1973) *Management: Tasks, Responsibilities, Practices*. New York: Harper & Row.

Goldhammer, R. (1969) *Clinical supervision: Special Methods for the Supervision of Teachers*. New York: Holt, Rinehart, and Winston.

Haefele, D. L. (1980) "How to evaluate thee, teacher—let me count the ways." *Phi Delta Kappan*, 61: 349–352.

Harris, B. M. (1975) *Supervisory Behavior in Education*. Englewood Cliffs, NJ: Prentice-Hall.

Lewis, J., Jr. (1973) *Appraising Teacher Performance*. West Nyack, NY: Parker.

McNeil, J. D. and W. J. Popham (1973) "The assessment of teacher competence," in R. M. W. Travers (ed.), *Second Handbook of Research on Teaching*. Skokie, IL: Rand McNally.

Odiorne, G. S. (1975) *Management by Objectives*. New York: Pitman.

———— (1974) *Management and the Activity Trap*. New York: Harper & Row.

Redfern, G. B. (1980) *Evaluating Teachers and Administrators: A Performance Objectives Approach*. Boulder, CO: Westview.

Sergiovanni, T. J. (1974) "Synergistic evaluation." *Teachers College Record*, 75: 540–552.

Teel, K. S. (1978) "Self-appraisal revisited." *Personnel Journal*, 57: 364–367.

Zimmerer, T. W. and T. F. Stroh, (1974) "Preparing managers for performance appraisal." *S.A.M. Advanced Management Journal*, 39(3): 36–42.

CHAPTER 13

EVALUATION-BASED TEACHER DEVELOPMENT

STEPHEN C. BROCK
Temple University

"Many receive advice; few profit by it" (Publicus Syrus, maxim 149, 1st century B.C.). This chapter explores some of the ways in which teachers receive advice about their teaching and considers the conditions that produce a likelihood of profit from it. The aim is to offer busy professionals an orientation to the issues about evaluation-based teacher development by addressing three main questions:

(1) What is an evaluation-based teacher development?
(2) How effective is it?
(3) What factors are likely to influence its effectiveness?

WHAT IS EVALUATION-BASED TEACHER DEVELOPMENT?

Measures of the effects of our educational practices (evaluation) can be used to make personnel decisions (summative evaluation), and/or evaluation can be used to improve subsequent educational practices (formative evaluation). When evaluation is used formatively, the image of a cycle of educational practice takes shape. The cycle begins with planning, moves to implementation, and ends with evaluation. Evaluation is the process by which we gauge the effects of the educational plans that we implemented; evaluation then serves to refine planning for subsequent educational implementation.

Evaluation of the results of our practices is only one type of evaluation activity that can inform planning. Planning decisions might also be aided by an evaluation of the entry competencies or interests of the learners in our educational program or by an evaluation of the curriculum needs of the learners or our society (Diamond et al., 1975). Therefore, if we wish to consider evaluation-based teacher development in its broadest sense, we must examine the variety of ways in which evaluation contributes to educational planning. For the purposes of this chapter, however, we focus only on evaluation of teaching performance, that is, on the ways in which individual teachers learn about their own performance and the ways in which this evaluation may influence subsequent teaching.

Models of Teacher Development

The evaluation-based teacher development activities described here are of two general types, those that provide teachers with the written results of student ratings of teaching and those that supplement data about teaching (student ratings, classroom visits, video/audio recordings) with consultation.

The end of each semester is an occasion for instructional stocktaking. Teachers must make judgments about student performance, and students are often asked to provide information about aspects of their teacher's performance. Whether organized on an occasional, voluntary, or systematic and required basis, one purpose for collecting information from students is to provide teachers with information useful for instructional change. As a variation of this theme, students are sometimes asked to rate teaching after the first several weeks of instruction. This midterm approach gives teachers early feedback on student opinion, so that midcourse corrections might be considered.

A teaching consultation approach was described recently by Erickson and Erickson (1979). A teaching specialist and a teacher work through a process in which (1) data about the teacher's performance from a variety of sources (student ratings, consultant classroom visits, videotaped teaching episodes) are reviewed, strengths are identified, and goals for improvement activities are established; (2) the consultant and the teacher agree on specific activities to achieve the improvement goals and then plan methods for subsequent data collection about teaching performance; and (3) in follow-up discussions, the teacher and the consultant review the additional data, determine the degree of progress toward achieving the improvement goals, and plan for continued work or termination of the consultation cycle.

Cogan (1973) described a similar cycle of consultation, which differs, however, in some critical respects. First, the process involves the teacher and the consultant in the design of a specific teaching episode rather than in the identification of an aspect of the teacher's performance that, from analyses of existing evaluation data, needs improvement. After an agreement has been reached on a strategy for classroom observation, which may include students' ratings as well as direct observation or video/audio recording by the consultant, data about the teaching episode are gathered and analyzed separately by the teacher and consultant. Then, in a conference session, the teacher and the consultant discuss the effectiveness of the teaching episode. In this conference the teacher and the consultant identify aspects of the teacher's performance that require alteration. The criteria used to identify an aspect of teaching warranting change are that (1) the teaching behavior in question is not an isolated event but constitutes a pattern of teaching behavior and (2) the consultant and the teacher judge that the pattern of teaching behavior has unwanted consequences for student learning and/or behavior. Conference time is always set aside for planning a subsequent teaching episode in which the identified teaching behavior will be changed. Thus, the cycle begins anew.

Evaluation-based teacher development that links data gathering to consultation may not always involve a teaching specialist in a consultant role. A peer development model (Sweeney and Grasha, 1979) involves volunteer trios of teachers representing expertise in different subject matter. The process begins with each member of the trio individually writing down instructional goals. At their first meeting, the trio discuss their most important goals, looking at similarities and differences. Later they establish dates for the observation of each member's class and identify the teaching behaviors about which each seeks feedback. In addition, they agree on the methods by which data about the observed teaching will be gathered (student ratings, video/audio tapes, observer notes). After gathering the data about the designated class, the trio reconvenes. The teacher-observers first describe the observed teaching. They identify positive aspects of the teaching and make any critical comments that relate to the teacher's request for feedback. The teacher who was observed is then asked to name one or several teaching problems discovered in their discussion. It is expected that solutions to the problem(s) will be evident in the next observed class session. The trio's conference concludes with a discussion of the strengths and weaknesses of the observers' data and of their skills in aiding their colleague.

These consultation approaches are designed to identify teacher behaviors that need alteration and to work directly on the behaviors of interest. This practice-centered approach assumes that a direct and frontal assault on teaching behaviors (practice followed by review followed by practice) is the best means for altering teaching behaviors. Teacher educators involved in the design of concept-centered approaches to teacher development hold a different view. They have designed protocols that provide teachers with written descriptions and film or videotape exemplars of a particular teaching concept (e.g., teacher-student interaction). Then, through a series of exercises and tests, the teachers learn to apply the concept. These educators hold that through such concept-centered protocols the teachers will develop critical teaching skills, which will be evident subsequently in their teaching (Borg and Stone, 1974; Gleisman et al., 1979).

These concept-centered protocols may be introduced as teacher development opportunities for teachers using a workshop/seminar (low-threat) strategy or using evaluation-based development strategy. For instance, all teachers in an institution may be invited to attend a concept-centered seminar on a topic of presumed general interest, or, as a result of evaluation data, those teachers with an identified teaching weakness may be offered the opportunity to undergo concept-centered training. Conceivably, a consultation process might supplement the protocol training by combining peer or expert observation, data analysis, and support for the teacher who has identified a teaching problem. In this fashion the concept-centered training may be followed by data gathering to determine the extent to which classroom teaching has been modified.

Somewhere between the evaluation-based development approach, which relies solely on the teacher's use of end-of-course student ratings, and the consultation processes is the Instructional Development and Effectiveness Assessment System (IDEA). In this approach to teacher development, referenced also in Chapter 8, p. 287, teachers are to select their important course objectives from a list of objectives before students' ratings. Students are asked to rate their progress on all the listed objectives (e.g., "gaining factual knowledge," "increasing creative capacities," etc.) and are asked to rate the frequency with which the teacher has used various teaching methods (e.g., "summarized in ways that aided retention," "promoted teacher-student discussion," etc.). Research has found that these "teaching methods" have a strong and varying relationship to student progress toward course objectives. The report that the teacher receives organizes student ratings, identifies those objectives important to the instructor for which student progress ratings are low, and points to teaching methods used infrequently that are strongly related to student progress ratings on those objectives. This organization of student ratings identifies teaching behaviors that may need improvement. In addition, written materials have been developed to guide the teacher toward activities designed to improve the teaching methods identified as important for the teaching of a particular objective. The IDEA approach can be used by teachers without consultation assistance or it may be supplemented by such assistance (Brock and Cashin, Note 1).

The time required of teachers to participate in evaluation-based development activities can vary greatly. Teachers who receive only written feedback from student evaluations may spend variable amounts of time in data analysis and planning, depending on their motivation and the richness of the data. The consultation process described by Erickson and Erickson (1979), as well as the peer consultation process, involves the teacher and consultant(s) in roughly 20 hours of planning, data gathering, and discussion. The clinical supervision model suggested by Cogan (1973) is one of long-term collaboration between teachers and consultants and has as its ultimate objective the preparation of the teachers to act as their own consultants.

In summary, evaluation-based teacher development, as it is conceived here, is likely to be more threatening to teachers than are other kinds of development attitudes. Depending on the blend of ingredients that are selected, evaluation-based development may incorporate written, peer, or expert consultation and may require small, moderate, or large commitments of resources, both in teacher time and other costs. Its key characteristic is its demand upon the teacher that systematic assessment of classroom teaching be undertaken, that these data be analyzed, and that the steps taken to overcome any identified weaknesses in teaching be the focal points for subsequent evaluation.

Nonevaluation-Based Development

Teacher development activities may be nonevaluation-based as well as evaluation-based. Nonevaluation-based teacher development is not based on specific diagnoses of teaching strengths and weaknesses. Among the most frequently offered development activities available to teachers are workshops (sometimes called seminars). Teachers are invited to explore such topics as "improving teacher-made tests," "the use of questioning in teaching," "the application of gaming and simulation to teaching," "computer-assisted instruction," and so on. The better seminars provide opportunities for teachers to get hands-on experience and, in this way, provide some feedback to the teacher about the learning that has resulted from the seminar. Although in some sense this feedback may be considered evaluation-based development, the teacher's participation is not prompted by the identification of a specific teaching weakness, which is addressed in the seminar.

In addition to seminars, other nonevaluation-based activities include (1) sending teachers information on educational innovations, (2) holding brown-bag lunchtime meetings for teachers to discuss informally issues of teaching, and (3) offering the services of audio-visual technicians to enhance instruction. When financial resources are plentiful, teachers may be invited to apply for institutional minigrants for course development. These minigrants might offer the teacher released time from other duties and offer other kinds of material support (Bergquist et al., 1975; Brock and Cashin, Note 1).

Because these sorts of activities do not require teachers to examine critically their strengths and weaknesses before participating in them, they are relatively nonthreatening. They offer teachers satisfaction of their curiosity about some aspect of instruction rather than a compensatory treatment for a diagnosed teaching problem. Because these activities are nonthreatening, they are acceptable to the teachers for whom they are designed. In the best of all possible worlds, an institutional strategy for teacher development might start with these kinds of low-threat activities. After teachers have begun to accept them and have developed a habit of participation, development opportunities can be introduced that are evaluation-based and, possibly more threatening (Debloois and Alder, 1973).

HOW EFFECTIVE IS EVALUATION-BASED TEACHER DEVELOPMENT?

Levinson and Menges (Note 2) recently completed a comprehensive and critical review of the research on methods for improving college teaching. They reached several conclusions about evaluation-based development procedures. With regard to the effectiveness of providing teachers with the results of student ratings, they concluded that studies comparing feedback conditions with no-feedback conditions "provide more evidence for than against written student feedback alone, but many of the studies are poorly designed and analyzed" (p. VI-3). Relatively few studies of feedback versus no-feedback were conducted over longer periods than a single semester. The studies that did involve more than one semester yielded contradictory results, and no clear conclusions are yet possible. However, one well-designed study (Centra, 1973) yielded encouraging findings for those who offer continued rating feedback to teachers.

Studies that compared feedback alone with feedback in conjunction with consultation varied in design and analysis. Although studies have suggested that the addition of consultation to written feedback holds promise (Hoyt and Howard, 1978), the findings were far from conclusive. As consultation is an expensive strategy, Levinson and Menges recommended further rigorous investigation of this strategy.

In addition to the variability in the methodological rigor with which these studies were conducted, another kind of variability in these studies should be considered by the practitioner interested in evaluation-based teacher development. The variability of rating forms used in research studies may diminish the extent to which findings may be generalized simply because information from different rating forms may have different effects on teacher behavior.

Not only are instruments that students use to rate teaching different but also approaches to consultation are diverse. Even if studies on the effects of evaluation-based teacher development meet the criteria for rigorous social science research, variability in the actual interventions investigated can present problems for conclusive generalization. Conclusions about the benefits of evaluation-based development activities will continue to be project-specific. Individual judgments about costs and benefits will continue to rely on experimentation with interventions, the satisfaction of teachers who are affected, and judgments made from observation or other evaluation about the extent to which teaching has been improved.

WHAT FACTORS ARE LIKELY TO INFLUENCE THE EFFECTIVENESS OF EVALUATION-BASED TEACHER DEVELOPMENT?

The following observations result from empirical inquiry as well as from clinical intuition and experience. Therefore, they make claims on different criteria for their "truthfulness." They are offered as leads to practitioners who are either considering an investment in the kinds of activities described above or who, having experience with these approaches, wish to consider adjustments in their practices.

Contextual Factors

The institutional climate for evaluation-based teacher development is affected by many organizational variables, including the availability of active support from senior administrators; modest financial resources; assurance of teacher privacy; expertise in such areas as learning psychology, media, group processes, and such; appropriate support services (media, library, well-equipped classrooms, etc.); and a reward system that is sensitive to teaching performance as a criterion for advancement based on a systematic process of personnel evaluation (Debloois and Alder, 1973).

Often the introduction of evaluation-based teacher development occurs as an afterthought to those who introduce systematic assessment for making personnel decisions. When this happens, two legitimate purposes for teaching evaluation are blended, often with unfortunate consequences. If systematic assessment for personnel decisions is used as a method by which the weakest teachers are identified and eventually "relieved" of teaching responsibilities, the net effect on instruction may be its improvement. On the other hand, if all teachers receive evaluation information that identifies strengths and weaknesses in performance, and if teachers make effective use of teacher development opportunities, then the net effect on instruction is, likewise, improvement. However, teachers often feel an adversary relationship is established when evaluation is introduced for personnel decisions. When the institution tries to communicate a commitment to the professional development of individuals in their offers of development activities, teachers are often deaf to the message.

It is difficult, therefore, for administrators to design procedures that effectively integrate two functions for evaluation. Careful attention needs to be given to the design of the procedures, to the inclusion of teachers in the process of design, and especially to clear and repeated communication with teachers about the procedures. In this way, the adversary relationship may be minimized. With the reduction of threat comes the increased likelihood that teachers will effectively use evaluation data to make decisions about changes in their teaching practices.

Procedural Factors

Characteristics of the evaluation instrument. A major source of evalua- tion data that teachers might consult is student ratings of their teaching. Many different kinds of instruments may be used to collect student perspec- tives. The particular items used on a student rating instrument strongly influence whether the results will promote improved teaching. Menges (1973) has identified several approaches to selecting items for student rating instruments. For most "home-grown" rating forms, and for many that are commercially available, items that have face validity for distinguishing effective from ineffective teaching are selected. Most such forms are com- posed of questions such as "speaks clearly," "promotes teacher-student dis- cussions," "relates material to real-life situation," and so on. The teacher must assume that all of these items are equally useful in discriminating effective from ineffective teaching and that all are equally important. Be- cause each item that appears on the questionnaire is based on a consensus about the elements that constitute effective teaching, it is not surprising that a teacher might react to a low-rated item, such as "relates course material to real-life situations," with a statement/question, "So what!" This item de- scribes a teaching method valued by those who consented to the face validity of the item, but in considering this item for a particular course, or by rationalizing about the "real" merits of such an item, the teacher can simply withdraw consent. The teacher may argue that making this particular course "relate to real-life situations" is inappropriate and, therefore, that low ratings on this item are meaningless in relation to teaching modifications that might be warranted. Thus, rather than provoking the teacher to consider alterna- tives for teaching, the results are rationalized to justify the status quo.

In a criterion-group approach to selecting items for a student rating instru- ment, a large number of items with face validity for discriminating between stronger and weaker teachers are given to the students in classes taught by teachers who are judged to be the "best" and "worst" by independent criteria, for example, peer and student nomination. Those teaching methods that are found to be used by the "best" teachers and not by the "worst" teachers comprise a set of items that appear on a refined questionnaire. With the feedback from a criterion groups instrument, the teacher with a low score on "relating material to real-life situations" has a more restricted latitude for rationalizing the students' perceptions of teaching. The teacher must reckon with the fact that this item is included on the questionnaire not because many people believe that it reflects successful teaching, but because "best" teachers use the method whereas "worst" teachers do not. A greater degree of confidence can be placed on the results of each item, and, therefore, the likelihood that they point to a modification worth making in teaching is heightened.

Another type of student rating form that Menges (1973) identifies is the instructor's goals approach. The IDEA system is an example. The criterion of teaching effectiveness for this instrument is students' ratings of their progress toward course objectives rated as important by their teacher. Rather than selecting teaching behavior items from those that differentiate "best" and "worst" teachers, as in the criterion-groups method, behavior items are identified according to how highly they relate to student progress toward objectives. If teachers are committed to an objective, they tacitly commit themselves to methods that relate to student achievement of it. If students give low ratings of progress toward an objective that the teacher rated as important, and if methods that relate to that progress are identified, the teacher will have some stake in improving those methods.

Both the criterion-groups instruments and the instructor's goals instruments are characterized by criteria of teaching effectiveness that are more likely to be compelling to the teacher than is the criterion of effectiveness built into the consensus approach. It is because these criteria are compelling that they are likely to affect the teacher's use of feedback from such instruments to alter teaching methods. Thus, the selection of the appropriate rating form for evaluation-based development is not a trivial choice.

Two other characteristics of student rating forms deserve brief attention. Instruments that provide a teacher with descriptive information about teaching as well as with judgments about its effectiveness will probably prompt changes in teaching practice. Although the students' overall judgments of teaching effectiveness may motivate teachers to alter their practice, items that describe specific teaching behaviors give direction to possible alterations.

The usefulness of a particular item for the teacher who is considering changes in teaching methods also depends on the extent to which the teacher needs to make inferences from the item to actual teaching behavior. For example, an item that asks students to rate the frequency with which the teacher "promoted teacher-student discussions (as opposed to mere response to questions)" is a relatively low-inference item. A picture of what the teacher is doing comes easily to mind. On the other hand, "introduced stimulating ideas about the subject" is a relatively high-inference item. This item may have many and complex references to the teacher's classroom behaviors. It is likely that a teacher will find it easier to change behaviors that relate to low-inference items rather than to high-inference ones. However, it is clearly better to provide the teacher with information that is important, even though it is high-inference information, rather than to supply only trivial information simply because it requires little inference.

Finally, teachers should be encouraged to construct their own items for student rating instruments, which are specifically targeted to instructional decisions that they are considering. By designing questions of their own, teachers can gather fuller and more detailed information about some aspect of their teaching, which may have been touched on generally in a prior evaluation or may have been unexamined by a standard instrument. Such teacher-designed items have great potential for guiding improvement efforts.

Teachers who ask students for feedback at midterm often encounter difficulties, which may be minimized if attention is paid to advice attributed to Seneca, "Do not ask for what you will wish you had not got." Frustration for both students and their teachers can result from midterm feedback. Students may be asked to rate their satisfaction with an aspect of the course that the teacher is either unwilling or unable to alter. For example, asking students at midterm to express their opinion about readings, when no change is possible, creates a situation ripe for student frustration. Teachers whose global perceptions of their effectiveness are dramatically more positive than are their students' perceptions often experience a shock and frustration that lead either to rigidity or disorientation rather than to orderly and specific changes in teaching approach. For these reasons, then, midterm student evaluations should be conducted with care.

Rather than soliciting student reactions at midterm, it may be more appropriate for the teacher to request that a colleague or other consultant review course materials and sit in on several classes early in the course. Based on these observations or on videotapes of several class sessions, the teacher and colleague may identify the aspects of teaching that warrant and are amenable to immediate change.

Characteristics of video/audio feedback. When video or audio feedback is used in teacher development, it is most effective when the recorded events are accepted by the teacher as representative of the teacher's classroom behavior (Fuller and Manning, 1973). When multiple recordings are called for in a teacher development project, a mix of audio and video recordings has good results. Videotape is dramatically involving and arouses the teacher's interest and, therefore, has benefits as an initial self-confrontation exercise. If aspects of the video-recorded teaching require alteration, then follow-up recordings to evaluate changes may be made on audiotape. Continuing audio playback is useful to teaching improvement (Lauroesch et al., Note 3), whereas video playback has diminishing effects (Stoller, 1968).

Characteristics of the consultant. Consultants whose academic and professional experiences specifically prepare them for the role are likely to be conversant with a wide range of educational inquiry. Generally familiar with educational psychology and with methodologies for evaluating teaching, the consultant may have special interest and competence in such diverse topics as audio-visual technology, ethnography, group dynamics, instructional evaluation, attribution theory, gaming and simulation, computer-assisted instruction, personalized systems of instruction, and philosophies of education. However, the attributes of greatest consequence for the consultant's effectiveness may be a commitment to student learning; an abiding curiosity about the relationship between teacher, student, and subject matter; an empathic disposition; a knowledge of local resources; a tendency toward self-disclosure; and effective interpersonal communication skills (Lindquist et al., 1978; Brock and Cashin, Note 1). These attributes are not the sole province of specially trained consultants. Because most teachers possess some or all of these attributes, they may be asked to assume a consulting relationship with their peers. In this instance, institutional support for their professional development in this new role is highly desirable.

Cogan (1973) presents a thorough and convincing examination of the consultant-teacher relationship. How is it like, and different from, a teacher-pupil relationship or a counselor-client relationship? Both of these relationships are clearly helping ones, and certainly the consultant is motivated to be of assistance to the teacher. But there are problems in constructing the consultant-teacher relationship as a "helping" relationship. Cogan (1973) describes an inventory of the pitfalls in helping relationships developed by Nylen (Note 4):

(1) Some helpers become so fond of giving advice that they forget to check the relevance of their advice.
(2) The helper may be unaware of resistances in the helpee, who may aver that he has no problems or blame them on someone else.
(3) The helper may over-praise the helpee in an effort to establish a good relationship. He may be reluctant to confront the helpee with the hard realities of this situation.
(4) The helpee may not relish exposing his problems.
(5) People are generally afraid of what others will think of them. The more helpless and inadequate an individual feels, the more likely he is to be afraid of the opinions of others.
(6) People who receive help may lose a sense of independence and become dependent.
(7) The helpee may set up defense mechanisms, rationalization, projection, logic, tight-thinking, repression, and withdrawal [p. 66].

Given these pitfalls, Cogan suggests that an effective consultant-teacher relationship should be collegial. The emphasis is on collaboration and complementary work with a shared goal of increasing student learning by improving the teacher's autonomy. The role of the consultant-colleague is a difficult one to achieve and to maintain, for the tendency to establish ascendant-nonascendant relationships is strong. The consultant must give serious thought to the consultant-as-colleague role and must be observant of its maintenance. The consultant can also benefit from systematic supervision by a fellow consultant.

The consultant-as-colleague receives a severe test when videotapes of a teacher's performance are the subject of discussion. Because video self-confrontation has powerful affective possibilities for the teacher, the consultant needs to create a psychologically safe situation in the discussion. However, to increase the likelihood of teacher change, the videotape review must also be sufficiently focused to be confrontational. Focus helps the teacher to address what is known to others but not to the teacher.

Teacher Factors

A supportive institutional climate, thoughtfully designed evaluation procedures, and competent consultation contribute significantly to the likelihood that evaluation-based development will affect teachers positively, but characteristics of the teachers also play an important role. Teacher motivation is probably a key characteristic. Those who naturally seek to understand their effects on students and who are committed to finding improved methods of teaching are likely to benefit from evaluation-based development. Motivation can be increased by effective rewards for participation in projects.

Research on attribution theory, reviewed by Wittrock and Lumsdaine (1977), suggests another important teacher characteristic that contributes to the success of evaluation-based development. Some teachers attribute instructional outcomes (student learning, behavior, and satisfaction) to characteristics of their teaching. These teachers are aware of the differences among their students, differences of talent, interests, social status, and so on, but when these teachers think about a student's difficulty in performance, they look to their teaching practices for a probable cause. Other teachers look first and primarily at characteristics of the students to explain the difficulties in their performance. Those who believe instructional effects to be principally a function of their teaching rather than a function of student characteristics are likely to use feedback about their teaching to alter their practices. Teachers oriented otherwise will be less inclined to do so. Attribution orientation can be altered through consultation, which brings this orientation and its consequences to the teacher's attention.

Two other teacher characteristics deserve brief mention. Teachers who receive moderately favorable evaluations are more likely to change than are very low-rated teachers (Pambookian, 1974). Strategies of evaluation-based development need to be different for teachers who are evaluated as moderately effective and for those who are rated as not effective. In the latter case, much more attention should be given to increasing teacher motivation, which is likely to be at a nadir.

Finally, teachers who believe that their performance is somewhat better than student ratings indicate are more likely to be influenced by student evaluations than are those whose self-ratings agree with evaluation scores (Pambookian, 1976; Centra, Note 5). Because moderate discrepancies frequently occur, it is highly desirable that an evaluation-based development strategy include teacher self-assessments. When teachers complete a self-assessment before examining other sources of data, they can benefit from an initial discussion of their self-ratings with a consultant. In this process the teacher and consultant can develop hypotheses, based on the self-ratings, about the strengths and weaknesses of the teacher's performance. Then they can turn to other sources of data to find support for their hypotheses or discrepancies that lead to new hypotheses. At this point, they may decide that further data-gathering is needed to develop a clearer picture of the teacher's performance, or they may move to discussions of avenues for teaching improvement.

In projects that use video/audio recordings rather than student ratings as the evaluation base, the same kinds of characteristics are predictive of the likelihood of change in teaching behavior. The motivated teacher who can identify deficiencies before playback, or who experiences a moderate discrepancy between observed performance and desired performance, is one who will benefit from teacher development.

SUMMARY

In general, giving teachers information about their teaching performance appears to be effective in inspiring some to improve their teaching. When feedback about performance is supplemented with consultation, teacher change in a desired direction is more likely than when feedback alone is given. Student rating forms differ in their construction and content, and not all are equally effective in improving teaching. Teachers should conduct a self-rating of their teaching before reviewing feedback from student ratings or before reviewing audio/video tapes of their teaching.

Patience and persistence are required to alter the complex set of behaviors that comprise a teacher's style. An effective program of evaluation-based teacher development requires a climate that provides collegial consultation that is nonthreatening, knowledgeable, and empathic. Those who are most likely to be influenced by a program of evaluation-based development are teachers who are moderately successful but whose self-assessment is more favorable than students' ratings or the assessment from focused video self-confrontation. They attribute the causes of student learning to their teaching and are motivated to enhance continually their students' learning and their own professional satisfaction. The challenge to those engaged in evaluation-based development is to give guidance and support to those teachers who meet these criteria and who are ready for development activities and to discover creative approaches to engaging others in them.

REFERENCE NOTES

1. Brock, S.C. and W.E. Cashin (1976) *IDEA system handbook*. Manhattan: Kansas State University, Center for Faculty Evaluation and Development.
2. Levinson, J.L. and R.J. Menges (1979) *Improving college teaching: A critical review of research* (Occasional paper #13). Evanston, IL: Northwestern University, Center for the Teaching Professions.
3. Lauroesch, W.P., P.D. Pereira, and R.A. Reyan (1969) *The use of student feedback in teacher training* (Final Report, Project No. 8-E-115, ERIC Ed 035 588). Chicago: University of Chicago.
4. Nylen, D., J.R. Mitchell, and A. Stout (n.d.) *Handbook of staff development and human relations training*. Washington, DC: National Training Laboratories Institute for Applied Behavioral Science.
5. Centra, J.A. (1972) *Strategies for improving college teaching*. Washington, DC: American Association for Higher Education.

REFERENCES

Bergquist, W.H., S. Phillips, and G.H. Quehl (1975) *A Handbook for Faculty Development*. Dansville, NY: Dansville Press.

Borg, W.R. and D.R. Stone (1974) "Protocol materials as a tool for changing teacher behavior." *Journal of Experimental Education*, 43: 34–39.

Centra, J.A. (1973) "Effectiveness of student feedback in modifying college instruction." *Journal of Educational Psychology*, 65: 395–401.

Cogan, M.L. (1973) *Clinical Supervision*. Boston: Houghton-Mifflin.

Debloois, M. and D.D. Alder (1973) "Stimulating faculty readiness for instructional development: A conservative approach to improving college teaching." *Educational Technology*, 13: 16–19.

Diamond, R.D., et al. (1975) *Instructional Development for Individualized Learning in Higher Education*. Englewood Cliffs, NJ: Educational Technology.

Erickson, G.R. and B.L. Erickson (1979) "Improving college teaching: An evaluation of a teaching consultation procedure." *Journal of Higher Education*, 5: 670–683.

Fuller, F. F. and B. A. Manning (1973) "Self-confrontation reviewed: A conceptualization for video playback in teacher education." *Review of Educational Research,* 43: 469–528.

Gleisman, D., R. C. Pugh, and B. Bielat (1979) "Acquiring teaching skills through concept-based training." *Journal of Educational Research,* 72: 149–154.

Hoyt, D. P. and G. S. Howard (1978) "The evaluation of faculty development programs." *Research in Higher Education,* 8: 25–38.

Lindquist, J., W. Bergquist, C. Mathis, C. Case, C. Clark, and L. Buhl (1978) *Designing Teaching Improvement Programs.* Berkeley, CA: Pacific Soundings Press.

Menges, R. J. (1973) "The new reporters: Students rate instruction," in C. R. Pace (ed.), *Evaluating Learning and Teaching.* San Francisco: Jossey-Bass.

Pambookian, H. S. (1976) "Discrepancy between instructor and student evaluations of instruction: Effect on instruction." *Instructional Science,* 5: 63–75.

——— (1974) "Initial level of student evaluation of instruction as a source of influence on instructor change after feedback." *Journal of Educational Psychology,* 66: 52–56.

Stoller, F. F. (1968) "Use of video tape (focused feedback) in group counseling and group therapy." *Journal of Research and Development in Education,* 1(2): 30–44.

Sweeney, J. M. and A. F. Grasha (1979) "Improving teaching through faculty triads. *Educational Technology,* 19: 54–57.

Wittrock, M. D. and A. A. Lumsdaine (1977) "Instructional psychology." *Annual Review of Psychology,* 28: 417–459.

CHAPTER 14

SUMMATIVE TEACHER EVALUATION

MICHAEL SCRIVEN
Evaluation Institute
University of San Francisco

INTRODUCTION

Teacher evaluation is a disaster. The practices are shoddy and the principles are unclear. Recent work has suggested some ways to clarify the issues and to make the procedures more equitable and reasonably valid, but one cannot yet point to a single exemplary system in which the practices come near to matching our knowledge. This state of affairs is a terrible indictment of the universities since the problems are sufficiently tractable that a modest investment of only approximately 2% to 3% of their *internally* controlled research funding would have solved them 50 years ago. That the great research and teaching centers of learning never put serious efforts into research on teaching, though they had to evaluate teachers all the time, is one more scandal in the history of the guilds, of professions that fail to practice what they profess, in this case, research-based decision making. Once more, the pressure to reform is coming from outside, from the Congress and the courts, not the conscience. But belated is better than never, and these notes sketch the traps and paths in the jungle, for those who want to avoid impotence, inefficiency, and inequity.

The emphasis throughout the chapter is on teacher evaluation for personnel decisions (summative evaluation), but there is some explicit reference to evaluation for faculty development (formative evaluation), and, since the two are not intrinsically distinct, there is substantial *indirect* relevance to formative evaluation. But summative evaluation is primary because (1) human careers are at stake, not "mere" improvement; (2) if it is not possible to tell when teaching is bad (or good) overall, it is not possible to tell when it has improved; (3) if it *is* possible to tell when it is bad or good, personnel decisions can be made even though it is not known how to make improvements. In short, diagnosis is sometimes easier than healing, and an essential preliminary to it.

The chapter in general applies to elementary and secondary teacher evaluation as well as to postsecondary; where key differences exist, they are discussed. To avoid cumbersome circumlocutions, the language is sometimes simplified, and the reader with, for example, K-12 interests will occasionally have to translate "dean" into "principal" and ignore references to the evaluation of research.

INSTITUTIONAL PREREQUISITES

It is improper to proceed with a system for evaluating teaching that is supposed to operate well or ethically regardless of the administrative and legal context. The following are some of the conditions that must be present in that context.

1. A system for the evaluation of administrators must be *in place* in order to avoid the entirely justifiable resistance of the "serfs" to being evaluated by those in the castle, who are above such things themselves. Administrator evaluation, if it occurs at all, is chiefly remarkable for being even worse than the evaluation of faculty. Where it is done in what is thought to be an especially enlightened fashion, it is usually based upon some bastardized version of management by objectives (MBO) which, even in optimal form, is totally inappropriate as a basis for the evaluation of administrators. But that is another story.

2. The evaluation of teaching must be part of a system that also has an appropriate process for evaluating research (if research is valued at all) and service (defined clearly), and a specific commitment to their relative weighting. Otherwise one is playing in a game for which only a few of the rules have been stated. It is notable that, for example, personnel manuals for the University of Texas system and the University of California at Berkeley (UCB) have (as of September 1980) no such commitment to the relative worth of teaching and, hence, no binding commitment toward its having *any* worth. The fact that UCB requires, and enforces the requirement, that data on teaching merit, including student evaluations, must be included in a dossier before it will be considered for personnel decisions looks as if it shows a valuing of teaching, but it does not. The data may show that the teacher is a *bad* teacher, yet the data requirement does not specify any penalty; if the data show the teacher to be a good teacher, no determinate benefit results. Specified relative weightings of all the relevant criteria of faculty assessment is the only nonvacuous procedure for objective evaluation and, not incidentally, the only equitable one. It is hardly surprising that in the two systems mentioned (and in most others), the standards vary by campus and department and, indeed, by who happens to be the current chair

or provost or vice-president. One cannot say that Berkeley does or does not value good teaching; one can only say that the official personnel manual, despite a page or two of rhetoric, does not require it for favorable action. Systems in which the weightings vary from individual to individual (and even from year to year) are fine *if* each individual's contract specifies them explicitly. It is not rigidity that is desirable, only clarity.

3. The institution must have clearly understood and defined the difference between the evaluation of worth and the evaluation of merit, with respect to the evaluation of teaching in particular. (The distinction also applies to the evaluation of research and service.) The impact of this distinction is crucial in half a dozen areas, but two examples should suffice. Suppose that an institution employs a teacher whose teaching is superlative by every reasonable standard and who is also producing substantial quantities of absolutely first-rate research, while rendering impressive service to the profession, the campus, and the community. If the institution is not absolutely clear that in spite of all this, and even though money is available, it may have to deny tenure to this teacher, the institution does not understand the difference between worth and merit.

The decision whether to make an initial appointment, the decision to grant tenure, and the decision to push for early retirement by the various means available for that should all depend upon the worth of a faculty member to the institution and not merely upon the faculty member's *professional merit*. The worth to the institution is essentially connected with such issues as the income generated and likely to be generated by the student enrollment (or grant support) that the instructor produces, the special services to the institution's general mission that are provided by the instructor (e.g., an uniquely talented Latin scholar or teacher at a Jesuit institution, a woman mathematician in an otherwise all-male department that was anxious to recruit women as mathematics majors, etc.). Neither private nor public institutions can today afford to be awarding tenure on merit alone as if the enrollments were irrelevant, but many of them are locked into a system of faculty evaluation that makes it impossible to deviate from merit considerations even in extreme cases (except at the appointment decision). Several other cases of worth are important; for example, an interesting case can be made that multidisciplinarians are worth more to an institution than most specialists, in these uncertain times, because they are less likely to be left high and dry by the tides of changing interests and emerging new disciplines.

If worth is to be given any weighting at all, as it should be, then the exact size and limit of this weighting must be as carefully defined as possible in order that one does not get into obvious abuses—such as firing teachers whose political activities lead to complaints or the loss of support from alumni, school boards, or legislatures—the sort of abuse that results from thinking that worth means only financial worth. Worth also has something to do with the integrity of the mission of the school. There is no worth left in an institution that sells its curriculum content to the highest bidder.

Incidentally, salary level will commonly involve yet another value dimension, namely, market value (or cost, or external worth). It is as well to specify the limits on these market adjustments, for example, in separate schedules for various areas.

4. There should be an independent support system of some kind (e.g., a consultant or teaching services unit) available to faculty to assist them in the effort to improve, so that the system of faculty evaluation is neither merely punitive nor seen as merely punitive. This support system should be independent of both administrators and peers, including (where relevant) department chairs and deans or assistant principals/curriculum specialists, and so on in order to avoid the disincentive to use it that results if instructors know that administrators will know (or can find out) when this support system is being used by a particular instructor. The consultations must not only be absolutely confidential but also professionally based and supportively oriented. Finding somebody who can provide the appropriate kind of assistance is very difficult because few might be said to be qualified in the first place, and many of them are too inclined to think that there is one true solution to the problem of how best to teach.

The cost of providing this support system is low. One professional and one secretary/assistant for several thousand students can do this and also do a number of other jobs that should be done in any college or school system, such as keeping up with research and practice in the fields of faculty evaluation and teaching research, maintaining a small consulting library for faculty, improving the student questionnaire (if one is used) and managing its administration, and supervising the data synthesis process in any multidimensional evaluation. That involves research-reading competence, not research performance. The helping role that works with the prima donna type of faculty is not something with which prima donna teaching researchers are familiar, so a nice balance of skills is required. It is therefore rash to make appointments to this job for more than a trial period at first.

5. The background system must have consistent and appropriate practices, not just consistent and appropriate rhetoric. A typical (college) example of how not to achieve consistent practice is to have a system in which the quality of teaching is said to be important, whereas in fact, departments are issued new positions and replacements for retiring or departing old appointees almost entirely on the basis of enrollments. Although this is admirable in the sense that it reflects an attention to a reasonable consideration that a decade or two ago was almost totally disregarded, in many contexts it amounts to rewarding the departments for, among other things, inflated grading, which is inconsistent with the rhetoric of respect for high standards.

The same type of inconsistency in a K-12 setting occurs when teachers are called in to justify failing grades but not passing ones. Another example is the use of a student questionnaire that attends to the extent to which instructors get to know the names and personalities of individual students, provide ample office hours, and so on, all of which are results easily achieved for small classes but not for large classes. Having thus provided an incentive for faculty to restrict enrollment in their classes, administrators then cry about declining enrollments, which this approach reinforces. Consistent systems are hard to set up, but the inconsistencies in systems are extremely expensive.

6. A reasonable *modus vivendi* with student government must be worked out so that both parties obtain mutual benefit from student evaluation.

7. The use of evaluation must not only be consistent but also comprehensive. In particular, each type of personnel decision must use it, especially the major ones: selection, retention, promotion/demotion, salary action, tenure and its revocation, early or postponed retirement, and layoff. In the many systems in which contracts restrict the administrator's options with respect to the major decisions, careful study always reveals a large second set of benefits or penalties, which are also options. They should be distributed with care and with regard to merit/worth; the effect of doing so can be great, and the effect of not doing so speaks loudly of the true values of the administrator and the system.

THE DEFINITION OF GOOD TEACHING

The best teaching is not that which produces the most learning, since what is learned may be worthless. There is a connection between teaching and learning, but not a simple one.

No definitions of good teaching in the literature avoid a series of counterarguments and counterexamples. The following definition avoids the so-far-identified counterexamples, but possibly has some of its own. Teachers are meritorious to the extent that they exert the maximum possible influence toward beneficial learning on the part of their students, subject to three conditions: (1) the teaching process used is ethical, (2) the curriculum coverage and the teaching process are consistent with what has been promised, and (3) the teaching process and its foreseeable effects are consistent with the appropriate institutional and professional goals and obligations.

The intent of the three qualifications can be illustrated with some examples of what they are intended to exclude. (1) Unethical processes include not only cruel and unusual punishment but also those processes that are completely nonuniversalizable, for example, putting so much pressure on the students that they abandon their work for other classes in order to do the work for this one. Since it would be impossible for all teachers to do likewise, it is an unethical procedure. (Getting students to do more home-work at the expense of an already extensive leisure is, on the other hand, admirable.)

It is often argued on weak a priori grounds that the use of a reward system such as a token economy or grades is unethical; in fact, the *failure* to use some kind of "reward system"—at least a grading system—is usually both unethical and unprofessional. It is unethical because it fails to inform the students about their progress or competence, and it is unprofessional be-cause it fails to show that the institution (or profession or future employer) values quality work as opposed to minimally competent work. It also hap-pens that grades provide a legitimate incentive for many students; not to use them is thus poor pedagogy unless the teacher has direct evidence for a better approach. Grading can even be arranged to make interstudent competitive-ness impossible, while retaining the feedback required in striving for excel-lence. So, even if grading did reduce learning, it would have to be done and done properly. Properly managed it should increase learning.

(2) Certain contracts are made by instructors and institutions, both expli-citly and implicitly, to which they frequently do not adhere. Such contracts are involved in promises as to what a course will cover, made in, for exam-ple, a course catalogue, school or departmental handouts, the faculty hand-book, the union contract, the class handouts or in the language of the opening presentation in class, or at a parents, faculty, or counselors meeting. Apart from misleading advertising, much of the hierarchical structure of sequential curricula has been made laughable by the failure of instructors to adhere to these commitments. Maximizing learning cannot be given auto-matic and complete precedence over these obligations.

(3) It would usually be appropriate, if the maximization of learning were the only obligation of an instructor, to adjust the level of instruction to the class average so that more people would be able to benefit from it. But there are institutional and professional commitments that transcend this commit-ment. For example, if one is faced with a class of medical students who will graduate at the end of this year, and if one's obligation is to instruct them in professional procedures that they will be practicing at that time, and if it is clear that most of them are so far off the pace that no instruction within the time available can get them to a level of competence, then it is professionally obligatory to focus the instruction upon those who *can* be brought up to the appropriate standard and fail the rest.

Other obligations that are important and must be considered very se-riously include the problems of providing compensatory justice for minori-ties and women, which may mean focusing more effort on them than would maximize total class learning; providing knowledge that will be expected by the instructor of a higher level course; and so on. Ultimately there is always an obligation to quality of learning rather than to quantity which precludes any simple maximization criterion from legitimacy, since it is essentially a quantitative criterion.

Note that the learning referred to in the definition above can certainly cover attitudes, in the rare cases in which it is possible to justify the claim that teaching a certain attitude is an appropriate part of an instructor's obligations. Teaching the scientific attitude might be a case in point, as might be teaching the motivation to learn. Note, too, that teaching can often be done, and often is done to a very important extent, outside the classroom; hence, evaluating it must involve looking for and at this out-of-classroom teaching. Remember also that the value of a teacher must include worth as well as merit, and worth involves very different considerations from maximizing learning.

The most important feature of our definition of teaching is that it does not *identify* good teaching with the production of (even good) learning, though it does not break all connections either. I have discussed several overriding considerations already, but there is yet another type of example that should be mentioned. If you have a number of students in the class who for various reasons unconnected with your own performance are not working hard enough to keep up with the class, you should not be downgraded as a teacher for the failure of these students to learn. If you happen to get half the basketball team in your class, it should not count against you if they are not planning to graduate or are not capable of it. A teacher's task is only to provide the *best possible* environment, not to guarantee that the results will be effective no matter how little effort is made by the students. It follows that one must never use on a student questionnaire the question "How much did you learn from this class (that you think was valuable to you)?" or cognates of that question. One must instead use questions such as "How well do you think the instructor taught the course?"

It is partly for the above reasons that the answers to student questionnaires are not to be regarded as intrinsically inferior to or as substitutes for studies of the learning gains of students in class. They are *more valid* in one respect, in that they address the correct question.

Another incorrect definition of good teaching which has some supporters, perhaps deserves a footnote. This involves the identification of teaching with the transfer of learning from the teacher to the student. But, as has often been pointed out, inspiring the student to seek learning elsewhere may be the best approach for maximizing learning even in the short run and more likely in the long run.

√ HOW NOT TO EVALUATE TEACHING

It will be clear from the preceding discussion that any method of evaluating teaching that simply identifies teaching merit with the amount learned is oversimplified and can be extremely unfair to some teachers, in particular to teachers of slow learners. It should also be clear that evaluating a teacher's worth only, or merit only, is, on occasions, also entirely inappropriate. And in the absence of certain institutional requirements, good evaluation is either difficult, inappropriate, or impossible. We should now look at a number of other attractive errors that have also been widely incorporated into systems for evaluating teachers.

Classroom Visits

Using classroom visits by colleagues (or administrators or "experts") to evaluate teaching is not just incorrect, it is a disgrace. First, the visit itself alters the teaching, so that the visitor is not looking at a representative sample. This defect is exacerbated by preannouncing the visit. Second, the number of visits is too small to be an accurate sample from which to generalize, even if it were a random sample. Third, the visitors are typically not devoid of independent personal prejudices in favor of or against the teacher, arising from the fact that visitors are normally administrators or colleagues of the teacher and in their other role are involved in adversary proceedings with them, alliances with them, and so on. Fourth, nothing that could be observed in the classroom (apart from the most bizarre special cases) can be used as a basis for an inference to any conclusion about the merit of the teaching. That this is so follows inexorably from the results of the enormous number of studies on style research that have been done and summarized on various occasions (see Centra, 1979). These result in the conclusion that no style indicators can be said to correlate reliably with short- or long-term learning by the students across the whole range of subjects, levels, students, and circumstances. (Anything less could scarcely be defended for personnel evaluation.) Fifth, regardless of the fact that no observations of teaching style can legitimately be used as a basis for inference about the merit of the teaching, the visitor normally believes the contrary. This is often because visitors have their own preferences as to a certain style or have many years of experience in teaching this same type of course or student. Consequently, they believe that not doing it their way, or perhaps in one or two other ways that they approve, is doing it badly. These prejudices are without foundation, to the best of our knowledge, and should not be allowed to come into the evaluation of teaching in any normal case. Among the hypothetically possible exceptions are the possibility that what the teacher is saying is known to be false by a visitor and is so grossly false as to constitute an impossible vehicle for teaching the truth, that the visitor observes racist or sexist or other immoral practices by the teacher, or that the visitor observes a total lack of classroom discipline to a degree that cannot possibly be reconciled with the continuance of a learning process of any kind. Since none of these events has ever been recorded on any of the classroom visiting sheets of the many thousands that I have either inspected directly or of which I have seen summaries, this cannot be taken seriously as a reason for making classroom visits part of teacher evaluation. It is scarcely surprising that the research studies (see Centra, 1979, pp. 74-76) show that colleague reports are not even mutually consistent; hence they are unusable as evidence.

Ultimately, the problem about the visitor is the lack of similarity between the visitor's thought processes and those of the student. They are generally separated by several decades in their learning maturity; thus, they may have substantially different vocabularies and cognitive repertoires, and they certainly lack many cultural similarities. Because of this, the visitor's empathic impressions are not likely to be a good indicator of how much learning is going on in the heads of the students (quite apart from the corrections that have to be applied to this first approximation to the key process in good teaching). Since the secondary indicators in teaching style (i.e., everything else you can see, leaving the empathy aside) turn out to be invalid as indicators of teaching effectiveness, this leaves the visitor—or should leave the visitor—at a loose end.

In spite of these staggering objections, the method of classroom visitation is of course the universal method whereby teachers in the elementary and high school are evaluated and is—depressingly enough—being quite steadily implemented at the postsecondary level, on the grounds that it represents an improvement over past practices. No variation of this kind of observation is of any value either; visits by experts are no better, and visits by peers are no better, for purposes of personnel evaluation. There are no valid indicators to be seen, no matter who looks. Visits by a consultant are defensible in the effort to provide *help to improve* teaching if it is already known that the teaching is very unsuccessful, because the consultant may be able to suggest some options. However, the (costly) classroom visit is usually unnecessary; a tape recording, or even a verbal report by the teacher, along with the student evaluation forms, is more than enough basis for consulting recommendations in most cases.

Course Content

Teaching is usually evaluated without any serious attempt at evaluating the quality of the content of the course. This is one side of the "methods-madness" that has made schools of education a laughingstock in the intellectual community, and increasingly in the total community, for many years. From what we have said about the definition of good teaching, it is clear that one cannot make one's judgment of teaching merit entirely on the basis of the content of *what is learned by* the students, but to do so is much better than making the judgment on the basis of merely inspecting *what is presented to* students. Both should be considered, but with the emphasis upon student performance. Here is the one place where peer evaluation of a limited kind is appropriate—evaluation of materials (both texts and student work) not process—and even here it is better to use people from another institution but in the same subject-matter area, eliminating costs by trading services in kind with that institution. Such an arrangement, with its attendant social pressure, tends to do more to improve standards than in-house evaluation of materials does anyway, apart from increased validity.

Teaching Processes

If one half of methods-madness is not looking at content, the other half is looking too hard at process. This not only involves the obvious traps of substituting style preferences for validated merit criteria but it also often involves making the formulation of behavioral objectives (or lesson plans) an end in itself. Yet the very best teachers (e.g., Socrates), on any criteria we can justify plausibly often eschew a predefinition of coverage because of the advantages of picking up on what turns out to be of current or great interest or difficulty to the particular students being taught, the "targets-of-opportunity" approach. Excesses are possible here, too; neither approach should be unbridled or totally excluded.

Enrollments in Further Courses

Another popularly acclaimed, though infrequently employed, measure of teaching success is checking on the relative number of enrollments in further courses in the same subject matter by "graduates" of the instructor being evaluated. This is an unethical indicator, and its use cannot be countenanced by central administration because it is nonuniversalizable. That is, one can only score points on this dimension by stealing, buying, or seducing students from other departments. It is exactly like the process of getting more work out of the students by having them give up their homework for other courses. However, reducing dropouts—the other end of the effects spectrum—is a highly legitimate criterion of merit, if the education missed can be shown to be a truly serious loss.

Student Questionnaires

Most student questionnaires are improper bases for faculty evaluation, despite the great potential of the approach, either because they involve ratings on style or ratings on nonuniversalizable indexes or because of the way in which the data from them are synthesized. If only mean ratings are used, then the important case of the instructors who are tremendously successful with a subgroup of the class, perhaps the best students, is overlooked. Although their mean score may be no different from those of other instructors who receive weak ratings from everybody in the class, their teaching potential is obviously different, and a sensitive administration should be making some provisions to tap such a promising source of inspiration in a more appropriate situation than the type of class that resulted in a low overall score. Or the consultant may be able to work out a way to generalize from this promising basis to success with the rest of the students. Similarly, averaging the means from courses taught at different levels may be unfair to teachers who are good at one grade level and not at another or good with introductory but not with graduate courses.

Alumni Surveys

More honored in principle than in practice, alumni surveys are essentially useless for normal formative and summative evaluation of teachers though they can sometimes be used for course or program evaluation. They have extremely low response rates; they relate to the ancestors of present performance and, hence, may exaggerate or underestimate the merit of the only performance that should be used for current personnel decisions, namely, current performance; they involve a perspective as to what will be valuable that may no longer apply to new graduates; and the attributions of causation involved are suspect. These reasons do not exclude some use of alumni surveys in selecting Distinguished (Elderly) Teacher Awards.

Overkill

Evaluation done every term on every course is likely to produce hostility from both faculty and students and stereotyped responses or low response rates, especially if a long form is used. It is also unnecessarily expensive, takes up too much class time, and is unlikely to achieve the best results because it allows no chance for experimentation, for example with new texts or approaches. Of course, undersampling (once every five years) and letting the instructor choose which classes are to be evaluated are worse alternatives.

HOW TO EVALUATE TEACHING

Student Questionnaires

The student questionnaire should be a key component in the evaluation process from about grade six. The piece of paper itself is only part of the story. Preparing students as evaluators is another part, and the methods for administering the questionnaire are a third. These methods must be proof against complaints about the possibility of selective return and prompting. A good straightforward approach is to have assistants from the central administration staff (a cheaper fallback system is using secretaries) take the questionnaires out to each class, have the instructor leave the room for a few minutes, provide a brief explanation of the process and how the results are to be used (possibly in writing), encourage questions, and pass out questionnaires to be filled out by every member of the class. One should get a 99% return rate from those present, and one should worry if it is less than 75% of those who complete the course.

At the college level, the date for distribution should be announced in advance if one wants most of those enrolled for the class to attend, since knowing that the questionnaire will be distributed on that date is sometimes an incentive to attendance. This does weaken one's defenses against certain types of preparation of the students by the professor, but this can be controlled by asking about it on the form so it is a less worrying problem than low attendance rates. "Absentee ballots" are not a good idea, logistically or for inferential purposes. One can get that 99% response rate and tolerance from the faculty for taking time out of their classes, if the whole process takes less than five minutes. This is the first of three interlocking reasons for using a very short questionnaire.

The second is the cost, which goes up quickly with length of printing, collating, keypunching or scanning, synthesizing, reporting, and interpreting. The third is that all the apparent justifications for using a long questionnaire are unsound. The usual questionnaires with 20 to 70 items are fishing expeditions of an entirely improper kind. Unless it is demonstrable that some possible answer to each particular question indicates merit or demerit in teaching, then the question has no place on the personnel evaluation questionnaire. Detailed questions may be used in a questionnaire designed by the instructor with the assistance of a teaching support consultant, or vice versa, when the instructor wants to get feedback on some specific effort or style venture of personal concern. But no such style choices can be legitimated for purposes of personnel evaluation, and no such questions should ever be on a form seen by anybody except the instructors and the consultants of their choice. If placed on a form along with legitimate questions, they will be likely to bias the response of somebody who favors or disfavors the style that they uncover, and such biases are illegitimate. For this reason they would be certain to affect seriously the legitimacy of any personnel decisions that were appealed in court, for example, but the ethical point is more serious than that.

Since one cannot help but be worried by the contamination of instructor ratings by irrelevant personality factors and by factors connected with like or dislike of the subject matter or course content, one should make some effort to syphon off those considerations. A simple way is to stress the contrast between these considerations in the verbal and written introduction to the basic judgmental question on the questionnaire, that is, the difference between liking or disliking the instructor as a person and thinking well of him or her as an instructor and between liking or disliking the course content and thinking that the instructor did or did not do a good job of teaching it. Another approach would consist in asking specifically for an expression of liking (1) for the instructor as a person and (2) for the subject matter, and *then* asking for (3) an evaluation of the job done by the instructor in teaching this course. The content rating (2) could then be torn off the form and sent to the relevant administrator for *course* evaluation; the personal evaluation (1) could be torn off and thrown away or given to the instructor if requested, and one would then use the rest of the form (3) for personnel evaluation.

Special thought must be given to the cases in which the instructor *is* responsible for course content (e.g., graduate level specialty courses) and cases where attitude toward subject matter is important (e.g., in K-3 reading instruction). A promising approach is to divide the "attitude toward content" question into two parts: "general attitude" and "attitude improved because of this teacher's approach to it," and add the latter rating to the instructor's file. It is also possible that the latter will be picked up on the holistic rating of goodness of teaching. We need some empirical research to find out whether this is true; meanwhile, the safest approach is to add the extra question.

The crucial question is a simple request for an overall judgment of the merit of the instructor as an instructor, and this question is enough. There are some other possible questions on such a form of a kind not often encountered. They should come before the requests for an overall rating, since they tend to depress it (and probably increase its validity). Technically this is desirable, because the main problem with the usual results is that the scores are too high to allow adequate headroom within which exceptionally good teaching can distinguish itself. These other possible questions are of two overlapping but loosely distinguishable kinds. The first concerns matters that can be described as ethical or professional obligations of the instructor and can be phrased in either a positive or a negative way or alternately. They may concern such matters as the match between the preannounced content of the course and the actual content, the match between the content of the course and the content of the tests or assignments, the extent to which the reasons for grades were explicitly and adequately justified, the extent to which the possibility of appealing a grade or disciplinary action was explained, the reliability with which scheduled class and conference hours were met, the use of racist or sexist or other bigoted remarks or materials (in and out of class), and so on. This is the so-called Black Marks list (when phrased negatively), and the extent to which it reminds instructors, as well as students, of the minimum professional obligations of the instructor is surprising. These are obligations that can be discharged rather easily and that one constantly finds are an underlying cause of dissatisfaction and bad holistic ratings.

The second kind of legitimate question consists of a listing of the components of instruction for independent "microassessment," that is, "please rate the merit of the catalog description/text/quizzes/grading system/class handouts/sections/labs/fieldwork, etc." Probably the best general-purpose form includes these component-evaluation microquestions, the overall macroquestion, and (optionally) a request for suggested improvements in the form and in the process of administering it. But one can vastly reduce the effort by first using only the 1-3 macroevaluation question(s) and going to component analysis only when the instructor requests it or is seriously and regularly below the mean for comparable courses. At that point, when remedial action is appropriate, the components evaluation is an obvious source of help. When a crucial personnel decision has to be made, the "professionality" questionnaire can provide a useful and valid supplement to information from the other two. (The two can be rather easily combined, at some cost in length that is unimportant for occasional use.)

Data from these forms should be accompanied in the file by comments on them from the instructor. Note that in all of the preceding only student evaluations are used. Students are in the best position to judge, and the evidence suggests they are at least quite good judges (i.e., there is a strong positive correlation of ratings with actual learning), especially if some care is given to preparing them for the rating task and making its value and use clear. Below the sixth grade, student evaluations require more preparation of the class and perhaps can best be done in group discussions. Where possible, ratings by paraprofessionals should be used, either as a supplement to or (in K-4) a substitute for student ratings. Failing these, no substitution should be made of ratings by administrators.

Quality and Professionality

The quality and professionality of content and process must be given careful consideration. The three key quality dimensions are currency, correctness, and comprehensiveness. These are picked up by peer or expert review. For professionality, the concern is with the implementation of a just and helpful teaching process. Ratings for both are made from a sample of (1) the materials provided, (2) the texts required and recommended, (3) the exams, (4) the term paper or project topics, (5) student performances, (6) the instructor's performance in giving appropriate grades for student work, and (7) the instructor's performance in justifying the grades to the students (via written material) and providing other helpful feedback, for example, comments on projects or term papers. The workload involved in this kind of evaluation is quite modest, contrary to appearances, because only a (matrix) sample is required. Other sources of data on these issues are the students' evaluations and the instructor's self-report. Major discrepancies among the data sources require further investigation.

Some traps exist. The text cannot gain points for the instructor unless the instructor chooses it; even then, since it may be little used, it can only account for a few points, perhaps 4 out of 20 or 30. The grades given to students might be all A's or all F's and justified, or they might be "on the curve" and unjustified, either because the performances in general deserved better or worse or because of particular inconsistencies (i.e., inequity). One needs to see the performances, the grades, and the justifications.

Although peers must be used for the evaluation of content, they are usually and culpably not competent to evaluate all that falls under this category, notably what we have here called professionality. This is the technical competence of the instructor in the small area of validated pedagogy, for example, in constructing examination questions that are unambiguous, involve adequate coverage of the intended target area, are not over-cued, and so on. This kind of quality is rather easily identified by somebody with good skills in test construction, and such a person should routinely review samples of the tests of those instructors that are up for (or a year from) particularly important personnel decisions like tenure. In the K-12 situation, this is only sometimes a key skill, but it should be checked whenever relevant.

Another point at which expert evaluation of professionality has some relevance concerns the way in which essays are graded or marked. There are professionally required standards here, with which virtually no faculty member at universities has the slightest familiarity; K-12 teachers are often better trained. As a remedy for this situation, when it is unsatisfactory, administrators should request that, in talking about self-improvement, the instructor fill out, as a normal part of the process, a form indicating how papers are in fact graded. The kind of grading that is legitimate involves at least the following requirements: the papers are graded "blind"; the papers are graded question by question, not paper by paper, to avoid the known large halo effect that results from having read a good or bad first question by the same author just before reading the second question; the exams are shuffled after each question is graded so that different students stand the brunt of one's fatigue (or initial optimism) for different questions; and when one has graded all the Nth questions in a given set of papers, one must then go back and grade the first 6 to 10 papers again in order to see whether one's grading standards have slipped, upward or downward. With multiple-choice exams, many of the preceding requirements are otiose, but the requirement for technical proficiency in constructing them becomes much more important and is something beyond the competence of most academic instructors at the moment.

Actual Learning Gains

Learning gains are useful in evaluating teaching only if one can, in advance, specify and justify the standards or comparisons that will be used. By themselves, they have no legitimate interpretation except, perhaps, when they are zero or negative. In the case of elementary schools that randomly assign pupils to teachers, or for multiply taught sections for an introductory college course, comparisons between sections can be extremely useful. In cases in which there are national norms, they can sometimes be useful. And, for purposes of instructional improvement, one can run a comparison against one's own previous performance and discover whether slight or large changes in approach or text turn out to have significant results.

The main aim of the comparisons is to try to determine what could reasonably have been taught to the students. Although it is always fairly straightforward to find out what was actually taught, that is evaluatively useless without some sense of what was possible and what was remarkable. If allocation of students between the afternoon sections of a large introductory class is random, then one can rather easily discover something quite important about what can be done, if several instructors are involved and prepared to experiment. Patterns of low or high performance by a particular instructor that extend across a couple of years or more become very significant. Shorter periods of study are likely to yield results that are due merely to unrecognized idiosyncracies of the particular classroom, time, groups present, and so on.

One must first realize that only highly salient performances deserve any attention at all and that there may be none of these. No rankings should be squeezed out of this kind of data but if someone consistently produces half the gain scores of five others, after warnings and help, it is time to fire him or her. (The 8th Circuit Court of Appeals in 1979 upheld a superintendent's right to do this.) Second, it is nice that just where student evaluations are least plausible (K-5), the measurement of learning gains is easiest. Third, this method also works on a posttest only basis, with random assignment, but of course the tests must be (1) secure, (2) reasonably comprehensive, and (3) professionally constructed. Fourth, superteachers do sometimes emerge from this process and should be given the opportunity to work as the teaching improvement consultants, with plenty of recognition and reward. They deserve every bit of it. Fifth, using this approach on sections of introductory courses at the college level gives a wonderful cross-check on the validity of student evaluations, at least at the first-year level.

Professional Development Dossier

Although the results of self-evaluation and self-improvement efforts should show up eventually in improved performance on the above scales, it is worth including them directly in a dossier since doing so encourages faculty efforts at professional development and hence speeds up the improvement. This procedure also improves the validity of decisions that have to be made under a time constraint. A professional development dossier should include a rationale for each course's or year's methods and coverage (where these are the instructor's option); evidence about professional development activity such as readings, courses, workshops, and consulting aimed to improve teaching; and, most important, a description of planned and performed experiments on the individual instructor's own teaching approach. A basic list of courses taught, enrollments, and grades; of committees (instructional, departmental, school and district); and of other formalized service should be included here, preferably as hard-copy output from the institutional data base. These four crucial types of data can be ramified usefully and without significant extra cost; for example, feedback from the student should be supplemented by feedback from teaching assistants or teaching aides when these are employed and when confidentiality of the responses can be preserved (as is usually the case).

For purposes of faculty self-development (only), the student questionnaire can be expanded to include an open-ended question in which there is a call for identifying particularly good and particularly bad features of the instruction. One should keep the volume of these responses down when teaching over 500 students a year, because it is so hard to simplify large numbers of these responses, by requesting that they be provided only when either the top or the bottom two scoring categories are used (i.e., only when an A or a D or an F rating of the instructor is given by the student). This also improves their utility, because it avoids the problem of, for example, interpreting favorable responses with long lists of criticisms attached. Responding to what are perceived as salient features is more sensible than trying to balance out large numbers of free-form responses.

Exit Interviews

In addition to the student ratings of the instructor during the class, another type of student rating is exceptionally valuable, at least when done sporadically, and that is the "exit" interview done at graduation. It falls midway between the in-class rating and the alumni rating and is vastly better than the alumni rating because: the rate of return can be around 100% instead of around or below 30%, memories are more reliable at the earlier time, it refers to more recent editions of the courses and the instructor, and causal inferences are more likely to be valid at that point. Exit interviews or questionnaires have sometimes turned up really interesting results, identifying instructors who are thought of as truly outstanding by a quite disproportionately large proportion of the students, but who do not show up in any other search. The "interview" may consist in no more than an additional short form to fill out when applying for the degree or certificate.

The approach outlined here does a great deal to protect faculty from two sources of injustice that are particularly pervasive in current systems. The first is the kind of injustice that makes it impossible for the teacher of a generally unpopular but absolutely essential prerequisite course, for example, calculus for architect students, to score really well compared to the usual norms. The other kind of injustice relates to the individuals who put an enormous amount of work into developing a course, keeping it up to date, and making it as effective a teaching device as they possibly can, at the expense of lots of happy friendly humanistic interchanges and socializing. When an evaluation system is used that does not pay a great deal of attention to the content of the course and that throws in irrelevant requests that ask students to rate the course on "touchy-feely" dimensions, these efforts are largely unrewarded. (Touchy-feely has a place somewhere sometimes, probably as a secondary advantage after the bases are covered; if we are careless in setting up a teacher evaluation system, we reverse these priorities.)

LOGISTICAL CONSIDERATIONS ABOUT STUDENT QUESTIONNAIRES

Much of the preceding refers to summative evaluation for personnel decisions. For that purpose, it is quite important to give out the class questionnaires, if used, at about the same time in the term for all instructors. What is the best time? The faculty at the University of San Francisco argued that the time from the 10th through the 12th weeks of class (semester system) is about right, not too near to the beginning to give a reading on the basis of inadequate experience and not too near to the end so as to interfere with the intensive review period for the examinations and the occasional drop in attendance while students work at home. Getting all the classes visited within this period is logistically feasible for a relatively small campus but would involve substantial difficulties in a large one. However, validity considerations suggest that administration of the questionnaire after final grades have been issued is preferable, and this procedure also increases headroom on the distribution.

How often should the evaluation process be run? Every second or third course given, or term of teaching (K-6), stratified by upper and lower division and graduate categories (college), is a good compromise. Moreover, it cuts the personnel and time requirements for distributing and collecting the forms by one-half or two-thirds and gives faculty a chance to do something about an unsatisfactory readout before the next evaluation is upon them. Student ratings are only one measure and an obtrusive one. Unobtrusive measures, such as reading a sample of student papers, assignment lists, and so on, could be used more often, though it seems unnecessary. More effectively, a matrix sampling across teaching assignments and evaluation components might be used.

On the issue of preserving confidentiality and the integrity of data collection, one could, especially in the precollege situation where consultant help is scarce, turn to secretaries to distribute and collect questionnaires, but there is still a credibility problem about that. It is much better not to use graduate students or indeed any students from the same campus, for similar reasons. The system of having each class elect a student who will do the job and take the materials over to the central administrative offices has worked quite well at some institutions, but it does not provide a person who can answer questions and exhibit authority and inside knowledge about the details and importance of the process and its results. Under no circumstances can one go to mail ballots, or "drop it in the nearest collection box" ballots, because the response rate deteriorates seriously. It is hard to justify validity with return rates under 75%, especially if they are variable between classes. One must select the best procedure in terms of the accessible resources at a particular site.

Although it is fairly easy to use optically scannable cards, this usually gets one into the business of providing the appropriate marking pencils, which can be a problem. It is better to use straightforward forms and have them keypunched; this approach, rather surprisingly, often turns out to be less expensive, even with an error check. The computer program for combining the data on the types of questions that I have been talking about is extremely simple and can provide a variety of interesting readouts. After investigating variations between small and large classes, required and optional classes, first-year and fourth-year classes, and differences between fields, one often gets a pleasant surprise, finding that most of these differences are not sufficiently important to be worth reporting separately, although one can run them through the machine for a check every time the system is operating. In general, however, the principle is always the same; teachers should only be compared to teachers with comparable tasks.

One should also have the computer automatically flag performances that are a half (or a full) standard deviation above the mean and those that are one (or two) standard deviations below the mean, not because a standard deviation means something in terms of traditional significance with the kind of skewed distribution one gets here, but because it is a convenient and quite appropriate flag. If one does not use a set of questions on components or professionality before the holistic question, one will probably have to set the upward flag at half or two-thirds of a standard deviation in order to get any success stories at all, but the top or bottom 15%, 10%, and so on should not be used because the system does not make a ranking meaningful. The standard deviation is just a convenient statistical measure that works well here; there may be better ones, for example, semiinterquartile range. It may well be the case that no teachers are two standard deviations down on any occasion, and none may be consistently down by as much as one. Such a situation is quite desirable, if the overall performance is about where it should be. The system described does not require that there be any losers, unlike a ranking system in which there must always be a bottom 10%, and there can still be winners.

The general issue of records-keeping deserves a mention here. Great universities and small school districts or private schools alike often have no record of what courses an instructor has taught over the years before, for example, a promotion review and, hence, no enrollment or grading data. School districts often have venerable central office records, defined by the board as the only official record and from which adverse comments disappear, hence no longer "exist." College administrators (and not just college faculty) are known to have falsified student responses in order to impugn or favor a particular individual. It is quite easy to avoid all these abuses with a little care: Faculty and administrators should regard this as a necessary duty for the needed fresh start toward satisfactory faculty evaluation.

Certain by-products of the questionnaire kind of approach are of some interest to administrators, especially at the college level. For example, one can get a very good readout on the actual teaching load of the faculty, in terms of numbers of classes and numbers of live bodies; it turns out that there is sometimes a startling number of "phantom" classes, that is, classes that are not in fact meeting although they have not been cancelled, usually because there weren't enough people to justify a scheduled class meeting but the instructor didn't want to convey to the department chair or dean the fact that the assigned teaching load had partly evaporated. A comparison of the number of grades awarded with the number present at the time of the official questionnaire will give an attendance ratio, which is also something that bears watching for faculty members who are trying to improve their performance. The number present for the evaluation should not be printed out on the summary sheets without a reference to the number absent, if the central administration's records or the registrar's computer can produce a current figure on that. Printing out some index of bimodal distributions is also easy but should, in general, be reserved for the situation in which someone is looking for help. Which brings us back to the "development connection."

HOW TO USE STUDENT EVALUATIONS IN
A FACULTY DEVELOPMENT PROCESS

Most of the preceding refers fairly specifically to summative evaluation; it is time to say something more specific about formative evaluation, partly because the summative system described above is often thought to be "hostile" to formative evaluation. In general, there is no need at all for the latter to involve the kind of rigorous supervision of questionnaire administration so far described. Nor need formative evaluation be done at any particular scheduled time, except when a rather careful evaluation of some new procedure is involved. The aim is simply to get useful suggestions for improvement; which leads to very different procedures. In my classes I have frequently used the following rather eccentric approach; although collegiate in specifics, much of it can be transferred to K-12. Evaluation forms are distributed to everybody who comes into the class the moment they walk in the door on the first or second or third day, while the tourists are still shopping around. These forms request the student to turn them in by putting them on the front desk or by giving them to another student to turn in, if they decide not to continue with the course after even one or two sessions. One wants to hear from them whether there was something misleading about the advertising, something needs-irrelevant about the content, or something offputting about the early presentations, and this is the best possible way to pick it up. Perhaps, for example, there was something about the way one outlined the proposed examination and assignment process that seemed particularly formidable. One will not pick these objections up from people that left because of them and hence are not there toward the end when the usual forms are distributed. Indeed, the usual process is heavily biased in favor of the instructor because of the highly self-selected population that stays around. One loses much of the critical and negative feedback, and I personally find that I learn a good deal from it, though I do not pretend that I like reading all of it.

With respect to students who stay around, one next requests that all of them should feel free to submit anonymous suggestions and criticism at any time throughout the term. One needs to make very careful and specific arrangements about this, to preserve their anonymity and to encourage them to see that one is going to do something with the results. One might issue feedback forms and put a collection box in the back of the room, perhaps passing it around once a week. Immediately after the midsemester test is returned, one requests that a full component analysis form, preferably including a Black Marks list, be submitted. A student volunteer may help with synthesis. Now one has the chance to show that this input really is valued, by discussing it and taking whatever steps seem best to improve the class in the light of it. This is also a very good time to demonstrate that some of the criticisms are contradictory and, hence, that one cannot satisfy everybody.

Next, one applies to the faculty senate or the appropriate administrator for permission to give an early final. The final is given during the last class (or two classes) and is quickly corrected so that it can be returned at the time originally scheduled for the official final in finals week. Attendance at that session is required, as it would be for a final, the penalty for absence being an incomplete in the course and possibly a lower grade. At that final session, the exam questions are reviewed in front of the class, an answer key with "model answers" is handed out, a sheet of actual but unsatisfactory answers that illustrate common mistakes is handed out with the appropriate commentary on it, an opportunity is provided to raise objections to the grade with the instructor and perhaps with teaching assistants, and then the students are required to hand in a final evaluation form on the class.

Now one finds out whether one's attempted remedies worked with those who requested them. The students who had been optimistically supposing that they were going to get an A and, in the light of this, had given the instructor quite a good grade in the 10th, 11th, or 12th week are now suddenly confronted with reality; unsurprisingly, their evaluation of the instructor is often affected. However, one cannot expect them to provide as accurate a judgment of the course before receiving a grade as after. Moreover this arrangement—apart from improving the evidential basis of the student evaluations and, probably, the validity of the ratings—makes the exams part of the learning process, not an arrow shot into the air and falling to earth one knows not where except for a grade. This scenario illustrates the point that improvement and effort should be directed by the most accurate evaluation that can be combined with good teaching practice, whether or not the institution uses the best system. Credibility here can be a trade-off for validity, since one does not have to persuade anyone except oneself. That is a major feature of formative evaluation.

In the course of formative evaluation, it is entirely appropriate to ask questions of the students about style, when one is striving to achieve a particular style. But one's rationale for such striving needs very careful examination. It is even more appropriate to ask some microquestions that identify possible problem areas, such as the text, handouts, quizzes, midterm, assignments, grading process, treatment of questioners, availability in office and after class, and final exams. There are no style assumptions lying behind the belief that it is better to perform well than poorly in each of these areas. Whereas it is certainly possible to have all instructors ask everybody about these matters on the standard form, that is, to build them into the general form, such a procedure is not ideal; the consequent increase in the load on the computer and/or staff is not only costly but also the process is less effective because the rigid time for collection of that data does not provide one with the opportunity to see whether improvements can be implemented that work well with the class that registered the complaints. A one-shot feedback is never as useful formatively as the two in the above model. A reasonable compromise that makes the extra load worthwhile for the institution consists in instructors using the "long form" (with the micro questions, and so on) twice, once after the midterm test or assignment, for the instructor's own edification and to identify needed changes, and once at the official time, with only the holistic responses going into the official record.

Now we come to the sequence of external events related to formative evaluation. If an instructor is getting bad ratings overall on a short form that do not seem to be explicable in terms of, for example, the peculiarity that the course is required and has unpopular content, then the next step is to recommend the use of the components analysis ("long") form that I have just mentioned. Professional consulting provided at this point will often suggest a number of ways to improve performance. Only if all of that fails should one even consider going to an analysis of style and a discussion of alternative possible approaches to that, because the results of style research make this a last resort. The consultant has several nonstyle possibilities to worry about first, the professionality considerations, such as the giving of unusually low grades, which may precipitate a suggestion that the instructor alter a particular teaching process because it is unprofessional.

It seems probable that most people who have the requisite content knowledge are capable of becoming quite good instructors, but it is not clear that many of them do so. It is possible or likely that some faculty—including those with tenure—neither could nor will become or remain reasonable instructors. Hence, an evaluation system must, first, identify any unsatisfactory instructors, second, try to upgrade performance, and, third, provide evidence to remove them either from the faculty or from the instructional faculty if improvement does not occur.

Tenure is not an insurmountable obstacle to removal for nonperformance at an appropriate level, and tenure should be phased out anyway. We are now moving away from the legal model of the "master-slave" relationship in colleges and toward the legal model of "just cause" for dismissal, as a result of the affirmative action legislation and the gradual development of an orientation toward collective bargaining. Therefore, previous fears about violations of academic freedom, which were the most important basis for tenure, are somewhat less of a worry and can certainly be taken care of through protective contracts, whether formal or informal. The residual infamy of tenure, due to the number of people who are "burned out" (or wrongly tenured) but kept on by it, stands as a proclamation of lack of responsibility that is becoming increasingly prominent as the hard times for education develop. We cannot afford to continue that way, and we cannot move any other way without a rock-solid process for evaluating teaching and for improving it, which must be the court of first resort. But one must not forget that *valid summative-type evaluation is the essential basis for recommending and detecting improvement*.

INTEGRATING THE RESULTS OF
FACULTY EVALUATIONS

Whereas the results of formative feedback go to the instructor alone or to some consultant chosen by the instructor, the summative evaluations from students also go to the responsible first-level administrator. They must be combined, on appropriate occasions, with the information in the files, direct measurement of learning gains (if available) and appropriate comparisons, ratings by teaching assistants, the quality ratings by topic experts of the content and by process experts of the examining and certain other professional processes, and a pick-up of out-of-class contributions to teaching, for example, individual tutoring, science club talks, forums, campus newspaper articles, or curriculum revision work. In addition, considerations of worth must be brought in for the appropriate decisions. The integrative process is a very tricky one, and all the preceding work may be wasted if bias can sneak in, as it usually can and does. It is not possible to give a complete outline of what should happen at this point without excessive length, but the ideal toward which one should strive is clear enough: The integrative process should be one in which the relative importance of the components is clearly expressed in advance, so that the calculation of an overall score/ grade is automatic, given the grades on each component, that is, a simple weighting and summing procedure. In this respect it should be the same as the procedure used at the college level for combining the results of the teaching evaluation with the results of research and service evaluations. Evaluating teachers involves more than evaluating their teaching, though we have focused on that, as the hardest part. Extreme rigidity in the integrative process is far better (although not necessary) than allowing the department chair or the dean or the principal to do a seat-of-the-pants synthesis of the data at this point, a major way for bias to come in.

There are, of course, a variety of situations in which one does not want to use equal weighting for all these components, but it should be a matter of complete openness to all involved as to how the actual weights are determined and what they are. Where it is possible to arrange for individual variations in the "contract," this should be done at the time of appointment, subject to later revision, and in fact usually can be done.

This is an incomplete version of what is only a fairly complicated procedure. It is a perfectly comprehensible procedure and can readily be made a rather equitable one. One of the results to be avoided if at all possible is the pressure to go with different evaluative approaches by different departments or schools. It may be a useful political procedure to start off with that as a possibility in order to get people on board who cannot admit that their teaching process in a lab or a clinic has anything in common with the teaching process in a philosophy seminar or a basic statistics course. But the real truth of the matter is that the pluralistic view is without intrinsic merit. All essentials of the procedures recommended here work perfectly well in a kindergarten or on a university campus, for any course from finger-painting, through School of Music courses, to molecular biology. One may want to add an extra question or two here, drop one or two there, especially from the formative evaluation procedures and perhaps even from the Black Marks list, but these are very minor changes. At a given site, all of the questions should be on all of the forms that are generally distributed, with a "not applicable" option for the students. The backup use of other forms, with reference to style, where necessary or desired, may certainly be made as idiosyncratic as the instructor pleases, and schools or departments may have a preferred version of these. But those forms should not get into the personnel review process even at the departmental level, because of the legal, ethical, and scientific hazards.

KEY ETHICAL CONSTRAINTS ON
FACULTY EVALUATIONS

The underlying reason for taking such a firm line about excluding style-related questions and answers and observations from personnel evaluation procedures is not merely the absence of any scientific evidence that connects particular approaches to teaching with successful results; it is a much graver matter. It affects formative as well as summative evaluation, which is why it has been left to the end. The error in racism, or sexism, does not lie in the empirical falsehood of the claim, for example, that the crime rate among blacks is higher than it is among whites, or that management success with male subordinates is much less likely for women than for men; both these and many other similar generalizations are probable or true. However, their truth fails to justify the appeal to them in order to make a personnel decision adverse to a black or female candidate, not because it happens to be illegal or unethical, but because it is scientifically indefensible. Generalizations like this are very much less reliable as predictors than inferences made from the track records of the individual candidates. In addition, it is unquestionable that any use of such generalizations would lead to self-fulfilling and socially undesirable results, so on that pragmatic as well as ethical ground they must also be abhorred. One does not need the additional ground in order to see that, no matter what the results of research on teaching styles ever turns out to be, one will never be able to use those results for making decisions about individual instructors because to do so would be a case of guilt by association. One may well ask what the point of research on teaching styles is, if it can never be used in this way. The best answer is that it can increase our repertoire of possibly useful last-resort options. The guilt-by-association point is simply this. Even if high correlations between certain teaching styles and good learning did exist, there would be individuals who used a different style and were successful, since correlations are only statistical. One could not take adverse action against someone who shared the characteristics that tend to identify the unsuccessful group, since that person might be one of the exceptions. One can only use data that refer specifically to that individual's performance: the learning gains of that person's students, the student evaluations of that person, and so on. Not only does this avoid the ethical errors but also the evidential force of such data far overpowers any loose generalization about teaching styles; it is, in fact, exactly the kind of data on which the style generalizations are based. Hence, going to it in the actual case preempts the generalization. The student and content quality judgments are based on this exact case; the generalizations are based only on cases something like this case. Given the generally quite good validity of the student evaluations, when they are discrepant with style desiderata (if any) the student ratings would have to be treated as better indicators. In their absence, and the absence of other instructor-specific data, the case is undecidable. Personnel decisions require personal data.

The preceding result affects formative evaluation too. Because of the costs in time and psychic energy, teachers should not be subjected to any pressure to modify teaching style except as a last resort, after the failure of components and professional evaluations to turn up remedies. Hence, no style questions should appear on standard required questionnaires.

Ethics and, increasingly, the law require certain other steps when possibly unfavorable personnel action is contemplated. These include:

(1) a chance to review the evidence and react to it
(2) a chance to scrutinize the chain of argument from the evidence to the unfavorable conclusion
(3) advance warning that provides time for improvement and a clear description of what degree of improvement will be satisfactory (This should not be taken to mean that the administration must provide a sure-fire remedy—because that is not always possible—but only a clear definition of what would constitute acceptable performance.)
(4) the above events to be recorded as having occurred on specified dates, preferably with the log signed off by both parties (This is the "audit trail" requirement.)

(5) since age (till 70) will be disallowed as a criterion, we urgently need a sound evaluation system that can be used throughout the tenured years, or else no dotard can be dropped before 70 (and perhaps not then, in the future). Often a reduction in load, and salary, and a change of title is the kindest move, but it must be done using a system applied to everyone regardless of age, or it will be disallowed, and rightly so. "Applied" means enforced, not pantomimed, on younger tenured teachers.

A final point on the ethical side. It is not ethical, and it may not even be legal, to deny to the students who generate the key evaluation judgments in the process recommended above the opportunity to see the summarized results. One might certainly argue against it with respect to some detailed written-in remarks, because those cannot properly be used without balancing them against all the rest, something that students may not be in a position to do; but the summarized holistic responses, and their distribution, cannot properly be withheld from the students. In addition to questions of propriety, there is the thoroughly unattractive possibility that the students, frustrated in their attempt to get these results, will set up their own evaluation system and the administration will then either have to cooperate with it, which increases the chance of questionnaire overload with a reduction in response rate and validity as well as a loss of class time, or take the indefensible position that students are not allowed to poll their peers in order to evaluate instructors.

Some compromises will be necessary in negotiating a joint effort, because the kind of evaluation of instructors that students are interested in is as different from the kind described as formative is from summative. Students are interested in such questions as the assignment mode and load, the cost of the textbooks and whether they are really necessary, and certain teaching style variables, which can well be an appropriate basis for a student with a certain learning style to use in selecting in or out of a particular class. But compromises of this kind should and can be made in the interest of a campus-community approach. Student morale and cooperation are not well-served by leaving them out of this process, and, in the long run, faculty evaluation and faculty improvement suffers from not having the best input from students.

None of the above entails an obligation to publish the results. As Centra has pointed out to me, making them available might be enough. However, publishing may produce more substantial improvement by faculty and more learning by students.

CONCLUSION

Personnel evaluation is, in general, a field that requires some care and attention, and it is usually done with amazing incompetence, as one can readily discover by studying the forms used by the White House, by large corporations, or by the military. If it is to be improved, presumably the academies should be the source of the leadership. These institutions, after all, do most of the little relevant research and interpretation. In the key matter of the evaluation of teachers at the K-12 as well as at the college level, they have shown a disgraceful disinclination to work on it, and in recent years, when that indifference has partly evaporated because of heat from outside, there remains a depressing failure to do it in a defensible way. Perhaps the remarks in this and the opening paragraph of this article will prove sufficiently irritating to lead to improvement. It is easy to refute them: one need only produce a single school district or college in the country whose teacher evaluation procedures avoid the gross invalidity and injustice that results from the dozen sources of error discussed here. Or even if that has not been done, one need only show that there are good excuses for not doing it. I affirm that neither response is possible and that faculty, students, and taxpayers deserve better.

REFERENCES

Centra, J. A. *Determining Faculty Effectiveness,* San Francisco: Jossey-Bass, 1979.
Scriven, M. et al. "Do student ratings involve guilt by association?" *Evaluation Notes,* 1980 (Nov.) and 1981 (March).

CHAPTER 15

POLITICS OF TEACHER EVALUATION

JOHN D. McNEIL

University of California, Los Angeles

The inevitability of conflicting demands, wants, and needs is responsible for the necessarily political character of teacher evaluation. Politics is a process used when a conflict of interest exists. This chapter focuses on the activities and views of individuals and groups as they impose on decisions about teachers. Legal constraints and state and federal influences on these decisions are shown. Basic strategies for dealing with conflicting views of teacher evaluation are given, along with illustrations of the use of these strategies in designing evaluation systems at elementary, secondary, and higher educational levels. Finally, generalizations are made about political considerations in implementing an evaluation system.

VALUE BASES

Conflicts over the proper bases for evaluating teachers are numerous. Individuals and groups have different concepts of the desirable personal characteristics, institutional contributions, community services, and instructional effectiveness of teachers. They also have different purposes for evaluating teachers: instructional improvement, personal growth, and accountability and control, which include selection, placement, tenure, promotion, and dismissal. Each value base has its supporters and detractors, who use political techniques to broaden their position. At times, evaluation procedures reflect the intents of employers, who use evaluation for the purpose of promotion or dismissal. At other times, assessment plans, involving peers and union representatives, are aimed at the improvement of teaching performance.

MAJOR INFLUENCES IN TEACHER EVALUATION

Teachers are direct intermediaries between students and the values inherent in particular content and methods. To the extent that adherents of given political views can shape the decisions of teachers with respect to teaching goals, content, and processes, they stand a good chance of affecting changes in students in the desired directions. Teacher evaluation is a key way to exert influence over the teacher. The following section provides illustrations of some of the political forces influencing teachers and indicates the nature of the competition among these forces for control over the evaluation of teachers.

Influence means the ability to get others to act, think, and feel as one intends. The group or individual who can make a difference in the outcome of the conflict over teacher evaluation has influence. Influence is found at federal, state, and local levels of government and among special interest groups, such as the American Association of University Professors, the Parent Teachers Association, the American Federation of Teachers, and the National Education Association. Moreover, there is a configuration of influence within local schools involving teachers, department heads, supervisors, principals, and students. Cutting across all levels of government is the persuasive influence of journalists, commentators, and key public figures, who disseminate their views about the conduct and effectiveness of teachers.

External Influences

Federal Government. In their concern for equity, those in federal agencies support programs to increase fundamental literacy among the poor and minorities. Definitions of "good teaching" that arise from these programs follow a technological model: pretesting the learner with respect to specific skills arranged on a continuum; assigning each learner to material in an instructional sequence relevant to the appropriate skill level as indicated by the pretest; and administering a posttest to indicate the degree of mastery of the skill, followed either by further teaching of the skill or instruction in a subsequent one. This teaching model calls for persistent application to pre-specified tasks, highly structured learning situations, teacher direction, and control of events. Examples of federally supported activities that reinforce the technological model are: Right to Read's focus on diagnostic prescriptive skills; Public Law 94-142, which prescribes that each handicapped child have an individualized program, including short- and long-term educational goals and criteria to use in determining whether objectives are being reached; and regional educational laboratories (such as the Far West Laboratory), which conduct both evaluation studies of teaching and inservice training of teachers emphasizing the technological model of teaching as the standard for effective teaching.

Other federal influences on the evaluation of teaching are seen in federal enforcement policies on bilingual education and in the role of the U.S. Office of Education in the inservice education of teachers. The Office of

Civil Rights, for example, has been responsive to Hispanic groups by downplaying the methodology of English as a second language in teaching non-English speakers, prohibiting school districts from relying solely on the English-as-a-second-language method.

In addition to fostering concerns for equity and encouraging cultural pluralism by placing a high value on teaching procedures that are consistent with these concerns, federal agencies and legislators are influencing the criteria for judging teachers and weakening local domination of teacher development and evaluation. A National Teacher Development Initiative Survey (Smith and Feiztrizer, Note 1) shows that 21 of the U.S. Office of Education's 120 programs have a component for the development of educational personnel. Teacher corps and teacher centers, both authorized under Title V of the Higher Education Act, are concerned exclusively with the professional development of teachers. The political implication of these programs is seen in such legislation as Public Law 94-482, the teacher center legislation, legitimizing the position that teachers should be the controlling force in staff development. This law, which was lobbied for and supported by teacher organizations, provides that teacher centers come under the operation of a policy board whose members are represented by a majority of practicing elementary and secondary teachers (Yarger and Yarger, 1978).

Briefly then, federally sponsored activity influences teacher evaluation in two ways: (1) by promulgating models of teaching consistent with the values held by proponents of equity and cultural differences and (2) by weakening school district authority for evaluating teachers for purposes of teacher improvement, challenging the right of local authorities to control inservice training. This right has rested on the grounds that employers have direct responsibility for maintaining teaching standards through staff development and the improvement of classroom performance.

State Legislatures and Departments of Education. Concerned about higher, but apparently unproductive, school expenditures, state legislatures began in 1970 to enact laws requiring the appraisal of teachers. California's Stull Act, for example, requires that local school boards evaluate teachers yearly and provide recommendations for improvement. One requisite in the local district evaluation system is evidence of students' progress toward locally defined expectations. In practice, such laws are often implemented to comply with the letter of the law but not with the spirit. This may be because additional funds for implementing the legislation are not provided or because state legislatures cannot effectively carry out their own policies without persuading local evaluators of their value.

Through competency-based legislation, states have emphasized some goals at the expense of others. Highest priority is given to the basic skills of literacy, with tests serving as proxies for the goals. Having delimited the goals of education, the legislation assumes that teachers will direct their teaching in a more efficient manner. Some see minimum competency testing as a victory for state legislatures over the local school system, because minimum competency testing makes teachers better bureaucrats but causes them to lose the modicum of professional discretion they now hold (Wise, 1979).

State certification of teachers and approval of programs for teacher preparation are other ways in which states exert influence on teacher behavior. Increasingly, teacher-preparing institutions find it necessary to have competency-based programs to win state approval. Teachers are then certified on the basis of performance in a number of isolated teaching skills thought to be related to successful instruction in the classroom. As Harris documents in Chapter 5, there are signs that states are moving in the direction of requiring new teachers to take competency tests measuring both the basic skills demanded for high school graduation and general teaching skills, such as ability to select instructional materials, knowledge of subject areas, and special teaching techniques. Although leaders of teacher unions are more accepting of such tests for applicants than for working teachers, they generally oppose them, indicating that the tests are likely to discriminate against minorities and are of doubtful accuracy.

As a step toward winning from legislators the right to determine teacher entry into the profession, Albert Shanker, President of the United Federation of Teachers, proposes that new teachers should be required to take competency tests and complete a training program before they receive tenure (Shanker, 1979).

Teacher Organizations. The National Education Association favors evaluation of teachers for instructional improvement but not for accountability or control. It opposes the use of national teacher examinations for teacher licensure, selection, assignment, evaluation, retention, salary determination, promotion, transfer, tenure, or dismissal. This organization also rejects the evaluation of teaching on the basis of any outcome measure of student learning (Soar and Soar, 1977). Outcome measures are opposed on the grounds (1) that what goes on in the classroom is not the only influence on the child's achievement, (2) measures for many of the objectives for which teachers have responsibility are lacking, (3) statistical difficulties arise in the measurement of pupil change, and (4) the teacher may give attention primarily to a small portion of the students when held accountable for pupil achievement.

Teacher organizations prefer to focus on the conditions that teachers confront and on those changes in conditions that they think will help a teacher do a more effective job: smaller class size, paid inservice education, parent-teacher and regional conferences, and publications treating issues in education, such as testing, discipline, and the gifted. These organizations do not take responsibility for removing incompetent teachers from the classroom. They hold that hiring and firing are the responsibility of the employer. A position paper from the American Federation of Teachers puts forth the concept that the analysis and assessment of teachers should lead to self-growth and self-development through programs based on the specific roles that teachers are performing (Bhaevman, Note 2). Although teacher organizations oppose evaluation for accountability as quality control and assessment for purposes of comparing teachers and rewarding or punishing them, they are on record as favoring the use of multiple resources, such as peers, supervisors, college personnel, self-analysis, and even assessments by students, when these resources are for the purpose of helping the teacher. In spite of their general opposition to negative assessment by school authorities, which they tend to view as deficient, leaders of some teacher organizations blame school boards and administrators for being irresponsible in hiring and evaluating incompetent teachers. "Most districts make virtually no investment in the evaluation of teacher performance. The typical high school principal with 70 to 75 teachers does not have time to supervise them" (Herndon, 1979). Charles J. Santelli, Director of Research and Educational Policies for the New York State United Teachers, has been quoted as saying, "If there is an incompetent teacher; that means that the supervisor is not doing his job" (Santelli, 1979).

Teacher organizations are bidding for control of teacher licensing. State boards of education, such as those in Minnesota, Oregon, California, and New York, are at various stages in the classification of teachers as professionals, thereby allowing statewide examinations for teachers and uniform disciplinary procedures on the recommendation of a professional practice board. The domination of such a board by a teacher union is possible. Designating the teaching field as a profession not only provides it increased status but also gives the teacher organization a greater voice in determining who enters the field, the credentials required, and how teachers are disciplined. The president of the United Federation of Teachers has said that making teachers professional will correct the failure of the present system to test teacher competency. "In our state you have to take an examination to become a lawyer and to get a driver's license and to sell insurance. The fact that teachers are now exempt from such a test is a form of deprofessionalization" (Shanker, 1979).

Teacher organizations have already increased their influence on teacher evaluation through the collective bargaining process. Contractual provisions regulating teacher working conditions limit principals' latitude in managing teaching (McDonnell and Pascal, 1979). Sometimes this new emphasis on legal rights and duties creates an atmosphere that impedes the relations of administrators and teachers. Collective bargaining does not always affect significantly either classroom operations or the quality of educational services provided to students. Nevertheless, bargaining gains in such areas as time for preparation, inservice education, professional leave, and textbook selection offer the possibility of increasing tension between teachers' interests over the conditions of their work and public demands for control over the goals and results of that work. Sometimes bargaining works against the interest of teachers. As one principal put it, "With the advent of collective bargaining came a new perspective of teacher evaluation: that of the 'gotcha process.' In the 'gotcha process,' teachers live in constant fear of being caught in the act of doing something in the classroom that may violate a provision in the contract for what the principal may, during the course of the evaluation, say, 'Aha! I got you for _____" (Stone, 1978).

Courts. As indicated by Professors Strike and Bull in Chapter 17, numerous legal factors bear upon policies for the evaluation of teachers, including constitutional considerations, federal civil rights laws, state statutes, administrative regulations, and local collective bargaining regulations. Although the courts tend to apply procedural requirements of teacher evaluation laws strictly, they usually defer to the discretion and expertise of school authorities with regard to the substantive aspects of teacher effectiveness.

Much of the influence of the courts comes from their enforcing the provisions of legislation or contracts. Zirkel and Castens (Note 3) conclude the following from their study of teacher evaluation and statuary and case law:

(1) The law of teacher evaluation is largely a state matter.
(2) The state must decide if teacher evaluation is permissive, mandatory, or illegal. The answer determines whether specific procedures for teacher evaluation will be locally established beyond state and federal standards.
(3) States differ in their provisions for what evaluation procedures are formulated (most leave the matter to the local board), which categories of teachers are to be evaluated (most evaluate all teachers), when evaluation takes place (most evaluate beginning teachers more frequently than experienced teachers), the scope of the evaluation (most use a categorical approach, that is, personality, preparation, techniques, pupil relations), and how the evaluation is to be conducted (most states leave it to the local board).
(4) Courts are strict about compliance with procedures mandated in the legislation on teacher evaluation, although there is some flexibility in applying procedures when the teacher does not have tenure.
(5) Where local discretion is permitted, districts should establish clear standards and procedures for determining competence.
(6) It is dangerous to base unsatisfactory evaluations leading to dismissal entirely on student test scores. Evaluation of a teacher's work compared with other teachers and evidence of low achievement of students can be introduced as additional evidence.
(7) Nonracial criteria must be used in judging the performance of teachers.

Evidence has been reported that the courts are filling in the gaps left by legislatures in requirements for evaluating teachers (Norden, 1978). For example, courts have determined that administrators have the right to forbid the conduct of a teacher when it materially and substantially interferes with appropriate discipline in the operation of the school. State laws allow school boards to discontinue the contracts of those who pose unacceptable moral and ethical influences on students.

The impact of the courts' concern about strict compliance with due process can be seen in the procedures for teacher evaluation, taken from a longer list, recommended by a state study council (Erickson, Note 4):

(1) Provide written standards of minimum teacher performance and expectancy.
(2) Inform teachers of district standards and requirements.
(3) Inform teachers in writing of changes in purpose for the evaluation.
(4) Inform teachers of the personnel file and its use, of the dismissal law, and of their rights and responsibilities.
(5) Involve a number of diversified qualified people in evaluating a teacher under fire. Get signed evaluation statements from them.
(6) Observe time schedule for dismissal cases.
(7) Use general delivery or certified mail; get a signed receipt.
(8) Know the law and its implications, for example, material from the personnel file that is admissible for evidence.
(9) Be sure that charges are documented in the personnel file and that, if these charges are to be used in the hearing, the teacher has a copy.
(10) Include measurable statistical data when possible.
(11) Word charges carefully, avoiding cause-and-effect statements. Choose the stated charges carefully, for example, inefficiency, inadequate preparation, insubordination, neglect of duty.
(12) Be specific as to days, dates, times when possible.
(13) Be sure your witnesses are available.
(14) Plan preventive measures carefully—job orientation, counseling, assistance.
(15) Consider all possible alternatives to dismissal.
(16) Do not depend on statements placed in the personnel file during the probationary period as evidence in tenure case.
(17) Do not refuse legitimate requests for transfer.

Briefly, then, the influence of the courts on teacher evaluation is greatest in ameliorating the conflict among local authorities, individuals, and teacher unions over control of the basis for evaluating teaching and when the purpose of evaluation is dismissal. School administrators complain that when they take steps to declare a teacher incompetent, they run up against a cumbersome and expensive legal process; it requires thousands of dollars in legal fees and indirect costs to rate one person as unsatisfactory. The issue does not turn so much on whether there is an incompetent teacher but on whether the record is solid:

(1) Does a legally permissible cause exist; for example, lack of student progress is both a reasonable and a substantial cause.
(2) Were data collected in a constitutionally permissible way?
(3) Is there a record of observations and evaluations of the teacher and of efforts to help the teacher improve?
(4) Does the process allow for an overlay of good faith?

Parents and the Public. According to a 1979 Gallup poll, parents and the public want "better teachers" and define them as those who take a personal interest in each student, trying to understand students and their problems, encouraging students so they get high grades, and inspiring students to set high goals in life for themselves. The public is demanding the establishment of authority, an authority of values, standards, and guiding purpose.

Parent and community representatives are now participating in the preparation of teachers. The California legislature, for example, mandates parent-community membership of at least 20% on all assessment and monitoring evaluation teams for the basic teacher credential programs. California legislation also mandates school site councils composed of 50% parents with real authority for determining school programs, including the evaluation of teaching. Parents are encouraged to bring reasonable complaints and concerns about teaching practices, as well as praise, to the council meetings.

Declining confidence in schools has been associated with the public's more negative or critical opinion of teachers. Collective bargaining has contributed to bad images of schools and teachers. In trying to improve their bargaining position, teachers portrayed boards and administrators as wasteful, incompetent, petty, tyrannical, political, and unconcerned about public welfare. School board members sought public support against teachers by labelling them lazy, incompetent, overcompensated, and concerned only with their own welfare. The public believed both sides. Comments about the deterioration of schools by writers such as James Michener have contributed to the declining esteem for teachers and schools. "The fact is that many classrooms are arenas in which purposeful learning can't take place. The incompetence of teachers, lack of discipline, the failure of society to support education. All of these are worrisome" (Michener, 1979).

Internal Influences

Teachers. Teachers fear evaluation. Appraisal usually arouses their anxiety. They want to feel that their worth as teachers is unconditional, not contingent on how they score on someone else's scales of merit. Teachers believe that the standards for evaluating what is effective teaching are too vague and ambiguous to be worth anything, that appraisal techniques fall short of providing information accurately characterizing their performance, and that judgments made about them depend more on the idiosyncrasies of the rater than on the teacher's own behavior in the classroom.

In his survey of teachers' feelings toward evaluation, Wolf (1973) found two kinds of teachers—those with positive concepts of evaluation and those with negative ones. Examples of positive concepts are views that (1) teachers welcome communication with parents, administrators, and peers about their own classroom program; (2) teachers are the most important audience for the results of evaluation studies; (3) assessing the results of one's own teaching is important; and (4) teachers want to take time to learn about how they can effectively evaluate their work. Examples of negative concepts are views that (1) there is no need for better communication with other groups about classroom programs; (2) the opinions of students are not valuable in evaluation of the classroom; (3) assessing the results of their teaching and the progress of the class is not important; and (4) they cannot spare the time to learn more about how they can effectively evaluate their own program.

Wolf concluded that if teachers are to develop more positive and broader views of evaluation, the threat of evaluation must be reduced. Threat might be reduced by working with parents, board members, administrators, supervisors, and individual teachers to show how evaluation can improve existing programs. It is important that evaluation not just assign blame but that it identify strengths and weaknesses. Also, it might be helpful to give rewards to teachers for participating in evaluation: systematic instruction, feedback from parents, and more teacher autonomy in evaluation.

It may be shortsighted to regard resistance to evaluation as a mere technical problem solvable by a new instrument, organization, system, or political ploy. To the extent that evaluation is judging, punishing, and controlling, it will produce anxiety. Although teachers are not opposed to observing other teachers, modeling a teaching practice, and sharing ideas with others, teachers seldom see each other in the act of teaching. Hence, their judgments of other teachers are based on observations of interpersonal competencies and ability to influence school decisions. High-status teachers are seen as helpful, as willing to share resources with others, and as preparing students well in terms of subject matter and classroom behavior (Smith and Sandler, 1974). Social power, the ability to influence the rewards for other teachers, is also a basis of status, at least in those schools in which the supervisor lacks power.

Supervisors. Consultants, coordinators, and department chairmen are among the titles of supervisors who are expected to assist teachers in ways that will improve their teaching. Blumberg (1974) has described the "cold war" that exists between supervisors and teachers. His book is an analysis of the behavioral and organizational dimensions that cause distrust on both sides. Similarly, Crews (1979) documented the sources of satisfaction and dissatisfaction among supervisors. Sources of supervisors' dissatisfaction are having suggestions ignored by teachers, receiving negative comments from teachers who want more expert assistance, being blamed by teachers when supervisors enforce state and local policies, being assigned responsibility for telling teachers they are to be dismissed, being responsible for supervising so many teachers that effective supervision is impossible, being held responsible for teacher performance without a voice in teacher selection, and seeing teachers released despite the supervisor's recommendation to allow more time for improvement. Sources of supervisors' satisfaction are providing teachers with support, suggestions, and experiences that enable them to improve teaching performance and being complimented by principals for helping teachers improve teaching. Clearly, supervisors get much more satisfaction from and prefer to spend their time in planning workshops and other staff development activities for teachers (improvement purposes) than they do from enforcing evaluation policies for accountability purposes. Without pressure from superintendents, boards of education, and organized parents, there is little likelihood that supervisors will become directly involved in the hard-edged evaluation of teachers.

Principals. Principals are responsible for selecting, training, guiding, and evaluating the teachers in their schools. This responsibility is mandated by tradition—community acceptance of the principal's role—and by law. Principals are charged with ensuring that subjects are well-taught. Principals get pressure for better quality teaching from board members, parents, students, community members, and teachers. An underlying assumption made by these groups is that the principal must present more demanding expectations for teachers than they set for themselves.

An acute dilemma for the principal is reconciling the two major functions of teacher evaluation. In order to fulfill the function of helping teachers, the principal must establish an open climate in which the teacher feels free to show incompetence. How can such a climate exist when the teacher knows that the principal must assess the teacher's fitness?

Some principals divorce themselves from one of the roles. For example, to fulfill the function of helping teachers, the principal may establish an *informal* evaluation procedure for the purpose of diagnosing instructional problems and offering suggestions in which the principal does not participate. The teacher seeks help on a specific problem from an outsider—parent, coordinator, fellow teacher. In addition to the informal procedure, there may be a formal one in which the principal takes an active part by observing in the classroom at least three times a year, filling out an appraisal form, and commenting on work in different subject areas and on the teacher's relations with parents, other teachers, and children. Strengths, weaknesses, and observed difficulties are described, and the entire report, with a copy to the teacher, is filed in the personnel office to be used in consideration of tenure and other decisions. Generally, elementary and secondary school principals differ in their biases regarding effective teaching. Elementary principals view warmth and acceptance as essential criteria, principals in intermediate schools prefer creativity, and high school principals favor dynamism. Principals at all levels value organized behavior (Hyman, 1979).

Faculty Colleagues. In higher education, faculty peers make judgments about teaching effectiveness. Peer judgments of the professor as a scholar are common and employ relatively well-defined criteria. Colleagues are often asked to assess their peers with respect to service, research and publications, knowledge of subject, recognition by others in their profession, and ability to cooperate with other members of the department. Classroom activities are seldom the basis for evaluation. Peer judgments of the professor as a teacher can be improved by making observations with respect to the following:

(1) knowledge of subject—observing the candidate's discussions of recent developments in a field, consulting with others, and assessing the candidate's sense of problems or ideas
(2) quality of teaching materials—observing the currency and appropriateness of the candidate's materials for course goals, including tests, syllabi, reading lists, and course outlines
(3) student performance—observing the kinds of tests and the quality of projects and assignments and collecting evidence of what students have learned
(4) departmental responsibilities—observing the quality of service on committees and the supervision of graduate students.

Chapter 6 contains further discussion of these and other indicators.

Students. Student participation in the formal evaluation of teachers is a function of the maturity they have and the nature of the particular community. Usually, it is a privilege granted by higher powers and subject to revocation. Student ratings are an important source of information in decisions about tenure and promotion in higher education. The political value of forwarding these ratings to administrative officers should not be overlooked. They are offered as proof to legislatures that the institution is interested in teaching, not just in research. In addition, they represent a convenient response to student desire for power.

In giving direct feedback to the instructor, students are influential in effecting changes in teacher behavior. In evaluating teachers, students are concerned about knowledge of subject matter and classroom interaction but lack insight about planning competencies such as assessment of student entry skills and evaluation of learning. Their ratings often measure student satisfaction, attitudes toward teachers in general, psychological needs of students, and the personality, popularity, and speaking quality of the teacher.

Students exert other influences on teacher evaluation. Often they "vote with their feet," refusing to enroll in courses taught by particular instructors. The issuing of student publications describing individual faculty members and their courses is not uncommon.

STRATEGIES FOR DEALING WITH CONFLICTING POLITICAL VIEWS OF TEACHER EVALUATION

There are two conflicting views of teacher evaluation. The accountability view is partly expressed in public concern that teachers are not paying enough attention to individual pupils and that they are not sufficiently dedicated. There are accountability demands for evaluation to assure the public that incompetent teachers will be removed. The accountability view is also expressed in legislative acts, federally funded programs specifying teacher role definition, and instructional procedures.

The noncontrolling view is that evaluation should be nonjudgmental, that it avoid the crushing pressure of judgments from supervisors, principals, students, parents, and peers. This view, which is prevalent among teachers, teacher organizations, and staff development agencies, favors self-evaluation and a professional supportive culture. Accordingly, instructional improvement is emphasized through development activities in which teachers are considered to be skilled professionals who help each other by bringing unique abilities to improvement activities. Teachers are not regarded as weak teachers who need improvement because they are lacking in the skill for doing an effective job. Rather, they are seen as competent persons whose creativity can be enhanced when additional resources are made available to them.

The noncontrolling view of evaluation usually results in informal evaluation plans. However, most informal, nonjudgmental evaluation plans have serious weaknesses. At the elementary and secondary school levels, staff development agencies, teacher centers, and other forms of inservice education initiated by federally funded activities and promoted by teacher unions are aimed at political goals. They aim at a technological view of teaching. That is, they have an equity bias, and they seek to enhance teacher union views of educational issues and of what teachers themselves perceive as problems. All of these purposes may be valid but are not sufficient for improving teaching. Informal evaluation seldom attracts the teacher most in need of improvement and runs the risk of being a random activity, unrelated to other instructional improvement activities and remote from the goals of the school. Further, without the participation of school administrators, administrative cooperation is lacking for effecting the institutional support necessary for implementing whatever teachers have acquired from the programs.

The question of location of staff improvement programs is itself a political concern, a decision about control. Ideally, the school or department is the best unit for staff development, allowing active participation by teachers, principal, interested parents, and students.

Informal evaluation plans can be strengthened to improve participation and focus. Institutional policies should enhance attendance by both good and apathetic teachers by linking staff development to the formal evaluation systems, for example, by placing a record of accomplishment acquired from the development program in one's résumé for promotion and by granting released time for attendance.

Through the use of performance objectives in staff development, teaching competencies can be tied to school goals. Informal evaluation is strengthened by specifying the kind of help that is necessary, the data that will be collected to assess achievement, and a statement of what constitutes an acceptable level of accomplishment.

The conflicting views of teacher evaluation lead to three different strategies for planning evaluation systems.

The first strategy advances the argument that nonjudgmental improvement activities serve the accountability objective of evaluation in the most effective manner. To the extent that the plan has a systematic staff development program emphasizing intrinsic rewards and following developmental, not deficit models, administrative officials can show that they are interested in good teaching and that total staff participation in the program is the best way to ensure quality teaching.

The second strategy recognizes the two foci of evaluation and designs separate evaluation systems for accountability and for improvement. Provision should be made to overcome the criticisms that under dual systems the informal improvement plans are not taken seriously and that the separation of functions makes it difficult for the teacher to reconcile the expectations of the separate systems.

The third strategy gives major attention to the need for exercising authority in school administration, to tighten up evaluation procedures to ensure that they meet laws and court decisions about evidence that can be used in cases involving rehiring, transfer, and dismissal.

EXAMPLES OF TEACHER EVALUATION SYSTEMS

The Salt Lake City Model

This model follows most closely the third strategy. The school administrators and the teacher union have created a highly structured evaluation program aimed at improving or terminating the weak teacher. All certified employees are required to write individual accountability plans and performance objectives each fall for the coming school year. Each teacher's plan is approved by the principal at an individual conference.

Any member of the school community—parent, employee, student—can request in writing a "review of service." This is followed by an informal remediation phase and, if necessary, a formal remediation phase. Cues that a teacher needs help are poor classroom management, lack of planning, low test scores consistently below other students', inability to keep students on task, lack of rapport with students, teacher screaming, and complaints from parents.

Informal remediation begins with the principal making several observations, informing the teacher of problems identified, and making suggestions. The teacher may ask for special resources in order to improve. If less than adequate improvement occurs after a reasonable period of time, the principal initiates formal remediation.

Once formal remediation is decided on, a remediation team is assembled consisting of the principal, the district learning specialist, and two teachers chosen by the union. One of these is appointed for strength in the pertinent grade level or subject; the other is the union's representative, whose primary function is to ensure due process. Team members observe in the classroom, conduct an improvement conference with the teacher, and give assistance as appropriate. The specific resources that the teacher wants to call on—aides, consultants, special materials—are determined. Scheduled visits are made to the classroom, and periodic progress reports are given to the principal and teacher. After two months, if the teacher has substantially improved, the testing by performance is over. If not, there is another three months of team-directed remediation. During this period, there are unannounced visits to the classroom, and some teachers get "counseled out." One way to get a teacher to resign is to offer to destroy negative personnel records upon resignation. If team standards are not met, the teacher is terminated with 30 days' notice. Each case takes a different character depending on the teacher and the situation: A bad teacher resigns and lets his file be destroyed; an improved teacher plans better and feels better about his work; another learns to judge better how long classroom activities take.

The technique of using peers in the process is useful. The teacher in need is assigned to another's classroom for three days, during which time the teacher observes and helps the host teacher, finally taking over the class. In spite of the stress, most teachers on remediation appear satisfied with their progress (Divoky, 1979).

Newport-Mesa Performance-Based Appraisal Plan

This plan follows most closely the second strategy. Operationally, this plan separates the functions of improvement and accountability by creating two types of evaluation. There is an *improvement cycle*—an informal, formative evaluation, which provides all teachers with opportunities to practice instructional skills with the assistance of colleagues who compose an observation, analysis, and conferencing team. Requirements for the improvement cycle include these elements: The teacher and the evaluators agree on what should be appraised and on how the appraisal is to be made; the focus is on the results obtained; processes and methods are recorded and analyzed in relation to obtained results, as means to be appraised not prized as ends. The second type of evaluation is the *appraisal cycle*—a formal, summative appraisal. This cycle calls for a teacher to submit each semester for the principal's approval instructional objectives covering two subject areas. At the end of each semester, data are collected documenting the extent to which the objectives were attained. Information from this evaluation is used by the principal in writing the teacher's end-of-year evaluation report. Requirements for the appraisal cycle include these elements: The plan must operate within the legal requirements of the local board and the state; adequate resources must be made available so that the operational requirements of the plan may be carried out; the plan must provide data to aid in making decisions about staff utilization, teacher improvement, clarification of the teaching assignment and results obtained, and continuation of the teacher's services. In addition to providing data on the teacher's performance in working with students, the overall appraisal plan calls for information about a teacher's performance with four other populations: the consumer community (e.g., future employers of students), the social community (e.g., neighborhood councils), the school environment (e.g., fellow teachers), and the professional self (e.g., self-improvement).

Higher Education Evaluation Patterns

The second strategy, dual systems of evaluation, is frequently followed in higher education.

Summative evaluation. The control variables of promotion and dismissal are largely left to departments, colleges, and standing committees. Faculty and administrators jointly participate in decisions about the candidate.

Through scheduled faculty reviews for purposes of retention and promotion, teachers undergo socialization into the values of the institution, including the relative importance of teaching and the mode of teaching desired, for example, didactics, actions to teach facts and principles; heuristics, actions to develop problem solving skills and strategies; and philetics, actions to help learners develop interpersonal skills and relationships.

The Center for Faculty Evaluation and Development at Kansas State University has developed a summative assessment system based on two propositions: (1) that effective teaching is best recognized by its impact on students and (2) that the amount of impact is a function of the instructor's classroom behavior. Teaching effectiveness is determined by reports by students of their progress toward teaching objectives that the faculty member specified as important for that particular course. Monitoring of results makes it possible to determine whether certain teaching techniques are associated with higher student gain. The system also provides for many different models of instruction reflecting the wide range of objectives deemed important by individual instructors. Adjustments are made for differences in the motivational level of students and class size (Hoyt and Cashin, Note 5).

Guidelines for improving summative evaluation procedures call for systematic assessment. There should be sufficient time, two or three years, to collect evidence of the teacher's work. As discussed by French-Lazovik in Chapter 6, enough data should be collected to ascertain trends and improvement, and the process of evaluation should guarantee the anonymity and independence of the raters.

Formative evaluation. The provision of resources for faculty development is getting increased recognition as a possible way to improve teaching quality. Federal funding allocated to states for upgrading teaching has resulted in increased emphasis on evaluation for purposes of teaching improvement and growth. The emphasis takes the form of instructional development, that is, curriculum development, teaching diagnosis, and training; personnel development or interpersonal skill training and career counseling; and organizational development or improvement in the institutional environment for teaching. In general, faculty attitudes toward instructional improvement favor personal development. Popular practices are provisions for visiting scholars, sabbatical leaves, grants for instructional improvement through travel, and temporary reduction in teaching load. Only a small number of faculty are involved in these practices at any one time.

The instructional improvement programs in higher education are characterized as "meek medicine for a major affliction" (Popham, 1974). The commitment is largely political, stemming more from a desire for good public relations than from a genuine desire to bring about increased faculty effectiveness. Campus improvement agencies have few personnel and limited financial resources. Typically, faculty participation is voluntary, resulting in active participation by good teachers who want to get better. The least active are those who need to improve, older faculty, and those in their first year of teaching (Centra, Note 6). Highest faculty involvement is found in programs run by the faculty rather than for them. In these programs, experienced teachers work with the inexperienced, and those with special skills offer assistance to others. A key feature is that both successful and unsuccessful teachers participate. However, there is little likelihood of increasing faculty participation in improvement activity without linking involvement to the formal reward structure. Institutions that have done this by requiring reports of satisfactory participation in staff development activity or professional courses get such participation.

IMPLEMENTATION OF EVALUATION PLANS

The present political climate approves of evaluation for both accountability and improvement. Arrangements for accommodating these two purposes remain problematic but appear to entail collaboration between groups of different persuasions.

Climate for Accountability

Public sentiment favors school boards, superintendents, and principals exercising legal authority to establish appraisal systems based on student progress and order in the classroom. The implication is that principals must become quality control officers and communicate clearly to the faculty goals deemed important by the school board. Teacher input is important, but the principal should not negotiate with teachers if negotiation results in unacceptable or less demanding outcomes of evaluation. The principal must represent the community and expect results related to the community's desires, differentiating good instruction from bad. Those emphasizing accountability believe there is a shortage of bastards among principals—more principals want to be a nice guy or gal and hand out outstanding performance ratings—and that principals should use their power in evaluation, even if it means taking a chance on leaving teachers bitter, angry, and hostile.

Courts are unwilling, except in most unusual circumstances, to substitute their judgment for that of school administrators or teaching colleagues about whether teachers are good or not. It is true, however, that principals have to learn how to build a case. As indicated in the Salt Lake City Plan, some teacher unions will support appraisal plans that involve teachers in the design, comply with due process procedures, and do not violate union positions on such matters as extra pay for extra hours. Shared responsibility with the teachers is necessary for political and practical reasons. Except for critical dismissal cases, the principal and supervisors cannot spend sufficient time with all teachers. Evidence of a teacher's ability is needed from the teacher (self), peers, students, and parents, as well as from administrators. A useful strategy for gaining teacher participation in the formal evaluation system is through peer participation, beginning first with opportunities for teachers to help and support each other, continuing with opportunities to learn and apply clinical analysis and feedback in observing in classrooms, and finally going on to responsibility along with the principal for decisions on retention, assignment, and the like.

Gaining Teacher Acceptance

In order to gain teacher acceptance of appraisal plans aimed at accountability and involving observation, the plans should have the following features:

(1) participation and agreement (The appraisal program is worked out with teachers. There is agreement on the form, the nature, and the timing of assessment. For example, will lessons be videotaped? What students are involved? The purpose of evaluation is stated, and it is clearly understood who will receive the data.)
(2) enabling resources (Roles in the evaluation process are specified, and those accepting these roles have the essential knowledge, skills, and attitudes to fill them. Sharing of responsibility for teacher evaluation also requires alleviating overburdens on teachers, such as large classes and heavy course loads.
(3) instrumentation (Instruments used in observation have sufficient definition and detail to provide a good record and to document judgments made. Items draw attention to what can be seen and heard rather than requiring inferences.)
(4) amenability (It is often counterproductive to assess characteristics that the teacher cannot change, for example, a high-pitched voice.)
(5) saliency (Selecting an area for improvement should be based on critically demonstrated effects and theoretical significance. Useful criteria for evaluating are the following: Do the teacher and the students have goals? Are students aware of teacher objectives and of the reasons for what they are doing? Do students contribute to the class? Is the teacher in control of the class, yet flexible in planning? What is the teacher's knowledge of subject matter? Does the teacher set an example?)

In higher education, cooperation between faculty and administration in formal evaluation has increased the validity and reliability of judgments about teachers and contributed to warranted decisions for retention and promotion. Merit review policies are strengthened by a broad definition of teaching and requirements for a variety of evidence about it.

The Southern Regional Education Board (Note 7) reported on its study of faculty evaluation practices in 536 postsecondary institutions in 14 states.

This study, involving the development and implementation of faculty evaluation strategies, led to the conclusion that four major conditions must be present for the plan to work:

(1) strong administrative support, either from the institution's president or chief academic officer (It is no accident that at institutions nationally recognized as leaders in teaching evaluation, there are one or more academic officers who understand and stimulate these developments.)
(2) full and extensive faculty involvement
(3) a base of expertise that the faculty and administration can draw on in developing or revising their system
(4) a generally recognized need for change in the faculty evaluation system.

The challenge facing education centers on the assigning of value to faculty activities so that such activities contribute to the overall worth of the institution.

REFERENCE NOTES

1. Smith, W. L. and C. E. Feiztrizer (1978) *Analyses of U.S. Office of Education discretionary programs having a professional development of educational personnel*. Washington, D.C.: National Teacher Development Initiative.
2. Bhaevman, B. (1970) *A paradigm for accountability* (AFT Quest Paper No. 12). Washington, D.C.: American Federation of Teachers.
3. Zirkel, P. A. and C. Castens (n.d.) *Teacher evaluation: A legal memorandum*. Reston, VA: National Association of Secondary School Principals.
4. Erickson, J. A. (1973) "Fair dismissal procedures." *Oregon School Study Council Bulletin* (Vol. 16, No. 5, pp. 1–26). Portland: University of Oregon, College of Education.
5. Hoyt, D. P. and W. E. Cashin (1977) "Faculty evaluation (IDEA Technical Report No. 1)." Manhattan: Kansas State University, Center for Faculty Evaluation and Development in Higher Education.
6. Centra, J. A. (1979) *Faculty development in higher education, faculty development in U.S. colleges and universities*. Princeton, NJ: Educational Testing Service.
7. Southern Regional Education Board (1977) *Faculty evaluation for improved learning*. Atlanta: Southern Regional Education Board.

REFERENCES

Blumberg, A. (1974) *Supervisors and teachers: A Private Cold War*. Berkeley, CA: McCutchan.

Crews, C. (1979) "Instructional supervision: The winter and the warm." *Educational Leadership*, 36: 519–521.

Divoky, D. (1979) "Evaluation: It can lead to teachers helping teachers." *Learning*, 7(8): 28–32.

Herndon, T. (1979) "Removing incompetent teachers is growing problem for schools." *New York Times* (March 4): A18.

Hyman, R. T. (1979) "Judging the effectiveness of teaching style." *Education Administration Quarterly*, 15: 104–116.

McDonnell, L. and A. Pascal (1979) "Rand report says board give away money and power." *American School Board Journal*, 166(6): 32–33.

Michener, J. (1979) "James Michener." *Los Angeles* (August 20): 110.

Norden, V. D. (1978) "The legal protection of academic freedom," in C. P. Hooker (ed.), *The Courts and Education*. Chicago: University of Chicago, National Society for the Study of Education, 77th Yearbook, Part 1.

Popham, W. J. (1974) "Higher education's commitment to instructional improvement programs." *Educational Researcher*, 3(11): 11–13.

Santelli, C. J. (1979) "New York teachers are gaining in the battle for professional status." *New York Times* (July 31): A1.

Shanker, A. (1979) "Teacher licensing considered." *New York Times* (July 3): C1.

Smith, K. E. and H. M. Sandler (1974) "Bases of status in four elementary school facilities." *American Educational Research Journal*, 11: 317–331.

Soar, R. S. and R. M. Soar (1977) Problems in Using Pupil Outcomes for Teacher Evaluation. Washington, DC: National Education Association. (ERIC Document Reproduction Service No. ED 150 187).

Stone, R. (1978) "The principal as chief negotiator: Some concerns for the supervision of teachers." *Educational Leadership*, 35: 577–579.

Wise, A. (1979) "Why competency testing will not improve education." *Educational Leadership*, 36: 546–549.

Wolf, R. L. (1973) "How teachers feel about evaluation," in E. R. House (ed.) *School evaluation: The politics and process*. Berkeley, CA: McCutchan.

Yarger, S. J. and G. Yarger (1978) "And so we asked ourselves about teacher centers." *Theory into Practice*, 37: 248–257.

CHAPTER 16

THE POLITICAL REALITIES OF TEACHER EVALUATION

MARY LOUISE ARMIGER
New Jersey Education Association

Many who attempt to initiate and implement teacher evaluation policies proceed headlong into the technical aspects of the task without considering political processes and interests. Yet political forces often determine the course that the evaluation program takes. To develop the technical aspects of evaluation with little or no regard for political interests is like building a technically sound automobile with no roads upon which to operate it. Any trip taken in the vehicle will be rough and bumpy despite the proficiency of the mechanism.

THE POLITICAL ARENA

Politics, as used in this chapter, involves not only the governmental system but also those groups or individuals who either attempt to influence or are affected by the policies, practices, or actions of government. The governmental system encompasses the organization, machinery, agencies, and persons through which authority is exercised.

A discussion of the politics of teacher evaluation draws upon perceptions related to the politics of education itself. At first, teacher evaluation may appear to be strictly a personnel matter between employer and employee. When viewed in the political context, however, the issue of teacher evaluation is both a contributor to and a result of the status of education in America today.

The Changing Character of Teacher Evaluation

Evaluation as a personnel process usually indicates that management appraises its employees to achieve two purposes:

(1) the formative purpose, designed to improve performance by aiding employees to identify areas for specific improvement or professional growth

(2) the summative purpose, designed to assist employers in making administrative decisions about employees.

It is the view of this author that the character of teacher evaluation is shifting from the formative, almost clinical model of assistance, to the summative, decision-making function. The transformation has much to do with the politics of education. The new attitudes about teacher evaluation have emerged from the broad accountability movement, declining student enrollment, and the systems approach to education.

The emphasis on program accountability over the last 15 to 20 years has created a thrust toward a more rigorous assessment of personnel given the conditions of a shrinking job market, declines in enrollment, and increased government regulations. The accountability movement extended the realm of teacher evaluation beyond the proverbial little red schoolhouse. No longer is teacher evaluation used only to help guide teachers to improve instruction. Evaluation serves to reduce staff and to prove cost-effectiveness. Those involved in the process are not only supervisors but also legislators, bureaucrats, and the courts. Kerr, as quoted in Miller (1972), predicted the phenomenon and stated, "Cost-effectiveness of operations will be more carefully examined. If this is not done internally, it will be done externally by the new experts working for legislators and governors" (p. 5).

The phenomenon of increased dollars flowing into state and local education agencies has raised two related questions: Who controls education? Whom can the consumer of education hold responsible for the quality and quantity of services? Wildavsky (1976) indicates that the answer to the first question is unclear. State governments hold constitutional responsibility, but all states except Hawaii have delegated significant discretionary authority over revenues and expenditures to local schools while retaining control over broad areas such as standards and certification. After court rulings on several cases of equal opportunity and educational finance (e.g., *Serrano v. Priest* and *Robinson v. Cahill*), however, authority in these areas was shifted back again to the state level. State governments were ordered by the courts to broaden the financial base of education on a statewide level and to decrease the local property tax burden. As states increased their fiscal commitment to education, state legislation and regulation proliferated.

The second question is equally complex and unclear: Whom can the consumer (students, parents, and taxpayers) hold responsible for the quality and quantity of educational services received or denied? Wise (1979) observed the politicians' movements within the last decade:

> I notice that for the last 10 years or so, state legislatures have been trying to get a handle on education. There have been numerous innovations during that

period, all proposed as ways to improve education . . . . They are all systems approaches devised elsewhere and brought to education. And they are not just ideas being developed; every one of them is embodied in state law in one or more states [p., 546].

Wise illustrated several developments within the legislative and judicial arenas that have undergone a transformation from school finance to account-ability issues. He pointed to the *Robinson v. Cahill* case in New Jersey, for example. It began as a lawsuit for the reform of school finance, which was to equalize educational resources throughout the state. The case emerged sev-eral years later in a considerably different form. The court called upon the legislature to define the portion of New Jersey's Constitution that requires a "thorough and efficient education," and accountability for schools was legis-lated throughout the state.

In this case, attention of the legislators, the media, and the public was drawn to assessment and accountability rather than to the weighty educa-tional and social issues of the day. Equal educational opportunity and school finance reform were reduced to the results of student tests and the evaluation of teachers.

Parallel to legislated accountability was a move toward specific program objectives. Planning, programming, and budgeting systems—an industrial approach to product cost-effectiveness—were plunged into the human ser-vices. Educators began dealing with terms such as "input variables," "behav-ioral objectives," and "output measures."

Goldman (1979) indicated that educators became concerned about politi-cal efforts to redirect education toward a fixed mechanical system of specific goals and objectives that could force children into molds, since the objec-tives derived must call for specific behavioral responses. Educators reasoned that if children's learning were measured in behavioristic terms, then the teacher's role and responsibility would likewise be reduced to measurable behaviors.

The accountability movement and systems approaches to education brought new attitudes about teacher evaluation. No longer would teachers feel that evaluators were helping them to improve instruction in a non-threatening manner. Evaluators were faced with new considerations beyond the tenets of clinical supervision and guidance.

DEVELOPMENT OF EVALUATION REQUIREMENTS

Role of the State

Several state legislatures have mandated the evaluation of teachers and state boards have approved state regulations, which have usually been formulated by employees of the state's department of education. For example, California's legislation, commonly termed the Stull Act, requires the evaluation of all certified employees from district superintendent to credentialed teacher assistants. The Pennsylvania School Code mandates an annual rating of all professional and temporary professional personnel in the public schools. Various state regulations in New Jersey call for the evaluation of all certificated public school employees, with different rules for tenured and nontenured staff.

Initiation and development of state requirements for the evaluation of teachers within school districts are politically expedient. They are the state government's attempt to show the public that local districts are being held accountable for the quality of education. The regulations give the appearance that legislators and boards are concerned about teacher competence. They are held up to the public as though they alone will somehow improve instruction. Moreover, the state government is relieved of the responsibility for the implementation of the regulations, and no additional tax moneys are expended for programs to assist teachers to improve their performance. Riessman (1978) stated that the temptation to tinker with public education is enhanced by the fact that state and federal officials are not, in the last resort, held responsible for what happens within local schools.

Role of Teacher Associations

Teachers have recognized over the years that they have little political clout as individuals. Teachers often feel that they are first in line when it comes to accountability and last in line for professional rights and monetary reward. It has been no surprise that organized teacher associations have stepped in to fill the perceived power vacuum.

In recent years, teacher organizations have emerged as effective influences upon public policy. While one teacher may have little authority to affect educational decisions, organized teacher associations have become major forces in local, state, and national issues. The teacher association exists to further the interests of its members in areas related to job security, compensation, working conditions, instruction, and, of course, organizational security. A major interest of these organizations is to protect the employment security of the members. Associations believe it is the secure employee, free from anxieties about the future, who will be able to pursue professional tasks to the utmost.

Teacher organizations have long supported evaluation. Teachers initiated the development of evaluation policies and procedures before the accountability movement. At that time, teacher leaders viewed evaluation primarily as an opportunity to enhance job satisfaction, to receive guidance, and to provide due process.

Associations emphasize the importance of due process and fair treatment in their recommendations about teacher evaluation. It is their belief that evaluators should presume teacher competence, based upon the lengthy training and certification requirements completed by the teacher. The onus, then, is upon management (ultimately the school board) to prove otherwise, if deficiencies are noted.

Because the general accountability movement has led to greater centralization of school decision making at the state level, state teacher associations have recognized in recent years the need to expand their influence beyond the local negotiations level. Their initial reaction to central educational authority was to lobby state legislatures. It soon became apparent, however, that state policy was often formulated in arenas beyond the chambers of elected officials—by the growing state departments of education, state boards of education, state task forces, and other special interest groups and by vast numbers of bureaucrats and appointed officials, all with views of education based on their individual experiences and, more important, on their perceived survival and possible advancement within the bureaucracy.

Now teacher associations organize to monitor and shape educational policy that is formulated by agencies and boards as well as legislatures. Teacher associations also inform and train their members about current developments at the national and state levels and how to cope with them.

The organization of professional judgment through state associations has served two purposes. First, teachers are significantly more aware of federal and state issues and their potential impact on the classroom. Previously, the reaction of classroom teachers occurred long after policy was fixed. Second, state officials are more sensitive to the judgment and input of teachers about educational issues. Many successful bureaucrats recognize that it is prudent to hear the professional judgment of organized teachers before developing regulations.

Many teacher organizations have developed guidelines for local evaluation procedures. These recommendations are usually prefaced by the reminder that evaluations and related procedures should adhere to the elements of due process. Rudimentary fair play and humane supervisory techniques provide for the individual's right of access to files, availability of assistance, options for requesting documentation, provision for response to and expulsion of inappropriate information, and opportunity for a fair hearing.

Negotiations

In many states, the local board adopts a teacher evaluation policy as the result of collective negotiations with the recognized representative bargaining units of the teaching staff members. Evaluation policies developed through a collective negotiations process represent a commitment on the part of both parties to the implementation of a satisfactory evaluation process. Both employer and employees have recognized the significance of evaluation and have agreed to participate in its execution.

In most states, evaluation procedures are negotiable as a term and condition of employment. That is, if either management or the teachers' representative asks for the issue to be negotiated, then negotiations can occur on the basis that they may affect the employees' terms and conditions of employment. The impact of teacher evaluation is another negotiable item. "Impact" is a term that relates to the affect, if any, of evaluation policies or decisions upon the terms and conditions of employment.

In some cases the criteria for evaluation are negotiated, and in other cases a procedure that provides for developing criteria is negotiated. It is generally recognized, however, that evaluation tends to be more successful when the teachers participate in developing the criteria by which performance will be judged. This process may extend beyond the bilateral contract of the school board and the representative organization.

Dilemma of Evaluators

It is ideal to involve those who will actually be conducting the evaluation, as well as those who will be evaluated, in the development of all evaluation policies. All too often this does not occur because evaluation emerges from political, rather than from professional, forces. Thus, the evaluator is in a dilemma. The evaluator is often called upon to implement policy that has been developed by outside groups. Moreover, if problems occur as the result of the language, concepts, or procedures of the regulation, the fault will usually be cited as that of the evaluator rather than as the fault of the policy itself.

The evaluator's dilemma is illustrated by the issue of pupil progress as a criterion for teacher evaluation. Most leading educators reject the notion that a teacher can be evaluated fairly on the basis of pupil progress. Most would agree with Soar and Soar (Note 1), who showed that the influence of the teacher on pupil progress is minor when compared to out-of-the-classroom influences. Yet some states and local districts require the use of pupil progress as a criterion for teacher evaluation. The evaluator's professional judgment may be compromised before the process of observation and evaluation even begins because he/she is expected to conduct evaluations through a policy or procedure with which he/she may not agree.

The evaluator's dilemma is exacerbated by the state of the art of evaluation. No conclusive research exists that determines what characteristics of the teacher lead to learning on the part of the student. In fact, there is no scientific basis to support the notion that one particular teaching style is superior to another (see Chapter 14).

Most evaluators of teachers are sensitive to the fact that they evaluate professionals. As such, the evaluator may be able to provide information about the teacher's job and methods. At the same time, however, the evaluator must respect the teacher's right and responsibility to develop professionally on an individual basis.

There is a need for the combined professional expertise of educators in the development of policies and procedures for evaluation on a local level. Communication within the educational community may result from cooperative decision making, negotiations, or informal networks. Regardless of how formal or informal the communication process is, effective evaluation cannot take place without it.

IMPLEMENTATION OF TEACHER EVALUATION

The implementation of teacher evaluation usually begins with the formulation of evaluation procedures. Good evaluation procedures generally foster good evaluation practices.

Procedures for Teacher Evaluation Recommended by the National Education Association

The National Education Association (Note 2) has developed a set of procedures to assist in avoiding arbitrary or capricious administrative action. The purpose of their procedures is to afford fair treatment to teacher members. Included are the following:

(1) the right to open appraisal: A teacher who is the object of administrative data gathering for the purpose of appraising performance should be informed that such data gathering is taking place.
(2) the right to fair consideration of work effort: Administrators charged with classroom observations should be fully apprised of the methodology, plans, and objectives of the teaching being observed and should observe the teacher often and long enough to obtain as accurate a picture as possible of the work performance of that teacher.
(3) the right to correct deficiencies: A teacher who is declared deficient should be given the opportunity to correct the deficiencies, and the administration should give all the support necessary to help the teacher do it, including time, resources, and consultant services.
(4) the right of access to information: A teacher who has information collected about him or her on matters related to his or her total work performance should be afforded the opportunity to monitor the collection of that information.
(5) the right to notice: A teacher who is declared deficient in his or her performance should be apprised of this judgment immediately, with the reasons set forth in a clear and detailed manner.

(6) the right to representation: The teacher charged with, reprimanded for, or stigmatized by an administrative judgment of deficient performance must have the right to be represented by the association and should begin at the time of the judgment of deficient performance.

(7) the right to a fair hearing:
   (a) If a teacher is judged deficient by an administrator, he or she ought to have the opportunity to question the administrator as to the reason for such a judgment.
   (b) If a teacher is judged deficient, fairness dictates that the teacher be allowed to give his or her side of the story in as complete a manner as necessary.
   (c) Another element is the right to have laid before the neutral party only the information that will be considered by the trier in his or her deliberations for arriving at a decision.
   (d) The final element of a fair hearing is the right to a neutral trier of fact.

(8) the right to fair punishment: A teacher who is judged deficient in performance and who is acted against as a result of that judgment should not have to suffer because the action taken is out of proportion to the deficiency.

(9) the right to equal treatment: Invidious discrimination is condemned in our society by equal protection concepts. A teacher cannot be singled out for special treatment in evaluations on the basis of irrational or unreasonable distinctions.

Local Guidelines for Teacher Evaluation

The following guidelines for local evaluation policies serve as a basis for discussion between management and teachers. They are adapted from the policy developed by the New Jersey Education Association (Note 3):

(1) Local procedures and criteria for the evaluation of all teaching staff members should be developed in accordance with state labor law.

(2) Evaluation criteria for each position should be approved by the representative teacher organization.

(3) Evaluators should be properly trained in the techniques and criteria for evaluation.

(4) Evaluators should be certified to teach in the instructional areas that they are evaluating.

(5) Teaching staff members should be evaluated only by persons designated by the board of education, certified by the state licensing board to supervise instruction, and employed by the district on a regular full-time basis.

(6) At the beginning of the year, teaching staff members should be given the names of their evaluators and the criteria for evaluation.

(7) A preobservation conference should be held to enable the evaluator to become aware of the teaching-learning situation to be evaluated. The teaching staff member should also be made aware of the instructional period within which the observation will take place.

(8) Observations and evaluations should be limited to the performance of the teaching staff member in the instructional process.

(9) All observations should be conducted openly within the classroom. An appropriate parallel setting for observation should be used for teaching staff members who are involved in other than direct instructional processes.

(10) Each observation of teaching staff members should be for at least one instructional period.

(11) All observations should be conducted openly.

(12) Nontenured teaching staff members should be evaluated at least three times annually.

(13) Evaluations for nontenured teaching staff members should be spaced throughout the year but completed before the submission of recommendations about continued employment.

(14) Tenured teaching staff members should be evaluated at least once annually.

(15) A teaching staff member should have the right to receive upon request a demonstration, observation, or evaluation by a properly certificated supervisor employed by the district on a regular full-time basis.

(16) Each evaluation should be given in writing to the teaching staff member within at least five days of the observation and at least one day before any conference to discuss it.

(17) The written evaluation should be written exclusively by the properly certified supervisor involved in the evaluation.

(18) Evaluations should include in a narrative form:

(a) strengths of the teaching staff members as evidenced during the period since the previous report

(b) areas of improvement, if any, identified in specific terms

(c) specific suggestions about measures that the teaching staff member might take to improve his/her performance in those areas in which weaknesses, if any, have been indicated.

(19) The observer-evaluator should demonstrate any specific suggestions for improvement.

(20) Areas in need of improvement that are not noted in subsequent reports should be deemed to be corrected.

(21) Each evaluation should be followed by a personal conference between the teaching staff member and the observer-evaluator for the purposes of identifying areas of strength and needed improvement, if any, and of extending assistance for improving instruction. Evaluations should be issued in the name of the observer-evaluator.

(22) The teaching staff member's signature—which indicates awareness of, but not agreement with, the report—should appear on the evaluation form.

(23) No part of the evaluative procedure should interfere with the normal teaching process.

(24) No evaluation reports should be submitted to the central office, placed in the teaching staff member's file, or otherwise acted upon or transmitted until after a conference with the teaching staff member.

(25) No material derogatory to a teaching staff member should be placed in the personnel file without the teacher staff member's knowledge.
(26) Teaching staff members should have the right to review their personnel files.
(27) Teaching staff members should have the right to file written responses to evaluation reports for the file and to submit complaints through the grievance procedures.
(28) Inappropriate information in the personnel file should be corrected or expunged through a fair and equitable process.
(29) Failure of the district to follow the provisions of the agreement should result in restoring any teaching staff member against whom action has been taken.
(30) Refusal to offer or renew the contract of nontenured teaching staff members should be grounds for a grievance.
(31) When a nontenured teaching staff member is not continued in employment, upon request the board should provide specific reasons why within five days and should give the teaching staff member an opportunity for a hearing before the board with representation.
(32) The final evaluation of a teaching staff member, whose employment has been terminated, should be concluded before severance, and no documents and/or other material should be placed in the personnel file of that teaching staff member after severance.

SUMMARY

In recent years the purpose of the evaluation of teachers has shifted from formative, designed to improve performance by aiding employees, to summative, designed to assist employees in making administrative decisions. Declining enrollments, the accountability movement, and systems approaches to education have contributed to the change. Participants in the process have taken positions on this issue based upon their interests.

Teacher evaluation is a sensitive issue. Successful implementation depends not only upon proficient assessment instruments and adequately trained evaluators but also upon the political interplay of those involved in the process.

REFERENCE NOTES

1. Soar, R. S. and R. M. Soar (1973) *Classroom behavior, pupil characteristics, and pupil growth for the school year and for the summer* (NIMH Grant Nos. 5 ROI MH 15891 and 5 ROI MH 15626). Gainesville: University of Florida.
2. National Education Association (1972) *Fair treatment of teachers: Teacher evaluation and collective bargaining* (No. 381-11996). Washington, DC: Author.
3. New Jersey Education Association (1977) *Teacher evaluation*. Trenton, NJ: Author.

REFERENCES

Goldman, N. (1979) "Implementing T&E," in S. R. Laccetti (ed.), *The Outlook on New Jersey.* Union City, NJ: William H. Wise and Company.

Miller, R. I. (1972) *Evaluating Faculty Performance*. San Francisco: Jossey-Bass.

Riessman, F. (1978) "The service society and the crises in education," in E. K. Mosher and J. L. Wagoner, Jr. (eds.), *The Changing Politics of Education: Prospects for the '80s*. Berkeley, CA: McCutchan.

Wildavsky, A. (1976) "The strategic retreat on objectives." *Policy Analysis*, 3: 499–526.

Wise, A. (1979) "Why minimum competency testing will not improve education." *Educational Leadership*, 36: 546–549.

CHAPTER 17

FAIRNESS AND THE LEGAL CONTEXT OF TEACHER EVALUATION

KENNETH STRIKE
Cornell University

BARRY BULL
Wellesley College

The legal context of teacher evaluation has a moral point. It is designed to promote fairness. It is, thus, important to see the legal aspects of teacher evaluation against the background of the moral concepts that they are intended to realize. Moreover, it is important to avoid the extremes of allowing the legal context to define one's moral sense about teacher evaluation or of treating the legal context as though it had no moral point. The law is not synonymous with morality. Neither is it simply a nuisance.

In the first section we briefly describe something of the moral context that seems relevant to teacher evaluation. In the second section we describe current federal law that applies to evaluation. In the third section we describe relevant state regulations, and in the fourth section we describe some typical contract provisions. Finally, in the light of these considerations, we describe the procedural features of a model teacher evaluation system. This model system reflects not only the legal constraints but also the authors' sense of justice concerning fair evaluation practices.

Most of the discussion concerns what is described elsewhere in this volume as summative evaluation. Legal rules are, after all, intended to promote fairness in decision making. Formative evaluation is, thus, less likely to generate legal attention. Our attention is also focused on public elementary and secondary schools. Most of the legal points we make do not apply to private institutions. The federal law we discuss applies both to public higher education and to public elementary and secondary schools. State statutes are usually applicable to elementary and secondary schools, and most of the contractual material discussed is from contracts that concern elementary and secondary teachers. Much of this material, however, is potentially illuminating for higher education in that it suggests some general points about the problems to be solved in designing a fair evaluation system and some models for how these problems have been dealt with. Perhaps the major difference between evaluation in much of higher education and in elementary and secondary schools is the importance of peer evaluation in higher education. We do not deal with this. The reader who wishes to apply what we say to higher education should, however, keep it in mind.

THE MORAL CONTEXT OF TEACHER EVALUATION

Here we look at two components of fairness, equal respect of persons, and reasonableness and suggest how these values relate to effectiveness. As we understand them, these values represent some of the central commitments of our society.

The Central Values of Evaluation

Equal Respect. This notion can be described as the conjunction of two ideas. The first is that human beings are objects of intrinsic value; they are ends in themselves. As such they deserve respect and are possessed of rights. The second idea is that insofar as this intrinsic value is concerned, everyone is of equal worth. Although some individuals may be more competent, attractive, or stronger than others, such empirical differences do not imply differences in individuals' fundamental human worth.

The notion that people are of intrinsic worth requires evaluation procedures that respect the dignity of teachers as human beings. It thus precludes the use of evaluation to harass or belittle a teacher and weighs against evaluations that are gratuitous in that nothing turns on them. It may also preclude some methods that are potentially useful sources of information, such as covert surveillance.

The notion that people are entitled to equal respect does not generate a demand that people be treated in every respect the same. Obviously, when teaching is being evaluated and decisions are made on the basis of such evaluations, people will be treated differently depending on the results of the evaluation. Rather, the demand is that people be treated as equals, that they be accorded equal respect when they are being evaluated (Dworkin, 1977).

The requirement of such a demand in the context of evaluation is that people have a right to have decisions about them made on the basis of relevant, rather than irrelevant, criteria. (This demand is similar to the requirements of the equal protection clause of the 14th amendment and can be regarded as its philosophical basis.) In the context of teaching, relevant criteria are those that have a plausible connection to achieving some legitimate educational goal. Irrelevant criteria do not. Normally we include in the latter class properties such as race, sex, or religious background. There are, of course, a host of other irrelevant characteristics, which are of less interest because they have less frequently been the basis of discrimination.

An evaluation or a decision made on the basis of some irrelevant characteristic exhibits a lack of respect for the individual so evaluated. For example, an evaluation linked to race says, in effect, that despite the fact that race is unrelated to teaching ability, persons of a given race are deemed less worthy of teaching positions than others. Such a judgment exhibits contempt for individuals of that race. Since race is not a relevant criterion, to incorporate it into a judgment implies that persons of that race are in some fundamental way less worthy of respect and fair treatment than others. It is a failure to treat them as equals. The value of equal respect thus leads to a requirement that people be evaluated on relevant, rather than irrelevant, criteria.

We do not, of course, pretend that it is always easy to decide what is relevant and what is irrelevant. What counts as relevant varies with one's educational values. Moreover, some of the characteristics, such as race, sex, or religion, that our society has identified as paradigm cases of irrelevant characteristics for any decision can become relevant given certain educational goals or concepts of good teaching. The desire for teachers to function as role models might make race or sex a relevant consideration. A desire to promote patriotism can likewise generate an interest in whether the religious preferences of teachers preclude their participation in the pledge of allegiance. Herein lies the philosophical source of much legal conflict.

Reasonableness. Here the word *reasonable* is used to express the demand that the decisions resulting from evaluation practices not be arbitrary or capricious. The demand for reasonableness can then be divided into two components, which in conjunction and when translated into requirement of fairness comprise the larger part of the notion of due process. The demand that decisions not be arbitrary we treat as equivalent to the demand that decisions be warranted by available evidence. This standard requires procedures for collecting and employing evidence that insures that decisions are rooted in the best available relevant evidence. The right to a hearing, the right to refute negative evidence, and, generally, rules of evidence are intended to achieve this ideal.

Decisions can be capricious in ways that do not depend on their being unwarranted by the evidence. They may, for example, be based on an unknown or unannounced standard, achieved in an untimely or irregular way, or constructed to pick out particular individuals. The demand that decisions be reasonable thus also involves the requirement that standards be public, general, and applied in an orderly and regular fashion.

The value embedded in the demand that decisions not be capricious is perhaps best captured in the time-honored belief that government should be by the rule of law, rather than by the rule of men. Human beings have a right to be governed by known and systematically applied rules, and they have the right not to be governed by whim.

These requirements, that decisions be made on the basis of evidence and that they be made according to known and systematically applied standards, are the essence of the concept of due process. Here it is important to note that the demand for reasonableness, as it is translated into due process requirements, is not equivalent to the demand that decisions be correct. One cannot challenge a decision morally or legally on due process grounds simply by claiming that it is mistaken. Due process, rather, requires procedures that promote decisions conscientiously and objectively reached. One offends against due process, then, not by being mistaken, but by being unfair, that is, by failing to follow procedures that promote objective and conscientious decisions.

Effectiveness. The prior comments on equal respect and reasonableness serve largely to express the rights of teachers in evaluation. But the point of evaluation is to promote good education by selecting or retaining competent teachers or by improving the skills of the current teaching staff. Procedural rules for teacher evaluation cannot, therefore, simply address the rights of teachers. They must also consider the interests of the evaluator in promoting good education and in pursuing the legitimate aims of the school and the society. That is to say, an evaluation program must not only be fair but it must also be effective.

The values of fairness do not, of course, conflict in principle with those of effectiveness. Indeed, they seem prima facie to promote effectiveness. Decisions that are nondiscriminatory, based on relevant criteria, and generally reasonable should, other things being equal, promote competent decisions and thereby good education. Thus, objections to fair evaluation procedures which see them as restricting administrative discretion so as to preclude the administrator from doing his or her job properly are suspect. At the same time, it must be recognized that it would be possible to design a set of procedures for the protection of the rights of teachers that would be so complex, time consuming, or threatening to the administrator as to reduce the effectiveness of evaluation. The point here is not that one can sometimes be more effective by being unfair. Rather, the point is that successful procedures must be "cost-effective." Schools should not be expected to conform to procedures that produce small increments of fairness at a high cost of effectiveness. Perhaps most important to success here are procedures that protect teachers from actual or likely abuses and the avoidance of procedures that protect against the merely possible. Fairness does not require procedures to defend against every imaginable evil, nor does it require that the systematic malevolence of administration be assumed. It must also be kept in mind that fairness does not preclude negative judgments. A system that makes a warranted negative judgment impossible is neither just nor efficient.

These remarks on the "cost-effectiveness" of procedural rules for evaluation assume that sometimes fairness and effectiveness, the rights of the teacher, and the interests of the school need to be balanced. One may also, however, view the effectiveness of an evaluation system not so much in terms of trade-offs of this sort as in terms of the inherent consequences of the system. A system can be just and produce reasonable personnel decisions and at the same time be ineffective because it is alienating or because it generates an excessive amount of litigation. Here, too, the overall fairness of a system is an asset. A system that is seen by teachers as fair is more likely to generate acceptance than one that is not. However, perceptions are colored by one's interests. It may well be, for example, that merit pay is a legitimate institution which can be administered in a fair way. Teachers, however, have found it offensive. Thus, it has a cost in alienation which any administrator will have to take into account.

Indeed, the very act of generating procedural rules to ensure fairness in evaluation can heighten suspicion and increase the alienation of school personnel. Certainly an effective system avoids procedures that generate unnecessary litigation. As a general rule, in an effective evaluation system the courts will be the last resort in settling disputes. An effective system prefers dialogue and mediation to litigation.

A Bill of Rights for Teacher Evaluation

The following list of principles should serve as a bridge between the abstract discussion of rights that precedes it and the discussion of the specific legal and contractual provisions surrounding evaluation.

Rights of Educational Institutions:

(1) Educational institutions have the right to exercise supervision and to make personnel decisions intended to improve the quality of the education they provide.
(2) Educational institutions have the right to collect information relevant to their supervisory and evaluative roles.
(3) Educational institutions have the right to act on such relevant information in the best interest of the students whom they seek to educate.
(4) Educational institutions have the right to the cooperation of the teaching staff in implementing and executing a fair and effective system of evaluation.

Rights of Teachers:

(1) Professional rights
  (a) Teachers have a right to reasonable job security.
  (b) Teachers have a right to a reasonable degree of professional discretion in the performance of their jobs.
  (c) Teachers have a right to reasonable participation in decisions concerning both professional and employment-related aspects of their jobs.

(2) Evidential rights
  (a) Teachers have the right to have decisions made on the basis of evidence.
  (b) Teachers have a right to be evaluated on relevant criteria.
  (c) Teachers have the right not to be evaluated on the basis of hearsay, rumor, or unchecked complaints.

(3) Procedural rights
  (a) Teachers have the right to be evaluated according to general, public, and comprehensible standards.
  (b) Teachers have the right to notice concerning when they will be evaluated.
  (c) Teachers have the right to know the results of their evaluation.
  (d) Teachers have the right to express a reaction to the results of their evaluation in a meaningful way.
  (e) Teachers have the right to a statement of the reasons for any action taken in their cases.
  (f) Teachers have the right to appeal adverse decisions and to have their views considered by a competent and unbiased authority.
  (g) Teachers have the right to orderly and timely evaluation.

(4) Other humanitarian and civil rights
  (a) Teachers have a right to humane evaluation procedures.
  (b) Teachers have the right to have their evaluation kept private and confidential.
  (c) Teachers have the right to evaluation procedures which are not needlessly intrusive into their professional activities.
  (d) Teachers have the right to have their private lives considered irrelevant to their evaluation.
  (e) Teachers have the right to have evaluation not be used coercively to obtain aims external to the legitimate purposes of evaluation.
  (f) Teachers have the right to nondiscriminatory criteria and procedures.
  (g) Teachers have the right not to have evaluation used to sanction the expression of unpopular views.
  (h) Teachers have the right to an overall assessment of their performance that is frank, honest, and consistent.

Principles of Conflict Resolution:

(1) Remediation is to be preferred, where possible, to disciplinary action or termination.

(2) Mediation is to be preferred, where possible, to more litigious forms of conflict resolution.

(3) Informal attempts to settle disputes should precede formal ones.

EVALUATION AND FEDERAL LAW

In this section we focus on the restrictions that federal case law and especially constitutional law place upon teacher evaluation procedures in public school systems. The application of such case law to teacher evaluation is, however, often indirect. American courts do not themselves initiate the review of legislative and administrative policies; such matters come before the courts only when particular individuals complain that the policies in question have violated their specific legal or constitutional rights *(Rescue Army v. Municipal Court)*. Moreover, courts have demonstrated a long-standing reluctance to interfere with the administrative prerogatives of governmental agencies *(Shelton v. Tucker)*. Thus, if teacher evaluation procedures were nothing more than mere administrative conveniences—like procedures for taking attendance or for taking inventory of school supplies—they would never come under judicial scrutiny. It is only when the uses to which such procedures are put affect the legally protected interests of teachers that they raise judicable issues. As a result, this section is organized around the types of administrative actions that may be based upon teacher evaluations.

Evaluation and Termination of Employment

The most substantial effect that evaluation reports may have upon the interests of teachers lies with their potential use in decisions to renew teachers' contracts or to dismiss teachers before their contracts have expired. In this essay we will use "termination" to include both failure to renew a completed contract and dismissal while a valid contract is still in effect. "Termination" thus ignores a distinction that is important in some legal contexts—a distinction which we will draw upon when appropriate. Since teachers' rights in these cases are relatively well-defined in both statute and case law, it is in this area that federal law has the clearest and most extensive implications for evaluation procedures. In particular we consider the implications of teachers' constitutional, personal, and due process rights and of their statutory civil rights.

Evaluation and Teachers' Personal Rights. The 14th amendment to the Constitution has been held by the Supreme Court to prohibit state legislation that penalizes individuals for their exercise of certain fundamental rights. Exactly how the 14th amendment accomplishes this prohibition and precisely what rights are thus protected are subjects of continuing judicial and academic controversy. Thus, whether this protection of personal rights proceeds from the 14th amendment's due process clause, its equal protection clause, or both and whether the rights protected are limited to or identical with those enumerated in the Bill of Rights are issues that current legal opinion has not definitively resolved.

Nevertheless, the general standards for constitutional review of the substance of state legislation or policy have been formulated rather precisely. All state regulations must meet the requirement of having a reasonable relation to a legitimate state purpose *(Nebbia v. New York)*. Since it has long been recognized in law that the state has a legitimate interest in the instructional competence of its teachers *(Shelton v. Tucker)* and since the Court has been extremely liberal in its interpretation of "reasonable relationships," any plausible administrative definition of competence is likely to meet this general standard.

When the legislation or policy in question regulates constitutionally protected activities, a more exacting standard is applied. In these cases, governmental regulation or action must be shown to be a necessary means to serving a compelling state interest *(Shapiro v. Thompson)*. Though the legal meaning of the key terms of this stricter standard is not entirely clear, in general it prohibits school officials from discharging teachers because of actions involving the exercise of rights explicit or implicit in the Constitution.

The rights involved are largely those protected by the 1st, 5th, 9th, and 14th amendments and include the rights of speech, press, religion, assembly, petition, protection from self-incrimination, and privacy. Of particular interest is that the Constitution provides protection for activities such as criticism of the school or of school staff *(Pickering v. Board)*, taking unpopular political positions *(James v. Board)*, the use of unpopular material in the classroom *(Parducci v. Rutland)*, and the discussion of controversial topics *(Sterzing v. Fort Bend)*. Courts do not, however, consider such rights as absolute. In judging a given case courts may apply the "material and substantial disruption" test of *Tinker v. Des Moines* (see *James v. Board*). Courts may also balance the rights of a teacher against the legitimate purposes of a school. The dismissal of a Jehovah's witness who refused to lead the pledge of allegiance to the flag has recently been upheld. Constitutional rights do not always excuse teachers from the performance of otherwise legitimate parts of their job.

While the definition of teachers' constitutional rights is not fixed or completely clear, at least four firm conclusions that affect teacher evaluation programs can be drawn. First, the requirement that a teacher participate in a teacher evaluation program or otherwise provide information that may enter . into a determination of instructional competence does not in general violate the teacher's constitutional right to protection against self-incrimination *(Beilan v. Board)*. Second, a teacher does retain the right to exercise professional judgment responsibly in the selection and use of instructional materials and methods to achieve the prescribed purposes of instruction *(Parducci v. Rutland* and *Mailloux v. Kiley)*. Third, the Constitution does not require school authorities to restrict findings of incompetence only to the consideration of a teacher's classroom performance *(Beilan v. Board)*. However, fourth, teachers do retain the right to express opinions outside the classroom so long as they do not substantially and demonstrably disrupt the educational process *(Pickering v. Board)*.

These rulings suggest that school authorities may compel teachers on pain of dismissal to participate in an evaluation program even though the results of the program will be used to make termination decisions and the program focuses on teacher performance outside as well as inside the classroom. Furthermore, in conducting such evaluations it may be both useful and perhaps unavoidable to record disagreements in professional judgments between the evaluator and the teacher as well as, for example, a teacher's publicly or privately expressed objections to broader school policies. Since, however, this type of information cannot, as a rule, be a constitutionally legitimate basis for termination, evaluation reports that will be used in termination decisions must be constructed in a way which allows the reviewing authority to separate these judgments and information from those upon which termination may legitimately be based. Thus the evaluation format, first, should require the evaluator to specify the particular observations upon which judgments of competence are based and, second, should not invite the evaluator to make unsubstantiated summary judgments of competence in which these two classes of information are likely to be inextricably interwoven.

Due Process for Terminated Teachers. The general purpose of the Constitution's due process requirement is to prevent government from affecting individual citizens' interests in an arbitrary or capricious manner (Abraham, 1972). The courts have sought to achieve this purpose through the enforcement of the legal doctrine of procedural due process. It is important to note the conceptual and legal link that the general purpose of due process establishes between teacher evaluation and termination decisions.

The first due process requirement, that government action be nonarbitrary, implies that there must be some factual basis for such action; it is unreasonable to treat an individual in a way specified under governmental policy unless he or she has, in fact, qualified for such treatment. In terms specific to this discussion, then, due process generally requires that teacher termination be predicated in some way upon established facts about the involved teachers, in particular, facts about their performance, behavior, or abilities. One of the common features of teacher evaluation systems is that they are designed to collect and record facts of this kind. Thus, one way for school officials to meet the nonarbitrariness criterion of due process is for them to base individual termination decisions upon the results of teacher evaluation programs.

Several limitations should be noted about this conceptual link between teacher evaluation programs and termination. First, not all such decisions *can* be based upon teacher evaluation programs since some legally legitimate causes for dismissal, like moral turpitude, for example, must be grounded in facts of a type not usually collected in this way. This use of evaluation programs is obviously most appropriate for making decisions about the teaching competence of school personnel. Second, even when teaching competence is at issue in a termination action, a commitment to base one's decisions upon evaluation reports is a sufficient but not a necessary condition of a school system's satisfying the nonarbitrariness criterion of due process. Thus, the simple fact that school systems do not maintain ongoing teacher evaluation programs does not necessarily preclude them from terminating teachers for incompetence, since appropriate facts may be collected in a less systematic manner. Nevertheless, when an evaluation system is in place, the commitment to base termination decisions upon the results of that system provides both a natural and an efficient way to meet the nonarbitrariness criterion of due process. Even though it is not legally necessary for school systems to make such a commitment, there are, however, persuasive legal and administrative reasons for doing so; in any case, the following discussion will assume the existence of this commitment. Finally, a policy of basing termination decisions upon evaluation reports does not meet all the requirements of due process, since the nonarbitrariness criterion is only part of the legal meaning of the doctrine.

The second general purpose of constitutional due process is to prevent government action from being capricious (22 Proof of Facts 617). This purpose may be further resolved into at least three requirements (cf. Rawls, 1971). First, the action should be based upon clearly formulated and publicly announced policies. Second, these policies should be general in their scope; that is, they must apply to all members of the class whose actions they are intended to regulate. Policies, thus, may not name particular individuals nor may they be rigged to single out such persons for special treatment. Third, these policies must be regularly applied; that is, they must be enforced in such a way that all those who qualify for the specified treatment receive it.

When a school system chooses to base its termination decisions on evaluation reports, these due process requirements have specific implications. The publicity requirement obviously suggests that teachers should be informed that employment decisions will depend upon the results of their evaluations. But, more important, the school system's personnel policies should specify in appropriate detail the types of evaluation findings that are likely to lead to termination. The generality and regularity requirements suggest that all teaching personnel should be evaluated; the exemption of certain individuals from evaluation implies that the school system is not in a position to apply its policies to everyone included under them. The regularity requirement suggests further that the same contract renewal decisions should be made for teachers who have received similar evaluations. In effect, past decisions set precedents for the future.

Once again, policies are legally sufficient to establish that decisions have not been capriciously made; they are not clear legal necessities. Nevertheless, the administrator accused in court of arbitrarily terminating a teacher can provide a nearly iron-clad rebuttal if he or she can demonstrate (1) that the grounds for this termination are contained in written school policy, (2) that all other teachers were submitted to a similar review, and (3) that other teachers have been terminated for similar evaluation-related shortcomings.

In addition to restricting the types of activities that government may regulate, the Constitution requires that the methods by which regulations are applied and enforced must be fundamentally fair. Since termination is not a criminal matter, however, federal courts have in general left the specification of procedures in such cases to the discretion of state and local authorities. As a rule, then, school authorities are deemed to have accorded terminated teachers procedural due process when they have followed the procedures outlined in state law or in their own official policies (68 American Jurisprudence 2d, 515–516). Thus, the primary effect of federal case law in this area has been to confer upon teachers a constitutional right to be accorded whatever formal procedures are already prescribed in the applicable state law or local policy.

The Supreme Court recently qualified this rule, however, in holding that, regardless of state and local policies, public school officials must allow a terminated teacher formal dismissal proceedings, including a hearing, if the termination deprives the teacher of a liberty or property interest (*Regents v. Roth* and *Perry v. Sinderman*). The precise legal definition of a liberty interest is unclear, however; the original Court stated that such an interest would be impaired if the termination "might seriously damage [the teacher's] standing or association in his community" or impose on him "a stigma or other disability that foreclosed his freedom to take advantage of other employment opportunities" *(Regents v. Roth)*. The definition of a property interest is somewhat more precise; such an interest exists when there is a clear and mutual expectation of continued employment, such as exists for the teacher who is dismissed before a contract has expired or who has achieved tenure as explicitly defined in state statutes or local regulations or as implied in the personnel practices of the employing agency *(Perry v. Sinderman)*.

Two features of the distinction between teachers who do and teachers who do not have a constitutionally protected property interest in their continued employment are notable for this discussion. First, the distinction is not so indeterminate as to convey such an interest upon all terminated teachers. In fact, in one of the two companion cases in which this new rule was first articulated, *Board of Regents v. Roth* (1972), a nontenured university teacher whose contract was not renewed at year's end was held to have no such interest and, therefore, not to deserve formal termination proceedings. Second, this distinction does not coincide precisely with that between tenured and nontenured teachers. In *Perry v. Sinderman* (1972), the second companion case, a teacher with 10 years' experience within the state college system of Texas was held to have a constitutionally protected property interest in his job even though there was no explicit provision for tenure in Texas statutory law. Here the Court found that the contract renewal practice in effect in the college system implicitly conferred upon long-term employees a legitimate expectation of future employment, which constituted a property interest sufficient to require formal procedures.

These decisions place some very general constraints upon the procedures that state legislatures and local school boards may prescribe in cases in which terminated teachers have a constitutionally protected liberty or property interest. Although the Supreme Court has not specified what formal procedures are due to teachers who qualify for them, their discussion of such procedures in another context *(Goldberg v. Kelly)* provides some general idea of what the constitutionally necessary elements of a procedurally fair administrative process for terminated teachers are likely to include:

(1) the right to be heard in a meaningful way
(2) appropriate notice and a statement of the reasons for termination
(3) the right to confront and cross-examine witnesses
(4) the opportunity to present evidence and argument
(5) the right to an attorney
(6) a decision resting on legal rules and the evidence produced at the hearing
(7) a statement by the decision maker of the reasons for the decision and the evidence on which it is based
(8) a record of the hearing.

The evidentiary requirements of this process, though not as stringent as those governing criminal or civil court cases, have clear implications for teacher evaluation programs. School officials are required to adduce evidence to substantiate a charge of incompetence, and terminated teachers must be given the opportunity to challenge such evidence. The burden of proof in such a hearing rests on the school authorities (68 American Jurisprudence 2d, 522), and, in the case of a tenured teacher, the evidence must be strong enough to overcome the presumption of competence that legally attaches to tenure (Rosenberger and Plimpton, 1975). The probitive value of evaluation reports in overcoming this presumption has been emphasized by legal commentators (Rosenberger and Plimpton, 1975; 22 Proof of Facts 616). When such reports have been systematically and periodically filed, courts to whom termination decisions have been appealed have relied heavily upon them. Since, in constitutionally mandated termination proceedings, performance evaluations are thus likely to carry particular evidentiary weight, it is especially important to ensure that reports used in this context have not been prepared in an arbitrary or capricious manner and that they are not based upon constitutionally inadmissible judgments.

In light, moreover, of the legal significance of evaluation reports and of the terminated teacher's right to challenge evidence presented at a hearing, a policy of allowing the evaluated teacher to enter objections to and explanations or clarifications of the reports into the personnel record at the time at which they are filed may be both prudent and fair. Challenges to those evaluations during a hearing are likely to be less persuasive if the teacher failed to enter objections when such reports were originally completed.

Roth and *Sinderman* have also raised some unresolved constitutional issues about the confidentiality of administrative findings of incompetence in cases in which the terminated teacher does not merit formal due process. The Supreme Court's description of the liberty interest suggests that, in some circumstances at least, the mere publication of the grounds for termination may convey upon the teacher a right to formal procedures, for a public announcement that a teacher has been terminated for some specific types of instructional incompetence may of itself damage standing in the community or limit opportunity to secure future employment. The logic of the *Roth* and *Sinderman* decisions implies that, when administrative actions have these effects, teachers have a constitutional right to defend themselves from the allegations, a right to be exercised in a formal hearing that meets the general requirements of procedural due process. The conditions under which public knowledge of a termination is legally considered to have had these effects are not entirely clear. Public knowledge merely of the fact that a teacher's contract has not been renewed does not constitute a violation of the teacher's liberty interests *(Regents v. Roth)*, but what additional public information is required to invoke the liberty interest criterion for formal due process is, as of now, basically a matter for speculation. These decisions, therefore, provide a constitutional reason for maintaining administrative confidentiality about termination decisions and, by extension, about the evaluation reports upon which those decisions might be based, particularly if school authorities wish to avoid a rash of administrative hearings on these matters.

Finally, because the teacher evaluation techniques used in schools are most likely to be exposed to judicial scrutiny in cases in which formal procedures have been accorded, school officials may be tempted to maintain a dual evaluation system, with one set of procedures that adhere scrupulously to the general and substantive requirements of due process for teachers whose termination will require a formal process and another set that do not adhere to these requirements for teachers who can be terminated without full formal procedures. Not only would such a policy contravene the moral underpinnings of fair evaluation, but it is likely to be legally inadvisable as well, for the *Roth* and *Sinderman* rulings have made it difficult to establish definitively in advance who will and who will not merit formal termination proceedings. First, the property-interest criterion implies that all teachers, not just the tenured, *may* under appropriate circumstances have a right to formal due process. Certain essentially unpredictable circumstances, such as the need to terminate a teacher for incompetence in the middle of a contract period, can confer such a right upon any teacher. Second, the currently unsettled meaning of the liberty-interest criterion makes prediction of who should be evaluated according to which set of procedures at least temporarily uncertain. But, more important, almost no matter how that criterion is eventually interpreted, its application is likely to depend upon the existence of specific unpredictable circumstances. If, for example, the Supreme Court accepts the interpretation that formal procedures are due when termination for the exercise of 1st amendment freedoms can be plausibly alleged (see *Carpenter v. Greenfield*), schools wishing to maintain a dual evaluation system will have to classify their probationary teachers according to whether they are or are not likely to speak out publicly against administration policy. In any case, the maintenance of such a dual system seems to us to be legally inadvisable under current constitutional law. Under a unitary evaluation scheme, a school system maintains the capability to accord formal procedures in all termination cases, whether or not it turns out to be legally necessary actually to do so in any particular case.

Statutory Civil Rights of Terminated Teachers. Both the Constitution and Title VII of the Civil Rights Act of 1964 prohibit discrimination in employment, but because the requirements of Title VII are in general broader and more stringent, we focus our discussion on that legislation. The Supreme Court has interpreted Title VII to hold that personnel policies that have a statistically disproportionate impact upon racial and ethnic minorities or women are illegal unless the employer can demonstrate legitimate and non-discriminatory reasons for them *(McDonnell Douglas v. Green)*. If it turns out, therefore, that the termination practices of a school district have an unequal impact upon the races or sexes, that district must be prepared to defend its practices in court.

In reviewing cases of this kind that had arisen before 1977, Holley and Feild (1978) noted that courts and the Equal Employment Opportunity Commission universally upheld dismissals, even though the members of a single race or sex were more frequently affected, when they were based upon systematic teacher evaluation procedures that had a reasonable and professionally supported rationale. In fact, the only case cited in which a school district's decision was overruled involved a district's purposeful failure to take such evaluations into account (EEOC Decision 74-106, 1974). Though legal standards in this area are still evolving, the potential need to defend termination policies against Title VII charges of race or sex discrimination thus seems to provide yet another legal reason for a commitment to base termination decisions upon systematic evaluation.

One specific area in which Title VII provides some suggestive but not yet firmly established guidance is in the use of standardized tests administered to teachers to help determine their competence. Since the members of some racial and ethnic minorities have traditionally scored lower on such tests, their use in termination decisions is likely to invite the application of Title VII. When these tests do have a disparate impact on the races, the *general* standard for their legitimate use is clear in both case law and federal regulation: Such tests must be validated to show that employee scores are positively related to on-the-job performance *(Washington v. Davis* and *Federal Register,* 12333–12336, 1970). However, there is little clear legal authority on the subject of precisely what sort of validation is acceptable; indeed, the Supreme Court recently refused to clarify these complex issues in ruling moot a case involving a screening examination for prospective firemen in Los Angeles *(Los Angeles v. Davis)*. Moreover, apparently no cases specifically involving the use of such tests in teacher termination have been litigated to date in federal courts. What can be gathered from the current case law is (1) that some sort of reputable validity study establishing the relationship between the test and teacher competence must have been undertaken and (2) that reputable testing authorities, especially the developers of the test in question, should agree that this use of the test is not inappropriate or unintended (Psychological Corporation, 1978). It should be noted that in one case, testing authorities testified that the strongest and most appropriate form of validation for this use of standardized tests, criterion validation, is infeasible since there is no firm professional agreement about the criteria for good teaching (Psychological Corporation, 1978). As a result, it may, depending upon the Supreme Court's eventual disposition of the validation issue, be impossible in practice to meet even these two loose requirements.

Other Uses of Evaluation Reports

In addition to termination, a variety of other personnel policies or actions may be tied to teacher evaluation. In this section we will review briefly the legal constraints imposed particularly by procedural due process requirements upon three such policies: salary determination, promotion and demotion, and employment recommendations. The reasons for this focus upon procedural due process requirements are two: First, the discussion of teachers' personal rights, the general criteria of due process, and statutory civil rights in termination cases apply straightforwardly and with little alteration to these other practices as well and, second, specific provisions of state tenure laws make the determination of procedural due process requirements in these cases a bit more complicated.

Salary Determination. Recurring concern over teacher productivity in public schools has stirred recent interest in merit salary schedules (e.g., Langerone, 1972). As a rule, the general power of school boards over teacher compensation allows them to institute such systems as long as they are "based upon reasonable distinctions as promotive of the progress and welfare of the school system" (133 ALR 1437) and are fairly administered (145 ALR 412). One possible basis for such a salary schedule is a teacher evaluation program constructed to meet the due process requirements.

However, certain features of tenure statutes may place restrictions upon the types of merit pay systems that are administratively feasible. Thus, in some jurisdictions, school boards are denied the authority to reduce the salaries of tenured teachers or to deny to teachers subsequent service increments as specified in the existing salary schedule (154 ALR 151). If, moreover, the salary schedule is set up in such a way that a reduction in salary effectively constitutes a demotion in rank, school officials may be required to show legal cause for such action and accord the affected tenured teachers formal due process procedures (68 American Jurisprudence 2d, 490–491). Even under such conditions, it would apparently be allowable to allocate merit incentives over and above the established salary schedule on the basis of systematic teacher evaluation.

Promotion and Demotion. Another possible use of teacher evaluation is in the assignment of individuals within a system of differentiated staffing. As suggested above, however, tenure statutes generally guarantee teachers assignments to the rank or grade in which their permanent status was acquired (68 American Jurisprudence 2d, 490–491). Thus, though the precise legal relationship between assignment levels not specifically mandated by state law and the ranks to which tenure statutes refer is not clear, this use of teacher evaluation may in certain instances require school officials to show cause for their classification of tenured teachers and to follow strict formal due process procedures.

Recommendations for Employment. Teacher evaluations may be used by supervisory personnel as the basis of reports to potential employers about the teaching ability of past or present employees. As a rule, statements imputing incapacity to teach are actionable; that is, they may form the legitimate basis of a slander or libel suit against the supervisor (40 ALR 3rd 493). The best defense in such a case is the demonstration that such statements are true and were rendered in good faith. These claims may be persuasively established if it can be shown that the report was a reasonable conclusion from a documented record of the teacher's performance. This requires in turn that the evaluations were conducted in a legally responsible manner, at least in accordance with the general requirements of due process, and that reasonable caution was taken in interpreting or generalizing about them.

STATE LAW AND TEACHERS' CONTRACTS

In this section we examine state sources of the legal context governing teacher evaluation. Since the topics discussed are matters of state law, they are subject to variation. We can at best describe their general or typical features and provide examples. Our description should not be treated as a substitute for detailed knowledge of actual state law.

Most states have clear tenure statutes. Moreover, tenure is something of a watershed as far as evaluation is concerned, in that the rights of teachers can change substantially as a consequence of their having obtained tenure.

The major role of tenure is to secure for the teacher the right of continued employment. Having achieved tenure, teachers may be removed from their positions only for cause and in a prescribed manner. Tenure thus divides employment into two phases, the probationary period (from one to five years, typically three) and the tenured period.

Probationary Teachers

For probationary teachers, it is important to distinguish between dismissal and nonrenewal. Dismissal refers to the termination of services during the period of a valid contract. Nonrenewal is the failure to provide the teacher with a new contract when the period of services specified under a prior contract has lapsed. Dismissal during the probationary period is analogous to the termination of a tenured teacher in that it must be for cause and must provide for reasonable due process. However, since nontenured teachers are not normally held to have a property right in the renewal of their contracts, they do not (except under unusual circumstances) have a constitutional right to due process under conditions of nonrenewal. Such rights as they do have are normally a function of state law or contractual provision.

State provisions as to the rights of nontenured teachers whose contracts are not renewed vary. Nebraska permits nonrenewal for "any cause whatsoever or for no cause at all" *(Schulz v. Board of Education of Dorchester)*. Several states require notice, but do not require that grounds for nonrenewal be specified or that the teacher be extended any right of due process.

Many states, however, have legislation that extends certain rights of due process to teachers whose contracts are not renewed. In other cases these rights are extended or expanded by contract. New York's "Fair Dismissal" Law, for example, requires that a teacher concerning whom a recommendation not to grant tenure is going to be made be given notice 30 days before the board meeting at which the matter is to be considered. The teacher is also entitled to a written statement of the reasons for not granting tenure and may file a written rejoinder. The law has been amended so as to require a board to give notice before negative action is taken on a teacher who has been recommended to tenure (Hageny, 1978).

Pennsylvania, while not providing statutory provision of due process for teachers whose contracts are not renewed (see *Travis v. Teter*), has legislated a review procedure which applies to all professional employees dismissed for incompetence, including temporary professionals. The statute reads in part,

> The professional employee or temporary professional employee shall be rated by an approved rating system which shall give due consideration to personality, preparation, technique, and pupil reaction. [Purdon's Pennsylvania Statutes Annotated, Title 24, sec. 11-1123].

Nontenured teachers may also obtain certain rights by contract. Contracts commonly specify certain evaluation or grievance procedures, portions of which may apply to nontenured teachers. Occasionally a contract provides nontenured or part-time teachers due process rights not provided for in state legislation. The United Federation of Teachers' contract with the New York City board provides probationary teachers with a review before the chancellor (Article 21C). The contract also contains the following provisions:

> Teachers on probation who have completed at least three years of service on regular appointment in the school shall be entitled, with respect to the discontinuance of their probationary service, to the same review procedures as are established for tenured teachers under Section 3020-a of the Education Law [Article 21C2].

Section 3020-a essentially specifies that tenured teachers can be dismissed only for cause and with due process. New York City teachers who have completed their probationary period, thus, are contractually entitled to the protection of the procedural components of this statute. A New York court has, however, held that it is beyond the power of a board of education to contract that a probationary teacher cannot be discharged except for just cause (*Morris Central School District Board of Education v. Morris Education Association*). There are, thus, limits to the contractual expansion of the rights of probationary teachers.

It is noteworthy that although some states have acted to extend due process rights to nontenured teachers, there has been no effort to specify what are permissible grounds for dismissal. The discretion of school boards here is thus extensive. Moreover, the consequences of violating such procedural rights as nontenured teachers possess are not severe. In cases in which proper notice was not provided or mandated evaluation procedures were not followed, courts have awarded back pay and temporary reinstatement but have not awarded tenure (*Feinerman v. Board of Cooperative Educational Services, Nassau County*).

In summary, the following generalizations can be made about the legal status of nontenured teachers.

(1) Probationary teachers have no property interest in their continued employment. They will not, therefore, receive the protection of federal courts under the due process clause of the 14th amendment. Federal courts will interject themselves into the nonrenewal of a nontenured teacher only when the grounds of dismissal are not constitutionally permissible.

(2) Some states have extended minimal components of due process to probationary teachers. Most common are the right to a statement of the grounds for nonrenewal and the right to respond.

(3) Additional rights may be secured by contract. Relevant provisions include appeals procedures, grievance procedures, provisions about the teacher's file, and rights to notice and appeal.

(4) There is little in state law or contractual provisions that specifies grounds for nonrenewal.

Continuing Contract Laws

Many states do not have tenure statutes. Such states often provide a degree of security for teachers by means of what are commonly called continuing contract laws, which provide for automatic renewal of a teacher's contract in the absence of nonrenewal. Continuing contract laws exhibit wide variation in the extent of the protection provided teachers. At one end of the continuum are statutes where only notification is required for nonrenewal. Other states require a statement of reasons along with notification. At the other pole, statutes can provide nonrenewed teachers with rights approaching those of a tenured teacher.

Arkansas provides an example of a continuing contract law affording minimal protection to teachers:

> Every contract of employment . . . shall be renewed in writing on the same terms . . . for the school year next succeeding the date of termination fixed therein, which renewal may be made by endorsement on the existing contract instrument; unless during the same period of such contract or within ten (10) days after the termination of said school term, the teacher shall be notified by the school board in writing . . . that such contract will not be renewed for such succeeding year [Arkansas Statutes, subsection 80-130f(b)].

By contrast, California provides substantial protection for a nonrenewed teacher:

> The employee may request a hearing to determine if there is cause for not re-employing him for the ensuing year.

> The governing board's determination not to re-employ a probationary employee for the following year shall be for cause only. The determination of the governing board as to the sufficiency of the cause shall relate solely to the welfare of the schools and the pupils thereof [California Statute, Education 13443(b) (d) (1975)].

Continuing contract laws and tenure laws may not always be sharply distinct. Connecticut provides for automatic renewal and requires that nonrenewal be for cause. It also provides for a hearing with right to counsel for any nonrenewed teacher; however, it distinguishes between teachers who have less than four years' service and those who have begun a fifth year by extending to the latter, but not the former, the right to an appeal to the court of common pleas.

Continuing contract laws may also render the applicability of the federal due process clause to cases of dismissal or nonrenewal less clear in that they make it less clear whether teachers have a property interest in their jobs. The basic standard is the extent to which the teacher has a reasonable expectation of continued employment. It is important to recognize that courts may look to more than state statutes in making a determination. Local policy or practice is also potentially relevant. Generally, any statute, policy, or practice that can be construed as granting de facto tenure or a degree of long-term job security will result in the application of the due process clause.

Tenured Teachers

Once teachers attain tenure, their legal status changes dramatically. Tenured teachers have a property interest in their job. The full protection of the due process clause of the 14th amendment thereby becomes available. The tenured teacher can be dismissed only for cause and has a wide range of due process rights. Additional rights may be secured by contract. In the case of tenured teachers, the failure to follow constitutional, statutory, or contractual procedures precisely is likely to result in a court rejection of any dismissal action. However, in our judgment the legendary impossibility of dismissing a tenured teacher is much exaggerated. The causes of dismissal specified in most state statutes provide sufficient latitude for any plausible charge. The procedural requirements normally require care, patience, and perhaps a bit of courage. They are, however, far from unexecutable. The protection afforded tenured teachers seems to us to be generally fair and reasonable to the teacher, the administrator, and the school.

Causes for Dismissal

The causes for dismissal are normally specified in a state's tenure law. A portion of Connecticut's statue will serve to illustrate.

> (b) Beginning with and subsequent to the fourth year of continuous employment of a teacher by a board of education, the contract of employment of a teacher shall be renewed from year to year, except that it may be terminated at any time for one or more of the following reasons:
> (1) Inefficiency or incompetence;
> (2) Insubordination against reasonable rules of the board of education;
> (3) Moral misconduct;
> (4) Disability, as shown by competent medical evidence;
> (5) Elimination of the position;
> (6) Other due and sufficient cause [Connecticut General Statutes Annotated, Title 10, Section 10-151].

Pennsylvania provides the following list: immorality, incompetency, intemperance, cruelty, persistent negligence, mental derangement, and persistent and willful violation of the school laws (Purdon's Pennsylvania Statute Title 24 Section 11-1122). New York adds failure to maintain certification.

Of this large range of statutory causes for termination, we focus on the charge of incompetence. Incompetence (or its legal synonym, inefficiency) is explicitly mentioned as a legitimate cause for termination in most state tenure statutes; even when not listed in those statutes, incompetence has been held to be implied in the concept of proper cause itself (4 ALR 1091). More important, incompetence is the charge to which teacher evaluation is most obviously and immediately applicable. However, incompetence is not normally defined by statute. Such judicial definitions as have been proposed are characterized more by their breadth than by their precision. One judge has provided the following definition:

> A grossly inefficient person would be one whose efforts were failing to an intolerable degree, to produce the effect intended or desired—a manifestly incompetent or incapable person [*Conley v. Board of Education of the City of New Britain*].

On the basis of such remarks, Rosenberger and Plimpton (1975) conclude that "There seems to have been no legal need to define competence" (p. 470), and that "conventional wisdom and common sense, rather than precise standards, have been used in judging incompetence claims" (p. 486).

It is instructive to note what has and what has not been permitted to count as incompetence. The following have been accepted as contributing to a finding of incompetence by some courts (see Rosenberger and Plimpton, 1975; Peterson et al., 1978; and 68 American Jurisprudence 2d): deficiencies of knowledge of subject matter, poor teaching methods, disorganized teaching or work habits, inability to maintain discipline or use of excessive force or other inappropriate methods, inability to motivate students, inflexibility or lack of adaptability, uncooperativeness, permitting or requiring vulgarities on the part of students, causing low morale, poor communication, poor attitude, violation of rules, mishandling of funds, low student achievement, unsatisfactory ratings, poor record keeping, arbitrary grading, and lack of self-control.

This omnibus list of teacher deficiencies does not suggest either the clarity or the distinctiveness of the various causes of dismissal. Rather, it appears as though almost any failure that is plausibly seen as relevant to teaching performance may count as incompetence. It does not follow that judicial opinion is unanimous on these topics or that charges of incompetence are lightly considered by courts. However, three conclusions may be drawn.

First, courts are likely to rely on the professional judgment of administrators in the substantive aspects of evaluation. In one recent case, a federal appeals court remarked as follows:

> It is possible that the discretion of a Board may, at times, to those more generously endowed, seem to have been exercised with a lack of wisdom. But the Board's decisions in the exercise of its discretion are not vulnerable to our

correction merely if they are "wrong," sustainable only if they are "right" . . . Such matters as the competence of teachers, and the standards of its measurement are not, without more, matters of constitutional dimensions. They are peculiarly appropriate to state and local administration [*Scheelhaase v. Woodbury Central Community School District*].

Second, however, judicial review of dismissal decisions is likely to be more restrictive when dealing with the procedural aspects of dismissal. Courts require that legislated or contractual procedures for evaluation or due process be rigorously followed. Moreover, they insist that evidence be produced that clearly demonstrates a significant failure on the part of the teacher. They may also insist, where the defect is remediable, that opportunity for improvement be given *(Yesinowski v. Board of Education)*. And granting tenure to a teacher creates a presumption in favor of the competence of the teacher, which must be disproven.

Third, despite the lack of an authoritative legal definition and despite jurisdictional variations in interpretation, a general and widely accepted core of meaning for teaching incompetence can be discerned in the case law. Incompetence may stem from deficiencies in the teacher's own knowledge of the subject matter to be taught, from inability to impart that knowledge, or from inability to maintain appropriate classroom discipline (4 ALR 3rd 1094). Moreover, incompetence is to be reflected in a pervasive pattern of teacher behavior that has proven to be irremediable (22 Proof of Facts 64–69).

The first part of this core of meaning places constraints upon the categories of information to be collected if teacher evaluations are to be appropriate grounds for legally sustainable findings of incompetence. Judgments must be based on evidence that is relevant to the three broad legally established criteria of instructional competence, knowledge, instruction, and discipline. Thus, for example, evidence of past psychological imbalance, obesity, and inability to maintain harmonious personal relations with other teachers have been found by courts to be irrelevant to teaching competence (Rosenberger and Plimpton, 1975). Therefore, if the connection between information collected and teaching effectiveness is not readily apparent, there should be some support in research or professional opinion that such a connection does exist *(Scheelhaase v. Woodbury)*.

The second part of the legal core of meaning of incompetence, that it involves a pattern of irremediable behavior, has two implications for the conduct of evaluations. First, evaluations should be undertaken periodically in order that they show the deficiencies upon which termination is based to have been continuously in evidence. Moreover, dismissal of tenured teachers requires a showing that the deficiency exists at the time that the action is taken; evaluations that are out of date or for assignments dissimilar to the teacher's current position will not support the charge of incompetence (22 Proof of Facts 619). Second, evaluation reports should be made available to the teacher involved. That the teacher has been informed of deficiencies provides evidence that the faults are irremediable if the pattern of behavior persists in subsequent evaluations (22 Proof of Facts 617). This policy is not strictly required under current case law; all that school authorities need to show is that the fault would not or could not have been corrected if the teacher had been warned. Nevertheless, the failure to share evaluation reports with teachers is likely to limit the authority of the school to dismiss incompetent tenured teachers to only the most flagrant cases.

Teachers may not be dismissed for cause when the cause specified involved the exercise of some protected right. Although most of the rights protected are constitutional rights, certain rights of political participation are sometimes protected by statute. Massachusetts law contains the following provision:

> No committee shall by rule, regulation, or otherwise restrict any teacher in, or dismiss him for, exercising his right of suffrage, signing nomination papers, petitioning the general court or appearing before its committees, to the extent that such rights, except voting, are not exercised on school grounds, or when their exercise would actually interfere with the performance of school duties [Massachusetts General Laws Annotated, Chapter 71, Section 44].

The preceding is by no means a complete discussion of the permissible grounds for dismissal. It should help, however, to provide a feel for the character of the substantive issues that can be generated by an attempt to dismiss a teacher for cause and the probable effect of these issues on teacher evaluation programs.

Due Process and Procedural Requirements. There are three sources of procedural requirements for taking action against a tenured teacher: the due process clause of the 14th amendment, state law, and contracts. For tenured teachers, due process requirements are normally laid out in state law. Such statutes typically include the constitutionally mandated components of due process but specify the mechanics of the process in considerable detail. Here, for illustrative purposes, is New York's system.

(1) Filing of charges: Charges must be filed in writing with the clerk of the school district or school board during the period between the opening and closing of the school year. No charges may be filed more than three years following the occurrence of the events to which the charges pertain.

(2) Disposition of charges: The clerk is to notify the board of the charges. Within 5 days the board shall determine by majority vote whether probable cause exists. If probable cause exists, the board must immediately notify the

accused by certified mail by means of a written statement which specifies the charges in detail and outlines the rights of the accused. The accused employee must then notify the clerk within 10 days whether he or she wishes a hearing. Failure to do so constitutes a waiver of the right to a hearing. If the hearing is not waived, the clerk, within 10 days, must notify the commissioner of education of the need for a hearing. If the hearing is waived, the board must, within 15 days, by majority vote determine the case and fix a penalty.

(3) Hearings: The commissioner of education must schedule a hearing within 20 days within the local district. Hearings are held before a panel of three persons selected from a list maintained by the commissioner. One member of the panel is selected by the employee, one by the board, and the third, who is chairman of the panel, by the other two. The third member is selected from a list maintained by the American Arbitration Association.

Hearings are conducted by the chairman according to rules determined by the commissioner. These rules do not require compliance with technical rules of evidence. Hearings may be public or private at the discretion of the employee. Employees must have the opportunity to defend themselves and to testify in their own behalf. Each party has the right to counsel and to subpoena and cross-examine witnesses. Testimony is taken under oath, and a record must be made, a transcript of which is to be available without charge to the employee on request.

(4) Posthearing procedures: Results of the hearing, including findings and recommendations of the panel, must be forwarded by the commissioner to the employee and the clerk of the board within 5 days of the conclusion of the hearing. The board must implement the findings within 30 days.

(5) Appeal: Either the employee or the board may appeal the findings of the panel to the commissioner.

Two points about these procedures are noteworthy. First, failure to follow the procedures outlined in the relevant state statutes is likely to result in the failure of the proceedings in state courts. Second, if charges are to be sustained, they must be proved by evidence, or documents, which can be presented and defended at a hearing of the sort described above. Again, the values of a systematic evaluation program in providing such evidence cannot be overstressed.

COLLECTIVE BARGAINING AGREEMENTS

Here we review some typical collective bargaining agreement which can affect teacher evaluation. Before beginning this task, however, it is necessary to make a few remarks about the statutory context in which such teacher contracts are embedded. Most states have collective bargaining acts which circumscribe the collective bargaining processes between teachers' unions and boards of education.

Two general rules can be laid down about negotiation and evaluation. First, most statutes specify that conditions of employment are a proper topic for negotiation. Typical is Connecticut's statute, which specifies that negotiations may be conducted "with respect to salaries and other conditions of employment about which either party wishes to negotiate (Connecticut General Statutes Annotated, Title 10, Section 10-153d). California's statute is more specific:

> The scope of representation shall be limited to matters relating to wages, hours of employment, and other terms and conditions of employment. "Terms and conditions of employment" mean health and welfare benefits . . . leave and transfer policies, safety, conditions of employment, class size, procedures to be used for the evaluation of employees, organizational security, and procedures for processing grievances [West's Annotated California Code, Government Code, section 3543-2].

The second general rule is that boards of education cannot negotiate away legislated board prerogatives. This is sometimes a result of court action, as in New York, where the Court of Appeals has ruled that matters that are not terms and conditions of employment may nevertheless be negotiated unless the resulting agreement would violate a statute or a strong public policy *(Susquehanna Valley Teachers Association)*. In other cases the limits of collective bargaining are specified by statute. California law holds that "All matters not specifically enumerated are reserved to the public school employer and may not be construed to limit the right of the public school employer to consult with any employees or employee organization or any matter outside the scope of representation" (3543.2). The actual limits placed on topics for collective bargaining by such statutes may be small. Phrases such as "conditions of employment" can be construed broadly enough to include many apparently excluded topics.

Concerning evaluation, first, in many states, boards of education may be obligated to negotiate procedures for conducting evaluation and grievance procedures. (In some cases the general structure of grievance procedures may be developed in state law. Some states also specify grievance procedures for districts which fail to negotiate them.) Second, the procedures and rules for doing an evaluation and for appealing the results are most likely to be negotiable. The substantive criteria of evaluation, however, are usually not negotiable. Third, the power of decision about hiring and retention generally cannot be negotiated away. A competent union may, however, succeed in significantly circumscribing board discretion even in such forbidden areas.

Collective bargaining agreements commonly contain provisions for evaluation and for the development of a teacher's personnel file. Contractual provisions vary just as statutes do. We will describe provisions that have occurred with at least modest frequency in our review of selected contracts. (Agreements reviewed are listed in the References.) Again, this summary is not a reasonable substitute for knowledge of the particular arrangements governing a given situation.

(1) Contracts commonly prohibit some kinds of procedures for collecting information and some sources of information. Some contracts forbid any secret observations or monitoring. Others forbid the use of electronic equipment in observation and require the teacher's permission for recording any observation or evaluation session. Some contracts prohibit the use of any anonymous material in an evaluation and prohibit its introduction into a teacher's file. A few contracts require that complaints about a teacher can be used in an evaluation or introduced into a file only if they are investigated.

(2) The timing of observations or evaluations may be specified. Many contracts require notice of any observation session. A few specify the content of the notice in considerable detail. Some contracts specify the frequency of evaluation or observation. Frequencies range from continuously to yearly.

(3) Contracts may contain provisions pertaining to the criteria used in evaluation. Although the actual criteria to be employed are typically not negotiable and, thus, are not found in contracts, contracts often specify that the teacher be informed of the criteria to be employed in an evaluation. Contracts also often prohibit the willingness to participate in or supervise extracurricular or outside activities from being employed as a criterion.

(4) Contracts often specify who can or who cannot participate in an evaluation. They frequently prohibit uncertified or unqualified personnel from participating. A few contracts set up mechanisms for teachers to participate in the evaluation of other teachers.

(5) Contracts commonly require a postevaluation interim report and sometimes a conference. Of those contracts requiring conferences, some require them only on the occasion of a negative evaluation. Others require them as a matter of course.

(6) Contracts usually regulate written evaluation reports. Teachers are normally entitled to see their evaluation reports. Contracts commonly specify that the teacher must sign the report if it is to go into the teacher's personnel file. Most contracts permit the teacher to respond to negative remarks. Some require negative remarks to be accompanied by suggestions for improvement. A few provide for a teacher's self-evaluation or other sources of information beyond the administrator's evaluation.

(7) Some contracts provide for some form of remediation for negative evaluations. Often a negative evaluation must be accompanied by suggestions for improvement. Some contracts require that the matter be worked out in conference and that some plan of action be agreed upon.

(8) The contents and construction of a personnel file are significant factors in contracts. The following provisions are reasonably common.

(a) Contracts often specify who may place material in the file.
(b) Contracts may forbid derogatory material from being included in the file unless it is job related.
(c) Teachers have the right to read and respond to material placed in the file.
(d) Teachers have the right to examine the file periodically and to copy material.
(e) The contents of the file must be kept private and confidential.
(f) Contracts often encourage administrators to include recognition of any special achievements or other significant positive contributions.
(g) Some contracts specify that derogatory material be removed after a certain period.

(9) Many contracts specify that the teacher may be accompanied by a union representative at any conference in which the teacher's evaluation is to be discussed.

(10) Many contracts require that any disciplinary procedures be for just cause.

(11) Many contracts specify that notice and reasons be given for adverse personnel actions, including nonrenewal.

Grievance Procedures

Failure to comply with legal or contractual provisions for evaluation is a common cause of grievances. Contractual provisions concerning what is grievable can differ. Some contracts limit grievances to violation of the contract. Most, however, provide for a wide class of grievable events. One contract puts the matter as follows:

> A grievance is a claim by any person or groups of persons in the negotiating unit based upon any event or conditions affecting their welfare and/or terms and conditions of employment, including but not limited to any claimed violation, misrepresentation, misapplication, or inequitable application of law, rules, or regulations having force of law, thus agreement, policies, rules, by-laws, regulations, director's order, work rules, procedures, practices, or customs of the Board of Education [Ithaca Teachers' Association].

Perhaps the conclusion to be drawn is that anything is normally grievable so long as it can be plausibly construed as a violation of a work-related rule. The source of such rules may vary substantially, ranging from law to common practice, and potentially to well-established moral sentiment.

What is grievable (or the extent to which something is grievable) may, however, be limited in three ways. First, an act may not be grievable if an alternative procedure is specified by law or contract. Second, some topics may be effectively precluded from grievance procedures by law or court action. Boards of education, for example, may be precluded from implicitly delegating personnel decisions or other decisions assigned to them by statute to the arbitration mechanisms found in some grievance procedures. Finally, a contract may specify the way in which or the extent to which an evaluation or its results can be appealed through grievance mechanisms.

Grievance procedures are usually characterized by a series of stages of deliberation at increasingly higher levels. The specific details of these stages vary considerably. We attempt to summarize a "typical" mechanism as a four-stage process. Most contracts specify some form of deliberation at each of these levels.

(1) Local-informal: Most contracts recommend that an aggrieved teacher attempt an informal settlement of a potential grievance before formalizing the matter as a grievance. This stage is usually optional with the teacher.

(2) Local-formal: If informal deliberations fail and the teacher wishes to pursue the issue, the next step is typically a written statement of the grievance to the building principal, who must then reply in writing within a specified period of time. Most contracts permit the teacher's union to become involved at this point.

(3) Off-site adjudication: If the teacher is dissatisfied with the result at this level, the matter may then be submitted to some higher authority. Appeals may be made to the superintendent, the personnel director, or the school board, depending on specific contractual provisions. Sometimes there is more than one level of off-site adjudication. At this level, many contracts permit attorneys for both sides and provide formal hearing mechanisms.

(4) Arbitration: Either side may appeal the result of the previous stage to binding arbitration. Since binding arbitration (depending on the topic) can be construed as an impermissible delegation of the authority of the school board, many contracts restrict what can be submitted to binding arbitration. Arbitration is often conducted under the auspices of the American Arbitration Association.

One of the contracts investigated (Philadelphia) also contains a provision requiring mediation under the auspices of the Labor Relations section of the

Personnel Division. Such mediation would be attempted between stages two and three of our model. We note this not because it is typical, but because it seems to us to be commendable.

We conclude our discussion of state law and local contracts by noting points in the administration of a teacher evaluation system at which problems are most likely to occur. Our discussion of the legal and contractual situation and the relevant literature on the topic (see especially French, 1978) suggest that certain areas are apt to be especially troublesome and are likely to be a common source of conflict, grievance, and litigation. Thus, here is a modest list of things to do to get into trouble.

(1) One may take action against a person when that person's records fail to make it clear that his or her conduct or job performance is regarded as unacceptable. One may do this by stating one's objections too tentatively, by balancing negative remarks with praise, or by failing to make it clear that some described behavior is viewed negatively. The teacher may thus raise the question as to whether reason was ever given to believe that overall performance was regarded as unsatisfactory. A teacher's record should make clear that a negative assessment is a negative assessment.

(2) One may fail to be consistent from evaluation to evaluation. An action taken on the basis of some deficiency sporadically or only occasionally mentioned can undermine the credibility of evaluators.

(3) One may give a negative evaluation in such a way as to make it unclear what exactly is being objected to or what is objectionable about what is being objected to. One may do this by using broad or vague phrases, such as "poor teaching" or "ineffective discipline," without providing any instances or descriptions of what particular acts are regarded as objectionable. Or one may fail to describe any clear standards or expectations that would indicate why the behavior in question was regarded as inadequate or what would count as adequate behavior.

(4) One may fail to acquaint a teacher with the evidence for a negative assessment. One may do this by introducing negative remarks into a teacher's file without the teacher's knowledge or by introducing negative evidence midway in a proceeding against the teacher.

(5) One may fail to provide feasible suggestions for improvement when providing a negative evaluation or fail to provide sufficient opportunity for improvement.

(6) One may fail to comply with the notification and scheduling requirements for conducting an evaluation.

(7) One may employ evidence obtained in an impermissible way or of a dubious nature, such as unchecked parental complaints, hearsay, or evidence gained through covert or unannounced observation.

(8) One may allow one's personal feelings or biases toward a teacher to affect one's evaluation of the teacher.

(9) One may use an evaluation to enforce adverse community or parental attitudes toward a given teacher.

(10) One may allow irrelevant criteria, such as race, sex, or lifestyle, to influence one's evaluation of a teacher.

The discussion of this section leads to a focus on developing an informative personnel file. The personnel file will be appealed to in any action taken with respect to a teacher. The administrator should thus focus on generating an evaluation system that produces a record about the teacher that is characterized by informative descriptions and clear assessments appealing to known and relevant criteria and collected according to a known and orderly process.

A GENERAL MODEL FOR TEACHER EVALUATION

The need to make personnel decisions in a legal and morally responsible manner is surely not the only justification for a systematic program of teacher evaluation; such a justification plainly overlooks the formative uses of teacher evaluation altogether and also ignores other respectable summative uses of teacher evaluation, such as its use in deciding whether to continue particular programs of inservice training. Moreover, a commitment to base personnel decisions upon evaluation reports is not an absolute legal or moral necessity. Nevertheless, the case for a school system's making such a commitment is strong, for, first, it declares formally the system's intention to respect teachers as persons by making decisions that affect their lives on the basis of performance-relevant criteria. Second, it declares the system's intention to make reasonable decisions based upon established fact. And, finally, it promises to protect the system's decisions against a wide variety of specific legal challenges, from allegations that they have been made for constitutionally proscribed reasons to claims that proper cause for termination has not been established.

As we have noted time and again, however, these benefits accrue to school systems that commit themselves to basing personnel decisions on teacher evaluations only when their evaluation policies and procedures meet specific requirements. In this section we synthesize these disparate requirements into a general model for a legally and morally acceptable program of teacher evaluation. We do not intend to offer a complete model for evaluation programs since they may serve a number of purposes in addition to that of forming the basis for personnel decisions; instead, our model will include a core of fundamental features upon which elaborations, modifications, and extensions may be made for other legitimate purposes.

We will confine ourselves to describe five general and, in our view, universal sets of characteristics of a legally and morally acceptable system of teacher evaluation to be used in making personnel decisions, particularly decisions about contract renewal and teacher dismissal. These characteristics are (1) the policy background, (2) the substance of the evaluation, (3) evaluation methods and procedures, (4) participation and mediation in evaluation, and (5) administrative review and use of evaluations.

Formal Policy Background

In keeping with the general purpose of due process to assure that judgments affecting individuals are made on the basis of publicly articulated rules, it is important that a school system's intent to use teacher evaluations in making personnel decisions be declared in the formal administrative policies of the school board. The policies in which this intention is articulated should meet some conspicuous formal requirements. First, these policies should be a matter of public record. Second, they should be written with as much precision, clarity, and detail as is consistent with the nature of the decisions to be made. The point of these rules, like any other public regulations, is to make it possible for individual teachers to comply with them. Neither the interests of the teacher in performing well enough to be retained nor those of the school system to promote instruction of an appropriate kind and quality are served by policies that are so indeterminate as to prevent teachers from conscientiously acting to meet their requirements. This criterion should not, however, be taken as a demand that evaluation and termination policies must be formulated as low-level behavioral rules, since the characteristics of good teaching may not be definitely specifiable in such terms and since it is perfectly possible for individuals to comply with more conceptually sophisticated rules.

A policy that meets this requirement of clarity might be constructed in the following format. Initially, the policy should include a statement of the criteria of acceptable teaching that will be used to make retention decisions. These criteria should be broad enough and detailed enough to encompass all characteristics of teacher performance that the administration deems relevant to teaching competence and that will, in fact, enter into personnel decisions. They need not, however, attempt to list exhaustively the infinitude of teacher behaviors in which competence might be reflected. Next, the policy should identify the information that will be collected, and its method of collection, under a teacher evaluation program upon the results of which judgments of whether these criteria have been satisfied will be made. This section of policy should indicate which information is relevant to the satisfaction of particular criteria but need not specify an artificially mathematical formula for translating data into judgments. Finally, the policy should indicate what types of evaluative shortcomings are likely to lead to termination; the purpose here is to illustrate in enough detail the application of the administration's rules of judgment and interpretation to allow teachers to comply with district policy. Again, there need be no pretense that these illustrations are exhaustive.

The third formal requirement is that these evaluation and personnel policies should be communicated to teachers. This requirement goes beyond that of making the policies a matter of public record; it reflects a commitment by school administrators to assuring that the ground rules for personal decisions are understood by those most immediately affected by them.

Beyond these formal criteria, evaluation policy should meet a few general substantive requirements as well. First, participation in the evaluation system should be mandatory for all. Popular misconceptions notwithstanding, tenure laws do not exempt any class of teachers from termination for instructional incompetence; evaluation reports are thus relevant to the personnel decisions that must be made periodically about all teachers. Moreover, the exemption of teachers from evaluation contradicts the purpose behind the school system's legal authority to dismiss teachers, the maintenance of appropriate instruction, and violates the spirit of due process, according to which rules are to be general in their scope.

Second, an evaluation program should be unitary in two senses. It should, on the one hand, collect similar information about all teachers and generate judgments based upon similar standards for all teachers regardless of their past experience or legal status within the system. This is not to deny that differences in legal status do exist or that these differences place differential constraints upon the personnel decisions that may legally be made about individual teachers. Rather, it reflects the general requirement of due process that rules be uniformly applied. As a general rule, state tenure statutes do not prohibit the evaluation of the performances of tenured teachers according to the same standards as those applied to probationary teachers. The different legal and practical purposes of evaluation that stem from tenured and probationary status may be adequately served by varying the schedules of evaluation and the administrative action taken upon evaluation results rather than by varying the observational focus or standards of judgment of the teacher evaluation itself.

On the other hand, a teacher evaluation system should be unitary in that it is a part of a uniform set of procedures for making personnel decisions about all teachers, procedures that meet the substantive and procedural requirements of constitutional due process. This policy prepares a school system to accord formal due process in all termination cases, whether or not it proves to be legally necessary to do so in any particular case.

Third, personnel policies should include a commitment to reaching similar termination decisions on similar evaluative grounds. Policies that meet the formal criteria outlined above are still likely to require administrative interpretation in individual cases; no matter how clearly formulated or detailed the district's criteria of acceptable teaching may be, evaluative judgments of the degree to which particular teachers have met those criteria are inherently unavoidable. This requirement recognizes that the decision process in personnel matters cannot be specified and regularized to the extent that it becomes the mere mechanical application of self-interpreting decision rules. Nevertheless, it does direct administrators to treat past and present decisions as precedents. In interpreting performance criteria, then, an administrator should rely, in the first place, upon relevant past interpretations. In the second place, in making a present decision the administrator should be bound to a particular interpretation of the performance criteria, which is to hold in similar present and future cases. This policy simply enacts the general due process requirement that the application of rules must be regular. It should be noted here that the legal status of the teacher is necessarily a consideration in classifying decisions as precedents. Tenure creates a legal presumption of competence which prevents the dismissal of a tenured teacher for short-term inadequacies that might be sufficient grounds for dismissing a probationary teacher. For the probationary teacher, such failings may more plausibly be construed as signs of chronic incompetence.

The Substance of the Evaluation

The evaluation itself should focus only on those aspects of a teacher's performance, behavior, and activities that are directly or indirectly relevant to the teacher's ability to execute the legitimate responsibilities that attach to the job. This general rule recognizes both the public's interest in maintaining an adequate standard of instruction within schools and the teacher's moral rights to privacy in life outside the school and to humane treatment on the job. The main difficulty in implementing this rule lies in distinguishing between legitimate and illegitimate teaching responsibilities on the one hand and between what is and what is not relevant to assessing the teacher's ability on the other.

The U.S. Constitution and a few state statutes provide some definition of what duties school systems may *not* legitimately impose upon teachers. Since teachers retain full citizenship rights within this society, their duties cannot, as a rule, include any that require them to forego or limit their exercise of the constitutionally protected liberties shared by all citizens. Beyond this, teachers have some extraordinary though narrowly restricted rights as members of the academic community. Thus, although teachers can be required to act in general in a professionally responsible manner, they retain the right to exercise their own judgment within the broad range of professionally acceptable activities. Teachers' duties, therefore, cannot be so narrowly construed as to preclude their exercise of professional judgment about, for example, the use of instructional methods and materials. Finally, because some state statutes protect teachers' rights to specific forms of political participation which go beyond the rights implied in the U.S. Constitution, teachers' duties in those jurisdictions cannot interfere with the protected activities. Although it may not be possible, or in some cases even desirable, to eliminate from teacher evaluation all information about these legally protected activities, the evaluation should be designed to prevent these considerations from figuring in summary judgments of teaching competence, because they apply to actions that fall outside the sphere of legitimate professional duties.

Even within the sphere of legitimate responsibilities, however, the evaluator must distinguish between information that is and information that is not relevant to judgments about teachers' abilities. The core of meaning in the legal concept of teaching competence provides a starting place for drawing this distinction. Competence consists of a teacher's command over the subject matter for which the teacher is responsible, the use of instructional methods for effectively communicating that knowledge to students, and the ability to establish a relationship with students and a classroom atmosphere conducive to effective teaching and the consistent operation of the school in general. As a rule, then, information is relevant to the evaluation of teaching competence insofar as it sheds light upon whether teachers meet these three criteria.

Several conclusions follow from this general principle of evaluative relevance. First, certain personal characteristics of teachers, such as race, religion, and ethnicity are generally irrelevant to teacher evaluation. Second, direct professional observations of classroom performance are unquestionably relevant to teaching competence. Neither the law nor common sense, however, requires that information relevant to evaluation be restricted to the classroom or even to the school. The relevance requirement for this external information is, however, still connected with the legal core of meaning of teaching competence: External information must be plausibly indicative of the teacher's capacity to fulfill central instructional responsibilities. Finally, certain indirect measures of teaching ability, such as student test results, teacher tests, or research-based instruments, may be held legally relevant to judgments of competence under a variety of conditions. In some cases, the connection between the observation, for example, of student performance or behavior and teaching ability may be so obvious as to require no specific corroboration. In cases in which this connection is not readily apparent, there must be a basis in professional opinion for its relevance. When, moreover, results on this measure vary systematically with race, religion, ethnicity, or sex of teachers, corroboration must go beyond simple professional opinion; here a reputable validity study of some kind must have been conducted to establish the relationship between the evaluation instrument and job performance.

Thus, the law itself does little more than to rule some considerations inherently irrelevant to the evaluation of teacher competence and to specify the conditions that must be met for some other types of information to be legitimately relevant. Beyond this, the law merely establishes a general test of relevance, plausible connection with the three criteria of competence; it does not tell the evaluator what specific items of information must be considered. Nor do general considerations of fairness take us much further, for these are matters for research, professional judgment, and good faith negotiation between teachers and administrators.

Evaluation Procedures

The law of due process itself applies specifically only to the procedures undertaken to terminate teachers; legal due process requirements do not apply directly to the procedures followed in teacher evaluation. One element of legal due process in particular, the giving of notice, seems to be required by a commitment to fairness in teacher evaluation. Moreover, there are several additional indirect implications of the law governing teacher termination for evaluation purposes.

The purposes of giving notice in the termination process are to inform the teacher of the specific charges and to allow him or her adequate time to prepare a defense against them. Since evaluation does not itself bring charges against a teacher or deprive the teacher of anything in which the teacher has a legal interest, there is no legal due process requirement that teachers be notified in advance that they will be evaluated. However, procedural due process is a practical instantiation of a fundamental aspect of fairness, the requirement that the decisions that affect people's lives be made reasonably. This requirement, in turn, implies a commitment to giving individuals feasible control over whether they violate the regulations for which they will be held responsible.

In terms specific to this discussion, teachers are given control over their compliance with standards of adequate teaching when they are informed of those standards and of the means that will be used to judge their compliance. Beyond this, however, teachers can, and should in our view, be extended more substantial control over their compliance through two additional measures. First, they should be given reasonable advance notice of when particular evaluation activities, such as classroom observations or testing of students, will take place. Such notice gives teachers an opportunity to plan instructional activities appropriate to the specific measurements of performance that will be taken. Second, teachers should, within administratively feasible limits, be consulted about the appropriate specific time for scheduling the evaluation activities. This is of special importance for the scheduling of class visitations when the exigencies of long-range instructional planning, the need, for example, to show a film on a particular day, may preclude fair evaluation. In such a case, the arbitrary scheduling of class visits either may disrupt a planned and natural sequence of instruction, if the teacher chooses to substitute an activity more suitable to observation than the one for which the students have been prepared, or may cause the evaluator to judge the teacher's competence on the basis of an activity unsuitable for that purpose if the teacher chooses not to change his or her plans. In neither case will the evaluation of the teacher be fair or reasonable.

Finally, there are five indirect implications for teacher evaluation procedures of the law governing teacher termination. First, evaluations should be undertaken on a regular basis. Second, permanent records of the results of evaluations should be maintained. Third, teachers should be informed of the evaluation results, including access to their personnel file. These policies allow evaluations to be used to establish the irremediable nature of the defects upon which a judgment of incompetence is based. Fourth, teachers should be given an opportunity to enter explanations and clarifications of or objections to particular evaluation findings into their personnel record at the time at which those findings are filed. Fifth, the evaluation record should be kept confidential.

Participation and Mediation in Evaluation

We have argued that it is not enough for evaluation procedures to produce results that are "correct." A good system is also humane in its treatment of individuals, is nonalienating, produces cooperative working relations in the schools, and is effective in increasing the professional skills of the teaching staff. The legal and contractual provisions that we have described are not altogether satisfactory in meeting these criteria. We shall note three areas of concern.

First, the legal and contractual provisions discussed are deficient in that they do not encourage, and may discourage, a sense of collegiality and participation in the evaluation process. Indeed, they tend to conceptualize the authority relations between administrator and teacher in a rather hierarchical fashion as a supervisor-employee relationship. Although to some extent this simply describes the legal state of affairs, teacher participation in evaluation is not thereby precluded, and finding meaningful roles for teacher participation in evaluation can have the benefits of establishing more cooperative working arrangements in the school and of bringing the teacher's expertise to bear on the difficult job of evaluation.

Second, typical provisions for evaluation do not involve teachers in the process of remediation for teachers whose performance has been judged deficient. Every school has on its staff teachers with a history of excellence in the classroom. It is only good sense to create a mechanism whereby the expertise and experience of these teachers can be brought to bear in cases in which less experienced or less competent teachers can profit from them.

Third, procedures for the resolution of conflict over evaluation often fail to provide for third-party mediation early in the dispute. They thus permit grievances to proceed to a more "contentious" forum without adequate attempts to settle them in less strident fashion.

These deficiencies have in common a perception of evaluation as an authoritarian and disputatious matter. That serious attempts to do systematic and meaningful evaluation often confirm this perception perhaps accounts for the fact that evaluation is often not seriously done. Schools would profit substantially from attempting to make evaluation a cooperative and helpful process in which conflicts are settled informally by discussion and mediation. While we do not underestimate the difficulties of moving in this direction in a litigious age when evaluation procedures are commonly the topic of collective bargaining, we do have some suggestions which we believe can be incorporated into publicly acknowledged evaluation procedures. Incorporating such suggestions into evaluation procedures may help to make evaluation into a more humane and effective and a less contentious matter.

First, teachers should be permitted official channels of input into the formulation of criteria for evaluation. Individual teachers should be permitted a statement of their view of their teaching and of the standards that they see as appropriate to its evaluation. Teachers collectively should have some mechanism for input into the formulation of whatever general criteria will govern the evaluation process.

Second, senior teachers with a history of successful teaching should have some recognized role in the evaluation process. Such teachers might well participate in the observation phase of evaluation and would be expected to share their reactions both with the administrator and with the teacher being evaluated. Senior teachers would also participate in working out a remediation plan for those whose performance is judged as substantially deficient.

Finally, grievance procedures should be modified to contain a phase of mediation by a neutral third party before disputes are permitted to leave the building. Mediation should be intended to promote meaningful communication between teachers and administrators who may be reluctant to communicate either because personal relations have become strained or because they wish to avoid saying anything that might jeopardize their chances or their rights in later proceedings. Given these factors, it is important to organize mediation so that whatever occurs in the process cannot become part of further proceedings. Moreover, it should be clear that no rights are waived by participation in mediation. Acceptance of any solution generated must be voluntary. Finally, it may be necessary to work out a role for the local union in mediation. Unions have a vested interest in solving teachers' problems and may be expected to resist conflict resolution strategies that appear to diminish the need for their services.

Administrative Review and Use of Evaluations

The conduct of teacher evaluations according to the recommendations made above in no way guarantees that evaluation results will be used wisely or even legally. Accurate evaluations conducted in good faith have the potential, for example, to lead to the improvement of instruction, but they will not do so in and of themselves. At least part of that potential may be wasted unless administrators are willing to discuss and explain their findings, to help teachers overcome instructional shortcomings revealed by the evaluation, and perhaps even to provide teachers with training opportunities to this end. Moreover, fairly and legally conducted evaluations do not indemnify a school system against the legal failure of its attempts to terminate teachers for incompetence. The U.S. Constitution and state statutes include requirements that go beyond the provision of appropriate evidence of incompetence. Failure to meet all these requirements in detail will lead to the legal miscarriage of termination proceedings.

REFERENCES

Court Cases

Beilan v. Board of Education, 357 U.S. 399 (1958).

Board of Regents v. Roth, 408 U.S. 564 (1972).

Carpenter v. Greenfield, 358 F. Supp. 220 (1973).

Conley v. Board of Education of the City of New Britain, 123 A 2d. 747 (Conn., 1956).

Feinerman v. Board of Co-op Educational Services of Nassau County, 1978—A.D. 2d., 404 N.Y.S. 2d. 37.

Goldberg v. Kelly, 397 U.S. 254 (1970).

James v. Board, 461 F 2d. 566 (1972).

Los Angeles v. Davis, 47 L.W. 4317 (1979).

Mailloux v. Kiley, 323 F. Supp. 1387 (1971).

McDonnell Douglas v. Green, 411 U.S. 792 (1972).

Morris Central School District Board of Education v. Morris Education Association, 1976, 54 A.D. 1044, 388 N.Y. S 2d. 371.

Nebbia v. New York, 291 U.S. 502 (1934).

Parducci v. Rutland, 316 F. Supp. 352 (1970).

Perry v. Sinderman, 408 U.S. 593 (1972).

Pickering v. Board of Education, 391 U.S. 563 (1968).

Rescue Army v. Municipal Court, 331 U.S. 549 (1947).

Scheelhaase v. Woodbury Central Community School Districts, 488 F. 2d. 237 (1973).

Scheelhaase v. Woodbury Central Community School District, 349 F. Supp. 988 (1972).

Shapiro v. Thompson, 394 U.S. 618 (619).
Shelton v. Tucker, 364 U.S. 479 (1960).
Shultz v. Board of Education of Dorchester, 222 N.W. 2d. 578 (Neb. 1974).
Susquehanna Valley Teachers' Association, 37 N.Y. 2d. 614 (1975), 8PERB7517.
Tinker v. Des Moines Independent School District, 393 U.S. 503 (1969).
Travis v. Teter et al., PA 326, 87H 2d. 188 (Pennsylvania, 1952).
Washington v. Davis, 12 FEP 1415 (1976).
Yesinowski v. Board of Education, 328 N.E. 2d. 23 (Illinois, 1975).

Statutes
Arkansas Statutes, subsection 80–1304 (b).
California Statute, Education 13443 (b) (d) (1975).
Connecticut General Statutes Annotated Title 10, sections 10–151, 10–153d.
Massachusetts General Laws Annotated, Chapter 71, section 44.
New York Education Law, section 3020-a.
Purdon's Pennsylvania Statutes Annotated, Title 24, section 11–1122, 11–1123.
West's Annotated California Code, Government Code, section 3543-2.

Collective Bargaining Agreements
Albany: Agreement between the City School District of the City of Albany, New York and the Albany Public School Teachers' Association.
Buffalo: Master Contract between the Board of Education of the City of Buffalo and the Buffalo Teachers' Federation.
Chicago: Agreement between the Board of Education of the City of Chicago and the Chicago Teachers' Union Local No. 1., American Federation of Teachers, AFL-CIO.
Eastern Michigan University: Agreement between Eastern Michigan University and the Eastern Michigan University Chapter of the American Association of University Professors.
Ithaca: Agreement between Ithaca Teachers' Association and Superintendent of Schools of the Ithaca School District.
Memphis: Agreement between the Board of Education of the Memphis Education Association, an affiliate of the Tennessee Education Association and the National Education Association.
New York: Agreement between the Board of Education of the City School District of the City of New York and United Federation of Teachers Local 2, American Federation of Teachers, AFL-CIO.
Onondaga: Central School District and the Onondaga Central Schools' Faculty Association.
Philadelphia: Agreement between the Board of Education of the School District of Philadelphia Federation of Teachers Local 3, American Federation of Teachers, AFL-CIO.
Wayne State University: Agreement between Wayne State University and the Wayne State University Chapter of the American Association of University Professors.

Books, Articles, and Legal References
Abraham, H.J. (1972) *Freedom and the Court.* New York: Oxford University Press.
Cowan, T. A. [ed.] (1976) *American Jurisprudence,* Dobbs Ferry, NY: Oceana.
Dworkin, R. (1977) *Taking Rights Seriously.* Cambridge, MA: Harvard University Press.
Federal Register, 12333–12336.
French, L. L. (1978) "Teacher employment, evaluation, and dismissal," in R. D. Stern (ed.), *The School Principal and the Law.* Washington, DC: National Organization on Legal Problems of Education.
Hageny, W. J. (1978) *School Law.* Albany: New York State School Boards Association.
Peterson, L. J., R. A. Rossmiller, and M. M. Volz (1978) *The Law and Public School Operation.* New York: Harper & Row.

Psychological Corporation (1978) *Summaries of Court Decisions on Employment & Testing*. New York City: Author.

Rawls, J. (1971) *A Theory of Justice*. Cambridge, MA: Harvard University Press.

Rosenberger, D. S. and R. A. Plimpton (1975) "Teacher incompetence and the courts." *Journal of Law and Education*, 4: 469–486.

For Further Work

Peterson, L. J., R. A. Rossmiller, and M. M. Volz (1978) *The Law and Public School Operation*. New York: Harper & Row. (A review of case law on numerous topics of education law, it is a reasonable substitute in education for a legal reference work, such as *American Jurisprudence*.)

Ware, M. L. and M. K. Remmlein (1979) *School Law*. Danville, IL: Interstate Printers and Publishers. (Contains a good section on teacher personnel problems, extensive illustrative material from state codes, and a short discussion on finding school law.)

INDEX

ABOUT THE AUTHORS

LAWRENCE M. ALEAMONI, Professor of Educational Psychology and Director of the Office of Instructional Research and Development at the University of Arizona since 1975, has the major responsibility for providing assistance and resources to all faculty in their efforts to improve instruction. He was invited to establish a Center for the Development of Teaching at the Technion-Israel Institute of Technology in 1974. In the area of instructional evaluation, Professor Aleamoni has had published 34 monographs and articles, participated in 40 symposia and workshops, and presented and served on 89 seminar and consulting assignments at 35 universities, colleges, and schools.

MARY LOUISE ARMIGER is Associate Director of Instruction for the New Jersey Education Association. Having taught at both the junior high school and university levels and having held several administrative and curriculum development positions, Dr. Armiger brings a wide range of experiences and perspectives to the problem of teacher evaluation.

STEPHEN C. BROCK is Assistant Professor and Director of Educational Services at Temple University Medical School, where his primary concerns are the educational development of faculty and faculty evaluation. They were also primary concerns during his previous assignments at Kansas State and Cornell Universities. He has authored several publications and films and presented many workshops on faculty development.

BARRY BULL is Assistant Professor of Education at Wellesley College. His main interest is the philosophy of education with an emphasis on the problems of ethics and educational policy. He has authored several articles concerning social justice in education on topics such as textbook bias and moral education.

J. GREGORY CARROLL is Director of the Office of Educational Services and Research, School of Medicine, and Lecturer in the Graduate School of Education at the University of Pennsylvania. His administrative responsibilities include programs for curriculum development, faculty development, and educational measurement and evaluation in medical education. His publications and professional interests include research on the preparation and evaluation of college teachers and on the teaching of problem-solving and interpersonal skills in the health professions.

353

CAROLYN M. EVERTSON is Coordinator of the Division of Research in Teaching and Learning in the Research and Development Center for Teacher Education at the University of Texas at Austin. Her major areas of concentration are conducting research in classrooms on a variety of observation methods, including behavioral coding systems and structured narratives; developing methods of refining research questions; gaining knowledge about classroom processes of interest to practitioners; and conducting programatic research leading toward theories of instruction.

GRACE FRENCH-LAZOVIK began work in the evaluation of teaching over 30 years ago with one of its earliest pioneers, Professor Edwin R. Guthrie. As director of offices of teaching evaluation both at the University of Washington (Seattle) and the University of Pittsburgh, she has developed instruments for student evaluation of teaching, as well as a methodology for their construction and validation. Her disciplinary training in psychological measurement underlies special concerns for the procedures that improve the quality of evaluation data and for the use of peer review in judging the "professor as teacher."

DONALD L. HAEFELE is Associate Professor at The Ohio State University, where he teaches graduate courses in educational research and evaluation. In addition to his primary interest in teacher evaluation, he is studying children's attitudes toward the aged.

WILLIAM U. HARRIS is Area Director for the Teacher Program Area and Program Director for the National Teacher Examinations, Educational Testing Service. His current responsibilities include the overall management, coordination, and development of existing and future teacher programs at the Educational Testing Service, including the National Teacher Examinations. Dr. Harris has taught in elementary and secondary schools and has served as an elementary school principal.

FREDA M. HOLLEY is Director of Research and Evaluation for the Austin (Texas) Independent School District. She has also served as program chairperson for the School Evaluation Division of the American Educational Research Association. Many of her articles and speeches have addressed issues in and approaches toward teacher evaluation.

EDWARD F. IWANICKI is Associate Professor of Educational Administration at the University of Connecticut, where he teaches courses in supervision, teacher evaluation, and program evaluation. In addition, Dr. Iwanicki works extensively with school districts and state agencies on policy, as well as procedural, issues in the design, implementation, and evaluation of teacher evaluation programs. Before coming to the University of Connecticut, Dr. Iwanicki served as Associate Director of the Center for Field Research and School Services at Boston College.

JEAN A. KING is currently Assistant Professor and Coordinator of Secondary Education at Tulane University. She has participated on faculty evaluation committees at both the secondary school and college levels. Her research interests include curriculum theory and utilization of evaluation.

BERNARD H. McKENNA is a program development specialist with the National Education Association where he works in the areas of teacher education and professional standards, professional development, and the evaluation of teaching, student learning progress, and educational programs. His writings include *Staffing the Schools,* "Minimal competency testing: The need for a broader context" (in *Educational Horizons*), and *Context/Environment Effects in Teacher Evaluation* (in press). Dr. McKenna has been recipient of a Ford Foundation grant to study evaluation in Europe and Asia and a United Nations Fellowship.

JOHN D. McNEIL is Professor of Education at the University of California, Los Angeles, where he has served as Director of Supervised Teaching. His major interests are curriculum, instruction, the teaching of reading, and educational evaluation. Professor McNeil is the author of many textbooks in supervision, curriculum, and instructional improvement. His book *Toward Accountable Teachers* was chosen as a Kappa Delta Pi best educational book for 1971.

JASON MILLMAN is Professor of Educational Research Methodology at Cornell University, where he specializes in educational measurement and evaluation. He has served as editor-in-chief of the *Educational Researcher* and the *Journal of Educational Measurement,* written several books and numerous articles on educational testing and research, provided consultant services to over 30 state and national agencies, been elected as an officer of three professional organizations, and conducted dozens of workshops on teacher evaluation and related topics.

MICHAEL SCRIVEN is Director of the Evaluation Institute, University of San Francisco. He has also held the posts of president of the American Educational Research Association, first president of the Evaluation Network, and editor of *Evaluation News* and *Evaluation Notes.* Author of numerous books and articles on evaluation, Professor Scriven has years of practical experience as a consultant and was chiefly responsible for overhauling the faculty evaluation system at the University of San Francisco.

KENNETH STRIKE, Professor of Philosophy of Education at Cornell University, has a wide range of interests in philosophy, education, and law. He has written numerous articles on subjects such as student rights and affirmative action, is an editor of *Ethics and Educational Policy* (Routledge and Kegan Paul), and is the author of *Education in Liberal America* (University of Illinois). He is currently working on a book entitled *Liberty and Learning* (Martin Robertson and Company).

ROBERT M. W. TRAVERS is Distinguished Professor at Western Michigan University. Other institutions at which Dr. Travers did graduate work or held professional appointments include Cambridge University, University of London, Teachers College—Columbia University, Ohio State University, University of Michigan, and Utah State University. Author or editor of 11 books and 150 journal articles and reviews, Dr. Travers served as editor of the *Second Handbook of Research on Teaching*.